The Institute for Diversity Certification would like to thank the following contributors:

Dr. Delmar Lee, CDE;

Dr. Deidra Dennie, CDE;

Susan Gordon, MBA, SPHR, CDE;

Karla Rodgers, PHR, SHRM-CP, CDP; and

Jasmine Smith, PMP, MSL, CDE

CERTIFIED DIVERSITY EXECUTIVE (CDE)®
EXAM STUDY GUIDE

Table of Contents

PERSONAL AWARENESS
& MANAGING BLIND SPOTS

Possessing personal-awareness, demonstrating authentic leadership, and managing blind spots are essential traits for effective 21st century leaders.

Personal-Awareness (self-awareness) *involves taking the time to reflect on and examine your experiences – your inner world. Powerful leaders work hard at developing this skill through persistent and often courageous self-exploration. It is within this realm that effective diversity leaders stay ahead of the curve.*

Authentic Leadership*, pertains to the nature of individuals to be true to themselves. Truth of oneself can be found through a deep exploration and reflection of the self, particularly in three areas of one's life: purpose, values, and relationships.*

Blind Spots *are areas in one's life in which a person continually fails to see himself/herself or a situation realistically. This unawareness often causes great damage to that person's career and those around him/her.*

OVERALL OBJECTIVES

The purpose of this competency is to empower leaders to develop authenticity as a leader; eliminate blind spots; and identify opportunities for empathy, compassion, care, and specialized focus. As a result, leaders will gain a better understanding of their personal strengths, weaknesses and opportunities for growth; thus, becoming more effective catalysts for change.

BACKGROUND & CONTEXT

Purpose. Values. Relationships.
Purpose, values and relationships are critical for Diversity and Inclusion (D&I) leaders to possess. When embraced and internalized, they can transform diversity thinking and inclusive practices on a personal, organizational, and community level.

Purpose.
Diversity leaders must be clear about their purpose for doing equity and inclusion work. Articulating the business case for diversity is critical when engaging key stakeholders but that is not enough. Purpose, in authentic leadership, is to understand oneself in relationship to what is being sought. It can also lead an individual to a specialized realm of D&I work.

In other words, understanding and exploring your motivation, your passion, and your personal journey serves as a foundation for reaching the desired vision. In order to understand your purpose, begin by asking:

- Why am I doing this work? How does my professional purpose align with my personal purpose?
- What do I value? Where do I draw the line?
- What relationships do I have with diverse groups? What biases do I have?
- Who am I really serving?
- What do I hope to accomplish? What is my ultimate vision?
- What presents a challenge for me in successfully accomplishing the organization's Diversity and Inclusion vision?
- What strategies will I employ to overcome the challenges?

The more virtual our lives become, the more people hunger for something genuine. What people really want now is not just a product or a service, it's an experience. An experience that is more honest and transparent…more authentic. But what does "authentic" really mean? To be authentic means that you are staying true to who you are, what you do, and who you serve. In an environment where human elements matter (such as in the field of Diversity and Inclusion), authenticity creates value and benefits for employees, as well as improves the organization.

Authentic leaders are interested in empowering the people they lead to make a difference-- more than they are interested in power, money, or prestige for themselves. They are guided equally by the heart and the mind, practicing heart-based guidance grounded in passion and compassion, as well as thoughtful leadership grounded in the qualities of the mind. They lead with purpose, meaning and values. And their people relationships are extremely strong. People follow them because they are consistent, reliable, and resilient. When they are pushed to go beyond their beliefs and values, they will not compromise. They are dedicated to personal growth and learning because they believe that becoming a leader takes a lifetime.

"If you want to be an authentic leader, you need to do the difficult inner work to develop yourself, have a strong moral compass based on your beliefs and values, and work on problems that matter to you. When you look back on your life it may not be perfect, but it will be authentically yours", says Bill George, author of *Discovering Your True North*.

A 2012 Goodpurpose study demonstrated that where quality and price were equal, the leading purchase driver for 53 percent of consumers was social purpose. This is also the case in some hiring decisions. Yet, most people struggle to understand the purpose of their leadership. In order to find their purpose, authentic leaders must first understand themselves and their passions. In turn, their passions will show the way to the purpose of their leadership. Without a real sense of purpose, leaders are at the mercy of their egos and narcissistic vulnerabilities. This phenomena has played out graphically over the last 100 years in the political arena which has been increasingly characterized by purposeless, self-serving leaders who are far more concerned with "I" than "we". Authentic Leaders must personally explore and identify what it would mean to the organization, and most importantly to its people, if diversity (of thoughts, ideas, people, systems, etc.) did not exist. Simply asking yourself and others, "if we didn't do this work, what would be lost?" can make a difference.

Values.

Leaders are often defined by their values, beliefs, and character. Authentic leadership in diversity work requires leaders to consistently review, revise, and reflect upon their personal value systems and how these systems impact the work they do. For example, authenticity means that one person can be an immigrant, while another individual is a citizen. The person who is an immigrant shouldn't have to pretend to be someone or something else so that the citizen can like him or her. Likewise, the citizen won't pretend to know what it's like to be an immigrant or expect the other individual to cover the fact that he/she is an immigrant. In spite of their differences, both can still work together to achieve common goals.

The idea of covering is a phenomenon that works in contrast to authenticity. A person will cover who they are or what they value for various reasons. In some cases, it could be due to fear of rejection and in other instances, it may be related to one's apprehension about discrimination. Diversity and authenticity can be tricky in this regard: its leaders must not become all things to all people, while at the same time, possessing the ability to promote the inclusion of characteristics that are valuable to the organization. Hence, Diversity and Inclusion leaders must understand that bringing your whole self to work defeats itself if you are not yourself.

Leaders must also understand and articulate which values drive their behaviors and attitudes. This means that leaders must question and challenge, they must explore the deeper stories that give life to their belief systems, and they must be courageous enough to give themselves a "reality check" for any dissonance surfacing between their beliefs and actions. Finally, they must distinguish between bringing their whole self to work and employing organizational standards for the sake of meeting customer, patient, or student expectations.

Most organizations that are as diverse as the relevant population find themselves armed with many perspectives, views, and ideas that add strength to their ability to strategize, communicate and deliver great products or services. While Diversity and Inclusion can also have its challenges in the workplace, it provides an opportunity for employees to reach out and discover the amazing commonalities beneath the surface differences. Successful leaders promote meaning in organizations by focusing on the following core values:

- *Excellence:* strive to do your best and meet the highest standards.
- *Respect:* treat all people with dignity, open-mindedness, and esteem.
- *Valuing Diversity:* appreciate and acknowledge differences.
- *Inclusion*: a dynamic state of operating in which diversity is leveraged to create a fair, healthy, and high-performing organization or community.
- *Integrity:* behave ethically, honestly, and fairly.
- *Accountability:* take responsibility for your actions.

These values work in harmony to produce better experiences for everyone who interacts with an organization, regardless of their differences. For example, excellence in the context of diversity, is not having a separate standard for the different markets in which you operate. For instance, some supermarkets in lower income neighborhoods offer vastly different products, inferior customer service, and substandard facilities in comparison to supermarkets in the suburbs. Public education is another example of an institution that allows variations in a person's experience based on one's perceived value to society. Excellence is then nullified because of its inconsistent application.

True leaders must guide and encourage others to make a positive difference in their own lives as well as in the lives of others, once again, irrespective of their diverse dimensions.

Core values are the guiding principles for our work and they exist on the organizational and personal levels. Employees will personally value something that is important to them. This phenomenon may be conveyed as "What's In It for Me (WIIFM)"? Simultaneously, what the organization values may differ from what its employees personally value.

Leadership occurs within the context of core values. When you help your workforce to focus on applying the qualities of the organization's core values, the competencies of leadership are activated – e.g., learned, developed, and practiced. By focusing on what people believe and value on an individual level, and then positively building on this understanding, we have the potential for impact on a far more wide-reaching scale than if we approached leadership development as a problem-solving activity.

Relationships.
Essential in authentic leadership is a person's ability to develop long-lasting and meaningful relationships. For this to happen, it's vital for leaders and organizations to change their thinking about, and practices in, relationships.

Keep in mind, people watch what you do more than they listen to what you say. If you are advocating for inclusion, but everyone in your close circle looks like you and thinks like you, then it may be difficult for employees to believe that you are truly authentic in your inclusion efforts.

Leaders can alter authentic Diversity and Inclusion work when they pay attention to the relationships that they develop. Authentic relationships can occur when the questions asked shift from "how can this relationship help me to reach my organizational goals" to "what can I (we) learn from this relationship, and how can the learning move us toward our organizational vision?"

There are several characteristics that make up good, healthy working relationships:

- ***Trust*** – This is the foundation of every good relationship. When you trust your team and colleagues, you form a powerful bond that helps you work and communicate more effectively. If you trust the people you work with, you can be open and honest in your thoughts and actions, and you don't have to waste precious time and energy watching others around you. Even if you have been "burned" a few times, you have to be able to press the 'reset' button because otherwise, your ability to have meaningful relationships will be impeded. Sometimes, this may include approaching the relationship differently.

- ***Mutual Respect*** – When you respect the people that you work with, you value their input and ideas, and they value yours. Working together, you can develop solutions based on your collective insight, experience and creativity.

- ***Mindfulness*** – This means taking responsibility for your words and actions. Those who are mindful are careful in what they say and don't let their own negative emotions impact the people around them. Mindfulness also implies that one is paying attention at that moment and possesses a certain degree of self-consciousness. Mindfulness is necessary in order to avoid labeling or judging what people say or do as right or wrong.

- ***Welcoming Diversity*** – People with good relationships not only accept different people and opinions, but they welcome them. For instance, when your friends and colleagues offer dissimilar opinions, take the time to consider what they have to say, and factor their insights into your decision-making. Likewise, if your friends and colleagues *never* offer divergent perspectives, it may be time to expand your circle.

- ***Open Communication*** – We communicate all day, whether we're sending emails and text messages or meeting face-to-face. The better and more effectively you communicate with those around you, the richer your relationships will be. All good relationships depend on open and honest communication.

Although we should try to build and maintain good working relationships with everyone, there are certain relationships that deserve extra attention.

For instance, you'll likely benefit from developing good relationships with key stakeholders in your organization. These are the people who have a stake in your success or failure. Forming a bond with these individuals will help you ensure that your projects, and career, stay on track. To find out who these people are, do a Stakeholder Analysis. Once you've created a list of key stakeholders who have an interest in your projects and career, you can devote time to building and managing these relationships.

A Stakeholder Analysis is the technique used to identify the key people in your organization who must be won over. The benefits of using a stakeholder-based approach include:

- Using the opinions of the most powerful stakeholders to shape your Diversity and Inclusion efforts will create shared ownership. In the early stages, a sense of ownership makes it more likely that key stakeholders will support you. Their input can also improve the quality of your work.

- Gaining support from key stakeholders can also help you win more resources – this makes it more likely that your efforts will be successful.

- Communicating with key stakeholders frequently ensures that they fully understand what you are doing and comprehend the benefits of your work – this means they can support you actively when necessary.

- Anticipating people's reaction to your work, and building that information into your strategy, will win support as well.

The first step in a Stakeholder Analysis is to identify the key stakeholders. The next step is to categorize them by power, influence, and interest so that you know who to focus on. The final step is to ascertain what is important to them. This will help you determine how they are likely to respond so that you can pinpoint how to win their support and you can record this analysis on a stakeholder map. An example follows in Figure 1.

FIGURE 1: STAKEHOLDER MAP

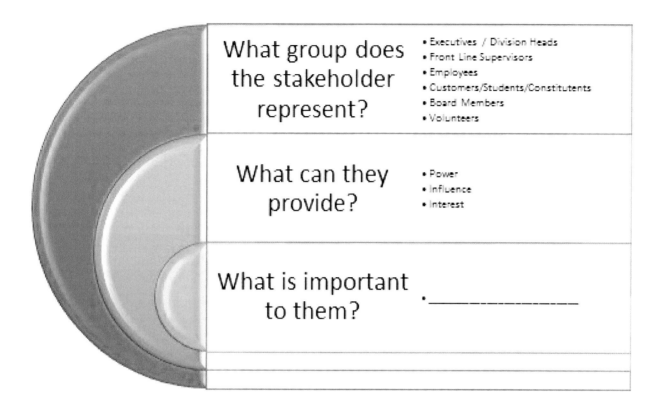

Students or customers are another example of a stakeholder group. Within these groups, various segments will view the value of your services or products differently. From this unique perspective, understanding what's important to them will go a long way toward delivering meaningful services and products. Although you may not be able to keep everyone happy 100 percent of the time, maintaining honest, trusting relationships with your students/customers can help you ensure that if things do go wrong, damage is kept to a minimum. Additionally, building relationships with people such as board members, alliance partners, suppliers, community groups, the media, and other stakeholders could be crucial to the success of an organization's future. Developing and customizing a stakeholder map for all of these group would be a great diversity training exercise.

By applying authentic leadership principles to diversity work, leaders can:

- Garner support and understanding for the work,
- Discover the discord between individual and organizational values,
- Recognize behaviors that serve as barriers,
- Develop meaningful relationships for organizational growth.

These principles are intended to heighten awareness and understanding for the value that diversity has on organizational life. Authentic leaders who dig beneath the surface to explore their purpose, values, and relationships will lay the foundation for a deeper commitment to organizational growth. That's because when attention is paid to purpose, values, and relationships, how we think about and act upon these elements will engage people-- not only with their minds but also their hearts.

MANAGING THE BIAS WITHIN

No matter how hard a person tries, we all have biases; we discriminate without even recognizing what we are doing. Therefore, an important element of authenticity is comprehending the diverse world around us and managing the biases that naturally arise when we are in various settings.

Most Diversity and Inclusion leaders would assume that they are fighting biases—they do not have any. A leader who is in tune with his/her self, however, will see things differently.

Susan Klopfer (2011) pointed out in her blog *Good Leaders Work Hard at Self Awareness*, that William Sonnenschein, a noted diversity expert and author, suggests overcoming the tendency to be oblivious to one's biases by "waking up tomorrow morning" and "try wondering what prejudice you will discover during the day, what assumption you will make that will be proven wrong, and what biases will affect your day."

By finding a daily bias, Sonnenschein believes a person will know they are continually working on self-awareness. Personal-awareness is the understanding that we all have biases and are working to eliminate as many as possible. It also includes knowing how others view you and how they perceive your efforts. As people work on personal-awareness, they become aware of things that are happening around them and they can adjust their behavior and leadership style accordingly.

This level of self-awareness can also help one uncover blind spots that are behind ineffective leadership practices and D&I strategies that are unintentionally exclusive. In many cases, the lack of self-awareness does greater damage to one's D&I career than the lack of senior leadership support. Hence, D&I leaders must be intentional, proactive, and confident about regularly operating on this level.

The Johari Window model is a simple and useful tool for illustrating and improving self-awareness and mutual understanding between individuals within a unit. The Johari Window model can also be used to assess and improve relationships between different groups. The model was devised by American psychologists Joseph Luft and Harry Ingham in 1955, while researching group dynamics at the University of California Los Angeles. It was first published in the Proceedings of the Western Training Laboratory in Group Development by the UCLA Extension Office in 1955 and was later expanded by Joseph Luft. Today the Johari Window model is especially relevant due to a modern emphasis on 'soft' skills in the workplace, such as: empathy, cooperation, emotional intelligence, dealing with ambiguity, and mindfulness. Additionally, like the Stakeholder Map, the Johari Window model is a great tool to use during training.

FIGURE 2

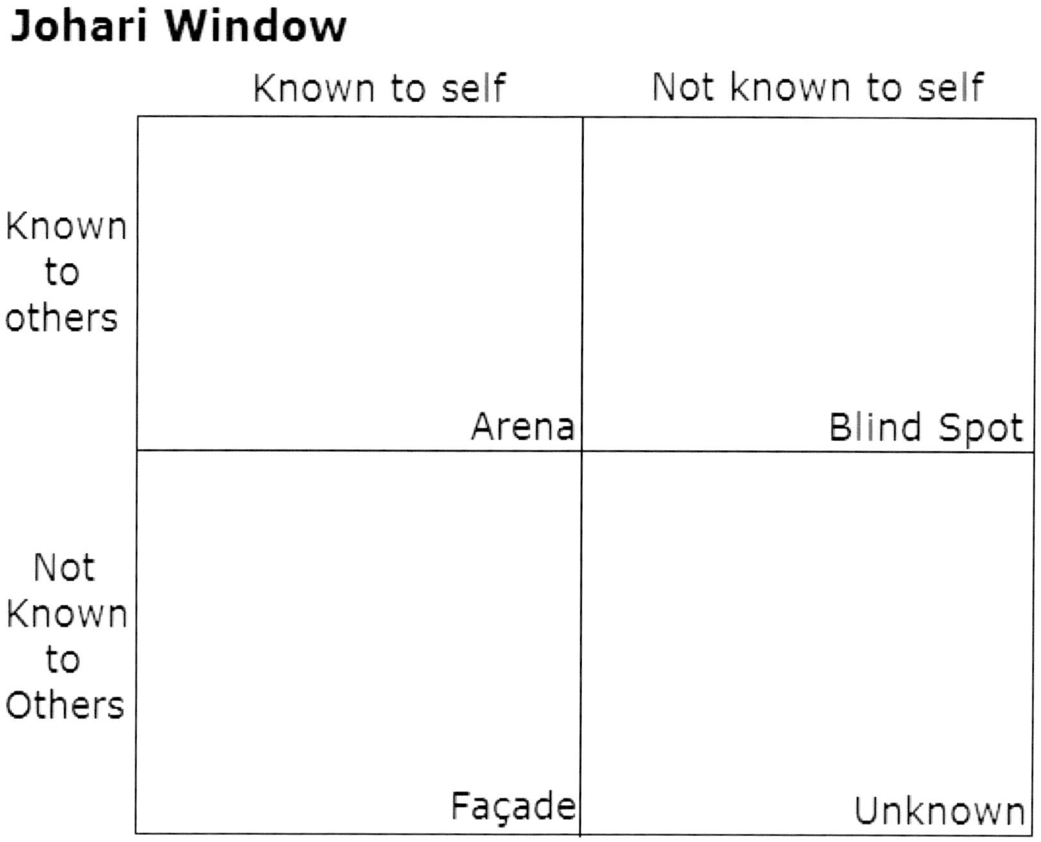

Johari Window

	Known to self	Not known to self
Known to others	Arena	Blind Spot
Not Known to Others	Façade	Unknown

Quadrant 1 – Arena

Johari Region 1 is also known as the area of free activity. This is information about the person - behavior, attitude, feelings, emotions, knowledge, experience, skills, views, etc. - known by the person (the self) and known by the group (others).

The aim in any group should always be to develop the open area for every person, because when we work in this area with others we are most effective and productive, and the group is most productive too. The open free area, or the arena, can be seen as the space where good communications and cooperation occurs, free from distractions, mistrust, confusion, conflict, and misunderstanding.

Quadrant 2 – Blind Spot

Johari Region 2 is what is known about a person by others in the group but is unknown by the person him/herself. By seeking or soliciting feedback from others, the aim should be to reduce this area and thereby increase the open area (i.e., to increase self-awareness). The blind area is not an effective or productive space for individuals or groups. This area could be referred to as ignorance about oneself or issues in which one is deluded. A blind area could also include issues that others are deliberately withholding from a person. We all know how difficult it is to work well when kept in the dark, or when subjected to "mushroom management". People who are "thick-skinned" tend to have a large blind area.

Quadrant 3 – Façade

Johari Region 3 is what is known to ourselves but kept hidden from, and therefore unknown, to others. This hidden or avoided self, represents knowledge, information, feelings, or any other thing that a person knows about him/herself, but is kept hidden from others. This arena could be considered a professional façade, and would include sensitivities, fears, hidden agendas, manipulative intentions, and secrets—anything that a person knows but does not reveal, for whatever reason. For example, a person may not have disclosed the fact that he/she received a job because of a personal connection to an executive; meanwhile, this individual is a staunch proponent of hiring/promoting workers based on 'merit'. Sharing information about how one received an employment opportunity could be useful in a conversation about privilege and unfair access to workplace benefits.

It's natural for very personal and private information or feelings to remain hidden. Indeed, certain information, feelings, and experiences have no bearing on work; therefore, it can and should remain hidden. Typically, however, most hidden information is not personal; it is work- or performance-related, therefore it is better positioned in the open area.

Quadrant 4 - Unknown

Johari Region 4 contains information, feelings, latent abilities, aptitudes, experiences, etc., that are unknown to the person and unknown to others in the group. These unknown issues take a variety of forms: they can be feelings, behaviors, attitudes, capabilities, or aptitudes. The unknown region can be quite close to the surface, positive and useful, or they can be deeper aspects of a person's personality, influencing his/her behavior to various degrees. Large unknown areas would typically be expected in younger people, or individuals who lack experience or self-belief.

The Johari Window model is a simple exercise that can assist groups in understanding the most effective way to optimize the value of different people. Explaining the meaning of the Johari Window theory to leaders empowers them to use the results in their own way, and to incorporate the underlying principles into their future thinking and behavior.

At the individual level, however, less is more. Rather than trying to be all things to their employers, people perform better and are more engaged when they focus on being their singular, authentic selves. When companies also encourage and reward this kind of authenticity and genuineness among their leaders, these individuals are more likely to create real value for the organization.

LINKING AUTHENTIC LEADERSHIP TO ORGANIZATIONAL PERFORMANCE

So, how does authentic leadership support organization performance? When people feel free to be whom and what they are (both privately and publicly) they have more energy to create and innovate. Authentic workers are more likely to bring their whole selves to the job, engage with the company's goals, and participate fully in the mission of the enterprise.

These same employees also recognize and are attracted to authentic leaders and follow them with greater dedication, leading to stronger teams and enhanced business performance. The challenge with Political Correctness (PC) is that it prevents individuals from revealing their true selves. By definition, PC is "the *avoidance* of forms of expression or action that are perceived to exclude, marginalize, or insult groups of people who are socially disadvantaged or discriminated against." PC workplaces are filled with fear of doing or saying the wrong thing, as well as rife with extreme concern over the consequences. If our policy is to avoid offensive language, behavior, and practices, we inadvertently create an environment that is negative and intolerant.

Organizational leaders can take steps to encourage authenticity in the workforce and in the process show their own authentic selves. By encouraging people to be whom they truly are, and welcoming differences, leaders create a more supportive, productive work environment. Employees then become more engaged and willing to take risks that will enhance their cultural competence. They channel their energy into innovation, which inevitably benefits the company.

Some leaders are concerned that authenticity will result in lowered standards where employees underperform. But true authenticity implies that the organization is meeting the public's and the community's expectations for excellence and abiding by organizational policies-- while at the same time providing employees with the freedom to bring their backgrounds, ideas, experiences, and knowledge to work in a meaningful way.

To accomplish these things, organizational leaders must pave the way by taking steps to become authentic themselves. Instead of striving to be seen as all-knowing and all-powerful, effective business executives must be prepared to show their own humanity through vulnerability. Dr. Brené Brown, a research professor at the University of Houston, who presented a powerful TEDx talk entitled, "The Power of Vulnerability," explains that at its core, leadership is really about relationships. And being in a relationship with anyone requires a certain degree of vulnerability. Leaders who display invulnerability create disengagement throughout the company culture. But embracing vulnerability, Brown says, is the key to creating an effective workforce for the future. "Re-humanizing work and education requires courageous leadership," asserts Brown. "It requires leaders who are willing to take risks, embrace vulnerabilities and show up as imperfect, real people."

Of course, overcoming a longstanding cultural preference for invulnerable executives and displaying our authentic selves is not always easy. Still, becoming a more authentic leader is a battle worth fighting. Leaders must be ever ready to overcome societal norms and organizational cultures that prefer more traditional yet less effective leadership styles. Leaders who fully embrace authenticity themselves and take steps to welcome it into their company culture can realize tremendous rewards, for themselves and their organizations.

Authenticity is especially important in the areas of gender and sexual orientation. The corporate world has long trained women to behave and even dress like men. Some executives coach women to negotiate like a man by using male body language, lowering their natural speaking voices, and avoiding feminine or frilly clothing so that they will be taken "seriously." Yet covering up natural female behaviors or appearances to seem more masculine does not help women lead effectively. "The women I see succeeding bring their whole selves to work," says Barbara Annis. Annis is founding partner of Gender Intelligence Group and the chair emeritus of the Women's Leadership Board at Harvard's Kennedy School. "They're empowered, and they're driven by their values," Annis continued. "The key is really to be authentic."

Similarly, many gay, lesbian, bisexual and transgender people in leadership positions believe they must mask their sexual orientation to be viewed as effective. Yet, businesspeople who feel they must hide something about themselves find it hard to relax and concentrate on their work. They spend precious energy covering up their differences and attempting to minimize the perceived stigma of what actually makes them unique. As a result, when they're in an executive role, they may be inauthentic leaders, and inauthentic leaders tend to be less productive and experience higher rates of burnout. In fact, some researchers suggest that inauthentic people may be as much as 20 percent less productive than employees who feel comfortable presenting their authentic selves to the world.

Worse, inauthentic leaders may breach the trust that is so essential to changing the organizational culture. People sense that they see an incomplete or misleading picture, even if they don't understand why. This disconnect can inadvertently create mistrust in working relationships among colleagues, suppliers, customers/students, and prospects.

One can increase personal awareness and authenticity in Diversity and Inclusion work by:

- Utilizing different tools to constantly explore how you have changed, both personally and professionally, over the years
- Being cultural bound-- careful about believing that your organizational culture and value systems are the best; realistic about the limitations of your culture; optimistic about change;
- Learning various facts about other cultures by participating in diversity or cultural education;
- Connecting your knowledge about the organization to your knowledge about the people with whom you work and serve.

Personal-awareness emanates from an honest self-appraisal about emotional strengths and vulnerabilities, values and attitudes, personality traits and unresolved conflicts.

AUTHENTICITY IN THE CONTEXT OF D&I'S ROLE

The Chief Diversity Officer (CDO) is one of the most integral roles in the organization, and therefore he/she must be strategically focused on change, as well as serve as an example of excellence. We also should ensure that our Diversity and Inclusion efforts are linked to strategic organizational goals, as well as indicate meaningful contributions to business results. This will eliminate the assumption that diversity is associated with unqualified workers/students, lower standards, and quotas.

Accordingly, a CDO must be aware of the challenges associated with this role and recognize that some people may not understand the role of CDOs.

Essentially, the role of a CDO is multi-faceted and involves oversight of all aspects of equity, diversity, and inclusion. It includes (but is not limited to):

- Providing acceptable definitions related to your organization's diversity and inclusion work (i.e., diversity, inclusion, equity, unconscious bias, etc.).

- Developing the Diversity and Inclusion business case, strategic plan and supporting documents (e.g., benchmarks, implementation plan, metrics, scorecard, etc.)
- Coordinating efforts of the Diversity Council and/or Employee Resource Groups
- Managing legal risks and compliance
- Designing, developing and implementing diversity and inclusion interventions
- Initiating partnerships with diverse suppliers and community-based organizations
- Creating a budget and ROI data
- Documenting office protocols and regularly reporting accomplishments
- Participating in succession planning
- Leading policy revisions, continuous improvement, and change management
- Conducting research, assessments, trend analyses, and cultural climate surveys
- Evaluating Diversity and Inclusion's impact; measuring how the organization progresses

Regardless of one's specific title, the most effective diversity leaders will create an elevator pitch that succinctly describes their role within the organization. For example, the pitch may be:

"My role as _____ (insert your title) is to help the organization leverage differences to support the achievement of organizational goals, outperform competitors, and exceed customer/client/student expectations."

OR

"As the _____ (insert your title), I create opportunities for our organization to better meet the changing needs of our students/clients with appropriate staff and programming interventions."

OR

"I help the organization meet the global demands of business and address the challenges that come along with changing demographics, differing points of view, and workplace fairness."

Presenting an elevator pitch will help you to clearly explain your work in a non-threatening manner, as well as establish the link to organizational objectives.

CONCLUSION

Research confirms that self-examination is critical for leaders' personal and professional development. Scott Keller, director at McKinsey & Company, described the importance of overcoming self-interest and delusion in the Harvard Business Review. Keller emphasized the need for openness to personal growth and development, because "deep down, (leaders) do not believe that it is they who are the ones that need to change..." and "the real bottleneck...is knowing what to change on a personal level."

Leaders understand that diversity is a journey that begins at the personal level. Authentic leaders continue to explore components used to evaluate the innate sense and provide much insight into the behaviors required for high-functioning organizations in today's multi-faceted and multi-dimensional society. Before exploring cultural dynamics and group differences, it is important to examine your unique worldview, which includes assumptions and perceptions.

With the benefits (and the necessity) of authentic leadership in mind – how can you demonstrate it convincingly in order to support an inclusive environment?

- Be real—maintain your true identity
- Always be consistent and avoid giving mixed messages
- Build Relationships - Get to know your key stakeholders
- Build trust
- Understand and effectively manage your personal biases
- Know your purpose

As Chief Diversity Officer or as a Diversity champion, you are responsible for helping the organization to leverage its differences to maximize opportunities, competitive positioning, and compliance. The most effective leader will understand his/her purpose, and tactically go beyond superficial expectations toward innovation, inclusion, interdependence, and excellence.

References:

Banaji, Mahzarin R.; Greenwald, Anthony G. (2016) *Blind Spot – Hidden Biases of Good People*

Brokaw, Leslie (2012). Sloan Review. MIT. *Self-Awareness – A Key to Better Leadership.* Retrieved From: https://sloanreview.mit.edu/article/self-awareness-a-key-to-better-leadership/

Brown, Brene (2011). *The Power of Vulnerability.* https://www.ted.com/talks/brene_brown_on_vulnerability

Chapman, Alan (1995-2014) adaptation, review and code, based on Ingham and Luft's original Johari Window concept [online] http://www.businessballs.com/johariwindowmodel.htm

George, Bill (2007). Discovering Your True North

George, Bill; Ibarra, Herminia; Goffee, Rob; Jones, Gareth (2017). *Authentic Leadership: Rediscovering the Secrets to Creating Listening Values.* Authentic Leadership Self-Assessment Questionnaire. Harvard Business Review: Emotional Intelligence Series. Retrieved From: http://people.uncw.edu/nottinghamj/documents/slides6/Northouse6e%20Ch11%20Authentic%20Survey.pdf

Keller, Scott (2012). *How to Get Senior Leaders to Change.* Harvard Business Review. Retrieved From: https://hbr.org/2012/06/how-to-get-senior-leaders-to-c

Klopfer, Susan (2011). *Good Leaders Work Hard at Self Awareness.* Diversity Officer Magazine

Medical News Today: https://www.medicalnewstoday.com/releases/247409.php

MindTools.com, Stakeholder Analysis [online] available from http://www.mindtools.com/pages/article/newPPM_07.htm

Musselwhite, Chris (2007) *Self-Awareness and the Effective Leader.* Inc. Magazine. Retrieved From: www.inc.com/resources/leadership/articles/20071001/musselwhite.html

Zenger, Jack (2014). Forbes. *The Singular Secret For A Leader's Success: Self-Awareness* Retrieved From: https://www.forbes.com/sites/jackzenger/2014/04/17/the-singular-secret-for-a-leaders-success-self-awareness/#54d281f24cb7

Sample Test Questions:

PERSONAL AWARENESS & MANAGING BLIND SPOTS

1. **Research confirms that _____ is critical for leaders' positive professional development.**
   A. Lifelong learning
   B. Self-examination
   C. High self-esteem

2. **Understanding Diversity and Inclusion is a journey that begins at the:**
   A. Personal Level
   B. Corporate Level
   C. Global Level

3. **You can increase personal awareness with all of the following EXCEPT:**
   A. Utilizing different tools to explore how you have changed
   B. Learning various facts about other cultures in training
   C. Serving as a reverse-mentor for senior executives

4. **Leaders must be ready to overcome societal norms and organizational cultures that prefer:**
   A. Traditional leadership styles
   B. Merit-based hierarchies
   C. Diversity and Inclusion

5. **The problem with Political Correctness (PC) is that it:**
   A. Eliminates organizational liability for offensive conduct
   B. Fosters open and honest dialogue on tough issues
   C. Prevents individuals from revealing their true selves

6. **People perform better and are more engaged when they focus on being:**
   A. All things to all people
   B. Their singular, authentic selves
   C. Code switching experts

7. **This Johari quadrant is "known to ourselves but kept hidden from, and therefore unknown, to others".**
   A. Blind spot
   B. Façade
   C. Unknown

Sample Test Questions:

PERSONAL AWARENESS & MANAGING BLIND SPOTS (cont'd)

8. **In Johari Region 1, the aim should always be to develop the:**
   A. Open area
   B. Blind spot
   C. Hidden area

9. **This is a technique used to identify the key people who have to be won over:**
   A. Relationship Map
   B. Partnership Model
   C. Stakeholder Analysis

10. **When embraced and internalized, these 3 elements can transform diversity thinking and inclusive practices:**
    A. Purpose, values, and relationships
    B. Equity, Diversity, and Inclusion
    C. Authenticity, awareness, and fairness

11. **Inauthentic leaders tend to be more productive and to experience lower rates of burnout.**
    A. True
    B. False

12. **Diversity and Inclusion leaders have biases too.**
    A. True
    B. False

IMPROVING YOUR APPROACH
TO THE BOTTOM LINE

The business case for Diversity and Inclusion theorizes that an organization which employs a diverse workforce is better able to understand marketplace demographics, is more proactive in managing costs and identifying opportunities, and is poised to thrive in a global economy—in comparison to an employer that has a limited range of employee demographics.

Beyond the business case, the notion of a triple bottom line references the realization that organizations can do more than utilize Diversity and Inclusion to make money or save money. As organizations look to the future, improving one's approach to the bottom line encompasses multiple components of sustainability.

OVERALL OBJECTIVES AND COMPETENCIES

The purpose of this competency is to help leaders construct a concise, data-driven approach to demonstrating the business benefits of equity and inclusion; communicate with internal stakeholders more effectively by distinguishing between Personal Value (What's In It For Me – WIIFM) and Organizational Value; and ensure that the organization is relevant to the needs of different groups now, as well as in the future.

BACKGROUND AND CONTEXT

Whether one works for a nonprofit, educational institution, or government agency, senior executives at these organizations are just as concerned about finance (i.e., the bottom line) as leaders at for-profit corporations. In fact, most organizations operate based on the "bottom line". The **business case** is known as one of the most effective techniques in helping high-level executives, board members, and other stakeholders to evaluate the benefits of Diversity and Inclusion from a bottom-line or reasoned (i.e., financial) perspective. Therefore, the business case for Diversity and Inclusion (D&I) must focus on one's strategic approach to making money, saving money, and/or achieving organizational goals.

This competency serves to explore the impact of going beyond the business case to validate Diversity and Inclusion interventions. The most obvious reason for improving your approach to the bottom line is to justify the resources and capital investment necessary to bring cultural competence and inclusion to fruition. However, this implies that the approach for supporting diversity is simply a financial document. While all business cases should include financial justification, monetary reasoning will not be its only function.

What does this mean? As the field of equity, diversity and inclusion evolves, the work must transition from helping organizations to *value different people* towards being perceived as an organization that is *valuable to different people*. This notion implies functioning as a vehicle for sustainability.

The term sustainability can be complex and take on different meanings. The most common definition originates from the 1987 United Nations (U.N.) Brundtland Commission:

Sustainability

Development which meets the needs of current generations without compromising the ability of future generations to meet their own needs.

Affecting meaningful change through sustainability and diversity are not merely trends but needs—especially when Millennials are key employees, customers, stakeholders, and increasingly managers. Millennials on college campuses, as well as in the workforce and marketplace are key drivers behind this evolution. From their perspective, diversity should be at the center of a sustainability strategy in which organizations partner with employees, suppliers, customers, and other stakeholders to make a difference in communities. Sustainability also entails ensuring that an organization survives demographic shifts, competitive pressures, industry changes, brand failures, and other risks.

THE VALUE PROPOSITION

Diversity, in and of itself, recognizes that each employee is different and can contribute to an organization in different ways by virtue of their individual experiences. While appreciating diversity may be an intrinsic individual value held by many employees, the reason for embracing the approach outlines how diversity adds value in an organizational context.

Most of us are familiar with how individuals are valued differently based on where they went to school, how old (or young) they are, or whether they are male/female, or by their race. Personally, each individual values things differently due to a variety of factors, and how that value is determined is subjective. This is what makes managing diversity complex.

Conversely, senior executives will pay the most attention to the areas that produce the most organizational value. This is what they are paid to do, regardless of their feelings. Hence, it can be said that leaders are valued for their ability to be objective. To be objective means that one is not influenced by personal feelings or opinions in considering the facts. This is very important because if one is going to increase the attention and focus on equity and inclusion, diversity practitioners must improve utilize objective data to illustrate organizational value.

In this instance, a dissertation about the lack of representation from different groups may not necessarily work: ethnicity and gender-based diversity initiatives result in a zero-sum ratio in some minds. This is where someone has to lose (us) in order for another to gain (them). It presents a divisive approach to establishing a culture where differences are valued. Accordingly, diversity will be viewed as a program for "others", "blacks", or the "less qualified", and not viewed as a business imperative.

The idea that employees and executives value the benefits of diversity differently implies that D&I leaders must present the concept of equity and Inclusion in a manner to caters to the needs and/or concerns of each group. For example, employees may be concerned about how they will be impacted by diversity initiatives. They may be apprehensive about losing workplace privileges, being excluded from promotional opportunities or key assignments, or trailing other groups in respect to pay or benefits. Essentially, the concerns boil down to a" What's in it for ME (WIIFM)?" type of attitude. Conversely, executives are worried about how much diversity initiatives will cost, how the organization will pay for these non-revenue generating programs, and whether inclusion efforts are veering too far from organizational objectives. If these concerns are placed side-by-side in a chart, it could be reflected upon in Figure 1.

FIGURE 1. Differences in "Value"	
Source: The Society for Diversity (2018)	
Personal Value (Employees)	**Organizational Value (Executives)**
• *Subjective* • What's In It For Me (WIIFM)? • Unique to the Individual	• *Objective* • Saving Money • Making Money • Achieving Organizational Goals

Indicating organizational value is not always a natural skill for D&I leaders. Because Diversity Champions are passionate and emotionally tied to this particular work, it can be challenging to indicate value in ways other than what is important to the Diversity Champion. Nevertheless, senior level executives expect D&I leaders to be adept in communicating value in organizational terms.

The most effective way to demonstrate organizational value entails:

- Presenting the business case
- Documenting cost savings
- Identifying growth opportunities by providing insight on demographic shifts
- Utilizing benchmarking data
- Calculating the DROI for everything
- Showing the triple bottom line impact

Improving your approach to demonstrating value stems from the need for business to promote the benefits of diversity. Since the 1960s, various models have advanced the field, ranging from:

- The **Compliance Model** - where organizations strived to satisfy Affirmative Action requirements and goals

- The **Social Justice Model** - where tokenism prevailed because it was the right thing to do

- The **Diversity Model** - where cultural competence and Inclusion leverage the skills and resources of diverse employees, and multicultural customers are attracted to high performing organizations

Today, there is a push for the **Inclusive Business Model**, where different communities are included in a company's value chain on the demand side as clients and consumers, and/or on the supply side as producers, entrepreneurs, or employees in a sustainable way. The concept was first formalized in an early United Nations report called *Creating Value for All: Strategies for Doing Business with the Poor (2008),* published by the Growing Inclusive Markets Initiative and guided by an international Advisory Board.

Inclusive business models build bridges between organizations and diverse groups for mutual benefit. The organizational benefits go beyond immediate profits and higher incomes. For business, they include driving innovations, building markets, and strengthening supply chains. Moreover, for traditionally disadvantaged groups, they include access to essential goods and services, higher productivity, sustainable earnings, and greater empowerment.

Inclusive business is not corporate philanthropy or corporate social responsibility, which have inherent limitations of scope, impact, and budget. Rather, it is the search for sustainable business models that "do well by doing good" and are a part of the organization's core business activities. Therefore, in addition to enhancing the bottom-line, Diversity and Inclusion can present value-added benefits to an organization.

Outside of economics, value-added refers to the *extra* features of an item of interest that go beyond standard expectations and offer something *more*, while adding little or nothing to its cost. Value-added features provide competitive advantages to organizations. The entire value-in-diversity notion rests on the assumption that outside of unique employees with knowledge, skills, and abilities that appeal to different groups, an inclusive organization is flexible enough to adjust to and survive external changes. This increases an organization's ability to:

- Reduce risks associated with lawsuits and negative publicity
- Decrease costs associated with lower productivity and turnover
- Innovate products and services
- Save money with diverse suppliers
- Demonstrate higher returns for investors
- Improve customer/student satisfaction
- Capitalize on greater sales (or grants, conventions, residents, visitors to a city, tuition, etc.)
- Gain an edge over competitors
- Strategically prepare for the future

In respecting the fact that value has to be positioned differently to fit the needs of dissimilar groups in the workplace, diversity leaders will be able to communicate in a way that is relevant and effective.

PRESENTING AN EFFECTIVE BUSINESS CASE

Diversity leaders should consider the fact that executives, board members, employees, and other stakeholders will have varying degrees of competence. The lack of cultural competence may manifest in the form of logical fallacies, rejection, extreme criticism, coordinated reverse discrimination claims, or other types of resistance. Do not confuse this behavior with feedback. At the same time, **do not** be afraid, **do not** ignore the behavior, and **do not** wait to address the issues. This is where an ally becomes valuable. In *How to be an Ally in the Workplace*, France Burks says, "Allies in the workplace provide assistance that helps support their coworkers, so you have to take an interest in other employees to be an ally. Such relationships can be mutually beneficial because accomplishing your goals at work may rely on having allies. However, you generally need to be an ally before you can expect to have allies."

In addition to securing the support of multiple allies, diversity leaders must learn to address backlash head-on. Many critics of Diversity and Inclusion efforts have strong personal feelings against its acceptance and delaying a response will cause their negativity to fester and spread. An excellent strategy to combat cultural incompetence is to use the facts and corresponding organizational data in the proper context. For example, if someone says, "All of the promotions are going to women and people of color." The diversity leader can remind the individual that women represent 5% of senior managers, and different racial and ethnic groups are not represented in the executive offices. The diversity leader must highlight the contributions of different groups while applying what is known about the antagonist's cultural competence.

Dr. Milton Bennett, co-founder of the Intercultural Communication Institute and director of the Intercultural Development Research Institute, created the Bennett scale, also called the Developmental Model of Intercultural Sensitivity (DMIS). This framework describes the different ways people can react to cultural differences and the degree to which they have adapted to them. In this framework, there is an emphasis on education versus training. According to Dr. Bennett, training changes skills, but education changes mindsets.

The Bennett Scale is depicted in Figure 2.

FIGURE 2.

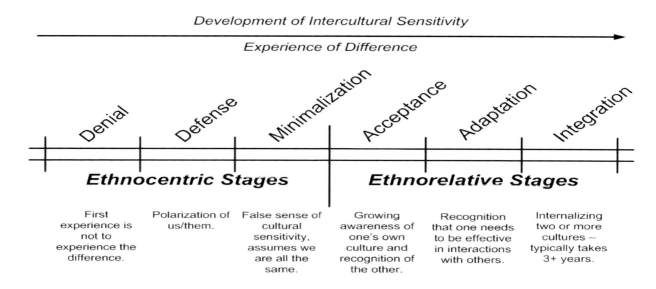

Source: Dr. Milton Bennett, Developmental Model of Intercultural Sensitivity (DMIS), 1986

Further, do not assume that everyone is racist, sexist, ageist, or homophobic. Perhaps the D&I leader could do a better job of explaining the business case or conceivably, the individual could understand the value of diversity if it was presented in a different way.

The broadest definition of diversity centers on our differences. Proponents endorse the idea that a diverse workforce allows for greater utilization of different perspectives, skills, ideas, and innovation. To advance this idea even further, Andres Tapia, Senior Partner at Korn/Ferry International, and Mary-Frances Winters, President of The Winters Group, espouse the concept of transitioning from a uni-dimensional to a multi-dimensional framework in diversity leadership. This framework assumes that no single dimension of diversity takes place in isolation.

What does this mean? Many people define diversity as a program for blacks, women, or some other singular dimension, consisting of the external descriptors (or primary dimensions) illustrated in Figure 3.

FIGURE 3: UNI-DIMENSIONAL FRAMEWORK

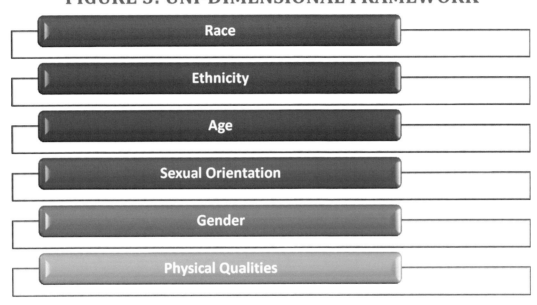

Instead, it may be more helpful to enable senior leadership and critics to define diversity from a multidimensional perspective. The multidimensional concept is also framed as intersectionality.

> Definition of **Intersectionality**:
>
> *"The interconnected nature of social categorizations such as race, class, and gender, regarded as creating overlapping and interdependent systems of discrimination or disadvantage; a theoretical approach based on such a premise."*
>
> *(Oxford Dictionary)*

According to a YW Boston Blog entitled *What is intersectionality, and what does it have to do with me?*, Kimberlé Crenshaw, law professor and social theorist, first coined the term intersectionality in her 1989 paper *Demarginalizing The Intersection Of Race And Sex: A Black Feminist Critique Of Antidiscrimination Doctrine, Feminist Theory And Antiracist Politics.* The theory emerged two decades earlier, however, when black feminists began to speak out about the white, middle-class nature of the mainstream feminist movement. Many black women found it difficult to identify with the issues of the mainstream (white) feminist movement, issues such as the pressure to be a homemaker. Black women, who often had to work in order to keep their family afloat and therefore did not have the luxury of being homemakers, did not feel as though these issues pertained to their experiences. At the same time, many black women experienced sexism while participating in the Civil Rights Movement and were often shut out of leadership positions. This intersectional experience of facing racism in the feminist movement and sexism in civil rights encouraged black women to call for a feminist practice that centralized their lived experiences." Intersectionality or multidimensional frameworks change the discourse from "this group will be the only beneficiary of diversity" to "I am diverse and will benefit from inclusion too."

Figure 4 provides a simplistic example of how the Multidimensional Framework might look in your organization.

FIGURE 4: MULTIDIMENSIONAL FRAMEWORK

Employee 1	Employee 2	Employee 3	Employee 4
• Ph.D. • Mother • Italian American • Baby-Boomer • Smoker • More	• Christian • Husband • Basketball Coach • Middle Class Suburbanite • Great Cook • More	• Gardener • Avid Cyclist • Southerner • Disabled • Extrovert • More	• Friend • Millennial • Facebooker • Traveler • Gay • More

This type of framework moves beyond external observations of groups toward multiple levels of human existence. A key assumption in this approach is that people cannot be understood or managed independent of complex determinants for human behavior (Ashford & Lecroy, 2009). It also assumes that the one-dimensional identifier may not be the dimension that the employee values most.

How to Construct the Business Case

Upon understanding the possible reactions, and developing the framework for Diversity and Inclusion, you are now ready to construct the business case. Keep in mind, that the process of approval for a business case will be thwarted if the Diversity and Inclusion leader is not prepared to handle objections. Figure 5 provides guidance.

FIGURE 5. BUSINESS CASE GUIDANCE

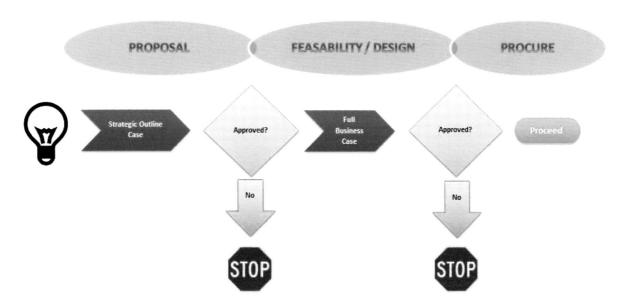

Your business case for diversity should be succinct and easy-to-understand. The following are tips to develop your business case:

- **Title**
  Everyone expects the title to briefly identify the case. An example of a good title would be "The Business Case for Employee Resource Groups".

- **Purpose**
  Generally, increased global competition supports the business case for diversity. Nevertheless, good statements include these objectives—business objectives, financial objectives, functional objectives, or operational objectives. It is important to note that your business case should not include the moral imperative or societal goals. The purpose will be designed to invoke action such as:

  - Developing a formal diversity plan
  - Conducting a diversity climate analysis, or cultural audit
  - Providing diversity training by business unit, or management level
  - Recruiting, promoting and retaining diverse talent
  - Preparing for a merger or acquisition, where two corporate cultures will mesh
  - Establishing employee resource groups, or a diversity council
  - Expanding operations internationally, nationally, or regionally, where the organization must understand customer's cultural nuances in the new market
  - Building a supplier diversity program
  - Creating multicultural curriculum or a multicultural marketing strategy
  - Designing a generational diversity or multi-cultural communications campaign
  - Pursuing socially responsible investors
  - Any combination of these or other Diversity and Inclusion objectives

The purpose should also align with the organization's strategic goals. Additionally, a short narrative description should identify the subject, scope, method of analysis, and major results.

- **Introduction**
  Position the case by telling the audience about the background, history, context, or track record. Again, do not use this as an opportunity to talk about slavery, ethnic cleansing, homophobia, or some other global issue, stay focused on the business task.

  Remind the audience about the problems, or business needs, such as lowering operating costs, improving customer satisfaction, developing professional skills, recruiting skilled human capital, and increasing capacity, production, or efficiency. Include other external factors such as competition or compliance with governmental regulations, as well as internal factors like policies or management directives. Briefly, describe alternatives.

- **Assumptions & Methods**
  What will it take for the business case to accomplish its purpose? Set the audience's expectations properly with a formal and diplomatic disclaimer, and at the same time, base your projections in terms of financial metrics. These metrics may include, but are not limited to:

  - Return on Investment (ROI)
  - Cost per employee, client/student/patient, or transaction
  - Legal costs and fines resulting from lawsuits
  - Lost client/student/patient or market share
  - Other specific metrics

  Include general assumptions pertaining to demographics, future trends, or competition. Senior leaders love to hear what other states are doing; how other healthcare organizations are faring; or how other law firms are coping. Whatever industry you're in, do the research. Equal Employment Opportunity (EEO) metrics and focus group data are popular sources to use to support the business case for diversity; however, these data sets are not as important to senior executives because the organizational impact is generally soft.

  On the surface, organizational culture appears to be a soft metric. However, when examining various aspects of the organizational culture, there are many opportunities to gather hard data. For example, cultural metrics may reflect the time it takes to deliver services to diverse customers. Alternatively, it may reflect harassment issues that result in lawsuits and turnover. Additionally, gaps in employee skills may be identified that result in lost customers or students.

  Using metrics pertaining to organizational culture will secure and maintain the attention of senior level executives more than EEO or focus group data. Nevertheless, EEO and focus group data can be helpful in providing background information.

- **Scope & Boundaries**
  Scope is the range of coverage encompassed by the business case along several dimensions. Boundaries define the scope of the business case more precisely, providing rules for which data belongs in the business case as well as guidelines for which data should be omitted.

One dimension that always needs bounding is time. Other dimensions are division or department, function, geography/location, and technology. Defining scope can help Diversity and Inclusion leaders push smaller, actionable strategies, versus sweeping entity-wide change that could be viewed as unrealistic or ineffective.

- **Scenarios**
The term scenario refers to a story showing one way that events may unfold. Scenarios are designed to make the business case clear and tangible. Business cases are built to answer questions such as:

    o Will the return justify the investment?
    o What will this action do for our business performance?
    o How will a Diversity and Inclusion strategy solve problems?

Such questions can only be answered if the business case is logically designed to address them. Use concrete details to illustrate marketing opportunities in the Hispanic community, or to describe the costs of brick-and-mortar buildings in making the case for flexible work-life programs. Also, compare scenarios to illustrate greater impact. For example: "If we continue along the current trajectory, here's what can happen: _____. However, if we make a slight adjustment, here are the opportunities that we could seize: _____."

- **Cost Model**
Cost refers to the expenditures of an organization. Financial impacts in each scenario that affect the business case include cost savings, avoided costs, continuing costs, and increased costs. For example, a Diversity and Inclusion strategy may reduce turnover costs. The cost associated with turnover can be calculated using the formula in Figure 6.

FIGURE 6: TURNOVER CALCULATION

Annual salary x the number of employees who terminated in the last year = X
X(0.30% in benefits*) = Y
X + Y = Z
Z x 0.25% = Annual Turnover Cost

$30,000 annual salary x 12 diverse employees terminating = $360,000
$360,000 x 0.30 in benefits = $108,000
$360,000 + $108,000 = $468,000
$468,000 x 0.25% = $117,000 Annual Turnover Cost

* 30% in benefits represents the industry average

When evaluating the cost, assess the price of NOT implementing a Diversity and Inclusion strategy. For example, an organization may occupy a large share of a non-diverse market; therefore, it believes that it can afford to resist broadening its appeal to different groups. Yet, the cost of not implementing a diversity strategy may exponentially increase in the long-term due to a surge in the size and buying power of diverse populations worldwide.

Thus, the current advantage in one market will not recover the cost of forgoing a Diversity and Inclusion effort.

- **Benefits**
  Although business is more than costs and savings, finances drive the business case. The following are objectives and contributions that may belong in the business case:

  - *Multicultural Sales and Marketing Objectives*
    - To increase sales revenue
    - To improve market share

  - *Financial / Business Performance Objectives*
    - To increase cash flow, margins or profits
    - To improve earnings per share

  - *Operational / Functional Objectives*
    - To shorten new product development time
    - To increase order-processing capacity

  - *Product / Service Objectives*
    - To improve customer/student/patient satisfaction
    - To update the product line or curriculum

  - *Image Enhancement Objectives*
    - To be recognized as a leading-edge product/service provider
    - To be known as a leader in social, educational or environmental issues

  - *Internal Objectives*
    - To improve employee morale and job satisfaction
    - To provide a challenging career path for employees

  - *Other Business Objectives*
    - To establish strategic alliances
    - To become a "total solution" provider

When the business case for diversity is presented via these objectives, the impact may be immediately recognized and measured in financial terms. Additionally, presenting the business case in this manner will avoid disagreements about "soft benefits".

Take supplier diversity for example. While supplier diversity provides economic benefits to the organization and the community by making bidding on contracts feasible for all vendors (the soft benefit), diverse suppliers can also provide significant ***cost savings*** on products and services in comparison to traditional vendors (hard or tangible benefits).

- **Results**
  Accordingly, there may be financial results and non-financial results. Nevertheless, if you assign no financial value to a real impact, it contributes nothing to the financial analysis. In this case, you run the risk of contributing to the bottom line but not receiving credit for doing so.

Financial results should be recorded as improvements to cash flow and compared to other scenarios. For example, your LGBT Employee Resource Group may invite other LGBT associations to your organization for a meeting to discuss strategic business opportunities. The result may be that your organization is selected as an exclusive partner by one of the associations. This partnership results in a 15% increase in new customers, new students, or new donors. A comparison could be made to equate the advantages of pursuing this business model over traditional methods, such as cold calls or direct mail.

When non-financial results are large enough to matter, and when they clearly influence a business objective, follow these three rules:

1. Be sure the impact is recorded. Describe it immediately after your financial benefits.
2. Make the impact tangible. Describe it in ways that can be observed or verified.
3. Compare the impact directly to the financial results, but in non-financial terms. Then illustrate non-financial results with a simple chart, graph, or picture (see Figure 7)

Figure 7: Diversity & Inclusion Benefits

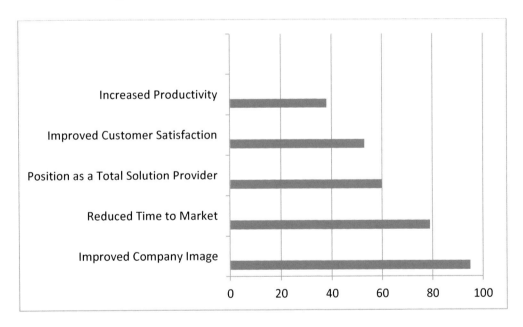

SAMPLE BUSINESS CASE FOR DIVERSITY

Chubb developed one of the best business cases for diversity. The company offers its clients more than 170 commercial insurance products, which are innovative, comprehensive, and tailored to individual customer needs. In addition, Chubb provides an array of property and casualty insurance products for individuals and families with fine homes and possessions. Their customers include many of the most affluent families in the world, CEOs of Fortune 500 companies, and art collectors.

Fortune 500 Chubb has a worldwide network of offices in 54 countries staffed by approximately 30,000 employees. After their merger with ACE Limited, the Chubb Corporation reported $37 billion in revenues in 2014 to become the world's largest publicly traded property and casualty insurer.

As stated throughout this competency, when organizations are particularly large and complex, the fundamental need for a Diversity and Inclusion strategy grows more profound.

Figure 8 encapsulates Chubb's business case for diversity

FIGURE 8: THE BUSINESS CASE FOR DIVERSITY
THE CHUBB GROUP

Those who perceive diversity as exclusively a moral imperative or societal goal are missing the larger point. Workforce diversity needs to be viewed as a competitive advantage and a business opportunity. That's why Chubb makes diversity a business priority and strives to achieve a fully inclusive diverse workforce.

Defining Diversity

Diversity is about recognizing, respecting and valuing differences based on ethnicity, gender, color, age, race, religion, disability, national origin and sexual orientation. It also includes an infinite range of individual unique characteristics and experiences, such as communication style, career path, life experience, educational background, geographic location, income level, marital status, military experience, parental status and other variables that influence personal perspectives.

These life experiences and personal perspectives make us react and think differently, approach challenges and solve problems differently, make suggestions and decisions differently, and see different opportunities. Diversity, then, is also about diversity of thought. In addition, superior business performance requires tapping into these unique perspectives.

Diverse Workforce

As our U.S. and global customer base becomes steadily more diverse, significant portions of Chubb's future growth must come from tapping into these diverse markets. If we are to form lasting business relationships with our customers and become a true global leader in the industry, we must understand our customers' diverse cultures and decisional processes, not merely their languages.

To do so, we must begin with a diverse workplace. It is well proven that diverse, heterogeneous teams promote creativity, innovation and product development. Only by fully embracing diversity and maximizing the well-being and contributions of our people can we fully maximize the strength and competitiveness of our company. We must encourage individuals to reach their full potential, in pursuit of organizational objectives, without anyone being advantaged or disadvantaged by our differences.

Demographics

Once a largely homogeneous group, the faces of customers, claimants, producers, employees and suppliers have been transformed into a dynamic mix of people comprised of various races, cultures and backgrounds. In 2008, "minorities" were roughly one-third of the U.S. Population; by 2042, "minorities" will be the majority.

Clearly, the U.S. population—and the world's—is changing dramatically. Forward-looking companies that recognize and understand the implications of these demographic shifts accordingly alter their customer focus, employee base and business practices to better manage the needs of current and future customers and employees.

Buying Power

To disregard the data on changing demographics, is to disregard the substantial growth in buying power of diverse markets. Not only are these diverse minority groups increasing as a percentage of the U.S. population, but so too is the buying power they wield.

From 1990 to 2007, minority market share and purchasing power doubled and in some cases tripled. By 2012, that buying power increased by another 30%. This economic power is not limited to minorities. Gay and lesbian consumers will control a 6.4% market share, or $835 billion. The present and future monetary power of diverse markets is more apparent each year.

Business Imperative

In order for Chubb to remain competitive for talent and for customers, it is imperative that we attract and value diverse talent and enable that talent to attract and value diverse customers.

This model can be followed when developing a business case for diversity for any organization. The data and objectives can be tailored based on whether your organization is a for-profit, nonprofit, government agency, or an educational institution.

TRANSITIONING D&I'S FOCUS TO SUSTAINABILITY

Diversity and Inclusion presents a viable opportunity for governments, educational institutions, corporations, and nonprofits to function more effectively, as well as prepare for the future. D&I leaders should actively seek examples of:

- **Cost Savings** can occur when organizations choose to utilize retired professionals or caregivers for certain part-time positions. These individuals may provide industry expertise and may not require as much training as a new employee in order to get up to speed.

- An **Avoided Cost**, on the other hand, is one that is not incurred. For example, spending on cybersecurity can avoid costs associated with data breaches, or in the Diversity and Inclusion space, providing training can help avoid the costs of a lawsuit and consent decree.

- **Opportunity Cost** is sustained when an organization loses future gain by choosing one action over another. For example, eliminating a Diversity Officer position may produce cash today, but a lost opportunity may manifest 3-4 months down the line when a multi-marketing or customer service mistake causes protests or boycotts.

There is another accounting framework that incorporates three dimensions of performance: social, environmental, and financial. It is called the **Triple Bottom Line**. This differs from traditional reporting frameworks as the Triple Bottom Line (TBL) includes ecological or environmental and social measures that can be difficult to assign appropriate means of measurement. The TBL dimensions are also commonly called the three P's: people, planet and profits. We will refer to these as the 3P's and it leads to sustainability.

According to Business News Daily, "Today's consumers are looking for more than just high-quality products and services when they make a purchase. They're prioritizing Corporate Social Responsibility (CSR), and holding corporations accountable for effecting social change with their business beliefs, practices and profits." In *What is Corporate Social Responsibility*, Nicole Fallon identifies four ways to practice CSR:

1. **Environmental Efforts:** One primary focus of corporate social responsibility is the environment. Businesses regardless of size have a large carbon footprint. Any steps they can take to reduce those footprints are considered both good for the company and society as a whole.

2. **Philanthropy:** Businesses can also practice social responsibility by donating money, products or services to social causes. Larger companies tend to have a lot of resources that can benefit charities and local community programs.

3. **Ethical Labor Practices:** By treating employees fairly and ethically, companies can also demonstrate their corporate social responsibility. This is especially true of businesses that operate in international locations with labor laws that differ from those in the United States.

4. **Volunteering**: Attending volunteer events says a lot about a company's sincerity. By doing good deeds without expecting anything in return, companies are able to express their concern for specific issues and support for certain organizations.

All of the areas are connected to Diversity and Inclusion work, as well as to consumer behaviors and decision making. Many diverse individuals make decisions about where to live and what to buy based on CSR. For this reason, some organizations have placed D&I within the purview of CSR. Following are three reasons why diversity is important to CSR and sustainability:

1. **Diversity is embedded in the definition of sustainability**
   Environmental impacts are as global as the carbon footprint and as local as litter in neighborhoods. There are so many ways diversity comes into the picture as we think about today's organizations. From the footprint of global supply chains to multinational locations

in communities around the world, employers are intrinsically linked to the people they employ and places in which they operate.

The costs and benefits associated with environmental impacts aren't always equally distributed among people. According to the National Resources Defense Council, people who live, work and play in America's most polluted environments are commonly people of color and disadvantaged communities. Increasingly, businesses have the duty to help reconstruct how resources and environmental impacts are shared among communities.

2. **There is strength in diverse voices and views**
   Diversity adds value across multiple perspectives. The more representation, inclusion and engagement there is in the workplace, the stronger the outcomes. As the number of diverse stakeholders who participate in global enterprise grows, so too does their need to account for and incorporate these diverse perspectives. For example, Coca-Cola had over 70 percent market share of fountain dispensers in North America, but it was seeing a decline in how often customers at restaurants and other locales ordered a drink with their meal. A manager by the name of Chris Dennis led a small team that operated like a startup, separate from the rest of giant Coca-Cola. Their sole task was to utilize their diverse perspectives to solve this real business problem. The team created the Coca-Cola Freestyle, which operates as a drink factory in a touchscreen box that lets customers choose from over 170 brands of beverages. In addition to boosting Coca-Cola sales, it also increased guest traffic at restaurants that offer the machines.

3. **Corporations, nonprofits and individuals can partner to better serve communities**
   Diversity enriches collaboration. When environmental progress stalls at a national level, creative and dedicated partnerships across sectors can step in to fill the void. For example, as profits hit 10-year lows, U.S. hospitals are heading overseas in search of growth. China is their top target, which is seeing an uptick in chronic diseases as its population ages. American hospitals are eyeing everything from consulting arrangements and franchise deals to outright acquisitions, according to The Wall Street Journal. Chinese hospitals get the prestige of American medical institutions, and U.S. hospitals get a fresh revenue source and new research partners. Some of these hospitals may be able to tap internal and external resources. Internally, diverse perspectives from Employee Resource Groups or Diversity Councils are invaluable to serving populations in China more effectively. Externally, partnering with educational institutions, state and local governments, Chinese-American suppliers, as well as community-based organizations would provide immense benefit to these healthcare organizations that are seeking to enter the Chinese market.

Bringing together the diversity in opinions, approaches and goals of various organizations and individuals can help bridge the divide at all levels – local, state, national and international. Caesars Entertainment is one of the companies taking the lead to embed sustainability across its business. Through innovative programs like CodeGreen at Home, Caesars incentivizes its employees to practice sustainable actions at both the workplace and at home. Their Diversity and Inclusion initiatives are a good approach to follow in order to achieve both personal vale and organizational value from your own business benefits.

References:

Burks, Frances. *How to be an Ally in the Workplace.* Chron. Available at: http://smallbusiness.chron.com/ally-workplace-35052.html

YW Boston (Mar. 29, 2017). *What is intersectionality, and what does it have to do with me?* Available at: https://www.ywboston.org/2017/03/what-is-intersectionality-and-what-does-it-have-to-do-with-me/

Ashford, Jose B. & LeCroy, Craig W. (Cengage Learning, 2009). *"Human Behavior in the Social Environment: A Multidimensional Perspective"*, 4th Edition. Belmont, CA.

Evans, Melanie. (Wall Street Journal, Apr. 22, 2018). *"U.S. Hospital Firms, Hungry to Expand, Look to China."* Available at: https://www.wsj.com/articles/overseas-markets-beckon-u-s-hospital-firms-hungry-to-expand-1524394800

Fallon, Nicole. (Business News Daily, Dec. 29, 2017). "What is Corporate Social Responsibility?" Available at: https://www.businessnewsdaily.com/4679-corporate-social-responsibility.html

Sample Test Questions:

IMPROVING YOUR APPROACH TO THE BOTTOM LINE

1. **The process of approval for a business case will be thwarted if the Diversity and Inclusion leader:**
   A. Is assuming a relatively new role
   B. Did not develop a strategic plan
   C. Is not prepared to handle objections

2. **The business case for Diversity and Inclusion is a:**
   A. Summary of corporate grievances
   B. Reasoned proposal for change
   C. Detailed description of EEO data

3. **The framework that assumes no single dimension of diversity takes place in isolation is:**
   A. Uni-dimensional
   B. Bi-dimensional
   C. Multi-dimensional

4. **The purpose of the business case for diversity is to:**
   A. Invoke action
   B. Educate employees
   C. Eliminate bias

5. **The following metric is a popular method for communicating the business case and impact, but is generally considered an ineffective metric by senior executives:**
   A. Return on Investment
   B. Legal costs and fines
   C. Internal EEO data

6. **Scope can be defined as:**
   A. The range of coverage encompassed by the business case along several dimensions
   B. The rules for which data belongs in the business case, and which do not
   C. The instrument that you use to create your Diversity and Inclusion vision

7. **The Triple Bottom Line consists of people, planet and _____.**
   A. Products
   B. Planning
   C. Profits

Sample Test Questions:

IMPROVING YOUR APPROACH TO THE BOTTOM LINE

8. **Which workplace model focused on using cultural competence and inclusion to leverage the skills and resources of diverse employees?**
   A. Social Justice Model
   B. Diversity Model
   C. Inclusive Business Model

9. **For some people, ethnicity-based diversity initiatives result in:**
   A. A zero-sum ratio
   B. Reverse discrimination
   C. Lower standards

10. **Financial results in the Business Case should be recorded as improvements to cash flow and:**
    A. Compared to other scenarios
    B. Described after non-financial results
    C. Detailed in chart or graph form

11. **All of the following are true regarding diversity's link to sustainability EXCEPT:**
    A. There is strength in diverse voices and perspectives
    B. Diversity is embedded in the definition of sustainability
    C. Inclusion empowers an organization to strive for equity

12. **An example of a uni-dimensional framework is gender.**
    A. True
    B. False

13. **Non-financial results such as increased productivity is always relevant to a business case.**
    A. True
    B. False

14. **Scenarios are designed to make the business case clear and tangible.**
    A. True
    B. False

15. **Financial justification is the only purpose of the business case.**
    A. True
    B. False

GLOBAL BEST PRACTICES

Diversity in itself does not create a model for inclusion—an inclusive environment must be intentionally designed, nurtured, and supported. Similarly, receiving an award for Diversity leadership does not necessarily mean that the organization is a great example of inclusion. This begs the question: **who can be a role model?**

Demonstrating a best practice in the field of Diversity and Inclusion does not exempt an organization from mistakes, nor does it translate into perfection. In order to improve organizational outcomes, it may be necessary to admit that Diversity is a journey and not a destination. It's also possible to elevate one's work by looking outside of traditional techniques and resources toward global best practices.

OVERALL OBJECTIVES AND COMPETENCIES

The purpose of this competency is to ensure that D&I leaders operate a best-in-class Diversity effort by adopting professional methods and/or techniques that have been globally accepted as superior in fostering equity, defining inclusive excellence, and achieving a discrimination- and harassment-free work environment.

OVERVIEW

A **Best Practice** is a method or technique that is generally accepted as superior or most effective. At one time, recent research data and best practices in the field of Diversity and Inclusion (D&I) were scant. Like most maturing industries, however, the D&I field has since evolved. For example, DiversityInc. has used a data-driven methodology to assess and track corporate best practices in diversity for roughly 20 years. Through their highly publicized Top 50 Companies for Diversity and other lists, organizations have begun to pay more attention to the use of best practices, as well as to their competitive standing.

According to DiversityInc., "Diversity management is the strategy of using best practices with proven results to find and create a diverse and inclusive workplace. Successful strategies link diversity progress directly to business results. Best practices include the effective use of executive diversity councils, mentoring and sponsorship programs, and employee resource groups to achieve desired results in recruitment, retention and management of diverse talent."

Google can help you find the answer to almost anything. However, in the Diversity and Inclusion space, it is not advisable to utilize a search engine to figure out how to do your job. Likewise, it is not recommended to copy random training programs, diversity plans, evaluation criteria, or other items because the organization does not have a current model for these materials. While Google can be helpful in many areas, for purposes of Diversity and Inclusion, there is a fundamental problem with copying someone else's work without knowing the corporate goals, context, or culture for which the work was done. In other words, copying and pasting a template is not necessarily a best practice.

While this study guide is not an all-inclusive list of every best practice as it relates to Equity, Diversity and Inclusion work, leaders can customize their approach, or even create their own model for internal departments or others to emulate.

THE DIVERSITY TOOLBOX

Achieving and advancing Diversity is a process that must be continuously evaluated, updated, and refined. Along the same lines, in order to enhance Equity and Inclusion, an organization must be purposeful, consistent, and cognizant of the many ways in which exclusion and bias can manifest.

It will be difficult to attain Equity, Diversity, or Inclusion if leaders deploy the same tools to fix every problem. It will be equally challenging if there are no strategic tools with which to create innovative solutions. **The Diversity Toolbox** is a proverbial set of equipment that one can utilize to fix problems or develop solutions. Traditionally, in the U.S., the primary tools are Diversity training and Diversity Recruiting. In fact, the American industry is shaped by an approach that leads with, and heavily relies on, these two tools. In Europe, however, organizations lead with: (1) staff-recruiting, retention and management; (2) organizational culture initiatives; and (3) work-life policies. See Figure 1.

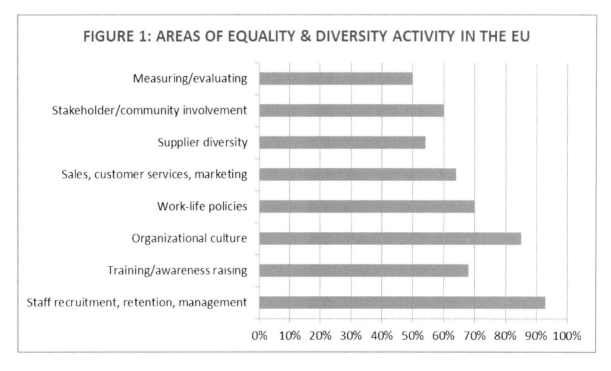

The European Community Programme for Employment and Social Solidarity conducted a survey of more than 330 companies with the European Business Test Panel (EBTP) between 2005 and 2008 on the subject of diversity management. Figure 1 illustrates where most Equality and Diversity efforts were concentrated in the European Union (EU). Since several of the top areas of focus do not involve making money, saving money or achieving organizational goals, the perceived benefits of Equality and Diversity are soft. The data also shows a disconnect from operations. According to the report, Equality and Diversity (E&D) "policies were slightly less likely to involve activities engaged with other areas of a company's business. While two-thirds of companies said their policies included a focus on sales, customer services, and marketing, only half responded to stakeholder and community engagement. Another half of company policies were related to supplier diversity."

Given that the majority of EBTP companies are at the beginning of their diversity journey – combined with the fact that very few companies set and measure targets – it is not surprising that the benefits they perceived from Equality and Diversity were still rather restricted (see Figure 2). Almost two-thirds of EBTP companies suggested that E&D policies made a positive impact on their business-- almost one-third claimed that they still could not tell how E&D efforts affected the organization.

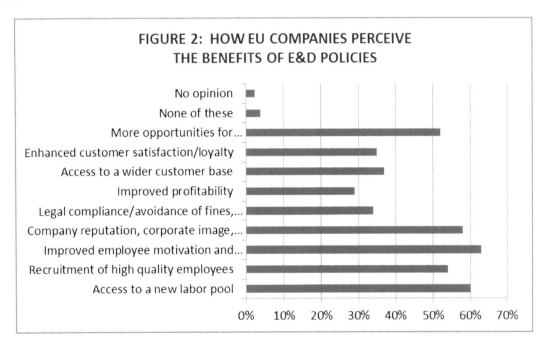

FIGURE 2: HOW EU COMPANIES PERCEIVE THE BENEFITS OF E&D POLICIES

It's easy to take for granted that everyone understands the value (or benefits) that Diversity and Inclusion brings to an organization. An effective D&I leader, however, will not assume that executives and employees understand Diversity terminology, the Business Case, or how Inclusion benefits everyone in the organization. Therefore, the D&I leader must not only be self-aware, but also intentional about their objectives.

According to the Stanford Encyclopedia of Philosophy, "in its philosophical usage, the meaning of the word 'intentionality' should not be confused with the ordinary meaning of the word 'intention.' As the Latin etymology of 'intentionality' indicates, the relevant idea of directedness or tension (an English word which derives from the Latin verb *tendere*) arises from pointing towards or attending to some target." Hence, D&I leaders will demonstrate the most value by focusing on a target. There are a variety of tools that leaders can use to hit organizational targets or achieve their D&I goals. Whether in the U.S., Europe, or elsewhere, Diversity and Inclusion leaders must explicitly connect the utilization of certain tools to the benefits that an organization will receive. A partial listing of equipment in the Diversity Toolbox is listed in Figure 3.

FIGURE 3. AN ARRAY OF EQUIPMENT IN THE DIVERSITY TOOLBOX

(Source: The Society for Diversity, 2018)

- Anti-Discrimination & Harassment Laws
- Anonymous Applications
- Benchmarking
- Best Practices
- Climate Analysis
- Communications & Reports
- Cultural Competency Education
- Defining D&I Terminology
- Diversity Councils
- Diversity Training
- Employee / Business Resource Groups
- Focus Groups
- Goal Setting
- Management Accountability
- Measurement Activities (e.g., goals to progress)
- Mentoring, Coaching & Sponsorship
- Multicultural Marketing
- Needs Analysis
- Onboarding
- Organizational Culture Assessment
- Pay Equity Analysis
- Performance Incentives & Rewards
- Policies and Procedures
- Product Development
- Quarterly and Annual D&I Evaluations
- Recruiting, Retention, and Management
- Research & Data
- Strategic Diversity Planning
- Succession Planning
- Supplier Diversity
- Surveys
- Work-Life Initiatives

Which tool should one rely on most? It depends on the situation. Diversity and Inclusion leaders must get comfortable utilizing many different tools and skills in order to execute strategy, as well as preempt or solve problems. Relying on one tool too much will result in the scope of Diversity and Inclusion work being limited to that particular tool. For example, the reliance on Diversity recruiting and training in America can be viewed as a cost center, which some organizations will undertake only if they have "extra" resources available. Because Diversity and Inclusion is viewed as an add-on in this scenario, it is not a strategic imperative.

The Toolbox is different from an Intervention. A Diversity and Inclusion Intervention is a strategy, program, or initiative that is put in place to:

- Prevent inequalities, biases, and harassment from impeding customer service, sales or collaboration at work
- Protect the brand by operating consistently and equitably across regions, nations, and communities
- Foster an environment with a sense of belonging, respect and tolerance in order to comply with legal requirements and/or achieve risk management objectives
- Educate management and/or develop employee competencies and skills that can contribute to the bottom-line

- Correct problem behavior or prevent problem behavior from occurring in the first place
- Diversify the employee population in order to successfully penetrate and serve diverse markets
- Customize products and/or offer high-quality services to unique groups who have different expectations for organizational effectiveness
- Improve the experiences of talented diverse employees, executives, Board members, etc. in order to increase retention and productivity, and decrease turnover and waste
- Build coalitions with partners and suppliers who represent various aspects of local communities
- Benchmark the organization's performance against direct and indirect competitors, as well as other internal functions

The toolbox is *what* you use to demonstrate value, while the intervention is *why* you use certain tools to achieve desired targets.

THE ROLE OF POLICIES IN PROMOTING EQUITY

Organizational policies are among the most important tools in one's toolbox. Policies help to ensure the consistent treatment of people and contribute to the uniform application of rules. Without policies, it will be difficult to take advantage of opportunities to positively impact the organizational culture. Policies also allow organizations to implement best practices.

Adapting best practices requires a re-evaluation of both written and unwritten rules. Undertaking this effort may entail partnering with Human Resources, as well as front-line supervisors, to determine which formal and informal policies advance, or hinder, the perception of fairness and belonging. D&I leaders must also ask the right questions when they observe that certain policies do not achieve expected outcomes. For example, a pharmaceutical company sent a sales representative to Diversity job fairs around the U.S. in order to interview diverse candidates for employment. After several job fairs and dozens of interviews with highly skilled professionals, the sales representative inquired why none of the candidates were considered for employment. The sales representative was told that his work at the job fairs allowed his manager to check a box that the task of interviewing diverse candidates was complete. There were never any intentions to actually hire these individuals. In this case, simply developing a policy of interviewing diverse candidates did not result in an increase in workforce diversity.

The ability to follow-up will distinguish effective leaders from mediocre ones. Savvy D&I managers must periodically follow-up and measure the impact of policy changes and/or other initiatives. Further, the enforcement of policies must be monitored as well. For example, police officers who use excessive force likely violate departmental policies in seemingly insignificant ways. Turning off a body camera, embellishing a report, or roughing up a suspect may not result in punishment in some departments. But because no-one monitors and reports on civilian complaints in many of these cases, accountability decreases and abuse may become rampant in the law-enforcement culture. According to the Governing Institute, experts endorse two core recommendations for departments looking to improve citizen oversight: (1) get rid of "special rules" protecting police officers and (2) increase the transparency of an officer's disciplinary proceedings and history. Transparency is the key. According to the New York Times, "there appears to be a higher level of concern about corporate transparency, philanthropy, and ethics in the Millennial generation than in older cohorts of shoppers and workers." Corporate transparency describes the extent to which information about an organization's actions are voluntarily shared with stakeholders. The process of transparency consists of information disclosure, clarity, and accuracy. Organizational efforts to achieve transparency are not only linked to sustainability, but also connected to governmental regulations, local norms, and the set of information, privacy, and business policies relative to corporate decision-making and operational openness.

A policy of transparency will also help uncover unwritten rules. In spite of written policies, unwritten rules govern how work actually gets done, and they also define the culture of an organization. Most unwritten rules can be observed. Examples of these rules include:

- **How time is managed.** Do employees eat at their desk or take a lunch break away from their desks? Do workers forgo vacations? Can a pregnant worker or veteran take time off?

- **What to do when the CEO is, or is not, around.** Do employees work more and talk less? Is the environment more or less formal? Will employees support diversity without visible CEO support?

- **When the work day really ends.** Should employees leave before the boss? Is overtime naturally expected? Can caregivers advance professionally if they don't work extraordinarily long hours?

- **Whether different people or new ideas are accepted.** Are "certain" workers frequently left out of important meetings? What happens when employees suggest new ideas?

It can be difficult to ensure that policies and practices are transparent. First, transparency is not a one-time occurrence. D&I leaders must continually update policies with a focus on current events and workplace trends. Second, key executives constantly come and go at some organizations—making administration and enforcement challenging. For all of these reasons and more, responsibility for updating and monitoring policies must extend beyond Human Resources and the Office of Diversity.

Policies are merely one tool in the toolbox. Relying too heavily on policies will cause employees to believe that Diversity and Inclusion is associated with political correctness, legal compliance, or other negative employment actions.

It's best to synchronize policies with a variety of different tools in order to achieve great results. In *Why Diversity Programs Fail*, authors Frank Dobbin and Alexandra Kalev assert that organizations should not outlaw bias and inequity. The 2016 Harvard Business Review article states, "Executives favor a classic command-and-control approach to diversity because it boils expected behaviors down to do's and don'ts that are easy to understand and defend. Yet this approach also flies in the face of nearly everything we know about how to motivate people to make changes. Decades of social science research point to a simple truth: You won't get managers on board by blaming and shaming them with rules and reeducation."

Further, changes to policies should be clearly communicated to all stakeholders. D&I managers should also provide ample time for the policy changes to go into effect so that stakeholders can make adjustments as needed.

BEST-IN-CLASS DIVERSITY & INCLUSION EFFORTS

Employers have policies, while governments have laws. Both are necessary in order to achieve genuine change. As more entities (e.g., government agencies, corporations, nonprofits, and educational institutions) work together, the systemic nature of diversity work will become more apparent. For example, a person who understands the power of inclusion in K-12 schools, may transfer cultural competency skills to a university, and then to a workplace, and ultimately to a residential community. Hence, the most effective Diversity efforts will extend beyond an organization's four walls and include external partners and other stakeholders.

Following are examples of global equity, diversity and inclusion efforts that have garnered outcomes that are worth emulating.

Europe: Gender Diversity Quotas

Gender quota laws have had a far greater impact than anticipated, resulting in European countries leading the way in Diversity on Boards of Directors. Konstantina Govotsos wrote a dissertation on the subject for the University of Pennsylvania entitled, *Gender Diversity in Corporate Boards in France: An Analysis.* Govotsos found that "since Norway passed the first quota mandate for women's representation on corporate boards in 2003, governments have looked to gender quotas as a tool to accelerate gender equality. Though the effects in Norway were at first mixed, as the so-called "golden skirt" problem resulted in only a few women occupying multiple board seats, several European countries followed Norway's footsteps and mandated some form of gender quotas on corporate boards."

According to Catalyst, one study found that countries with specific targets, quotas and penalties for not meeting regulations had nearly double the average percentage of women on Boards compared to countries without those measures. A 2011 French law required corporate boards to be at least 20% female by January 2014, or Directors risk losing their fees. In January 2012, women represented 22% of board members at France's biggest public companies. By 2016, females represented 34% of Board seats. Norway achieved an astounding 46% of women on Boards as of 2016. In addition to diversifying the Board of Directors, gender quotas simultaneously resulted in diversified senior leadership teams, where the largest companies saw an increase in women holding C-level positions.

Belgium, Spain, the Netherlands, Norway, Iceland and Italy recently enacted similar statutes. The U.K. and Swedish governments have embraced voluntary targets. The U.K. hoped women would occupy 25% of boardroom positions at the biggest companies by 2015, but without penalties, gender diversity efforts failed to materialize significant progress. As of 2016, the percentage of women on Corporate Boards was stuck at 16%, while women in C-level positions decreased 3%. In this scenario, the legislative mandate was effective, while the voluntary target was not. This is a prime example of how D&I results can vary if an entity does not make a full commitment to equity and inclusion. Nevertheless, keep in mind that mandates are not always successful.

Canada: LGBTQ+ Inclusion

Despite great progress in the last decade, homophobia and transphobia still exist in the workplace, and the topic remains underrepresented in Diversity and Inclusion conversations.

As previously stated, if organizations want to show that they are serious about tackling all forms of discrimination, it is essential to have a formal policy outlining the employer's position and the expected behaviors that should be exhibited by all workers. Accordingly, employers must have explicit policies protecting LGBTQ+ employees, customers, patients, and students from discrimination, harassment and retaliation. The key is to emphasize professionalism and the standards that the public generally expects from your organization, regardless of one's sexual orientation, gender identity, or gender expression.

One country in particular is a global model for how they integrated policies with laws. In Canada, same-sex relations between consenting adults was considered a crime punishable by imprisonment before 1969. That year, the Canadian government passed an omnibus bill decriminalizing private sexual acts between two people over the age of 21 – a breakthrough in treating gay men, lesbians and bisexuals equally under the law.

Almost ten years later, in 1977, Quebec became the first jurisdiction in Canada to amend its provincial charter of human rights to include sexual orientation as a prohibited ground for discrimination.

In 1996, the Act was amended to specifically include sexual orientation as one of the prohibited grounds of discrimination. This inclusion was a clear declaration by Parliament that gay, lesbian and bisexual Canadians are entitled to "an opportunity equal with other individuals to make for themselves the lives they are able and wish to have". Today, the Canadian Human Rights Act prohibits discrimination based on race, national or ethnic origin, color, religion, age, sex, sexual orientation, gender identity or expression, marital status, family status, genetic characteristics, disability and conviction for an offence for which a pardon has been granted or a record was suspended.

In 2000, Parliament passed Bill C-23 which gives same-sex couples the same social and tax benefits as heterosexuals in common-law relationships. Additionally, the enactment of the Civil Marriage Act in 2005 marked a milestone in sexual orientation equality rights by allowing same-sex couples to be married anywhere in Canada.

Nonprofit and corporate partnerships have been instrumental in ensuring that LGBTQ+ individuals experience the full intent of the law. For example, Pride-at-Work Canada develops a Cross-Canada Survey to assess job application data, interviewing and hiring statistics, as well as other LGBTQ+ insights. They also distribute a Best Practices Guide and provide benchmarking data to employers.

The Scandinavian Way to Work-Life
Whether one calls it work-life balance or work-life integration, allowing employees to alter work or life schedules has been recognized as an effective practice. In 2017, companies in France that have more than 50 employees have been ordered to implement "the right to disconnect" in an effort to reduce stress and help people balance work and personal life. Nevertheless, the top countries for work-life are Sweden, Denmark, and Norway. For these nations, the Scandinavian Way is all about balance.

Sweden, like Denmark and the Netherlands, has adopted a policy to improve work-life balance for its citizens. For example, Sweden has considered flexible working time arrangements and they tested sabbatical leave. The Swedish government has taken the initiative to reduce the work-life conflict experienced mostly by women, by promoting men's participation in housework and the upbringing of children. In this instance, inclusion efforts target both women *and* men.

Parental leave is structured so that it encourages men to stay at home more with their newborn babies, thus encouraging both parents to take care of their children. Moreover, the Swedish welfare system includes an extensive child-care system that guarantees a place in a public day-care facility for all children between the ages of 2 and 6 years old.

If companies plan to do business in Sweden during the summer, it is important to remember that most of the Swedes take their vacations between June and August. The minimum amount of vacation time per year is five weeks. Swedes are also not available during the Christmas holidays at the end of the year or at Easter.

Normal working hours in Sweden are 40 hours a week with an upper limit of 48 hours. Some companies in Sweden have started experimenting with 6 hour work days, or 30 hour work weeks. At Toyota's Swedish service center, shifts were cut for mechanics more than a decade ago. The company saw a swift uptick in productivity and profitability, although mechanics worked fewer hours.

Obviously, there is no limit for managers who sometimes have to work at home. Due to the development of telecommunications, more and more Swedes are used to working from home. Always keep in mind though that after 5 pm most Swedish employees are committed to taking care of their families or enjoying time with friends. Working overtime is neither valued nor seen as a necessity; in fact, it can be viewed as an indication of poor planning and time management.

While taxes are higher, Danes do not mind, according to a Bloomberg report. The report states that higher taxes support what people in Scandinavian nations treasure most: happiness. Work-life integration has been instrumental in improving the quality of life, education, health, civic engagement, earnings, productivity, and satisfaction.

Anonymous Applications

According to an article in the Economist entitled, *No names, no bias?*, "Discrimination against job applicants based on their names is well documented, particularly among ethnic minorities. An experiment in Germany found that candidates with German-sounding names were 14% more likely to be called for an interview than candidates with Turkish ones. A review of various studies, by the Institute for the Study of Labor (IZA), a German outfit, found that anonymized job applications boost the chances of ethnic-minority candidates being invited to an interview. A Swedish study found that it led to more ethnic-minority people being hired. However, the results from other trials are less clear. A second Swedish experiment found that only women, not immigrants, were boosted by anonymous recruitment." The results of the second study indicate that the process has to be tied to other interventions in order to achieve the best results. In particular, anonymous applications enable diverse people to get to the interview stage; but once the individual arrives for the meeting, then what?

The Economist adds, "Several countries have experimented with name-blind applications. In 2010 Germany's Anti-Discrimination Agency, an advisory body, sponsored a voluntary scheme to get businesses to try it. In France a law passed in 2006 made the anonymizing of applicants' CVs compulsory for firms with more than 50 employees. But the government was slow in laying down the conditions for how the law would operate, and only started enforcing it in 2014. In Sweden and the Netherlands there have been some trials." Applying best practices requires working out the fine details before executing a new initiative. This may entail engaging in a pilot or trial before rolling out a huge enterprise-wide program. Pilots will be discussed in greater detail later.

With anonymous applications, you must utilize more sources to pursue a broader pool of diverse candidates. Keep in mind, the full potential of anonymous recruitment can be realized only if there are no broad structural differences in qualifications or skills between applicant groups. While it can be very effective in reducing bias in the initial candidate sourcing process, removing the data can be a huge effort so you may want to work with a tech company that specializes in creating software specifically for this purpose.

As stated earlier, in addition to anonymous applications, organizations must consider other interventions to effectively recruit, onboard, develop, engage and retain diverse individuals. For example, the employer may utilize a trained interviewing panel; develop an onboarding program; offer cultural competency education to current employees; design mentoring and sponsorship initiatives; offer a broader array of employee resource groups; and track retention data, to name a few.

ELIMINATING WORKPLACE SEXUAL HARASSMENT

Harassment leaves its fingerprint on the organizational culture of any employer that allows it to persist.

In the wake of the Harvey Weinstein scandal, and all of the fallout from other entertainers and celebrities being implicated in sexual harassment complaints, there is a burning question: *with all of the Diversity programs and equal opportunity efforts around the world, why is sexual harassment still a workplace problem?* This question, and the inevitable answer, perplexes both Diversity leaders and organizational executives.

In June 2016, the U.S. Equal Employment Opportunity Commission (EEOC) held a public meeting where the latest Task Force report and recommendations on workplace harassment were released. The report notes that while more research is needed in this area, workplace harassment too often goes unreported, as "roughly three out of four individuals who experienced harassment never even talked to a supervisor, manager, or union representative about the harassing conduct." The report also acknowledged that training must change. In fact, "much of the training done over the last 30 years has not worked as a prevention tool-- it's been too focused on simply avoiding legal liability". The translation is that the law is for lawbreakers, and some people may think that because they are not breaking "the law", policies governing harassment do not apply to them. Nevertheless, training should address some of these "fuzzy" areas. Following are examples:

- *Jen hugs some of her male co-workers, but how should she handle the guys that she doesn't feel comfortable hugging?*

- *Bob normally tells jokes about all sorts of things-- although a few of his jokes may not be appropriate for the workplace. Are Bob's jokes really offensive if everyone always laughs?*

- *Tom often misses deadlines and some people in XYX department give him a gentle nudge right before a due date. He complains that they are harassing him. Should a supervisor step in?*

- *Everyone sees Gail, who is a Senior Vice President, engaging in unprofessional behavior. How can someone report Gail without jeopardizing their job or their ability to get a promotion?*

- *Nigel regularly makes outbursts in the classroom about political issues. If another student tells him to be quiet, he attacks them verbally. The teacher has sent Nigel to the Office, moved his seat, and called his parents. At what point should the teacher simply ignore Nigel?*

- *Everyone knows that you can always count on Tina for the juicy office scoop. There's no harm in a little workplace gossip, is there? Even if 1 or 2 people are (deservedly) frequent targets?*

Some D&I managers are reluctant to offer training that does not have the word "Diversity" in the title. However, this can work to your advantage as more employees may be interested in Diversity-related topics, but *not* generic Diversity training. Providing employee education in bystander interventions, workplace civility, and making harassment complaints are all crucial skills that workers/students can use.

Bystander Intervention Training
Bystanders may recognize a potentially harmful situation or interaction but they may not know how to respond. D&I leaders are in a unique position to empower Bystanders to respond in a way that could positively influence the outcome.

According to Psychology Today, "the Bystander Effect occurs when the presence of others discourages an individual from intervening in an emergency situation. Social psychologists Bibb Latané and John Darley popularized the concept following the infamous 1964 Kitty Genovese murder in New York City. Genovese was stabbed to death outside her apartment while bystanders who observed the crime did not step in to assist or call the police. Latané and Darley attributed the bystander effect to the perceived diffusion of responsibility (onlookers are less likely to intervene if there are other witnesses who are perceived as likely to do so) and social influence (individuals in a group monitor the behavior of those around them to determine how to act). In Genovese's case, each onlooker concluded from their neighbors' inaction that their own personal help was not needed."

The Bystander Effect often occurs in the workplace or on college campuses. Research has shown however, that bystanders can make a significant impact in preventing or stopping harassment and other inappropriate behavior. Before intervening, bystanders should use their best judgement to determine the level of danger that is present. In Portland, Oregon, three bystanders were stabbed on a train when they tried to intervene and stop a White Supremacist from taunting two young women because of their ethnic and religious diversity.

Like all other forms of Diversity training, employees/students should be able to walk away with skills that they can apply on the job or on campus. Depending on the situation, Lehigh University recommends three (3) strategies that individuals can employ in a Bystander Intervention:

1. *Involve Yourself*
   Students/employees can get directly involved in the situation. This is where an individual steps in and says or does something to stop the situation. For example, if someone is trying to take an intoxicated student to a room, the bystander can directly intervene by taking the person aside and saying, "Hey man, she looks drunk. I do not think that's a good idea." If an employee observes harassment, the bystander can say, "That wasn't funny. We're at work, let's act like professionals." In the classroom, teachers can stop bullying by using a firm voice to say, "This is not acceptable in my classroom. We have a rigorous agenda today and we must stay focused on the topic at hand."

2. *Interrupt the Situation*
   An employee/student can distract the harasser by redirecting the attention of those behaving inappropriately toward something else. For example, if one individual is berating another and things are getting heated, the bystander can call the victim's cellphone or the bystander can tell the victim that someone is outside urgently looking for him/her. Bystanders can also interrupt the harasser by making a simple (or elaborate) distraction to diffuse the situation. For example, the bystander can say, "Sue, let's go to the breakroom to get a cup of coffee." Walking away from the aggressor may temporarily diffuse the situation until the bystander and victim obtain more assistance.

3. *Initiate Help*
   This is a good option if a bystander does not feel safe directly intervening, the bystander is not sure what to do, or the individual simply does not want to get directly involved. For example, in New York, an unidentified man was recorded as he yelled at the employees of a Fresh Kitchen restaurant in Manhattan, berating the workers for speaking Spanish to customers. The bystanders did not feel comfortable intervening at the moment, but they sought help by recording the interaction and posting the rant on Twitter. The video went viral and within hours, the man was identified as a lawyer who touted his fluency in Spanish. Bystanders can also notify a supervisor/human resources, submit an anonymous report, advise a counseling professional, or call the police. The bystander training should explicitly identify these potential resources, as well as describe the scenarios in which employees should call the police.

Situations can escalate into violence or become more traumatic for the victim if bystanders do not act quickly. Thus, bystander training should stress the benefits of getting involved early.

Hashtag MeToo
The #MeToo Movement spread virally in October 2017 as a hashtag used on social media to help demonstrate the widespread prevalence of sexual assault and harassment, especially in the workplace. It followed public allegations of sexual misconduct by Harvey Weinstein. The phrase, long used by social activist Tarana Burke to help survivors realize they are not alone, was popularized by actress Alyssa Milano when she encouraged women to tweet it to "give people a sense of the magnitude of the problem". Since then, the phrase has been posted online millions of times, often with a personal story of sexual harassment or assault.

A University of Kent lecturer, Afroditi Pina, recently wrote an article for BBC News entitled, *How to Stamp Out Sexual Harassment in the Workplace*. Pina reports, "Research shows that the climate of an organization and tolerance are the strongest predictors of sexual harassment. How permissive the organizational climate is determines how risky a complaint appears to the victim, how likely the harasser is to be punished, and how seriously one's complaints will be received by the organization and their colleagues. A common theme in the Weinstein allegations is that his behavior was widely known. Other employees in his company were complicit in it too, so complaints were difficult and risky for the victims." This would explain a low incidence of formal reporting. Of course, enough cannot be said about bystander intervention techniques, but it is also important to ensure supervisors are equipped to identify harassment and bullying, as well as practice handling it effectively. For high-level or rainmaker complaints, get the Board involved so employees do not have to fear the repercussions of reporting a superior.

Although the BBC News featured Pina's article, some assert that EU laws and culture prevent Western European employers from experiencing harassment on the level that's in the U.S.

Excerpt from "How employers in European countries should deal with workplace sexual harassment" by Richard Lister | Ius Laboris, 12 Dec 2017

Within European jurisdictions, there is a degree of uniformity in laws concerning sexual harassment on account of European Union legislation. The issue was first addressed in a concerted way at EU level in 1991, with the adoption of a Recommendation on the dignity of women and men at work and a Code of Practice on measures to combat sexual harassment. The current EU definition of sexual harassment is set out in the 2006 Equal Treatment Directive (2006/54/EC): "where any form of unwanted verbal, non-verbal or physical conduct of a sexual nature occurs, with the purpose or effect of violating the dignity of a person, in particular when creating an intimidating, hostile, degrading, humiliating or offensive environment". While EU regulation has led to some measure of consistency in member states' laws dealing with sexual harassment, there are significant differences of emphasis and approach. Some of the key differences are described below.

In the U.K., the definition of harassment specifically covers unwanted conduct "of a sexual nature", which is prohibited if it has the purpose or effect of violating a person's dignity or creating an intimidating, hostile, degrading, humiliating or offensive environment. It is also harassment if the harasser treats the victim less favorably because of the victim's rejection of, or submission to, this conduct. Employers in the UK are liable for acts of sexual harassment committed by their employees, even if these were not authorized or known about. An employer has a defense in this situation if it can show that it has taken all reasonable steps to prevent the harassment from occurring.

Italy defines sexual harassment as a form of discrimination and, in particular, as unwanted conduct of a sexual nature expressed in any way which violates, or is intended to violate the dignity of an employee or which creates an intimidating, hostile, degrading, humiliating or offensive working environment. Even if the employer is not itself the perpetrator of the harassment, it could still be liable on account of the general obligation to ensure the health and safety of all employees.

Sexual harassment is a criminal offence in France. It is defined by the fact of repeatedly imposing behaviors or discussions with a sexual connotation on a person that either: offend his or her human dignity because of their degrading or humiliating characteristics; or create an intimidating, hostile or offensive situation for that person.

In Denmark, employers are required to take action when they become aware that an employee is alleging sexual harassment, but there are no specific legal obligations in relation to the investigative procedures that are to be followed. According to the Danish Working Environment Authority, it is advisable for the employer to talk with the alleged harasser as well as the alleged victim to determine the facts. As it may be difficult for the employer to be objective, it is also advisable for it to involve a third-party adviser in these matters. Most large companies have implemented a sexual harassment policy that provides guidelines on information regarding the type of behavior which will not be tolerated, specifying that sexual harassment is prohibited and laying down clear directions on how and where employees can file a report. However, it is not common that companies offer training courses for their managers to prevent sexual harassment.

In Belgium, Companies need to take measures to prevent sexual harassment. Such measures must be based on a risk analysis and will differ from one business to another, taking into account factors such as the activities, the context, and whether it is a large or small organization. Employers also need to implement internal procedures to enable employees who have been sexually harassed to contact a neutral and objective person of trust and/or a specialized prevention counsellor (usually someone who is external to the company and a certified psychologist). Employees who use these internal procedures are protected against dismissal. Finally, employers should provide psychological assistance and support to victims.

In other parts of the world such as in regions of Asia, Africa, and South America, sexual harassment is routine. According to a CNN report entitled *Sexual Harassment: How it stands around the globe*, the conduct could include "the words 'hey, beautiful' or 'hey, sexy,' or a woman may be instructed to smile. It may be more intentional such as standing in the way or blocking a person's path in hope of some interaction. It may get more aggressive—with a person's hands reaching to inappropriate places on another individual." Legislation may have been passed to prohibit harassment, but in many cases, the laws are not enforced. Harassment is a global phenomenon and multinational employers with workers around the globe must be prepared to address different customs, traditions and religions that may impede harassment prevention efforts. What is acceptable conduct in one culture may not bode well in another community.

STRIVING FOR INCLUSIVE EXCELLENCE

The Harvey Weinstein case illustrates the fact that our work is not done yet. In fact, throughout the U.S. and in the European Union, exclusion and discrimination have become mainstream concepts in communities where racist and sexist identities were previously relegated to society's fringes.

Nevertheless, before you adopt a new entity-wide Diversity and Inclusion effort, do your homework. Conduct an analysis of the organizational climate to determine readiness. Find out where you can anticipate resistance and then develop a plan to reduce it. Also, understand how well employees adapt to change.

Key Elements of Leading D&I Programs

In 2017, PwC conducted a global, cross-industry survey of business, D&I, and HR leaders who develop and execute their organizations' Diversity and Inclusion strategies to understand what programs their organizations have in place, and the impact they are having on the employee experience. The report entitled, *Diversity & Inclusion Global Benchmarking Survey*, consisted of 810 corporate respondents in 5 regions and 25+ industries.

PwC found that there are four elements to a best-in-class Diversity and Inclusion program.

1. *Understanding the facts of today*
   Initiating a continuous process for understanding the facts of what's happening inside the organization today. Examples include:

   - Gathering and analyzing data to remove bias and increase opportunity, including demographic data, performance and compensation data, and feedback from customers.
   - Sharing information on the Diversity of the company with employees

2. *Building an inspirational strategy*
   Creating a business-focused vision and strategy for D&I that reflects the reality of today and the real potential of tomorrow. Examples include:

   - Identifying D&I as a priority for driving business results
   - Publicly communicating progress toward meeting goals

3. *Developing leadership engagement*
   Engaging leadership around an inspirational D&I strategy by articulating the business case and establishing supportive governance, policies and procedures. Examples include:

   - Leaders communicating regularly about D&I as part of broader discussions about business priorities and results
   - Holding leaders accountable for D&I results
   - Placing oversight for D&I with senior leadership and the Board of Directors

4. *Creating sustainable movement*
   Executing the D&I strategy across all elements of your business and talent ecosystem. Examples include:

   - Embedding a diversity lens into talent management, training, and supply chain operations and programs
   - Embracing a broad definition of diversity that includes a focus on inclusion of all differences
   - Leveraging affinity networks to inform strategic priorities

Testing Programs & Initiatives with a Pilot

From an Information Technology (IT) perspective, new software is always tested. For example, a beta test is the second phase of software testing in which a sampling of the intended audience tries the product out. Beta testing can be considered pre-release testing, user acceptance testing, or end user testing. In this phase of software development, applications are subjected to real world testing by the intended audience for the software. The experiences of the early users are forwarded back to the developers who make final changes before releasing the software commercially.

Can Diversity and Inclusion leaders do a Beta test? You bet! It's called a pilot and you can test your D&I program, curriculum, or other initiatives with a small group before rolling it out enterprise-wide. The steps to a pilot are:

- Identify the Anticipated Outcomes
- Choose a Small Group to Participate
- Gather Feedback
- Collect Data, Regarding Effectiveness, Over Time
- Assess and Correct any Problems
- Report Your Findings and Successes

After the pilot, the Diversity practitioner can gather meaningful participant feedback to make improvements to the program, or to share the program's successes. The D&I leader can also institute and test support mechanisms in order to reinforce learning or change management practices after the pilot concludes.

Piloting a program can eliminate costly mistakes that will make or break a Diversity initiative. It can also help D&I leaders ascertain the answer to questions such as:

- Beyond planning for an event, how can we create an experience that participants will find relevant, useful, and impactful?
- How can we show that this intervention will work better if more resources are invested?
- What should we do to improve this initiative so that we can get better results?

Seeking Intentional Targets
As Diversity and Inclusion leaders, we must continually strive for inclusive excellence– going beyond our traditional framework and including those that we inadvertently left behind. There are many models that are working. We just need to find the right strategies for our organization and build upon our successes.

References:

Diversity Inc. *Diversity 101: Definition of Diversity-Management Best Practices.* Available at: https://www.diversityinc.com/diversity-management/diversity-management-101

The European Community Programme for Employment and Social Solidarity. *Diversity Management in 2008: Research with the European Business Test Panel.* Pages 12-13, 17-19

Stanford Encyclopedia of Philosophy. *Intentionality.* First published Thu Aug 7, 2003; substantive revision Wed Oct 15, 2014. Available at: https://plato.stanford.edu/entries/intentionality/

Govotsos, K. (2017). *Gender Diversity in Corporate Boards in France: An Analysis*, Joseph Wharton Scholars. Available at https://repository.upenn.edu/joseph_wharton_scholars/29

Catylst (2017). *Women on Corporate Boards Globally: Quick Take.* Available at: http://www.catalyst.org/knowledge/women-corporate-boards-globally

Cox, Josie (2017). *UK push for gender diversity on corporate boards stalls, new study shows.* The Independent. Available at: https://www.independent.co.uk/news/business/news/uk-gender-diversity-equality-corporate-boards-stall-push-for-new-study-the-pipeline-a7832756.html

Delgadillo, Natalie (2017). *Civilian Oversight of Police Appeals to Many. But Is It Always Effective?* The Governing Institute. Available at: http://www.governing.com/topics/public-justice-safety/gov-civilian-oversight-police-charter-amendment.html

Dobbin, F. and Kalev, A. (2016). *Why Diversity Programs Fail.* Harvard Business Review. Available at: https://hbr.org/2016/07/why-diversity-programs-fail

Revkin, Andrew C. (2016). *With Imposed Transparency and Concerned Millennials, A Boom in Corporate Responsibility?* The New York Times. Available at: https://dotearth.blogs.nytimes.com/2016/01/25/with-imposed-transparency-and-concerned-millennials-a-boom-in-corporate-responsibility/

McLeod, Lea. *The 6 Unwritten Company Rules You Won't Find in the Employee Handbook.* The Muse. Available at: https://www.themuse.com/advice/the-6-unwritten-company-rules-you-wont-find-in-the-employee-handbook

Gray, Alex (2017). *Denmark has the best work-life balance. Here's why.* World Economic Forum. Available at: https://www.weforum.org/agenda/2017/03/denmark-best-work-life-balance-oecd/

The Economist (2015). *No Names, No Bias?* Available at: https://www.economist.com/business/2015/10/29/no-names-no-bias

U.S. Equal Employment Opportunity Commission, "EEOC Select Task Force on the Study of Harassment in the Workplace". June 20, 2016. Available at: https://www.eeoc.gov/eeoc/task_force/harassment/index.cfm

Lehigh University Student Affairs. *What is Bystander Intervention?* Available at: https://studentaffairs.lehigh.edu/content/what-bystander-intervention

Psychology Today. *What is the Bystander Effect?* Available at: https://www.psychologytoday.com/us/basics/bystander-effect

Lister, Richard (2017). How employers in European countries should deal with workplace sexual harassment. Globe Business Media Group. Available at: https://www.lexology.com/library/detail.aspx?g=5ab39cb3-f3ac-4981-b444-1ddb1d1dd7d0

Pina, Afroditi. University of Kent (2017). *How to Stamp Out Sexual Harassment in the Workplace.* BBC News. Available at: http://www.bbc.com/capital/story/20171103-how-to-stamp-out-sexual-harassment-in-the-workplace

Senthilingam, Meera (2017). *Sexual harassment: How it stands around the globe.* CNN News. Available at: https://www.cnn.com/2017/11/25/health/sexual-harassment-violence-abuse-global-levels/index.html

PwC (2017). *Global cross-industry survey of diversity and inclusion programme leaders.* Available at: https://www.pwc.com/gx/en/services/people-organisation/global-diversity-and-inclusion-survey.html#anchor1

GLOBAL BEST PRACTICES

1. **Piloting a program can eliminate costly mistakes that will make or break a Diversity initiative.**
   A. True
   B. False

2. **In its philosophical usage, the meaning of the word intentionality is the same as the ordinary meaning of the word intention.**
   A. True
   B. False

3. **This term describes the extent to which information about an organization's actions are voluntarily shared with stakeholders:**
   A. Executive briefing
   B. An annual report
   C. Corporate transparency

4. **All of the following are strategies that individuals can employ in a Bystander Intervention EXCEPT:**
   A. Involve yourself
   B. Interrupt the situation
   C. Identify the victim

5. **Over-relying on one tool in the D&I toolbox will result in:**
   A. A limited scope of Equity, Diversity and Inclusion work
   B. The Diversity and Inclusion leader demonstrating expertise
   C. Outcomes that do not sufficiently illustrate qualitative benefits

6. **A _____ is a method or technique that is generally accepted as superior or most effective.**
   A. Best practice
   B. Diversity strategy
   C. Diversity toolbox

idc Institute for Diversity Certification™

Sample Test Questions

GLOBAL BEST PRACTICES

7. Policies help to ensure the consistent treatment of people and:
   A. Contribute to the uniform application of rules
   B. Are solely responsible for eliminating harassment
   C. Allow managers to use their discretion when necessary

8. Unwritten rules define the organizational culture and may not reflect written policies such as:
   A. How many people are hired annually
   B. What time the work day really ends
   C. Customer expectations for great service

9. A D&I Intervention is a strategy, program, or initiative that can be put in place to:
   A. Ensure employees do not violate 'safe space' requirements
   B. Leverage affinity networks to protest working conditions
   C. Protect the brand with consistent and equitable operations

10. The systemic nature of D&I work requires the most effective efforts to:
   A. Include external partners and other stakeholders
   B. Ensure that unity is the underlying framework
   C. Develop a socialist approach to equity and inclusion

11. It is called _____ when one executes the D&I strategy across all elements of the business and talent ecosystem.
   A. Developing leadership engagement
   B. Creating sustainable movement
   C. Building an inspirational strategy

GLOBAL BEST PRACTICES

12. Research shows that these two items are the strongest predictors of sexual harassment:
   A. Organizational climate and tolerance
   B. Cultural competence and policies
   C. Accountability and inclusion

13. Which tool in the Diversity Toolbox is most effective?
   A. It depends on the situation
   B. Diversity & Inclusion training
   C. Diversity recruiting and management

14. Many European employers are researching ways to eliminate irrelevant ethnic or personal information from being used in hiring decisions by testing:
   A. Enhanced job descriptions
   B. Virtual interviews
   C. Anonymous applications

THE ELEMENTS OF LEADING
A LARGE-SCALE D&I EFFORT

Unlike other business functions, Diversity and Inclusion appears to be a relatively easy task. Anyone can do it, right? Wrong.

Leadership, in the Diversity and Inclusion space, is complex. When one considers all of the different preferences, expectations and styles of each group, and how they can overlap, it's easy to see why managing diversity efforts at an organization with 10,000+ different employees, and millions of diverse customers can be full of surprises and challenges.

OVERALL OBJECTIVES AND COMPETENCIES

Mastering this competency will allow Diversity and Inclusion practitioners to develop a formal framework from which to advance D&I work. Leaders will be equipped to choose the right approach, delegate, and plan effectively.

BACKGROUND AND CONTEXT

As more organizations hire Chief Diversity Officers, there are many components that are rooted in leading a large-scale Diversity and Inclusion effort that are oblivious to employers who are novices in this realm. The most important fact that many overlook is that individuals who serve in this capacity, formally or informally, will ultimately determine how the organization's D&I efforts are perceived.

For example, Apple hired its first Vice President of Diversity and Inclusion in May 2017. After six months on the job, the inaugural Diversity Chief stepped down. Why would anyone want to leave a position with a fat salary, great title, and loads of publicity? For one, 20 years of worldwide Human Resources experience may not necessarily prepare one to lead a large-scale Diversity and Inclusion effort. Second, Apple's decision to internally promote someone for the role may not have been the best choice. Accordingly, this inclusion chief was totally blindsided by the backlash that she received by saying something that is taught in both the Certified Diversity Executive (CDE)® and Certified Diversity Professional (CDP)® programs:

> *"There can be 12 white, blue-eyed, blond men in a room and they're going to be diverse too because they're going to bring a different life experience and life perspective to the conversation. Diversity is the human experience. I get a little bit frustrated when diversity or the term diversity is tagged to the people of color, or the women, or the LGBT."*

The critics showed no mercy. Apple's D&I Chief apologized for those remarks and resigned shortly thereafter. The role was subsequently downgraded so that the next D&I Chief does not report directly to the CEO. *It only took 6 months on the job for the future of the position to be devalued.*

What could have been done differently? First, Diversity work at a large scale organization must never begin with a discussion about race. The problem with race is that most organizations want D&I leaders to address it; yet, they are not culturally competent to handle the realities of racial discrimination and bias in the workplace or on campuses. To illustrate this point, babies often want to eat solid food when they lack teeth or the ability to digest certain things. Good parents will not give a baby food that he/she will choke on; they will feed the baby milk or other meals that a baby can easily digest. In the same manner, a good diversity leader will not give in to the desires of an entity that is just beginning this journey. The organization will choke—the underrepresented groups will think diversity is too soft, and the White males will think diversity is too hard. Therefore, it is best to stick to non-threatening topics (e.g., the changing family, different generations, the shifting industry landscape, etc.) until the organization is ready to digest the harder concepts.

Second, D&I leaders must always communicate the business value—which is, making money, saving money, and achieving organizational goals. Focusing on the mission will give employees a broader vision with which to work together as a team, and it will allow them to connect Diversity and Inclusion to their day-to-day work. It is through group cohesion or unity that individuals are empowered to move from me-to-we over time, assuming that everyone wants to belong to something bigger than themselves. In *How to Energize Diversity & Inclusion Work with Mindfulness*, Dr. Nika White, CDE, asserts that "you need to develop the right mindset for inclusion and belongingness, because if you don't intentionally include, you will unintentionally exclude."

The unfortunate part about this work is that the actions of one person can have a negative impact on Diversity and Inclusion efforts for years to come. After the Apple debacle, detractors began to assert that being a woman or a person of color alone should not qualify a professional for a diversity leadership role. Yet, if gender or color are not job criteria, what do individuals need to know before they lead a large-scale Diversity and Inclusion effort?

Diversity and Inclusion work requires dispelling the myths about the nature of the D&I profession, and dismantling fallacies about the ability of practitioners to achieve desired results. An educational approach can help negate many fears that people have when it comes to addressing diversity. For example, both managers and employees may fear that they may say the wrong thing, be perceived as discriminatory, or become stifled by rigid rules of political correctness. Employees need to know that while there are standards and expectations for professional behavior in the workplace, a focus on diversity isn't about being perfect. Diversity and Inclusion is best nurtured in an open workplace where mistakes can be used for learning – not for embarrassing or shaming individuals.

In an era where activists, cell phone videos, and social media work together to keep the public informed and hold people accountable, organizations cannot afford to be flippant about a critical component of the organization's strategy. Diversity and Inclusion leaders, with various titles and roles within the organization, play an important role in setting the tone for the shift towards increased equity and cultural competence. Additionally, some organizations have recently seen Diversity Officers transition to other leadership roles. For example, Ithaca College, Savannah State University, Eureka College, and University of Houston Downtown are just a few of the educational institutions that have hired a former Chief Diversity Officer as a College President. These institutions have found that the skills and issues within the Equity, Diversity and Inclusion space are relevant to successful senior executive work.

The full scope of diversity work goes beyond gender, race, and ethnicity alone. Organizations must consider the myriad of unique ways in which people look, think, feel, believe, solve problems, communicate, and interact with others, to name a few. In order for an entity to include this full spectrum of differences in business operations, it must be open to change as well as accept the fact that cultural competency can advance organizational goals. Of course, each organization will start this journey from a different place and in their own unique context, but every employer has room for improvement. Nevertheless, improving the ability of managers to lead Diversity and Inclusion efforts presents an opportunity for innovative ideas, better service delivery models, advanced brand loyalty, or other quality of life enhancements.

LEADERSHIP VS. MANAGEMENT

Diversity and Inclusion only produces great outcomes when leaders manage it well. But what exactly is management and who is a leader? Let's explore the Theory of Adaptive Leadership to clarify these questions.

In the books "*Leadership without Easy Answers*" and "*Leadership on the Line*", Ron Heifetz and Marty Linsky, believe that leadership is, at its essence, about influencing change that builds and enables the capacity of individuals and organizations to thrive. Specifically, that leadership is the practice of mobilizing groups of people to tackle tough challenges and thrive. The bottom line is that leaders need to understand the importance of adaptation and are able to employ the relevant processes and tools to build the adaptive capacity of organizations.

The word "adaptive" in adaptive leadership is drawn from evolutionary biology and refers to the process that organisms follow if they are going to survive and thrive. The three components of this process (applied to organizations) are to:

1) Reserve the organizational elements necessary for survival,
2) Remove (or modify) the elements that are no longer necessary or useful, and
3) Create (or innovate) new arrangements that enable the organization to thrive.

In adaptive leadership, to thrive is to develop new capabilities and strategies to address changes in the environment (e.g., industry) and realize the strategic vision and goals. The key for an adaptive leader is to understand what it means for a specific organization to thrive, and then help make that happen. To thrive is to successfully adapt to circumstances, make desired changes, and stay anchored to what is best about the organization in the process. This requires an appreciation for the core values, purposes (whether explicit or implicit), and the history of the organization.

The adaptive leadership approach views leadership more as a process than a set of competencies. Having said this, below are some skills, attitudes, and implied qualities that align with adaptive leadership.

- *The adaptive leader needs to be able to connect organizational change to the core values, capabilities, and dreams of relevant and diverse stakeholders*
- *The adaptive leader seeks to foster a culture that collects and honors diversity of opinion and uses this collective knowledge for the good of the organization*
- *The adaptive leader knows that change and learning can be painful for people, and is able to anticipate and counteract any reluctant behavior related to the pain*
- *The adaptive leader understands that large scale change is an incremental process and that he/she needs to be persistent and willing to withstand the pressure to take shortcuts*

The theory that informs adaptive leadership appears to be more about the nature of organizations than about the nature of leadership. In the writings of Heifetz and Linsky, the clearest theoretical underpinning is the speculation that organizations adhere to the same processes outlined in evolutionary biology. It is the task of the leader to understand this theoretical framework and use it to guide and strengthen the organization.

As we consider the theory of adaptive leadership, it becomes clear that any employee can be an **organizational leader**. These are the people who use either formal or informal authority to influence the future of the organization, to promote change, and to generate a consensus for impacting the community in positive ways. Nonprofit leaders may include program managers who lead from the middle or board members who lead from the top. Nonprofit leaders may also include volunteers who are passionate about the organization or the future of the community. Within government agencies, leaders may be civilians or military personnel, union or non-union. They can also work on the federal, state or local level. Educational leaders can be students, faculty, staff, alumni or parents. In respect to inclusion, anyone can become a diversity leader.

An **organizational manager**, on the other hand, relies on formal authority to make decisions that are required for organizational sustainability. These decisions often revolve around day-to-day operations, processes and policies, and involve hard-skills related to programming, staffing or scheduling. Managers may include staff or board members who focus on technical skills that create the foundation upon which leaders can operate. Managers may also rely on their leadership skills in order to carry out their management responsibilities. A Diversity Officer would fall under the category of an organizational manager. This individual must have a rigorous skillset with specific abilities to design change management strategies, serve as an internal organizational development consultant, and connect Equity, Diversity and Inclusion to sustainability efforts. Also, the Diversity Officer must continually ensure that D&I efforts impact the bottom line.

Clearly, managers and leaders share some of the same attributes. And most managers and leaders fall on a continuum, incorporating aspects of both leadership and management.

A few ways to think about the distinction between managers and leaders are outlined in Figure 1.

FIGURE 1: THE DIFFERENCE BETWEEN MANAGERS & LEADERS

Manager	Leader
Formal authority	Informal authority
Manage things, processes and products	Lead people and ideas
"Do things right"	"Do the right things"
Focus on how things get done	Focus on what things mean to other people
Focus on tasks and things	Focus on ideas
Use hard skills: planning, policy making, scheduling, staffing, etc.	Use soft skills: communication, motivation, inclusion, team building, etc.
Seek stability (comfortable with order)	Seek change (comfortable with disorder)
Focus on the day-to-day work that leads to achieving the vision ("the trees")	Focus on the vision that impacts the day-to-day work ("the forest")
Technical skills	Adaptive skills

Organizations require both effective managers and effective leaders in order to thrive over the long-term. Management and leadership are intrinsically intertwined and no absolute distinction exists between these two aspects of organizational oversight and impact. The same can be said for a Diversity Officer and a Diversity Leader—both are needed in today's organizations.

The reason why a distinction must be made between management and leadership is because today, an organization's success depends on its cultural competence. The most effective organizations are those that don't simply use their diversity in order to have legitimacy with clients; they use their diversity to increase the cultural competence of their workforce.

To achieve cultural competence, both leadership and management skills are necessary to build the cultural dexterity of all employees. Cultural dexterity is the ability to connect across a myriad of areas, backgrounds, and priorities that are different. It's difficult to be a true leader in today's world without a minimum level of cultural dexterity. Ultimately, organizations must make sure they're creating a culture where every individual is valued for their unique contributions and that they are able to achieve their highest potential.

For example, it is difficult to determine a person's gender identity or sexual orientation simply by looking at them. Additionally, someone who is heterosexual may not understand or be concerned with the difference between the terms cisgender, pansexual, nonbinary, and gender nonconforming. Therefore, if a manager is going to create an inclusive environment for LGBTQ+ workers, supervisors should follow these guidelines:

- Don't assume everyone is heterosexual
- If specific significant days or events are highlighted for other employees (such as disability employment awareness month in October), annual Gay Pride celebrations (usually held during the month of June) should be similarly marked
- Acknowledge the relationships of staff equally by ensuring that anniversaries, births and marriages/union ceremonies are celebrated in the same way

- Use the term 'partners' when inviting spouses to social activities. This is a more inclusive and non-gender specific term for same-sex couples

- Never reveal a LGBTQ+ person's sexual orientation or gender identity without permission

- In training or information sessions for employees or other managers, use concrete examples of situations that pertain to LGBTQ+ persons

- Learn about the different LGBTQ+ groups. A person's sexual orientation, gender identity, or gender expression will not change because one becomes an ally or an accomplice for the LGBTQ+ community. It simply means that you are better equipped to support and advocate for individuals who are not like you.

As stated earlier, identifying the nuances that apply to each group is an educational process—one that no individual will ever fully master. For instance, there are 30,000 – 40,000 Christian denominations alone. They each have their own beliefs, customs and rituals. When you factor in Muslims, Jews, Buddhists, Hindus, Sikhs, Atheists, Agnostics, and thousands of other religious and non-religious groups, it's easy to understand why managing lots of people in the workplace can be intimidating.

It can also be challenging as one learns what to say and what not to say to different groups. For example, a disability descriptor (e.g., schizophrenia) is simply a medical diagnosis. A person's medical diagnosis should not be used to identify the person (e.g., a schizophrenic woman).

People First Language respectfully puts the person before the disability because a person with a disability is more like people without disabilities than they are different from them. Kathie Snow, author of *People First Language* suggests the following:

FIGURE 2. PERSON FIRST LANGUAGE	
Instead of:	**Say:**
The handicapped or disabled	People with disabilities
She's confined to a wheelchair	She uses a wheelchair
Normal or healthy kids	Children without disabilities
He's learning disabled	He has a learning disability
Excerpted from Kathie Snow's People First Language article (2009), available at www.disabilityisnatural.com	

Using language that demonstrates cultural competence has nothing to do with political correctness. It has everything to do with cultural humility, or the ability to maintain an interpersonal stance that is other-oriented (or open to other individuals) in relation to aspects of cultural identity that may be important to the other person.

Managing different viewpoints in the workforce is challenging, but today's supervisors must own responsibility for maximum productivity and inclusion for all. The question is whether management and leadership in your organization is congruent or contradictory? Likewise, are diversity efforts meaningful interventions or symbolic gestures? Does the sound of diverse voices go beyond the halls at work, towards the homes in the communities that are being served?

Delegation

Managing diversity requires delegation. Leaders must determine which tasks can only be done by the D&I manager, and which duties can be performed by someone else. Potential individuals who could help D&I managers include volunteers (i.e., Diversity Council or Resource Group members), supervisors, and Office of Diversity staff, to name a few. Delegation entails equipping other leaders to execute key tasks. This may involve recruiting skilled volunteers and professionals, developing these individuals, and creating standard operating procedures.

Standard Operating Procedures (SOP) are used in industries such as food services and manufacturing to ensure excellence and consistency. Essentially, the SOP is a detailed explanation of how a procedure is to be executed. An effective SOP communicates the responsibilities that are to be performed in the Office of Diversity (i.e., which tasks are a priority, what materials are necessary, where the tasks take place, who performs the tasks, and how to evaluate the outcomes, etc.). The details in a SOP standardize the processes and provide step-by-step instructions so that anyone in your organization can perform certain D&I tasks in a consistent manner.

A standard operating procedure can also be applied to the strategic diversity planning process if one is necessary for the Office of Diversity or supporting plans must be developed for other entities (e.g., divisions, schools, employee resource groups, or countries of operation). Additionally, a SOP can be created for job descriptions, employee training, recruiting and interviewing, corrective action and discipline, performance reviews, coaching, mentoring, policy creation/revisions, and exit interviews. The SOP can apply to anything that needs a systematic approach or that must be duplicated in the future. The objective is to create best practices for the organization and the Office of Diversity.

Step-by-step written procedures can increase employee accountability and improve the chances of success in the Office of D&I. The SOP document serves as an instructional resource that allows the successor to act with minimum directions, reassurance, or guidance. Communicating procedures that are clearly understood, and easy to replicate, will ensure the organization continually provides high quality Diversity and Inclusion interventions.

Critical to the success of standard operating procedures is creating a system for periodic review. Care must be taken to design a review that prevents the SOP from becoming outdated without making frequent changes to the document. Incorporate as much feedback as possible in the SOP review process. Additionally, make sure the revision date is included on the SOP so that everyone knows that this is the most recent policy.

D&I managers may also need to break down key functions so that the Office of Diversity tasks are executed in accord with the strategic diversity plan objectives. Pertaining to the structure of the office, you may not have the resources to implement a fully staffed diversity office yet. And, if your organization isn't advanced in its diversity journey, it may be a few years before you achieve this level of organization. Certainly, you may have to get creative about getting work done if it is just you in the office, or if you have 1-2 staff support members.

A sample organizational chart is detailed in Figure 3. Note, that the ideal reporting structure is directly to the Chief Executive Officer.

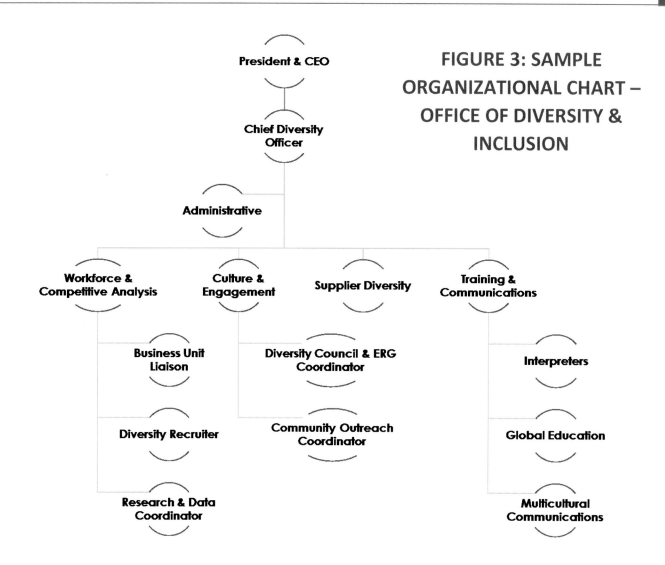

FIGURE 3: SAMPLE ORGANIZATIONAL CHART – OFFICE OF DIVERSITY & INCLUSION

STRIVING FOR FAIRNESS

At the heart of helping employees reach their full potential is this notion of fairness. In fact, fairness is contributing to a surge in activism by diverse groups. Since the Boston Tea Party in 1773, America has had protests. Nevertheless, for the last 40+ years, America has not had many major protests like the 1963 March on Washington for Jobs and Freedom or the Anti-Vietnam War Demonstrations through the early 1970's. In 2011 however, something changed. Protesters began to demonstrate on Wall Street to denounce financial greed and corruption. Images from Occupy Wall Street dominated the news for months. Then in 2013, Black Lives Matter coalesced to protest violence and systematic racism against African Americans. Unlike other protests, the message of Black Lives Matters was hijacked so that the focus shifted away from excessive force and discrimination to "All Lives Matter" or "Blue Lives Matter". Lawmakers in states like North Dakota, North Carolina, Florida, Tennessee, and Texas even proposed legislation that would offer limited protections for drivers who cause injury or death to protesters, according to CNN.

In 1995, the Nation of Islam led the Million Man March for African American men in Washington, DC, but the 2017 Women's March on Washington was the largest single day protest in U.S. history. There were 3-5 million protesters at 600+ marches throughout the U.S. and an additional 200+ protests occurring on all 7 continents around the world. The estimated total number of participants hovered around 7 million. The women advocated for human rights, including women's rights, reproductive rights, and LGBTQ+ rights, as well as racial equality, freedom of religion, and immigration reform. The Women's March illustrated how diversity intersects with many different dimensions and highlighted the fact that gender equity is not exclusive.

The 2018 Gun Control protests were equally diverse, where thousands of Generation Z students staged walk-outs from school, participated in marches, and registered youth to vote. Dissimilar from schools in American inner cities, where most students are subjected to uniforms and metal detectors, schools in the suburbs have no such restrictions. This scenario presents a prime opportunity for bullied kids and other disgruntled youth to bring guns to K-12 campuses and shoot innocent children. Nevertheless, students from the inner cities and suburbs joined together to protest the gun violence against young people that occurs outside of school in inner city neighborhoods, and inside of schools in the suburbs. The bigger question was: why would some call for arming teachers with guns, instead of placing metal detectors in suburban schools like they do in urban schools?

In the corporate sector, protests about unfair treatment and discrimination against African Americans have resulted in layoffs at American Airlines and Starbucks. According to the NAACP, "Since issuing a travel advisory for American Airlines on October 24, 2017, the NAACP has received testimonies from hundreds of concerned passengers and employees, regarding alleged racially discriminatory and racially-biased treatment." The NAACP national staff fielded approximately 600 phone calls on the subject, including nearly 50 from current and past American Airlines employees. In response, Black customers used their buying power to support other carriers, resulting in American Airlines making an announcement in June 2018 that it was reducing its headcount. In April 2018, a viral video sparked outrage over the frivolous arrest of two Black men at a Philadelphia Starbucks. Former Starbucks President Kevin Johnson quickly met with the two men and then closed 8,000 stores for unconscious bias training. Nevertheless, by June 2018, the cost of training and negative publicity prompted an announcement that 150 stores would close.

Educational institutions are not exempt. For several years now, protests have occurred on campuses around the world, both for and against diversity. Faculty members, who oppose diversity, further complicate these issues on campus.

Regardless of the organizational response, activism takes its toll on all employees, customers, and students. There is a high price tag for corporations who engage in activism as well. The Georgia legislature removed a $40 million tax break from Delta because the airline dropped the National Rifle Association from a discount-fare program that only 13 people used. The airline upset Georgia lawmakers when the company assumed a neutral stance in the gun control debate.

Activism can be defined as "taking action to effect social change" and is designed to send a message about an organization's culture and its leadership. Activism is led by individuals but done collectively through social movements. It is aided by social media, which allows large crowds to gather at once or provides instruction such as #GrabYourWallet, #MeToo, and #Boycott. The term activism is different from an activist.

While activism is what you do, the term activist is contentious because it is who you are. An activist campaigns to bring about change by any means necessary. This individual may protest, organize a petition, boycott, bring a lawsuit, demand a termination, or participate in all of these activities plus more. For example, Edith Windsor is known as a Gay Rights Activist. Her landmark lawsuit, United States vs. Windsor (570 U.S. 744 -2013 - Docket No. 12-307) resulted in equal tax treatment for same sex couples.

Activism and advocacy are different terms as well. Advocacy aims to influence decisions within systems and institutions (e.g., using the business case). It also works on behalf of others who may not have a voice. For example, in February 2017, individuals staged A Day Without Immigrants boycott and protest, in hopes of showing "American consumers what an economy without immigrant labor would mean for the services and goods many rely on". Some companies showed support, but other employers fired over 100 immigrant workers for violating "no show" policies. If these workers had an advocate in the executive offices, they would have had someone to influence senior management's decisions about their jobs.

Today, we need activists, advocates, allies, and accomplices. Everyone can't protest on the streets; someone needs to be in the executive offices influencing. Likewise, everyone can't have a seat at the table; allies and accomplices must ensure that different voices are heard in the absence of diverse groups. As a Diversity and Inclusion leader, your approach could be aggressive, passive or collaborative. Keep in mind, there are many ways to get results, and your approach will generally determine how long you are in that position, as well as whether your career advances once this role evolves.

If the diversity leader doesn't have hopes of building a career at the organization, perhaps a radical activist approach will achieve the goal of inclusion. Nevertheless, if a future relationship with the organization matters, it may be best to serve as an advocate. At some Fortune 500 companies, the person in the role of Chief Diversity Officer changes every 2 years. If you are aware of this going into the role, you can take an approach that will serve your career well, while at the same time working to get lots of great results. In the interviewing phase however, you want to find out if this is a new position. If not, you should ask what happened to the last Diversity Officer.

Where will activists draw the line? It's difficult to say. Walgreen's is facing a #boycott for allowing pharmacists to opt out of providing birth control pills for women based on religious beliefs while enabling men to obtain prescriptions for erectile dysfunction—even if the prescription allows some men to cheat on their partners. These types of issues require organizations to walk a fine line.

As stated in a previous competency, instead of organizations simply valuing diversity, they must transition to being perceived as valuable to different groups. This means that a diverse team may need to engage in a design thinking session to determine how different groups perceive current, new, or changing policies. How will customer or student perceptions change if 'X' occurs? How will the brand be impacted? Is there a work-around or back-up plan that can be quickly implemented? From a communications perspective, how will the organization ensure that the internal and external messages are consistent?

Globally, equality has roots in government and legislation. The Equality and Human Rights Commission in the U.K. states, "Equality is about ensuring that every individual has an equal opportunity to make the most of their lives and talents, and believing that no one should have poorer life chances because of where, what or to whom they were born, what they believe, or whether they have a disability. Equality recognizes that historically, certain groups of people with particular characteristics e.g., race, disability, sex and sexuality, have experienced discrimination." Equality is different from equity.

Equity involves fairness or justice in the way that people are treated. John Stacy Adams, a workplace and behavioral psychologist, put forward his *Equity Theory* on job motivation in 1963. The *Equity Theory* focuses on determining whether the distribution of resources is fair to relational partners. Equity theory thus helps explain why pay and conditions alone do not determine motivation. In terms of how the theory applies to work and management, it asserts that each person seeks a fair balance between what he/she puts into a job and what one gets out of it.

Equity, and thereby the motivational situation one might seek to assess using the model, is not dependent on the extent to which a person believes reward exceeds effort, nor even necessarily on the belief that reward exceeds effort at all. Rather, equity, and the sense of fairness which commonly underpins motivation, is dependent on the comparison a person makes between his or her reward/investment ratio with the ratio enjoyed (or suffered) by others considered to be in a similar situation.

This is why the notion of *privilege* is so hard to identify and eliminate. For example, in school admissions, students may focus on the apparent diversity of the student body through affirmative action admissions. Nevertheless, they neglect legacy admissions, student-athlete admissions, and other admissions that allow students to gain admittance without meeting or exceeding entrance requirements. Everyone is on the campus to obtain a high-quality education, but certain students and faculty members proliferate the idea that some people should not be there because of that individual's race or ethnicity.

The workplace functions in the same respect. Some individuals gained employment because of who they knew (e.g., a friend, family member, neighbor, or a politician) without necessarily meeting job qualifications. However, if another person, with qualifications, is hired because of a Diversity and Inclusion effort, a discussion about "merit" or "lower standards" ensues. Thus, the historical context behind fairness and race, in particular, cannot go unnoticed. But the same applies for every dimension of diversity—there will be a history of exclusion, discrimination or inequity. Modern-day Diversity and Inclusion efforts may attempt to whitewash the past with equality.

Figure 4 illustrates that it is not enough to seek "equality". Equity is better; but removing systemic barriers is best.

FIGURE 4:
EQUALITY VERSUS EQUITY

In the first image, it is assumed that everyone will benefit from the same supports. They are being treated equally.

In the second image, individuals are given different supports to make it possible for them to have equal access to the game. They are being treated equitably.

In the third image, all three can see the game without any supports or accommodations because the cause of the inequity was addressed. The systemic barrier has been removed.

According to the U.S. EEOC, "Systemic discrimination involves a pattern or practice, policy, or class case where the alleged discrimination has a broad impact on an industry, profession, company or geographic area. Examples of systemic practices include: discriminatory barriers in recruitment and hiring; discriminatorily restricted access to management trainee programs and to high level jobs; exclusion of qualified women from traditionally male dominated fields of work; disability discrimination such as unlawful pre-employment inquiries; age discrimination in reductions in force and retirement benefits; and compliance with customer preferences that result in discriminatory placement or assignments."

The Manitoba (Canada) Civil Service Commission asserts that "Systemic discrimination produces hidden barriers that appear neutral but which negatively impact on a designated group. They are generally unintentional. Systemic barriers thus are measured not by intent but by impact."

It's important to remove systemic barriers so as not to transfer discrimination or unfairness from one group to another. Unfairness precludes individuals from reaching their full potential. Fairness, on the other hand, can be defined as "the quality of making judgments that are free from discrimination". Fairness, or the perception thereof, leads organizations, management teams and employees to greatness. This means that Diversity and Inclusion leaders must ask the questions that make other folks uncomfortable about the realities of workplace equity efforts. For example, "if we change our policies and practices to benefit non-dominant groups, but the majority groups are now at a disadvantage, how is this fair?" Accordingly, it must be said that fairness requires balance. For instance, in our efforts to include women, are we excluding men?

IS THIS A REPLACEMENT STRATEGY OR INCLUSION?

Research has shown that in comparison to ethnic or generational diversity, gender diversity feels better and easier-- especially when the organization can hire, advance and retain individuals who look like those in senior leadership. Japan provides a prime example of this approach, as the country hesitantly embraces immigrants and refugees. In fact, the Japan Times reported that, "Out of the 7,533 people who applied for refugee status in 2014, or appealed earlier refusals, only 11 were approved." Facing a huge, projected labor force shortage, Japanese companies have extended the olive branch to women.

Replacement work is not inclusive. The bias of gender diversity becomes evident when an organization creates a replacement strategy. Currently, replacement occurs on two fronts:

(1) Replacement manifests in respect to women generally displacing men in the workplace and in society. Some universities, employers and marketing initiatives have taken an 'either/or' approach instead of 'AND' in respect to males and females. Consider the enrollment of men and women on college campuses in a recent Pew Report entitled, *Women's College Enrollment Gains Leave Men Behind.*

The report's authors, Mark Hugo Lopez and Ana Gonzalez-Barrera assert that "Even though college enrollment rates among young people have risen in recent decades, a Pew Research Center analysis of U.S. Census Bureau data shows that females outpace males in college enrollment, especially among Hispanics and blacks."

This growing gender gap is illustrated in Figure 5.

FIGURE 5:

Women Outpace Men In College Enrollment

Share of recent high school completers enrolled in college the following October

Hispanic	Women	Men	% point gap, women/men
1994	52%	52%	0
2012	76	62	+13 women
Black			
1994	48	56	+9 men
2012	69	57	+12 women
White			
1994	66	62	+4 women
2012	72	62	+10 women
Asian			
1994	81	82	+1 men
2012	86	83	+3 women

Source: Pew Research Center analysis of the October Supplement to the Current Population Survey. Note: % point gap calculated prior to rounding. White, black and Asian include the Hispanic portion of those groups. Due to the small sample size for Hispanics, blacks and Asians, a 2-year moving average is used.

PEW RESEARCH CENTER

(2) Replacement also occurs in transferring the plumb line for discrimination. The plumb line occurs when an organization transfers power to one group under the condition that it is not bestowed upon anyone else outside of that group. The expectation is that this group will maintain status quo. For example, an organization touts:

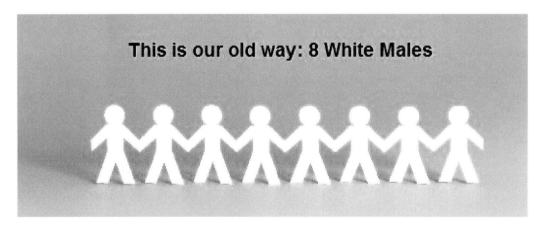

Slack Technologies is a great example. According to the International Business Times, Slack proactively released its workforce breakdown report, showing the company was "61 percent male and just 39 percent female. African Americans held 4% of jobs, while Hispanics held less than 1% of positions. The silver lining was that women held 45% of manager positions" in September 2015.

After receiving much criticism, Slack released another report in February 2016 showing that it was growing and including more African American, Hispanic, and LGBT workers in the mix.

Diversity, in its truest sense, is saying: We need White males and White females. But we also need people of color; individuals with different languages; folks with different ages, sexual orientations, abilities/disabilities, and marital/family statuses; as well as workers from various socioeconomic backgrounds, schools, and parts of the world. Utilizing a broader definition of diversity includes everyone so that White men and White women do not view themselves as outside of the scope of Diversity and Inclusion work. The key message should be: we are all in this boat together, and it benefits no one if bias transfers from one group to another (e.g., if it went from White men to White women to Black men; or from Christians to Muslims to non-religious, etc.).

In conclusion, gender diversity is not as biased and simplistic as including an assortment of thin and beautiful blondes, brunettes and redheads. We cannot allow the "frat-house" mentality to overtake workplace Diversity and Inclusion efforts. Our focus should be hiring, promoting and retaining the best and brightest-- even if they are a little, round, and hard to look at. This requires acknowledging the phenomenon of beauty bias-- but recognizing this type of bias doesn't make it right. In *Who Wants to Fight Beauty Bias*, Boston Globe Correspondent Ruth Graham says,

> ***"A drumbeat of research over the past decades have found that attractive people earn more than their average-looking peers, are more likely to be given loans by banks, and are less likely to be convicted by a jury. Voters prefer better-looking candidates; students prefer better-looking professors, while teachers prefer better-looking students. Mothers, those icons of blind love, have been shown to favor their more attractive children.***

So what can an organization do to correct course?

- *Determine if there is an imbalance in your diversity efforts by evaluating the data from the most recent year of Diversity and Inclusion work (e.g., if women are hired, do they represent one race? Are they in one age range? etc.)*
- *Appeal to and educate senior leadership about the benefits of ensuring a broader representation of the population in the workforce, management and executive levels.*
- *Don't exclude men. Ensure that your initiatives do not merely pit women against men, Blacks against Whites, gay vs. straight, Christians vs. Muslims, parents vs. single parents, etc.*
- *Create more opportunities for professional interactions among diverse groups in client service teams, crisis management teams, research teams, etc. Studies have shown that greater interaction improves communication and comfort between groups.*
- *Address inappropriate and unprofessional behavior before it escalates into full-blown discrimination or harassment.*
- *Go beyond workforce diversity or student diversity toward supplier diversity, diversity in philanthropy, and board diversity.*

If your diversity efforts feel too easy and too good, it's not inclusive enough. This 21st Century business concept can bring an organization great success, but there are no shortcuts to excellence through Diversity and Inclusion. Additionally, if bias is present in any way, it's time to go back to the drawing board and tweak your efforts. No need to scrap your entire work, just make it work better—as the ultimate goal is to reduce or eliminate bias, not transfer it.

CHANGING THE CYCLE

A diversity plan is central to doing diversity work, as well as evaluating the impact of that work. By nature, evaluation implies accountability. But accountability doesn't just apply to others; it also pertains to Diversity and Inclusion leaders. This is the piece that has to do with professional standards. Accountability is "to be answerable to oneself and others for one's own actions."

People who are passionate about Equity, Diversity and Inclusion have to overcome many pitfalls, which adds a layer of complexity to D&I work that other fields do not have. In addition to the highly charged and emotional nature of D&I work, there are pitfalls associated with: office politics, the organizational culture, personality clashes, the general political environment as in Washington, DC, or social issues of the day. Yes, diversity leaders have the missing piece to the puzzle, but if practitioners are not careful, they will accidentally tumble into a pitfall before their work is finished.

So D&I leaders have to navigate through all of these things, as well as demonstrate competence in strategic planning. The plan must be in laymen's terms (i.e., void of professional D&I terminology), as well as connect to the business of the organization.

Strategic Diversity Planning is an ongoing process that maps, controls and evaluates an organization's Diversity and Inclusion efforts. Most D&I leaders start the process by googling the phrase "Strategic Diversity Plan" and then copying what someone else prepared online. The problem with this approach is that the plan that was copied may have different workplace issues, distinct organizational goals, and be in a unique stage of the diversity journey. These nuances alone will derail your plan, as well as your ability to effectively demonstrate the skill of setting goals and executing them accordingly.

It's fine to review another plan for the purposes of finding out what others are doing; but your plan should be customized for your organization and its specific needs. If one changes jobs, a new and different plan should be developed. Additionally, D&I leaders should resist the urge to develop simplistic initiatives.

Simplistic initiatives are often reactive– i.e., there's a problem, training will fix it. This may or may not necessarily be true. Leading with training can be professionally dangerous because if it doesn't go well, that is one more snip against you that has to be overcome.

Strategic interventions require more thought, more time, more details, and more transparency because you're not doing things in a vacuum. Once again, it is tempting to apply a "check box" mentality in diversity planning: Once the plan is completed, we will simply check the box to show that it's finished, right? But remember, the definition of strategic diversity planning indicated that it was an ongoing process, which means that there will be changes, adjustments and periodic reviews. Additionally, this is where the implementation process begins.

Studies of for-profit companies done by Catalyst, Credit Suisse, The Center for Talent Innovation, and McKinsey demonstrate that diversity in the for-profit world can increase financial performance, boost an organization's reputation, help attract talent, and promote stability and innovation.

Many people believe the same is true in the nonprofit world: that greater diversity helps expand the pool of donors willing to support charities, improves the quality of strategic thinking at organizations, and makes them more responsive to the needs of clients and better able to attract the most talented workers. Some nonprofits postpone diversity work because they believe the organization is not large enough. However, if the nonprofit serves thousands or even hundreds of constituents, the organization has a huge opportunity to impact Diversity and Inclusion on a local level.

To solve complex problems, it is critical to understand the root causes of those problems. In the case of the growing and related issues of racial inequality and poverty, we must openly acknowledge that a problem exists, and then explore the factors at the root of that problem. Sadly, statistics from high school dropout rates to incarceration data point to the reality that in America, racial discrimination is one of the most significant root causes of inequality in education, health, and wealth outcomes. While most nonprofits have a mission and commitment to helping people who aren't in the majority, not all organizations reflect that in their employment policies. Consider this graphic from the Common Wealth Partners and Annie E. Casey Foundation:

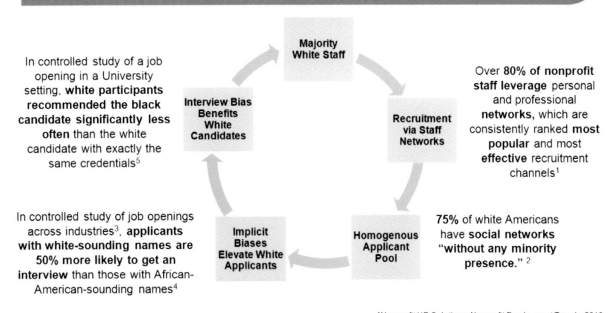

Self-reinforcing cycle causing majority white staff

In controlled study of a job opening in a University setting, **white participants recommended the black candidate significantly less often** than the white candidate with exactly the same credentials[5]

Interview Bias Benefits White Candidates

Majority White Staff

Recruitment via Staff Networks

Over **80% of nonprofit staff leverage** personal and professional **networks,** which are consistently ranked **most popular** and most **effective** recruitment channels[1]

In controlled study of job openings across industries[3], **applicants with white-sounding names are 50% more likely to get an interview** than those with African-American-sounding names[4]

Implicit Biases Elevate White Applicants

Homogenous Applicant Pool

75% of white Americans have **social networks "without any minority presence."** [2]

[1] Nonprofit HR Solutions. Nonprofit Employment Trends. 2013.
[2] Slate. Why It Shouldn't Surprise Us That Whites and Blacks Have So Little Empathy for Each Other. 2012
[3] The study included both private sector companies specializing in manufacturing, and financial and business services, and social sector organizations working in health, education, and other direct service delivery
[4] Booth School of Business. Are Emily and Brendan more employable than Lakisha and Jamal? 2002.
[5] The Nonprofit Quarterly "Color blind or just plain blind? The pernicious nature of contemporary racism." 2014

Community Wealth Partners

THE ANNIE E. CASEY FOUNDATION

Nationally, up-to-date research on nonprofit diversity is scanty, but recent research done for Green 2.0, a group that promotes diversity at environmental groups, found that "the racial composition in environmental organizations and agencies has not broken the 12 percent to 16 percent 'green ceiling'"; efforts to diversify have been lackluster; and "alienation and unconscious bias" hamper recruitment and retention of talented people of color.

A study by the Level Playing Field Institute, a group that seeks to get more minorities into science and math programs, found that "while almost 9 out of 10 employees believe their organization values diversity, more than 7 out of 10 believe their employer does not do enough to create a diverse and inclusive work environment."

It's not just ethnic and racial diversity that is a problem. A report on compensation issues in September 2014 by GuideStar confirmed a longstanding gender pay gap (11 percent at small organizations and 23 percent at large ones).

Commongood Careers and Level Playing Field Institute released a report in 2011 entitled *The Voice of Nonprofit Talent: Perceptions of Diversity in the Workplace.* The report finds, "Today's nonprofit employees are approximately 82 percent white, 10 percent African- American, five percent Hispanic/Latino, three percent other, and one percent Asian or Pacific Islander. The gap in representation is more pronounced in nonprofit governance, where only 14 percent of board members are people of color. Similarly, in specialized functions such as development, less than six percent of roles are filled by people of color. When examining organizational leadership, the gap persists. According to the 2006 report by the Nonprofit Leadership Alliance (formerly American Humanics), up to 84 percent of nonprofits are led by whites, and 9.5 out of 10 philanthropic organizations are led by whites."

While we wait to see what the most recent data show, nonprofits can take steps now to adopt what for-profits have already learned about diversity:

1. Define organizational culture by considering such factors as philosophy, policies and practices, interpersonal dynamics and work environment.
2. Articulate the benefits and motivations for becoming a more diverse organization.
3. Define what the organization will look like within the context of the mission. Ensure the message that diversity matters comes from the top. United Way is a good example: More than 125 years ago, the diverse community of leaders who founded the organization realized that the acceptance of cultural, religious, and economic differences was essential to its core mission of strengthening local communities. The founding leaders implemented a diversity vision, definition, and rational that continues to successfully foster diversity from the top down.
4. Identify other organizations, both locally and nationally, that might serve as models for diversity efforts.
5. Develop a realistic action plan for diversity efforts that takes into account ongoing operations and competing priorities.
6. Develop criteria to measure success. In other words, begin with an evaluation plan.
7. Create a safe environment for candid and honest participation.

In the nonprofit and government sectors, it is important to model inclusive leadership in community interactions. Inclusive leadership is the practice of leadership that carefully includes the contributions of all stakeholders in the community or organization. Inclusion means being at the table at all levels of the organization, being a valued contributor and being fully responsible for your contribution to the ultimate result. Inclusive leadership creates an organizational culture that consistently produces results that benefit all stakeholders.

Best practices for inclusive leadership development show that it is an ongoing effort incorporating learning, action and feedback as each organization discovers new ways to support the development of board, staff and program participants to become diversity leaders actively participating in an inclusive organization.

Through interviews and a review of national and international research, the Diversity Council Australia (DCA) published a study, *Building Inclusion: An Evidence-Based Model of Inclusive Leadership,* in October 2015. The study sheds valuable light on the need for inclusive leadership and what it takes to build more inclusive leaders. According to DCA, individuals can build their capabilities by adopting five mindsets of an inclusive leader, which involve being:

- ***Identity aware.*** *Believes diversity can significantly improve organizational performance, and learns about their own and others' identities.*
- ***Relational.*** *Creates teams and networks in which a diversity of people feel they belong, and are valued and respected*
- ***Open and curious.*** *Is curious about and open to new and different perspectives from a diversity of people*
- ***Flexible and agile.*** *Is flexible about, and responsive to, a diversity of people and perspectives*
- ***Growth-focused.*** *Challenges accepted practices and incorporates different perspectives into how business is done.*

For years, nonprofits have used the excuse, "we don't have the money, or the staff, or the resources" to pursue Diversity and Inclusion effectively. But in order for true change to occur in communities, nonprofits must commit to prioritizing inclusive leadership with diversity management. Not only is the sustainability of the organization at stake, but the vitality of talented and committed staff is at risk as well. Those organizations that intertwine these principles within their missions will achieve service oriented goals, as well as acquire an absolute competitive advantage.

Likewise, leading a large-scale effort at a university, government agency, or corporation entails acknowledging that there is a higher level of scrutiny for equity and inclusion work. It also comes with the expectation that the D&I leader will not simply try to impress people with fancy industry terminology, but that the practitioner will be able to properly distinguish between the terms in order to facilitate belonging, cultural competence, and inclusion.

Regardless of industry, D&I leaders must carefully choose their approach, delegate, and continuously plan if they intend to be successful in managing a large-scale effort. They must also be intentional about seeking partners and improvements to ongoing Diversity and Inclusion interventions.

References:

Steinbuch, Yaron (2017). *Apple's Diversity Officer Out After Outcry.* New York Post. Available at: https://nypost.com/2017/11/17/apples-diversity-chief-lasts-just-six-months/

White, Nika (2017). *How to Energize Diversity & Inclusion Work with Mindfulness.* Nika White Consulting.
Valbrun, Marjorie (2018). *From Diversity Chief to College President.* Inside Higher Ed. Available at: https://www.insidehighered.com/news/2018/05/07/chief-diversity-officer-position-new-path-presidency

Heifetz, Ronald A. (1998). *Leadership Without Easy Answers.* Harvard University Press, 1st edition

Heifetz, Ronald A. and Linsky, Martin (2002). *Leadership on the Line: Staying Alive through the Dangers of Leading.* Harvard Business Review Press, 1st edition

Snow, Kathie (2009). *People First Language.* Available at: www.disabilityisnatural.com

Andone, Dakin (2017). *These states have introduced bills to protect drivers who run over protesters.* CNN. Available at: https://www.cnn.com/2017/08/18/us/legislation-protects-drivers-injure-protesters/index.html

Chenoweth, Erica and Pressman, Jeremy (2017). *This is what we learned by counting the women's marches.* The Washington Post. Available at: https://www.washingtonpost.com/news/monkey-cage/wp/2017/02/07/this-is-what-we-learned-by-counting-the-womens-marches/?noredirect=on&utm_term=.58169b915f0a

NAACP (2017). *NAACP Travel Advisory for American Airlines Update.* Available at: https://www.naacp.org/latest/naacp-travel-advisory-american-airlines-update/

Rose, Joel (2018). *'I'm Not Aware Of That': Starbucks Employees Receive Racial Bias Training.* NPR. Available at: https://www.npr.org/2018/05/29/615263473/thousands-of-starbucks-stores-close-for-racial-bias-training

Matyszczyk, Chris (2018). Starbucks is closing 150 stores. Here's Why this might change your breakfast habits. Inc. Magazine. Available at: https://www.inc.com/chris-matyszczyk/starbucks-just-made-an-eye-opening-decision-thatll-change-many-peoples-breakfast-habits.html

Jansen, Bart (2018). *The number of Delta Air Lines passengers who bought tickets with NRA discount: 13,* USA Today. Available at: https://www.usatoday.com/story/news/2018/03/02/delta-reviews-all-fare-discount-programs-after-nra-dispute-costs-georgia-tax-break/388587002/

Levine-Weinberg, Adam (2018). *American Airlines Plan Some Much-Needed Job Cuts.* The Motley Fool. Available at; https://www.fool.com/investing/2018/06/22/american-airlines-plans-some-much-needed-job-cuts.aspx

Lam, Bourree (2017). *The Fallout From 'A Day Without Immigrants'.* The Atlantic. Available at: https://www.theatlantic.com/business/archive/2017/02/day-without-immigrants-2/517380/

Adams, John Stacy (1963). *Toward an understanding of inequity.* Journal of Abnormal Psychology, 67, 422-436

Equality and Human Rights Commission. *Understanding Equality.* Available at: https://www.equalityhumanrights.com/en/secondary-education-resources/useful-information/understanding-equality

U.S. EEOC (2006). *Systemic Task Force Report to the Chair of the Equal Employment Opportunity Commission.*

Manitoba Civil Service Commission (2004). *Principles & Policies for Managing Human Resources.* Available at: http://www.gov.mb.ca/csc/policyman/removbar.html

Osaki, Tomohiro (2015). *Asylum seekers in Japan soared to record level in 2014.* The Japan Times. Available at: https://www.japantimes.co.jp/news/2015/03/10/national/asylum-seekers-in-japan-soared-to-record-level-in-2014/#.WzHBrlVKjIU

Lopez, M.H. and Gonzalez-Barrera, A. (2014). *Women's College Enrollment Gains Leave Men Behind.* Pew Research Center. Available at: http://www.pewresearch.org/fact-tank/2014/03/06/womens-college-enrollment-gains-leave-men-behind/

Rodriguez, Salvador (2015). *Slack Diversity Figures Show Progress With White Women But Minorities Being Left Behind.* International Business Times. Available at: http://www.ibtimes.com/slack-diversity-figures-show-progress-white-women-minorities-being-left-behind-2293478

Graham, Ruth (2013). *Who Wants to Fight Beauty Bias?* The Boston Globe. Available at: https://www.bostonglobe.com/ideas/2013/08/23/who-will-fight-beauty-bias/Kq3pbfOy4VRJtlKrmyWBNO/story.html

Commongood Careers and Level Playing Field Institute (2011). *The Voice of Nonprofit Talent: Perceptions of Diversity in the Workplace.* Available at: http://commongoodcareers.org/articles/detail/the-voice-of-nonprofit-talent-diversity-in-the-workplace

Diversity Council of Australia (2015). Building Inclusion: An Evidence-Based Model of Inclusive Leadership. Available at: https://www.dca.org.au/research/project/building-inclusion-evidence-based-model-inclusive-leadership

Sample Test Questions:

THE ELEMENTS OF LEADING A LARGE-SCALE D&I EFFORT

1. **The adaptive leadership approach views leadership as a:**
   A. Behavior
   B. Competency
   C. Process

2. **This approach can help negate many fears that people have when it comes to addressing diversity:**
   A. Remedial
   B. Educational
   C. Divisional

3. **A _____ strategy transfers discrimination or unfairness from one group to another.**
   A. Flexible
   B. Inclusion
   C. Replacement

4. **_____ can be defined as "the quality of making judgments that are free from discrimination".**
   A. Equality
   B. Fairness
   C. Equity

5. **Inclusive leadership creates an organizational culture that consistently produces:**
   A. A workplace free from gender discrimination
   B. Opportunities to recruit diverse staff
   C. Results that benefit all stakeholders

6. **Only certain dimensions of diversity have a history of exclusion, discrimination or inequity.**
   A. True
   B. False

7. **Management is different from leadership in that leadership relies on:**
   A. Political correctness
   B. Formal authority
   C. Informal authority

idc Institute for
Diversity Certification™

Sample Test Questions:

THE ELEMENTS OF LEADING A LARGE-SCALE D&I EFFORT (cont'd)

8. **All of the following are examples of systemic barriers in the workplace EXCEPT:**
   A. Restricted access to high level jobs or management training programs
   B. Inclusion of qualified women in traditionally male dominated fields
   C. Age discrimination in reductions in force and retirement benefits

9. **Globally, equality has roots in:**
   A. Imperialism and military force
   B. John Adams' *Equity Theory*
   C. Government and legislation

10. **To achieve cultural competence, both leadership and management skills are necessary to build the:**
    A. Cultural dexterity of employees
    B. Cohesiveness of the community
    C. Business case for Diversity & Inclusion

11. **Delegation entails equipping other leaders to execute key tasks.**
    A. True
    B. False

12. **_____ is an ongoing process that maps, controls and evaluates an organization's diversity and inclusion efforts.**
    A. Strategic diversity planning
    B. A standard operating procedure
    C. A global best practice

13. **Diversity and Inclusion leaders must always communicate the business value which is:**
    A. Best demonstrated by hiring an innovative and diverse workforce
    B. Making money, saving money and/or achieving organizational goals
    C. Ensuring that all employees belong and are culturally competent

RACE, POWER & PRIVILEGE

Race problems in America are as traditional as baseball and apple pie. Nevertheless, the old way of diversity thought leadership assumed that White men were the problem. In the next generation of Diversity and Inclusion work, White men are part of the solution. Engaging White men in diversity efforts will ensure inclusion for all, as well as foster organizational cultures that value and support a long-term diversity strategy.

Diversity should be good for business for everyone—not just the traditionally underrepresented groups.

OVERALL OBJECTIVES AND COMPETENCIES

The purpose of this competency is to present alternatives to an outdated social and power construct in the workplace; identify the nuances behind the theory of privilege; and encourage White males to actively engage in a culture that is becoming increasingly diverse.

BACKGROUND AND CONTEXT

In America, race is the metaphorical elephant in the room. It's difficult and clumsy to work around, it's big and obvious, and no one wants to acknowledge or talk about it. Yet, because people are uncomfortable talking about race, they rely on conjecture or code words.

In *Matters of Race, Power and Privilege*, Carol Brantley et al asserts, "While there is no scientific evidence to support our notion of 'race', it has stood the test of time as a moniker that defines visual and/or cultural differences between Caucasians (White) and people of African, Asian, Aboriginal, Latin (Hispanic) decent, or natives of the continental Americas ("people of color" as a more appropriate term for non-whites). The Human Genome Project has shown that there are few, if any, genetic differences between the peoples we have come to identify as a particular race. All genetic differences are individual."

Keep in mind, the word individual is not the same as inferior. Individual implies that someone is unique, one-of-a-kind, or characterized by unusual qualities. It is in stark contrast to the meaning of inferior, which entails being lower in rank, status, ability, or quality. To some, the word diversity is synonymous with inferiority, which may improperly imply that people of color are powerless and dependent in respect to engagement and inclusion. D&I leaders hold the keys to creating a culture where people can genuinely talk about race but first, the conversation must be framed differently.

The use of code words is one such example of how ineffective communication can derail Diversity and Inclusion efforts. A code word is a word or phrase shared by a group which has a special meaning to that group. Code words are often used to hide meaning or intention from anyone not in the group. For example, one may say "inner city" or "thug" when the underlying meaning in the code word is Black people. Contrariwise, there are some who espouse that diversity is a code word for "White genocide" or anti-racist is a code word for "Anti-White".

In a blog entitled, *"What's in a word?"* Mary Frances Winters, CEO of the Winters Group, admonishes diversity practitioners.

"I want to challenge us to be mindful of code words. Diverse candidate or diversity hire are really codes for race/ethnic and/or gender diversity...especially women and people of color. It is understood by most of us that we are talking about the visible dimension of diversity for which companies get diversity credit.

If we claim to define diversity with a myriad of dimensions (e.g., age, sexual orientation or gender identity, sex, education, military status, etc.) that embody the term, everybody is a "diverse candidate" or a "diversity hire". Everyone comes with some aspect of diversity. A white male is not usually considered a diverse hire because white men often represent the majority and have not been historically underrepresented. But what about a white male hire in a historically female dominated industry like nursing?

One of the reasons that we are stymied in our progress in the diversity and inclusion field is we talk out of both sides of our mouth so to speak. On the one hand we argue that diversity is more than women and people of color and that everyone is included in the diversity mix. On the other, we perpetuate terms like "diversity hire" knowing full well that what we really mean is a hire that can be counted against our representation goals (usually women and people of color including Blacks, Latinos, Asians, Pacific Islanders, and Native Americans).

Be specific. If you want to hire a woman say so. If you want to hire a person of color make it clear but also make the business case so it does not appear that you are simply filling some arbitrary "quota". How will the addition of such diversity support your business objectives? For example, "our customer base increasingly includes Asian Americans and we do not have any Asians represented on our leadership team who can help us ensure we are meeting the needs of these customers." Or, "we want to develop products and services that meet the needs of individuals with physical disabilities and we have no one on our team who represents that community." Let's stop using code words that sound more PC but in effect continue to exclude."

In the workplace, the proper use of language is a key component of advancing diversity efforts and dispelling biases. How a D&I leader communicates, or doesn't communicate, will provide a model for all other employees and executives to follow. Similarly, if the diversity leader clumsily approaches the conversation around race, or avoids the topic altogether, the tone will be set for the entire organization. It's a precarious situation to be in, but this guide will provide some instruction.

The Continuing Legacy of Discrimination & Racism

According to the Equal Employment Opportunity Commission (EEOC), race receives the most discrimination and harassment complaints out of all protected categories. In celebration of its 50th Anniversary, the EEOC released a report entitled, *American Experiences Versus American Expectations,* which illustrates significant changes to the demographics of the workforce since EEOC opened its doors in 1965.

The new report is an update to EEOC's groundbreaking 1977 study, *Black Experiences Versus Black Expectations*. The American Experiences report examined changes in participation in nine job categories for African-Americans, Hispanics, Asian-Americans, American Indians/Alaskan Natives, and women between 1966, the first year for which EEOC collected data, and 2013, the most recent year for which data is available. The report draws on data from the EEO-1 survey.

According to former EEOC Chairperson Jenny R. Yang, "Despite notable progress in diversity and inclusion in the workplace over the past half century, the report highlights continued job segregation by race and gender, with women and people of color disproportionately occupying lower paying positions".

Race is a painful topic to address because of the historical context of slavery, disenfranchisement, the institutionalization of the "separate but equal" doctrine, National Labor Laws, exclusion from labor unions, glass ceilings in the workplace, and housing patterns. Many Caucasians are horrified by what their ancestors did, and some unnecessarily experience "White Guilt." The word unnecessarily is used because guilt can immobilize individuals, or cause some to overcompensate. At the other extreme is fear. Some believe they have to band together under the Confederate Battle Flag, lest people of color take over. In some small circles, the Confederate Battle Flag is a symbol of rebellion and indicative of rejection for diverse groups.

For African Americans, only a few individuals are still alive who have actually experienced slavery, Jim Crow, or sharecropping. Nevertheless, the remnants of these systems remain dominant in American society. Slavery led to systematic racism and negative stereotypes toward African American's in particular. Another remnant of this system is the extreme negative effects of the White Guilt phenomenon, where Caucasians' feel responsible and guilt-ridden for the past actions of their predecessors. Similarly, some African American's have used slavery as a justification to abdicate responsibility for bad choices or to relinquish accountability for empowering themselves to achieve a higher quality of life. At the other end of this extreme thinking are African Americans and Caucasians who choose to pretend that racism is a thing of the past.

Race is a social construct based on observable, physical characteristics. Race pertains to visible physical characteristics such as skin color, hair, bone structure, and eye color—as scientists have noted there are minimal genetic variations within the human species. This social categorization results in differences in virtually every aspect of American life, including socioeconomic, legal, educational, political, and other constructs through the institutionalized practice of preference and discrimination. The word institutionalized is key here. Institutionalized racism includes any system of inequality based on race. This term was introduced by Black Power activists Stokely Carmichael and Charles V. Hamilton in the late 1960s. In *Social Constructionism in the Context of Organization Development*, authors Celiane Camargo-Borges and Emerson F. Rasera assert that the key to altering a systemic social construct lies in fostering dialogue, imagination, and co-creation as partners in the change process (Sage Publications, 2013, Retrieved 2017).

Within the framework of race, there are many nuances. For example, colorism is the practice of discrimination by which those with lighter skin are treated more favorably than those with darker skin. Colorism is applicable to Hispanic, Asian, Black, and mixed raced communities. Within all communities of color, this concept mirrors "White Privilege" in that lighter skinned individuals are afforded benefits that darker skinned people may not receive. Where race and colorism are nuanced, race and ethnicity differ.

Race and ethnicity can obviously overlap, but they are distinct. For example, a Japanese-American woman would probably consider herself a member of the Japanese or East Asian race; but if she doesn't engage in any of the practices or customs of her ancestors, she might not identify with the Japanese ethnicity. Instead, she might consider herself American.

In the future, the traditional concept of race may be negligible due to net migration and the natural increase of mixed-race individuals, which means that America and Western European countries will become more diverse. Some people are very concerned about this probability and have resorted to changing laws, altering immigration patterns, and restricting birth control options. In other words, demographic projections currently dictate high level decision making to ensure that the present social construct rolls back one hundred years, or does not shift with the population.

While most Blacks in America have multi-cultural heritages, it is becoming evident that more individuals of mixed heritage are opting to identify with more than one culture. The fact that some people do not identify solely with one group presents another challenge the current social construct. In nations such as Central and South America, color gradients are used to identify people. In Brazil, there are "approximately 40 color groupings" for people of mixed races (Schaefer, 2015, p. 227). In the event that America's racial construct changes to Brazil's model, there may be attempts to classify individuals by color or class. Or worse, America may develop a structure similar to South Africa's Apartheid system. Just imagine what *could* happen if diversity leaders are not proactively engaged in redefining how the new social construct should look.

SHARING SPACE & POWER

In a recent New York Times article, U.S. Senator Corey Booker says, "many families in America made their wealth or secured their status as middle class through housing, and you have the government systematically devaluing neighborhoods—taking away that wealth, in effect—then concentrating poverty very consciously." Cities such as Detroit, MI; Gary, IN; and Newark, NJ are notoriously ascribed for their poverty, high crime, and sub-standard educational systems while surrounding suburbs flourish.

After the end of the Civil War and the abolition of slavery, Jim Crow laws were introduced. These laws led to the discrimination of racial and ethnic minorities, especially African Americans. Fifteen state courts obeyed ordinances that enforced the denial of housing to African American and other minority groups in "White-Zoned" areas. These ordinances were then made illegal in the 1917 Supreme Court case, Buchanan v. Warley. Following this decision, 19 states legally supported covenants, or agreements, between property owners to not rent or sell any homes to racial or ethnic minorities. Although the covenants themselves were made illegal in 1948, they were still allowed to be present in private deeds.

It was not until the Civil Rights Act of 1968, otherwise known as the Fair Housing Act, that the U.S. federal government made its first concrete steps to deem all types of housing discrimination unconstitutional. The act explicitly prohibited common housing discrimination practices such as filtering information about a home's availability, racial steering, blockbusting, and redlining. Nevertheless, in spite of the changes to the law, discriminatory practices still exist, exacerbating wealth disparities and urban renewal efforts.

Many will agree that wealth and power are the keys to success in modern-day America. In fact, in *The Black Power Imperative*, Theodore Cross asserts, "Power demands control of at least one of the following: private wealth, business or public wealth, organized crime, or state and local government. Power includes authority and domination, both of which were used to benefit Whites and deny equal access to Blacks."

Today's political narrative around "taking America back" is a flawed theory. These are code words for increasing the White population so that Caucasians can control the power and resources. Both Whites and Blacks came to America around the same time period. The first White colonists (or permanent European settlers) arrived in 1607, while the first Black immigrants unwillingly came to Jamestown, Virginia as slaves in 1619. In *The Half Has Never Been Told: Slavery and the Making of American Capitalism*, author Edward Baptist writes, "During the middle of the 1800s, cotton became the world's largest commodity. The cheapest and best cotton came from the southern U.S."

Slavery in the Americas triggered a revolution, civil war, and many rebellions before it was abolished in 1865. While slavery is documented as a common practice going back as far as the book of Exodus in the Bible, the institution of slavery in America was an enduring system that still shows vestiges 400 years later.

In a controversial 2018 interview with TMZ, Rapper Kanye West said, "When you hear about slavery for 400 years. For 400 years?! That sounds like a choice." Social media backlash caused West to clarify his statement on Twitter. "Of course I know that slaves did not get shackled and put on a boat by free will," he wrote. "My point is for us to have stayed in that position even though the numbers were on our side means that we were mentally enslaved." Blacks did fight enslavement. They ran away, organized uprisings, and educated themselves. They also established relationships with Whites who were instrumental in abolishing the institution of slavery. In fact, history is replete with examples of how Whites and Blacks worked together to enact social change in America.

Unlike slaves from other nations in prior eras, Africans did not return to their country of origin once slavery ended. Since arriving in America in 1619, these individuals have contributed to research, innovation, and productivity—although a majority of Blacks did not receive acknowledgement or compensation for their intellectual contributions and their work. They unwittingly became part of a discriminatory, but profitable, economic system in which wealthy Whites benefited from legal structures designed to advance their interests in everything from slavery and sharecropping to predatory lending and privatization of the prison industrial complex.

Today, the notion that Blacks are lazy, intellectually inferior, and deserving of separate but unequal systems and services, runs counter to the reality that America was built from the contributions of many groups. Without all of these diverse individuals, America would be vastly different. For example, beyond music and food, Latinos have significantly contributed to the nation as well. Instead of asking why there are so many Hispanics in America's largest cities, people should ask why some of these cities are Spanish words: Los Angeles, Las Vegas, San Antonio, and Miami.

Race is a powerful and debilitative social construct that affords privileges to some, but not others. It is also intentionally divisive so that certain individuals are continually motivated to take action to preserve the benefits afforded to them because of race or ethnicity. In other words, Whites are not the only individuals who are advantaged by America's social construct.

Equal access to resources is a debatable theory. Within this framework is the developmental approach, where there is a desire for rapid growth. The developmental approach is a study of influence and the influential. Within this framework, J. Owens Smith et al emphasizes, "Society can expect groups to struggle to obtain a position of power to influence the authoritative allocation of resources favorable to their self-interests. The natural outgrowth of this struggle is the development of tyranny among the dominant class, i.e., where the most powerful groups are going to undertake measures to limit choice possibilities for the less powerful groups."

In *"Land of Equal Opportunity? The Power of a Costly Myth"*, Jon Wisman explores the myth of social mobility. Wisman contends:

> "Americans are becoming increasingly aware that our society has become dramatically less equal over the past 40 years, with a very small elite taking most economic gains.
>
> First, it should be noted that many Americans greatly underestimate the degree of inequality. Second, some people still believe that anyone can get rich if they only work hard and save. Those who are rich have earned it, and those who are poor also get their just deserts.
>
> This view of fluid social mobility has deep roots in U.S. culture. For much of our history, thanks to abundant land and emigrants who fled Europe's rigid class structure, there was greater social mobility in America than anywhere else on Earth.
>
> In the 1830s, Alexis de Tocqueville noted an exceptionally high degree of vertical mobility in the U.S. and termed it "American exceptionalism." He exclaimed that "the rich are constantly becoming poor," adding, "To tell the truth, though there are rich men, the class of rich men does not exist...."
>
> Tragically, whatever might have been the case earlier in American history, such exceptionalism is no longer valid. Over the past decade, multiple studies have found that there is less vertical mobility in the U.S. than in other rich societies such as Canada, Sweden, Germany, Spain, Denmark, Austria, Norway, Finland, and France. A 2012 Pew Research Center report found that 43 percent of individuals born into the bottom quintile of the U.S. income distribution remain there as adults, and 70 percent remain below the middle quintile."

The underpinning for racial conflict is the notion that there are or will be benefits for a particular group now or in the future. Everyone knows that if you weren't born into wealth, the 'benefits' are limited. Yet no one wants to share or give up the potential to acquire more benefits. On a basic level, most Whites know that they receive an advantage because of their skin color. Likewise, some Blacks understand that African Americans are indeed advancing and they don't want the progress to stop or slow down. Additionally, some immigrants are aware that they are very fortunate to be in America, as their home countries do not offer as many opportunities. No one group has "enough". A conversation about benefits, and the perception that benefits are in limited supply, will present a non-threatening avenue from which to initiate a discussion about race and privilege. A skilled diversity facilitator can ask the questions: What do you hope to gain by working here? What have you been told about your ability to accomplish your goals? Who can help you achieve your personal and professional objectives? What threatens your ability to achieve your dreams? The responses from the different groups in the room will provide an opportunity to educate each group about one another. For example, some Whites may be surprised to learn that most of their Black co-workers never grew up in an inner city. Some African Americans are third and fourth generation college graduates and come from well-to-do families. African American employees may be surprised to learn that some Whites grew up in rural areas or were not born into wealthy, two parent households. It's important to establish an educational foundation that allows employees to see each other as 'someone like me' before moving into harder subjects like race and privilege. This framework can also apply in Canada with aboriginal people, in the E.U. with Eastern and Western Europeans, as well as in other regions.

While societal disparities may always exist in some fashion, the role of a Diversity and Inclusion leader is to help all employees focus on the shared opportunities, the common purpose, and diversity of thought. Otherwise, African-American and Caucasian work groups will remain polarized by the past, and other groups will remain excluded from the conversation but included as victims of discriminatory practices.

WHAT ABOUT THE WHITE GUYS?

Chuck Shelton, author of the *Study on White Men Leading Through Diversity & Inclusion,* conducted an anonymous survey consisting of responses from 700 leaders at eight major companies. In the study, he found that approximately 80% of all respondents rated Caucasian male managers highly on the ability to show respect for diverse co-workers. In contrast, only 36% of Caucasian male respondents rated Caucasian male leaders positively for saying just what needs to be said (candor) among diverse co-workers.

The project also found that the "what about the White guys?" conversation requires clear definition and purpose. In fact, even using the words "White men" operates in a contentious social narrative around demographic change and personal experience. All employees want to know why including Caucasian men is important, how everyone will benefit from the learning, and what the organization will gain by taking inclusion in such an unexpected direction.

Inclusion with integrity includes everyone—even White guys. The numbers for this particular group are eye-catching: 6 million Caucasian men in America lead for a living according to a 2009 article in Diversity Executive. Accounting for only 5 percent of all U.S. employees, these leaders wield decision-making influence far beyond their proportion. Yet, many Caucasian men have grown or remain quiet about diversity because it doesn't seem to include them. Further, it's not always clear to them what diversity involves.

Since there's momentum to galvanize and progress to praise, the Caucasian male disconnect is both a problem and an opportunity. Over the years, organizations have developed Diversity and

Inclusion (D&I) as a strategy to hire and retain employees, win and serve diverse customers, expand globally, improve innovation, save money through different suppliers, and avoid litigation. Doors are opening for women, people of color, and those with other dimensions of diversity. These achievements make us all proud. However, organizations seek to fuel such forward movement by including 100 percent of employees. Their intention is to expand the return on investment in Diversity and Inclusion.

Standing squarely in the way of sustaining progress is the low confidence in and weak commitment to Diversity and Inclusion among many Caucasian men who are leaders. Keep in mind, most Caucasian male leaders enjoy strong relationships with diverse colleagues and customers. However, many of them:

- Do not give constructive feedback to diverse employees in fear of being called racist or sexist. This results in wrong or incorrect work and does not allow diverse direct reports to improve professionally.

- Dismiss Diversity and Inclusion efforts as being a program for others. They may silently wonder why nothing is being done for White males when it appears that other groups obtain more opportunities or are advancing.

- Fulfill the minimum requirements for hiring, promotions, or professional development. They only do what they are told to do, versus coming up with ideas for how it could be done better.

- Are ostracized, or even punished, for voicing their feelings or objections about Diversity and Inclusion, so they learn to keep quiet and not voice any concerns.

- Lurk on the margins at diversity events and rarely volunteer for D&I initiatives. They visibly demonstrate their belief that inclusion excludes them.

- Settle for uninspired diversity goals that don't drive high performance. As a result, D&I is weakened as a credible business strategy.

- Anonymously post their dissatisfaction with diversity efforts online.

In most organizations, more than 50 percent of the leaders are Caucasian men, and this percentage increases as one ascends the hierarchy. When Caucasian male leaders disconnect, it represents a huge underperforming asset in many companies' Diversity and Inclusion investment portfolios. No business strategy, especially Diversity and Inclusion, can deliver significant results when more than half of the organization's leaders disconnect from it.

Instead of developing new ways to meet the challenges of globalization, competition, and scarce resources, many have reverted to a discussion about the value of Diversity and Inclusion. Hence lower standards, unqualified, merit, compromised values, and unfair, are all code words being used to describe modern-day Diversity and Inclusion efforts. These sentiments are reminiscent of the 1980's, when organizations first began introducing Diversity and Inclusion efforts en masse due to an increase in Equal Employment Opportunity (EEO) lawsuits, negative publicity, and compensatory and punitive damages.

There are two causes for the White male disconnect:

1. **The Inadvertent or Intentional Exclusion by Diversity Leaders:** Two generations of diversity work opened doors to those disadvantaged by various dimensions of difference. During this period, Caucasian men in leadership positions were often cast as default villains. More recently, D&I has largely left them alone. However, leaving Caucasian men alone can be considered inadvertent exclusion. This is where D&I officers are unaware of the fact that they need to actively include and engage Caucasian men.

   Exclusion is more intentional when diversity leaders make a conscious decision not to include Caucasian men. This may happen because the diversity officer finds it easier to exclude skeptics or he/she feels somewhat intimidated by unsupportive Caucasian males in leadership.

2. **Unformed Self-Interest in Diversity Among Caucasian Men:** While advantages accrue for Caucasian men due to their skin color, gender, education, and social class, the inclusion of everyone else unintentionally triggered a visceral sense of being excluded. Another inadvertent outcome: There is a severe shortage of Caucasian men who champion diversity from whatever level they lead.

   Today there's fresh motivation for Caucasian men to include themselves. Not only are there more professional opportunities for Caucasian men who are culturally competent, but they can positively contribute to the organization's bottom line by supporting inclusion and moving diversity efforts forward. White male diversity champions can answer the "what's in it for me" question with utter professional and personal clarity. Not only will they advance D&I work, but they will differentiate themselves from unengaged Caucasian men.

When Caucasian male leaders with position power detach from diversity, companies suffer higher costs, lower revenues, decreased productivity and innovation, more conflict, and diminished competitiveness. This occurs because Diversity and Inclusion only delivers superior results when it is managed well; otherwise, it can produce negative outcomes. Further, without Caucasian male leadership, D&I programming will be insufficiently allied to the operational side of the business. When that happens, line leaders may view the work as a low-performing cost, rather than perceiving diversity executives as high-performing partners in growing income and talent. In other words, it's bad news when Caucasian male leaders disengage from D&I efforts.

CHANGING DEMOGRAPHICS

Although Caucasian men are in the minority, they are in positions of power in some of the largest countries in the world—China, India, Nigeria, and Japan, per the 2013 Population Division of the United Nations.

According to the U.S. Census Bureau, non-Hispanic Whites made up 85% of the population in 1960. By 2050, individuals of color are projected to account for 54% of the population and non-Hispanic Whites 46%, down from their current 63.7% share (2010 U.S. Census).

While the Caucasian population is the largest racial group in America, it grew at a slower rate than the total population. According to the U.S. Census Bureau report *The White Population: 2010* (published September 2011), the majority of the growth in the White population was due to the growth among Hispanic Whites.

Throughout America, there is a broader demographic shift occurring. First, the White population is aging. By 2050, one in five residents will be aged 65 or over, up from one in nine today. Second, because of the Delayer Boom, where women delayed childbirth until their careers were more established, today's Caucasian families have fewer children. Meanwhile, immigration from Asian and Hispanic populations, as well as higher birth rates among these groups, especially Hispanics, are accelerating demographic changes in the U.S. Additionally, there has been an increase in interracial marriages. According to the U.S. Census Bureau, White Americans were statistically the *least* likely to wed interracially. Although in absolute terms, their number of interracial marriages is higher than any other group because their proportion of the population is greater. In 2010, 2.1% of married Caucasian women and 2.3% of married Caucasian men had a non-White spouse—with the majority of Caucasian men marrying Asian women, when they marry outside of their race. Nevertheless, there has been an increase in the number of Caucasian men marrying African American women.

According to the U.S. Census Bureau, there were 354,000 White female/Black male, and 196,000 Black female/White male, marriages in March 2009, representing a ratio of 181:100. This traditional disparity has seen a rapid decline over the last two decades, contrasted with its peak in 1981 when the ratio was 371:100. Pew Research Center analyzed this phenomenon in its 2017 report entitled, *Trends and Patterns in Intermarriage*. Pew found, "The share of recently married blacks with a spouse of a different race or ethnicity has more than tripled, from 5% in 1980 to 18% in 2015. Among recently married whites, rates have more than doubled, from 4% up to 11%." There have been several high-profile interracial marriages to substantiate Pew's findings, including Meghan Markle and Prince Harry, Serena Williams and Reddit Founder Alexis Ohanian, Mellody Hobson and Star Wars creator George Lucas, and Chirlane McCray and New York Mayor Bill de Blasio.

Pew adds, "intermarriage has ticked down among recently married Asians and remained more or less stable among Hispanic newlyweds. Even though intermarriage has not been increasing for these two groups, they remain far more likely than black or white newlyweds to marry someone of a different race or ethnicity. About three-in-ten Asian newlyweds (29%) have a spouse of a different race or ethnicity. The same is true of 27% of Hispanics."

Jennifer L. Bratter and Rosalind B. King conducted a sociological experiment to examine the role of gender in interracial divorce dynamics; specifically, looking at marital instability among Black/White unions. In their studies, it was observed that White wife/Black husband marriages showed twice the divorce rate of White wife/White husband couples by the 10th year of marriage. Their studies also found that Black wife/White husband marriages were 44% less likely to end in divorce than White wife/White husband couples over the same 10-year period.

This data is critical to Diversity and Inclusion officers and multi-cultural communications professionals who make decisions about marketing. While interracial unions are still controversial, as evidenced by the 2013 Cheerios commercial that sparked a racist backlash, there has been a slight shift from the traditional image of an American family.

From an employee engagement perspective, you cannot look at someone and tell who their spouse is, where they have traveled, or what they value. Therefore, to assume that Caucasian males do not care about diversity may not only be erroneous, but it could also derail the sustainability of your efforts.

Figure 1 illustrates the projected changes to U.S. demographics. The US Census Bureau's projections are based on birth, death, and current immigration rates.

FIGURE 1

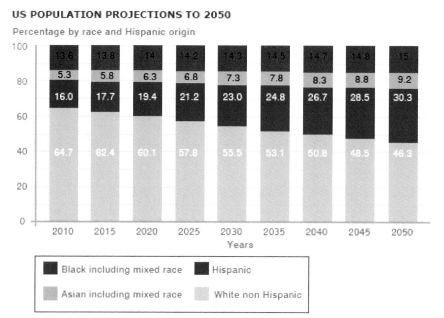

US POPULATION PROJECTIONS TO 2050

Percentage by race and Hispanic origin

SOURCE: US Census Bureau

In states such as Hawaii, Florida, Texas, and California, Whites make up less than half of the population. In large cities, such as New York, Los Angeles, Chicago, Houston, and Washington, DC minorities predominantly occupy these areas. Correspondingly, "White flight" (where Whites moved to suburbs to avoid contact with people of color) is not what it used to be.

Young Caucasians have had more contact with people of color than their parents or grandparents, putting them in a position where it is virtually impossible to avoid individuals who are different. Although more interracial contact is generally positive, it does not necessarily lessen prejudice or stereotypes.

Thus, it is up to Diversity and Inclusion professionals to address these issues when they arise in the workplace, as well as to ensure that Caucasian male employees understand how their majority status has translated into benefits for their group that may or may not exist in the future. For example, President Nelson Mandela's democratic election in 1994 marked the end of apartheid in South Africa. Under apartheid, the government enforced a system of segregation, classifying groups by four races: Black, 80% of the South African population; White, 9%; Coloured, 9%; and Indian/Asian, 2%. Today's South Africa struggles to correct the inequalities created by decades of apartheid. Despite a rising Gross Domestic Product (GDP), the end of the apartheid system left the country socio-economically divided by race.

According to the United Nations, while President Mandela's nomination signaled the beginning of a shift in the overall thinking of some South Africans, privilege still existed in education and employment causing Blacks to make up over 90% of the country's poor. Although apartheid ended, Whites were still privileged in South Africa's social construct.

WHAT IS PRIVILEGE?

A privilege is a special entitlement or immunity granted by those in authority to a restricted group, either by birth or on a conditional basis. By contrast, a *right* is an inherent, irrevocable entitlement held by all citizens or all human beings from birth.

A Caucasian man once described privilege in this sense: he asserted that because he is White, tall, and a male with gray hair, he can say things at meetings and do things at work, that other groups would be prohibited from doing. He also says that his mere appearance affords him leadership positions over diverse individuals who may be more educated or experienced.

For the purposes of this guide, we will define privilege as power.

DEFINITION	
Privilege	*"Privilege is the absence of barriers and the presence of unearned positive attributes."*

Everyone has varying degrees of privilege based on certain characteristics. In the field of D&I, White Privilege is an advantage provided by Whites' and afforded to other White individuals because of their race. It is an unconscious and invisible benefit. It is not a bad thing, but it can sometimes be misunderstood because so few Caucasians admit that it exists. Therefore, they neglect to use the power associated with privilege to advance Diversity and Inclusion initiatives.

White privilege is a sociological concept that describes advantages enjoyed by Caucasian persons beyond what is commonly experienced by people of color in those same professional, social, political, and economic spaces.

Tim Wise, author and educator, defines White privilege as any advantage, opportunity, benefit, head start, or general protection from negative societal mistreatment, which persons deemed White typically enjoy that others will generally not experience. These benefits can be material (such as greater opportunity in the labor market, or greater net worth, due to historical restrictions in which Whites had the ability to accumulate wealth to a greater extent than persons of color), social (such as presumptions of competence, creditworthiness, law-abidingness, intelligence, etc.) or psychological (such as not having to worry about triggering negative stereotypes, rarely having to feel out of place, not having to worry about racial profiling, etc.).

Privilege is closely related to affinity bias, which occurs when we feel more comfortable with and gravitate towards people who we perceive to be like us. Nevertheless, privilege differs from racism or prejudice in that a person benefiting from White privilege does not necessarily hold racist beliefs or prejudices themselves. Often, the person benefiting is unaware of his or her privilege.

Privilege provides context in the field of diversity in that privilege:

- Challenges Ideas About Race
- Uncovers Invisible Rules
- Diminishes the "Meritocracy" Mindset
- Motivates Individuals to Manage Their Power to Create Inclusion

Presently, there is significant global backlash against immigrants and people of color. Reactions from some individuals can range from a "wall of silence" to outright hostility. Current ideas about racism can be limited because of their tendency to focus only on minorities and the historic oppressive context/legal status (i.e., slaves, illegal immigrants, etc.). This approach overlooks how Caucasians are affected by race and indeed receive privileges through race. Thus, resistance to the idea of White privilege may stem from a tendency of Caucasians to see the inequality arising from privilege as a Black or Latino issue. However, unfairness resulting from privilege impacts Caucasians too. The reality is that Whites can be negatively affected by privilege due to their economic status, family upbringing, marital status, sexual orientation, age, ability, and other unique characteristics. This notion implies that White privilege has categorical levels of hierarchy and benefits are doled out based on affinity.

For example, White women are privileged by their race, but disadvantaged because of their gender. Organizations find it easier to develop programs that enhance gender diversity, but many of these efforts still leave White women feeling invisible and undervalued. Some Caucasian women may also be concerned about the impact of changing demographics on their fathers, husbands, and sons.

The theory behind White privilege in America may be seen as having its roots in the system of legalized discrimination that existed for much of American history. In her book, *Privilege Revealed: How Invisible Preference Undermines America,* Stephanie M. Wildman writes that many Americans who advocate a merit-based, race-free worldview do not acknowledge the systems of privilege which benefit them. For example, many Americans rely on a social or financial inheritance from previous generations. This inheritance—unlikely to be forthcoming if one's ancestors were slaves—privileges Whiteness, maleness, and heterosexuality.

An analyst of the phenomenon, Thomas Shapiro, professor of law and social policy at Brandeis University argues, "The wealth gap is not just a story of merit and achievement, it's also a story of the historical legacy of race in the United States."

Keep in mind, the privilege theory extends beyond mere wealth. A 2002 Department of Justice survey found that while the likelihood of being stopped by police did not differ significantly between White drivers and other races, Black or Latino drivers were three times more likely to be searched than White drivers. Young White offenders are also more likely to receive lighter punishments than minorities in America. Black youth arrested for drug possession for the first time are incarcerated at a rate that is 48 times greater than the rate for White youth, even when all other factors surrounding the crime are identical. According to a report by the Illinois Disproportionate Justice Impact Study Commission, Black men are eight times more likely to be imprisoned than White men.

Racialized employment networks are yet another facet of the economy that benefits Caucasians at the expense of African Americans. Deirdre A. Royster, Ph.D., author of "*Race and the Invisible Hand*", conducted a study that compared African American and Caucasian males who graduated from the same school with the same skills. She looked at the success of their school to work transition and subsequent employment experiences. What she found was that the Caucasian graduates were more often employed in skilled trades, earned more, held higher status positions, received more promotions, and experienced shorter periods of unemployment. Since all factors of these graduates' education and skills were strikingly similar, the differences in employment experiences could only be attributed to race.

Royster concluded that the primary cause of these racial differences was due to social networking. The concept of "who you know" seemed just as important to these graduates as "what you know." However, Devah Page found that Caucasians enjoyed an advantage in hiring when education levels were equal to other candidates of color, and they enjoyed an advantage when the minority person had more education. A dramatic finding was the fact that despite having a prison record, the Caucasian applicant received more callbacks than the African American applicant without a criminal record. "Race it seems, was more of a concern to a potential employer than a criminal background" (Schaefer, 2015, p. 232).

Since older Caucasian males predominantly control blue-collar trades, they are more likely to offer varying forms of assistance to those in their social network (other Whites). Assistance can range from job vacancy information, referrals, direct job recruitment, formal and informal training, or vouching behavior and leniency in supervision. The assistance available to Caucasians is a form of privilege, which consistently puts people of color at a disadvantage in the employment sector.

Other research shows that there is a correlation between a person's name and their likelihood of receiving a call back for a job interview. A field experiment in Boston and Chicago proved that people with "white-sounding" names are 50% more likely to receive a call back than people with "black-sounding" names, despite equal résumé quality between the two racial groups.

As stated previously, the Blackwell Encyclopedia of Sociology describes several tactics that afford real estate benefits to Caucasians—blockbusting, redlining, and steering. Blockbusting is an illegal practice. It occurs when real estate agents frighten Caucasian homeowners into selling their homes at low prices due to the fear that more minorities are moving into the neighborhood. It is expected that the value of a home will depreciate due to an increased diverse presence. Realtors then sell those homes to a minority buyer for an inflated price, making a large profit in the process.

Another pernicious practice is redlining, where banks and financial institutions designate certain neighborhoods as too risky for an investment. Redlining can happen for any number of reasons, but it is most prominent when there is an increased presence of minority residents in an area. Lastly, steering is the practice of directing homebuyers to neighborhoods already populated by their race, maintaining market values and stigmas. In all of these cases, commercial investments, such as top-grade supermarkets, are not made in certain neighborhoods and the general quality of the community declines.

White youth tend to go to schools where, on average, 80 percent of the other students are White as well. Contrary to popular opinion, at schools where race or ethnicity is considered in admissions, students of color are not competing against Caucasian students for admittance; they are competing against similarly situated students.

For example, if 75% of the new entrants are Caucasian, 15% are Asian, 7% are African American, and 3% are Hispanic, the top students in each group are considered for admission. In most cases, the standard for Asians is much higher than the standard for Caucasians, while the standard for African Americans is much lower than for all other groups based on negative stereotypes.

In the infamous Fisher v. University of Texas (UT) case, Abigail Fisher, who graduated from Austin High School in 2008, was rejected from UT. Fisher, a White female, said that she was rejected from UT because of her race. She believed that she should have been admitted because her father and sister graduated from UT, and she had a 3.59 Grade Point Average (GPA). However, the Supreme Court agreed that other factors could be considered in her rejection. For example, UT's current admissions policy is to automatically accept students who graduate in the top ten percent of their class, under the statewide Top Ten Percent rule. The Top Ten make up roughly 75 percent of new UT admissions. However, Fisher did not graduate in the top 10 percent of her class; therefore, she was subject to the affirmative action admissions policy where the remaining 25 percent of UT's incoming students were selected based on a variety of factors, including GPA and SAT scores, extra-curricular activities, and special circumstances, which included racial and ethnic representation.

In a TIME News article entitled, *Affirmative Action Has Helped White Women More Than Anyone*, author Sally Kohn notes, "As for Fisher, there is ample evidence that she just wasn't qualified to get into the University of Texas. After all, her grades were not that great, and the year she applied to the university, admissions there were more competitive than Harvard's. In its court filings, the university had pointed out that even if Fisher received a point for race, she still would not have met the threshold for admissions. Yes, it is true that in the same year, the University of Texas made exceptions and admitted some students with lower grades and test scores than Fisher. Five of those students were black or Latino, 42 were white."

Interestingly, K-12 schools that appear to be integrated, often segregated students based on income, and may have subjected students to unfair treatment in other ways. For example, the learning assessments used to evaluate diverse children in K-12 schools are culturally biased because they do not take different dialects and other ethnic characteristics into consideration. Evidence shows that traditional psychological and academic assessments are based on skills that are considered important within the White, western, middle-class culture, but which may not be salient or valued within other cultures. This cultural bias presents White students with an educational advantage, magnifying the unequal classroom experience of diverse students.

Another feature of privilege is preparation. Some White and Asian students have the resources to prepare for standardized tests years in advance, whereas many first generation Black and Latino students prepare for the SAT or ACT exams within weeks or days. White and Asian families typically employ more tools to prepare as well. For example, some may pay for expensive prep courses, hire a tutor, purchase the study guide, or pay to take the exam multiple times. While every Asian on the continent of Asia may not be able to afford these luxuries, individuals who score high on standardized exams in America can. Therefore, a difference in test scores cannot be attributed to intelligence. Cultural bias on the test, the ability to adequately prepare for the exam, and the school system's resources play a huge factor.

According to Rivera (2012), employers are often more focused on hiring someone they would like to hang out with, more so than finding the person who can best do the job. This finding was the result of research based on 120 interviews with professionals involved in undergraduate and graduate hiring in elite U.S. investment banks, law firms, and management consulting firms as well as participant observations of a recruiting department.

According to the study, evaluators at firms often valued their personal feelings of comfort, validation, and excitement over identifying candidates with superior cognitive or technical skills. In fact, more than half of the evaluators in the study ranked cultural fit—the perceived similarity to a firm's existing employee base in background, leisure pursuits, and self-presentation—as the most important criterion at the job interview stage. Yet, studies have shown that the individuals who are hired are more likely to believe that they achieved their new positions based on merit.

Authors Emilio Castilla and Stephen Bernard substantiated these conjectures when they coined the phrase "The Paradox of Meritocracy". They assert that our current notions of merit are flawed because they are subjectively based on factors such as communication, polish, and cultural fit. In order to change ideas about meritocracy, D&I leaders must define merit, identify stereotypes, and help people to understand the disadvantages of privilege. For example, Millennials and Baby Boomers have different definitions of diversity; Millennials view diversity as open participation and Boomers interpret diversity as equitable representation. When both groups hear the word diversity, they may assume that it will spark interpersonal conflict, but dialogue between the two groups could present an opportunity to identify how either group receives workplace advantages or benefits. The same principle can apply to conversations about race, ability, gender, sexual orientation, religion, or other areas where privilege may manifest.

In order to change the organizational culture regarding privilege and merit, one must engage in choice architecture, whereby you seek to go beyond "fixing people" toward altering the environment in which decisions are made. The best place to start is to identify unwritten rules within the organization that enable subjectivity. Then one can create formal policies, justify when exceptions are required, and educate employees.

Not recognizing personal privilege leads to:

- A distorted viewpoint of one's "Profile of Success"
- The belief that your own success was all earned and therefore others must earn theirs as well
- The inability to distinguish between attributes and value-added results

Similarly, unmanaged workplace privilege leads to:

- Lost productivity
- Lost relationships
- Stress & emotional strain
- Worker dissatisfaction
- Turnover

The indirectness of White privilege is what makes it so prevalent. If people are not educated on the matter, it is unlikely that they will take note of it. Secondly, those that are aware of it suffer under the stigma of benefiting from an unfair system. Some may ask, "How can I see myself as a just person when I willingly participate in a system that is inherently unfair?" The "White Guilt" formed by this opinion creates a spirit of inactivity in solving the problem and is an impediment to change.

In order to use privilege as power, it is necessary to take progressive steps in dealing with White privilege and its implications. After awareness, the easiest way to initiate a paradigm shift is through dialogue. Honest and multicultural dialogue is the first step to building alliances, which can then transform people and systems and turn intention into action; thus, slowly changing the persistence of White privilege. Education can also provide people with tools to use their privileges positively. For example, teaching Whites how to speak up or ask questions when they recognize differences in treatment is an effective tool to empower Whites to champion inclusion.

Some D&I Practitioners want the Office of Diversity to dedicate more initiatives to race, fearing the inclusion of everyone will water down parity efforts for African Americans—who by all accounts still experience the most discrimination of all racial groups. A potential solution is Employee Resource Groups (ERG's), who can coordinate vital forums to discuss issues of race and privilege in the workplace. Not only can they explore distorted viewpoints, peers can engage in transformative discussions in an intimate and safe environment; and a skilled facilitator should lead these discussions.

Resource groups can be instrumental in helping employees convert privilege into power. In a decentralized manner, they could discover where privilege exists in the workplace, such as: Is there privilege in team assignments, decision-making, performance reviews, hiring and retention, sharing of information, career development, promotions, and feedback? If there is, how can the organization initiate a conversation about the lack of inclusiveness or foster an environment where all receive equal benefits? Resource groups can also assist in identifying those informal rules and recommend formal policies that apply to all. Create the business case for inclusion; this will keep those who enjoy the status quo focused on organizational goals instead of personal agendas.

The key to managing privilege involves creating an environment of fairness in lieu of a web of informal benefits and rules, as well as fostering a workplace culture that values employee contributions and differences. As the organization becomes more culturally competent, the privilege conversation should eventually extend beyond White males receiving benefits, to uncovering why women may not advocate for other women in senior executive roles, or why African Americans or Latinos may not support their group in the C-Suite, or why some Asian-American or Indian-American citizens may not assist their culturally-connected immigrant counterparts. It is also a prime opportunity to explore the intragroup and external dynamics pertaining to the privileges afforded by colorism.

There are many advantages to managing the various manifestations of privilege:

- Accelerate Inclusion
- Increase an Employee's Understanding of the Organizational Culture
- Increase Knowledge of Informal Rules
- Increase Advancement & Development Opportunities
- Enhance Alignment Towards Goal Achievement
- Heighten the Organization's Reputation
- Boost Productivity
- Increase Loyalty & Commitment to the Organization
- Cultivate Leadership Throughout the Organization
- Level the Playing Field

HOW TO BUILD TRUST

Shifting the current racial paradigm requires changing the way that D&I leaders address the "race" issue and fostering an environment where **all** employees can trust that there will be equal opportunity to access limited benefits. Building trust adds another layer to the engagement of Caucasian men in the Diversity and Inclusion process. There are multiple ways to build trust. First, Diversity and Inclusion practitioners must get Caucasian men involved early in the planning process. In this type of inclusion endeavor, do not limit your efforts to complicit men, seek skeptics. Encourage them to voice their feedback, suggestions, and concerns. This will make your Diversity and Inclusion work better, and it will signify that you are serious about engagement. Second, include Caucasian men in all aspects of your Diversity and Inclusion journey. Ask them to serve as executive sponsors, mentors, coaches, guest speakers, volunteers, communications liaisons, and more. Third, continue to build trust in sharing how Diversity and Inclusion benefits them too.

Trust is a major part in the foundation of interpersonal and business relationships. It is just as easy to build trust, as it is to break it down on a daily basis. If your interpersonal relationships are plagued by those deadly elements of suspicion and fear, you might find more success if you put extra effort into building trust. The art of building trust is a learned skill and can be a great asset to engaging Caucasian men in today's business environment. To build trust, consider these steps:

1. **Volunteer information**. When an opportunity to be vague arises, do not take it. Volunteer information to Caucasian men to prove that you have nothing to hide.

   Example of breaking down trust: "How did the meeting with the lawyer go?" "It went fine."

   Example of building trust: "How did the meeting with the lawyer go?" "It went fine. The whole day was stressful, getting all the documentation together, and we barely made it on time. But we both signed, and he said it would get mailed out tomorrow."

   You are not saying anything different, the meeting with the lawyer went fine, but by volunteering additional details; you are proving that you have nothing to hide.

2. **Speak your feelings and tell the truth**. Many Diversity and Inclusion practitioners fear that honesty may jeopardize their job or their professional standing, as they do not want to be the complainer or the trouble maker. However, it's not what you say; it's how you say it. If you say things the right way, Caucasian men will begin to look to Diversity and Inclusion practitioners as a credible source and trustworthy partner. Choose your battles wisely.

3. **Show consistency in your behavior**. This relates to your reliability and predictability. It also determines your skill and good judgment in handling difficult situations. Display loyalty; this refers to your ability to protect others and to be on the same side in their presence but most importantly in their absence.

4. **Be competent**. Gain the respect and admiration of Caucasian men by displaying adequate interpersonal or professional ability. Learn the business and speak the language of senior leadership (i.e., finance).

5. **Demonstrate a strong moral ethic**. This is particularly important in relationships. Caucasian men must feel confident that you will not falter or show betrayal in any form.

6. **Affirm Your Values.** Trust starts with values. It's important to communicate that the commitment to Diversity and Inclusion starts at the top, and even more important to demonstrate that commitment through decisions and actions. Show Caucasian men that you are embracing these values, and you will go a long way towards building trust.

7. **Share Your Vision and Strategy.** It's also important to keep your vision and strategy simple. Caucasian men need to understand the direction of your diversity strategy and clearly see how their work contributes to the organization's success. When you share your vision for success, you acknowledge your trust in others who can help obtain good outcomes.

8. **Be Open, Honest, and Transparent**. Caucasian males recognize in an instant when a leader is being honest, and if you communicate frequently, you will earn their trust and respect. This is especially true when times are tough. That is when Caucasian men need to hear from you most.

9. **Offer Sincere and Genuine Thanks.** The simple act of saying "thank you" is incredibly powerful. Thanking Caucasian men is another trust-builder, as long as it's from the heart. It's important to recognize people by name and explain why you are so grateful. To paraphrase the famous quote, Caucasian men may not remember everything you say, but they will never forget how you made them feel. Sincere gratitude goes a long way toward building trust.

Demonstrating a strong moral ethic causes the Diversity and Inclusion practitioner to make sure initiatives for women, people of color, individuals with disabilities, older workers, and other underrepresented groups are not forsaken at the expense of engaging Caucasian men, but are part of a larger effort to create a level playing field for all—while simultaneously ensuring full inclusion and employee engagement.

CONCLUSION

The unequal distribution of power limits opportunity for everyone.

By using code words in lieu of transparent practices and excluding certain groups, diversity leaders inadvertently perpetuate racial divisions. Caucasian men are not the racist and sexist individuals that once dominated the workplaces in the 1960's. While there are small pockets of Caucasian men who intentionally or inadvertently discriminate, it's important for each person to be considered as an individual. Therefore, instead of the traditional approach to race, power and privilege, consider adapting the following principles as you seek to increase engagement and inclusion:

- Talk about inclusiveness, not just diversity.
- Help workers build relationships across difference.
- Identify influential White male leaders to help champion your efforts.
- Encourage powerful White men to serve as visible Champions for Diversity.
- Educate all employees about the business imperative.
- Help your organization to become aware of bias and hidden inequities.
- Be specific and assign tasks when you ask for help.
- Provide organization-wide incentives for D&I efforts.

References:

Baptist, Edward E. (2014). *The Half Has Never Been Told: Slavery and the Making of American Capitalism*. Basic Books

Brantley, C.l, Frost, D., Pfeffer, C., Buccigrossi, J., Robinson, M. (2003). *On Matters of Race, Power and Privilege*. wetWare, Inc. Rochester, NY. Retrieved from: https://workforcediversitynetwork.com/docs/Race_5.pdf

Camargo-Borges, Celiane & Rasera, Emerson F. (May 3, 2013). *Social Constructionism in the Context of Organization Development*. Sage Publications. Retrieved From: http://journals.sagepub.com/doi/full/10.1177/2158244013487540

Castilla, E. J., & Benard, S. (2010). *The Paradox of Meritocracy in Organizations*. Administrative Science Quarterly, 55(4), 543-676.

Cross, Theodore (1987). *Black Power Imperative: Racial Inequality and the Politics of Nonviolence*. Faulkner Books.

DeGruy, J. (January 13, 2014). Post traumatic slave syndrome [Video file]. Retrieved from: https://www.youtube.com/watch?v=XRQ-Ci6LwVw

Kohn, Sally (June 17, 2013). *Affirmative Action Has Helped White Women More Than Anyone*. TIME. Retrieved From: http://ideas.time.com/2013/06/17/affirmative-action-has-helped-white-women-more-than-anyone/

Leonhardt, David (June 24, 2015). *Middle-Class Black Families, in Low-Income Neighborhoods*. New York Times. Retrieved From: https://www.nytimes.com/2015/06/25/upshot/middle-class-black-families-in-low-income-neighborhoods.html

Livingston, Gretchen and Brown, Anna (2017). *Trends and patterns in intermarriage*. Pew Research Center. Available at: http://www.pewsocialtrends.org/2017/05/18/1-trends-and-patterns-in-intermarriage/

Rivera, L. A. (2012). Hiring as cultural matching: The case of elite professional service firms. *American Sociological Review*, 77, 999-1022.

Schaefer, R. T. (2015). *Sociology: A brief introduction, 11ᵗʰ Edition*. New York, NY: McGraw-Hill.

Winters, Frances (June 11, 2015). *What's in a Word*. Retrieved From: http://www.theinclusionsolution.me/whats-in-a-word-part-11-diverse-candidate-diversity-hire/

Wisman, Jon (February 25, 2015). *Land of Equal Opportunity? The Power of a Costly Myth*. Huffington Post. Retrieved From: https://www.huffingtonpost.com/jon-wisman/land-of-equal-opportunity-myth_b_6694354.html

Yang, Jenny (2015). EEOC Press Release. Retrieved From: https://www.eeoc.gov/eeoc/newsroom/release/8-3-15.cfm

Unknown (November 11, 2006). *Census Report: Broad Racial Disparities Persist*. NBC News. Retried From: http://www.nbcnews.com/id/15704759/ns/us_news-life/t/census-report-broad-racial-disparities-persist/#.Ws4iFojwbIU

Sample Test Questions:

RACE, POWER & PRIVILEGE

1. _____ are often used to hide meaning or intention from anyone not in that group.
   A. Contrasts
   B. Code Words
   C. Strategies

2. Of all protected categories, which of the following receives the most EEO complaints?
   A. Age
   B. Sex
   C. Race

3. Stokely Carmichael and Charles V. Hamilton introduced this term to describe a system of inequality based on the practice of preference:
   A. Discrimination
   B. Institutionalized
   C. Unconscious Bias

4. The practice of discrimination by which those with lighter skin are treated more favorably that those with darker skin is called:
   A. Colorism
   B. Racism
   C. White Privilege

5. The federal government made its first steps to declare housing discrimination unconstitutional with the:
   A. Jim Crow laws
   B. Fair Housing Act of 1968
   C. Civil Rights Act of 1964

RACE, POWER & PRIVILEGE (cont'd)

6. **This code word is used to describe the exclusionary effect of some modern-day workplace diversity and inclusion efforts:**
   A. Multiculturalism
   B. Undocumented worker
   C. White genocide

7. **Privilege can be defined as the:**
   A. Ability of wealthy people to gain more assets
   B. Presence of unearned positive attributes
   C. Right of Caucasian men to be treated differently

8. **All of the following are examples of unmanaged workplace privilege EXCEPT:**
   A. Lost relationships
   B. Worker dissatisfaction
   C. Failed leadership programs

9. **Race is a social construct, which means that people:**
   A. Have the power to change it
   B. Will learn to ignore it
   C. Can effectively adjust to it

10. **One advantage to managing privilege is the ability to enhance D&I alignment with the achievement of organizational goals.**
    A. True
    B. False

11. **The sandwich generation, where women delayed childbirth until their careers were more established, became a key driver in demographic change.**
    A. True
    B. False

BOARDROOM DIVERSITY

> *Constructing a quality board is about the caliber and perspective of individual directors chosen, as well as the deliberate creation of a group dynamic and chemistry that allows for effective execution of corporate governance and strategic organizational oversight. While the board's primary responsibilities can vary, it typically includes identifying and evaluating significant opportunities and risks.*

OVERALL OBJECTIVES AND COMPETENCIES

The purpose of this competency is to improve policies, management, and decision making at the board level to reflect inclusive leadership. This competency is also designed to ensure that there a pipeline of diverse board candidates and that D&I professionals are equipped to serve in board leadership positions.

BACKGROUND AND CONTEXT

A Board of Directors is a body of elected and/or appointed members who jointly oversee the activities of a company or organization. The body sometimes has a different name, such as Board of Governors, Board of Trustees, or Supervisory Board, to name a few.

Theoretically, control of a for-profit company is divided between two bodies: the Board of Directors and the Shareholders. A shareholder is an individual or institution that legally owns stock in a public or private corporation. This term is different from an investor, which is a person or group that takes an ownership interest in any type of venture, whether it is a corporation or other business structure. It is possible for one to be both a shareholder and an investor.

The demographic changes that have occurred in the workplace since the 1960's, as a result of global anti-discrimination legislation and other factors, have highlighted the importance of understanding the value of diversity in the workplace, and even more important, understanding the value of diversity in the boardroom. Thus, boardroom diversity is a relevant issue at for-profit corporations, nonprofit organizations, colleges and universities, as well as quasi-governmental agencies, such as City Councils, public housing agencies, and school boards, to name a few.

The primary difference between serving on a corporate board, or a nonprofit board, is that the corporate board is a paid position versus the volunteer seat on a nonprofit board. Some corporate boards pay as much as $45,000 a year up to $1.5 million a year depending on the size of the company. Quasi-governmental boards—such as school boards, city councils or housing boards— may compensate smaller amounts.

Over the years, leaders in for profit companies and non-profit organizations alike have become increasingly aware of the strategic value of having diverse boards. Yet, despite the increased awareness and resulting emphasis on the importance of diversity in the boardroom, there is still a lack of diversity in gender and ethnicity among board members, and progress occurs at a snail's pace. Answering why this shortage still exists, and why some boards have not taken proactive steps toward resolving this issue, is a valuable exercise in diversity learning.

One of the major developments to shape contemporary thinking about organizational governance targeted businesses and originated in U.S. legislation. The Sarbanes-Oxley Act (SOX) was passed in 2002 in the wake of Enron, Tyco International, Adelphia, WorldCom, and other corporate scandals. Boards of Directors, specifically Audit Committees, who were supposed to establish oversight mechanisms for financial reporting in U.S. corporations, on the behalf of investors, failed to fulfill their obligations. As a result, corporate accounting fiascos cost investors billions of dollars when the share prices of affected companies collapsed, shaking public confidence in the nation's securities markets.

These scandals identified Board Members who either did not exercise their responsibilities or did not have the expertise to understand the complexities of the business. In many cases, Audit Committee Members were not truly independent of management. Therefore, SOX was intended to strengthen corporate governance and deter fraud in the corporate sector. However, it quickly sparked questions about nonprofit governance and whether nonprofits should comply with its standards. It also caused governments and corporations abroad to consider their vulnerabilities.

DEFINITION OF BOARDROOM DIVERSITY

The U.S. Security and Exchange Commission (SEC) Governance and Executive Compensation Disclosure Rules that went into effect February 28, 2010, requires companies to disclose whether, and how, the nominating and governance committee considers diversity in its board composition. While this is critical, it is even more important to develop policies about diversity, and procedures for the board to successfully implement, assess, and sustain the effectiveness of the policies.

Although there is no SEC mandated definition about what board diversity is or is not, the SEC mentions factors that boards can consider:

1. Professional experience
2. Education
3. Race
4. Gender
5. National origin

In reality, the actual meaning of boardroom diversity can vary from organization to organization, but sensitivity to diversity throughout a company can dramatically increase its competitive advantage, productivity, and cost savings. An example of such is the dramatic turnaround by Denny's Restaurant Chain after the well-publicized lawsuits against them for racial discrimination.

What is clear is that all board members must understand their role as a director and know how that role contributes to helping the organization maintain a positive brand and reputation in the community.

A GLOBAL CONUNDRUM: DIVERSITY IN THE BOARDROOM

Many studies have shown that companies with more diverse boards perform better financially, on average, than companies with less diverse boards. Companies that have more women and minority board members also see greater diversity throughout the organization as well.

When BoardSource surveyed over 1,750 American executives in 2017 however, it found that 90% all nonprofit CEOs are white, as are 84% of board members. That's up from its 2015 findings, which were 89% and 80% respectively. Overall, within that time frame the total number of all-white boards rose too, from 25% to 27%, despite the fact that many leaders are clearly dissatisfied with the imbalance. The study showed that 65% of CEOs and 41% of board members reported being somewhat or extremely dissatisfied with their board's racial and ethnic diversity but only 20% considered it a top priority to actually fix it.

Some countries have begun mandating gender diversity on boards, while other nations enacted what they call "a soft target". The Harvard Law Forum on Corporate Governance and Financial Regulation recently conducted a study of global board diversity in 2017 and found that Regulation of Board Diversity matters less than the attitudes behind diversifying the board of directors.

FIGURE 1.

Source: Harvard Law School Forum on Corporate Governance and Financial Regulation (2017)

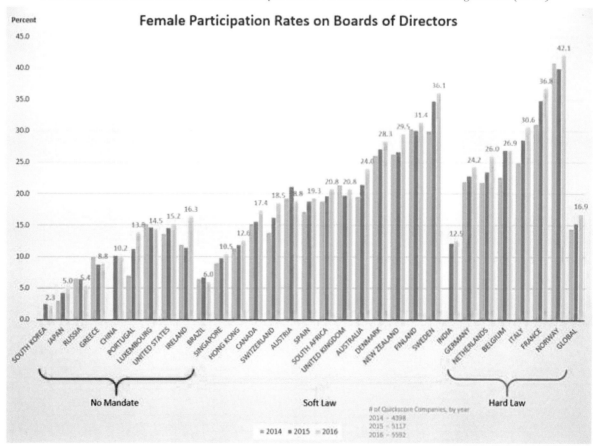

According to the report:

> *It is apparent that having a law requiring some mandatory minimum level of female board representation is effective in causing companies to bring female directors on at a rate that satisfies those legal requirements. It is also clear that countries without regulation tend to lag those with both hard and soft laws. However, the potency of these regulations, especially in terms of their ability to affect real change, is determined to a large degree by the general outlook of the locality where they are enacted.*
>
> *For example, Sweden has no quota for female board representation, but boards in Sweden are among the best in gender parity in the world. In fact, all the Nordic countries have much higher levels of female board representation than their global counterparts. Finland does not have a hard law, similar to Sweden, and so a willingness to comply with the soft law and enhance gender parity on boards is driving the relatively high number of female directors. Norway has a 40-percent minimum hard law and the highest degree of gender parity on boards in the world. The country was the first to pass a law—enacted in 2003 and enforced since 2006—reflecting a more progressive attitude toward female board representation.*
>
> *Contrast this with some of the lowest performing countries in terms of gender parity—for example, South Korea, where hermetically-sealed, family-contained chaebols run a significant number of companies, and traditional attitudes around gender roles run strong. South Korea has the lowest gender parity of any country in the Institutional Shareholder Services QualityScore universe. China, Russia, and Japan also fit this category. It is difficult to say if the commitment to the status quo is a result of a desire by executives and directors to maintain the control they have over these companies, as opposed to a traditionalist viewpoint that is skeptical of gender diversification, but the outcome of the resistance to change in these markets is clear in its imp on boardroom diversity.*

In order for men to make more room for others in the boardroom, they must understand "What's In It For Them?" They must also be assured that inclusion efforts will not inadvertently exclude them. In view of the evolving responsibilities and influences of boards, some studies show how boardroom heterogeneity is perceived and valued by directors. One focus is on gender, as there has been a significant amount of change regarding women in the boardroom over the last decade. Some are less interested in the often-quoted statistics and glass ceiling issues that have been analyzed and discussed by many, and instead sought to identify why it is important to have a diversity of perspectives in the boardroom. This topic often transcends bigger issues, such as: How do diverse perspectives in the boardroom lead to good team dynamics and better governance? How can boards better structure themselves to benefit their constituents? Finally, how can candidates and nominating committees respond to the opportunities and needs that already exist?

Fortune 250 boards include a large number of women directors from non-business sectors. Women from government services, academia, nonprofits, and legal professions currently account for nearly half of all female directors. Among women directors who have joined these boards more recently, there is an increase in those with corporate backgrounds. A decade ago, women with significant professional accomplishments were more likely to be found in universities, foundations, and government sectors that were quicker to lower the entry barriers to their most senior leadership ranks.

FIGURE 2

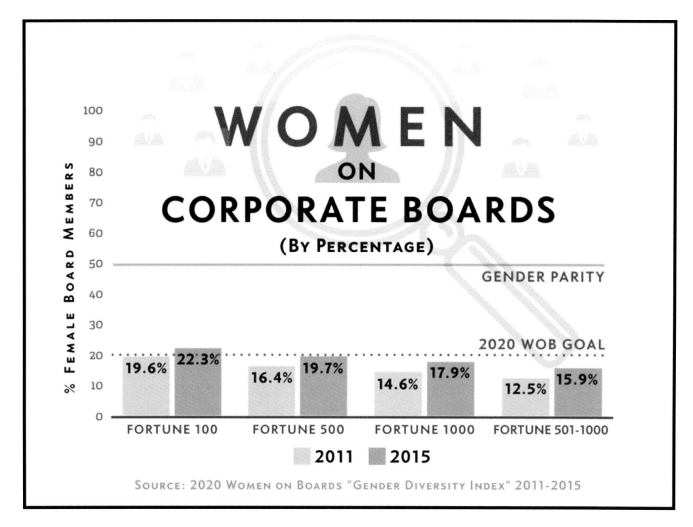

When most organizations discuss gender diversity on the board, in reality, they are referring to White women. If the numbers for White women are this dismal, you can imagine what the outlook is for multicultural women.

The benefits of having a diverse board are particularly powerful when there is a critical mass of varied perspectives to support broad thinking. One male director said, "A board is better off if the representation is as well-balanced as you can get it". The effects of critical mass were confirmed in a recent Wellesley College study focused on gender in the boardroom, which showed improved dynamics with three or more women on a board and consequent advantages in board governance. Nevertheless, organizations must go beyond mere representation toward inclusion and diversity management so that outliers can be engaged and heard.

Recent legislative efforts and other initiatives have helped bring women's representation in the boardroom to an all-time high. Despite this, nearly 90 percent of the world's board seats still belong to men. It's well known that people have a bias in favor of preserving the status quo; change is uncomfortable.

According to the Harvard Business Review, "This doesn't mean that companies haven't tried to change. Many have started investing hundreds of millions of dollars on diversity initiatives each year. But the biggest challenge seems to be figuring out how to overcome unconscious biases that get in the way of these well-intentioned programs."

In 2016, researchers Stefanie Johnson, David Hekman, and Elsa Chan found that when a majority of the candidate finalists were white (demonstrating the status quo), decision makers tended to recommend hiring a white candidate. But when there were two minorities or women in the pool of finalists, the status quo changed, resulting in a woman or minority becoming the favored candidate.

This means that when the candidate pool has 1 diverse candidate, the myths about the candidate's skills and abilities will be filtered through unconscious bias. If that person is hired, the unconscious bias persists because the assumption is that the individual HAD to be hired to fulfil the quota (or the diversity goal that was ill-defined).

As Figure 3 suggests, placing more diverse candidates in the hiring pool, greatly improves your chances of hiring diverse talent because of merit.

FIGURE 3.

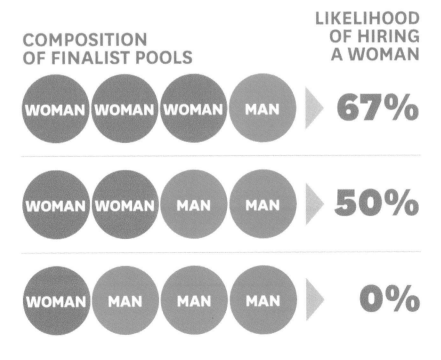

The Relationship Between Finalist Pools and Actual Hiring Decisions

According to one study of 598 finalists for university teaching positions.

COMPOSITION OF FINALIST POOLS	LIKELIHOOD OF HIRING A WOMAN
WOMAN WOMAN WOMAN MAN	67%
WOMAN WOMAN MAN MAN	50%
WOMAN MAN MAN MAN	0%

SOURCE STEFANIE K. JOHNSON ET AL   © HBR.ORG

THE ADVANTAGES OF BOARD COMMITTEES

Committees allow board members to be more productive and effective in their director duties. Committees have gotten a bad rap in the business world for supposedly wasting time and resources while ultimately achieving poor results. This is a long-held belief that many well-respected individuals have promoted over the past several decades. Many would agree with the viewpoint of legendary humorist Will Rogers, who joked in 1928: "Outside of traffic, there is nothing that has held this country back as much as committees."

When committees have an agenda, they can effectively achieve specific objectives. Committees have several advantages that make them a useful medium for an organization's board of directors:

1. They help the board identify and set priorities on key issues and establish a more definitive timetable for action.
2. They allow for a more detailed examination of key issues.
3. They empower the board to delegate certain projects to small working groups, increasing the likelihood that the projects will get done.
4. They allow a more equitable distribution of the workload, since committee assignments can be dispersed evenly among board members.
5. They enable individual directors to make a fuller, more meaningful contribution to the board.
6. They make the full board meeting shorter and more productive by allowing preliminary discussions and research to take place in a committee setting.

Examples of types of committees are:

- Finance
- Audit
- Governance
- Strategic Planning
- Diversity
- Marketing
- Community relations
- Nominating

The Importance of a Nominating Committee

One of, if not the most important committee, is the nominating committee. This committee is responsible for recruiting, nominating, and holding elections for new directors. The nominating committee is also responsible for board orientation and director development. The challenge for this committee is to stack the board so that the creative tension of different perspectives and personalities exist within a coherent framework that serves the needs of the organization.

According to R. Reynolds & Associates (2017), as one director put it, "Good governance, by definition, is having a breadth of perspective. It is about bringing in ideas from elsewhere. A board that is not getting the quality of input it needs will likely have a loose approach to governance and a less disciplined approach to business."

There are several ways in which nominating committees can successfully incorporate breadth of perspective into their candidate selection process:

1. **Determine which competencies, priorities and insights should be sought, and establish a process for screening individuals with those qualities.** In addition to needed functional or regional expertise, it is critical to include other competencies, such as conceptual thinking, resilience, and the ability to manage ambiguity. These are prerequisites to adding value to boardroom discussions. The list, of course, will vary for each situation and requires thoughtful analysis by the nominating committee.

2. **Conduct a gap analysis of the board that considers a full range of attributes.** A gap analysis can be a helpful tool to identify the experience and competence represented around the boardroom table—and those that are lacking. However, traditional gap analyses are usually focused on a select range of competencies and professional accomplishments, such as CEO experience or financial expertise. By expanding the analysis to include the full range of competencies sought and the experiential, demographic, and personal attributes that form perspective, a nominating committee can act with greater awareness of the variables at work in shaping a board.

3. **Place priority on effective communication skills and interpersonal expertise.** Effective communication is essential to competent directorship. This is essential in a diverse environment where shared perspectives cannot be assumed. Director candidates should have a track record of successfully working with multiple constituencies and building support for difficult undertakings. They should be able to succinctly and clearly express their point of view, probe and learn from the perspective of others, and extract solutions from the flow of boardroom dialogue. As one director put it, an effective board member is one who can "stand out for what you bring to the table and fit in so that you can be heard".

4. **Cast a wider net.** Conversations suggest that there is a substantial pool of developing female talent immediately below the C-suite level that can be tapped into if nominating committees are willing to look a little deeper. These candidates can contribute additional competencies and perspective, in addition to uncommon energy and drive. When diversity becomes a requirement for the candidate pool, it makes for a better search. Diversity forces the issue of people getting comfortable with people who are not like them to the forefront.

5. **Ensure a meaningful director evaluation process.** A diverse board is united by common organizational standards and goals. A thorough director evaluation process is central to maintaining that touchstone. According to R. Reynolds & Associates (2017), a veteran board member stated, "Boards need to get beyond the 'clubby' perspective that keeps them from providing robust direction and evaluation of their members". Evaluating individual members on an annual or bi-annual basis will allow the board to ensure high performance, as well as periodically compare member diversity with the needs of the organization. This evaluation process would work hand-in-hand with member terms.

WHY BOARD DIVERSITY CAN BACKFIRE

As much as diversity is something that we value, the truth is that people often feel baffled, threatened, or even annoyed by persons with views and backgrounds very different from their own. When directors are appointed because their views or backgrounds are different, they are often isolated and ignored. Constructive disagreements then spill over into personal battles. However, the solution is not to give up and avoid diversity. Rather, boards need to minimize the friction that diversity often introduces. To unlock the benefits, in short, boards must learn to work with colleagues who were selected not because they fit in—but because they do not "fit in". Next, the board must actively manage the diversity that arises in different individuals' communication, thinking, leading, and operating styles.

The Wall Street Journal published an article entitled, *"Why Diversity Can Backfire on Company Boards"*, pertaining to the challenges that diverse boards face. The article found that boards fail in the area of diversity because of:

- **Initial Encounters**. The problems start on day one. At the very first meeting, directors will scrutinize the words and behavior of new and atypical colleagues for signals about their competence and personality. Depending on why they were appointed to the board, the newcomers run the risk of being saddled with all sorts of stereotypes. "Typical woman", "Impersonal accountant", "Politician", "Activist", and so on.

  If the new member asks too many basic questions, for instance, (s)he becomes "clueless" or "high maintenance"; if (s)he says nothing, (s)he's "insecure". Unbridled enthusiasm, meanwhile, particularly coming from a specialist, could be seen as posing a threat to an existing director's expertise in a given area.

- **Lasting Impressions**. Once a label is on, it can be all but impossible to remove. Directors who quickly take a dim view of a colleague will tend to process all subsequent information in ways that support their initial opinion and block any information that does not fit. If a new member's commitment is doubted, for example, a non-reaction to an issue on the floor might be read as disinterest, even though the member actually agreed.

- **Cultural Differences.** Signals are easily crossed due to cultural differences. Directors with broadly different experiences will behave in unexpected ways that may be misinterpreted. Behaviors like interrupting or excitability may raise eyebrows where they generally aren't the norm.

- **Confirmation from Others.** Current board members will also compare notes about the newcomer in an attempt to define his or her character. Confirmation bias makes perfect sense at this stage. Nevertheless, it is important to realize they are usually turning to like-minded colleagues, who may not only confirm the view but also reinforce it with their own observations that support the bias.

- **Reinforcing Behavior.** When people are regarded as difficult or unimportant, some of their colleagues may begin to interact with them in a brusque or forceful manner. Once judged unfavorably, such people are usually excluded from informal interactions that take place before and after meetings, which further limits their involvement. Having contact only when it is required also means there is less opportunity for directors to develop well-rounded views of that individual.

  The reactions of the new members themselves can be a source of friction as well. They may be defensive or overly sensitive to stereotyping seeing slights where none was intended. In addition, they may succumb to stereotyping themselves.

  The bottom line is, when a lack of trust or respect develops, the new director can become reluctant to contribute, or he/she may become more strident. In either case, such behavior is likely to move them to a fringe status on the board.

- **Groupthink.** Existing directors may unite in a defensive reaction to the new member and become more entrenched in groupthink. Groupthink is a psychological phenomenon that takes place within groups of people. It occurs when group members try to minimize conflict and reach a consensus decision without critical evaluation of alternative ideas or viewpoints.

  Conflicts that affect only a few members can spread to and impair the performance of the entire board—inhibiting discussion, innovation, and decision-making. In the worst cases, the situation turns into a vicious circle that cannot self-correct. Part of the problem is that boards infrequently gather in formal settings leaving few opportunities to correct false impressions and iron out the tensions.

- **A War Between Factions.** Sometimes, boards become polarized or split into factions determined by how the different members perceive the new director and his or her contributions. For instance, the appointment of a foreign national may sharpen differences between domestic and overseas directors. Over time, a relational pattern of "us-vs.-them" evolves.

The good news is that there are ways to handle all of these potential conflicts. Most of the friction can be avoided, or at least kept to a minimum, by following some simple strategies.

- **Choose Members Carefully.** When board members are choosing a new director who will bring more diversity, they should think carefully about personality. Newcomers need to be savvy and aware of how they come across to others. The more different they are from the rest of the group, the more they will need to work at winning over skeptical colleagues.

  The ability to disagree constructively should be high on the list of desired characteristics, as well as experience dealing with new kinds of people and situations. The newcomer needs to become part of the group even as he or she challenges it.

Board members looking to hire a new director should also guard against biased thinking—by themselves and their colleagues—as early as the interview stage. When interviewers catch themselves thinking, "she/he just doesn't get the business", they can remind themselves that this will also allow the newcomer to ask questions that the board stopped asking long ago.

- **Assist Newcomers.** The chairman or chairwoman should pay close attention to the way new directors are introduced, especially if they have divergent profiles. Newcomers must have a chance to make a favorable first impression and to connect with others in a benign setting—before their first official board meeting.

  The chairperson should identify an existing board member likely to connect best with the incoming director and ask him or her to make a friendly phone call or meet for coffee. Giving newcomers insights into the board's operating philosophy and culture up front can help avoid gaffes early on. Debriefings after the meetings can also help.

  At the first official board meeting, the chairperson can help the newcomer get off to a good start by calling on him or her to comment about a particular issue. This can signal the new director's area of expertise, helping them contribute right away without seeming presumptuous. However, the chairperson must be careful not to pigeonhole the new director—for example, by inviting the newly appointed female director to "give us a woman's perspective on this issue."

- **Don't Give in to Get Along.** Dissenting voices can be necessary to notice issues that chief executives may be missing. Nevertheless, sometimes diversity inhibits pushback. Some directors, for example, may hold their tongues so as not to trigger hostilities between warring factions.

  Diverse boards must not be afraid of conflict, as long as it is constructive and civil. Boards that have difficulty discussing their differences, or reconciling them, make it easy for the chief executive to either dismiss what they are saying or to listen exclusively to their supporters on the board. The board thus fails in its governance role.

- **Encourage Initial Dissenters.** New directors sometimes tire of the struggle to make themselves heard. Feeling isolated and ignored, they end up self-censoring. Sometimes they will not speak up for fear of being alone in their opinion, even though they were placed on the board for their unique perspective. Other members may have the same opinion but will also remain silent, not realizing that another person was thinking the same thing.

  The chairperson or lead director must go out of his or her way to make it easy for board members to express vague concerns as a way of finding out whether those views are more widely shared.

The chairperson may have to draw out the newcomer, particularly on issues outside of their comfort zone: "Mary, you haven't said anything". If Mary responds, "Well, I'm not an expert", the chairperson may need to insist: "I understand, but we still value your candid way of looking at things".

- **Have Members Share the Role of Devil's Advocate.** Boards often have need of a "devil's advocate". However, it should not always be the same person, and particularly not a director who was appointed because his or her views differ from the groups' traditional perspective. Anyone who always looks at issues critically may end up being typecast as an "oddball" or a "cynic," one whose comments should not be taken too seriously.

  One way around the problem is to choose a different director to play "devil's advocate" at each meeting. The choice can depend on the issues to be discussed, or the chairperson can ask for volunteers. This is also a great way to help reluctant lone dissenters test whether others share their opinion.

- **Go Beyond "Just One".** As with diversity recruiting, adding just one diverse candidate to the interviewing pool will not likely result in a diverse new hire. However, when there are a few diverse candidates, the likelihood of hiring a diverse employee increases exponentially. In the same fashion, adding just one diverse person to the board will not likely achieve the desired result. The organization must go beyond having one diverse person, and include two or three individuals with different characteristics, attributes, backgrounds, and skills to the board.

- **Review the Role of the Chairperson.** Increasing a board's diversity is ultimately a test of leadership. If the process is not managed well from the start, it is not going work.

  Sometimes the role of the chairperson has to change from chief strategist to that of a facilitator. Required skills for this role include the ability to keep discussions on track, bridge gaps between people, elicit the viewpoints of those who are less opinionated, and cut to the heart of issues without bruising egos. Such a role can be challenging for a chief executive who doubles as chairman or chairwoman. Patiently encouraging views that run counter to the mainstream, or those of leadership, is not something that comes naturally to many CEOs.

CASE STUDY: How Macy's Quietly Created One of America's Most Diverse Boards

By Caroline Fairchild | Fortune Magazine, Feb. 18, 2015
Retrieved from: http://fortune.com/2015/02/18/macys-board-of-directors/

Macy's CEO and Chairman Terry Lundgren likes to fill his board with members who have diverse perspectives. As the head of a major U.S. retailer, he's adamant that the board reflects his customer base so he can stay attuned to trends in how different people shop.

What Lundgren looks for in board members hardly sounds radical, but the results have been: Half of Macy's 12 board members are women. When he appointed Leslie Hale from RLJ Lodging Trust to the board, Macy's reached this milestone. Less than 1% of companies in the Fortune 500 have achieved or surpassed gender parity on their boards, according to a recent Fortune analysis in collaboration with S&P Capital IQ.

Reaching the 50% mark brings Macy's into an elite group that includes three other companies as of Fortune's January analysis: Avon (AVP) 1.00% , Xerox (XRX) 2.04% and TravelCenters of America (TA) -0.32% (which only has four board members in total). These companies have each demonstrated a serious commitment to changing the male-heavy gender dynamics on corporate boards. It's worth noting that Macy's board diversity extends beyond gender as well — two members are African-American, one is Asian-American and another is Hispanic. Nearly 30% of Fortune 500 firms have just one female director and 23 have none at all.

"We talk a lot about diversity, but the first criteria is that each and every board member has a unique skill set and experience that they can bring to the board," said Lundgren in an interview with Fortune. "The women have a lot of choices. They could go on any board because they have lots of demand for their skills."

The women Lundgren is referring to are powerhouse executives like Deirdre Connelly, the former North American president of pharmaceutical company GlaxoSmithKline; Marna Whittington, the former CEO of Allianz Global Investors Capital; and Joyce Roché, the former CEO and president of Girls Incorporated. Yet a common sentiment among executives with fewer women on their boards is that there are just not enough qualified candidates like Connelly, Whittington and Roché out there. After all, in the Fortune 500, just 25 CEOs and roughly 18% of directors are women. A lot of boards strongly prefer candidates with prior board or CEO experience, making the pool of female candidates appear very small.

Craig Weatherup, a member of Macy's board and the former CEO of PepsiCo, said Lundgren has fought hard against the notion that every board candidate must fall into this narrow category. As a member of the nominating and corporate governance committee, Weatherup also has worked tirelessly to ensure Macy's isn't solely considering candidates whom he refers to as a part of the 'old boys club.' "Boards that aren't looking for younger, digitally savvy female and ethnic board members are really going to fall behind. It's a key part of staying relevant in today's market," Weatherup said. "I agree that if you're just looking for a sitting CEO or a recently retired CEO it is almost impossible. But there is no reason why that should be a limiting criteria."

Annie Young-Scrivner, an EVP at Starbucks and the president of Teavana, is the epitome of the type of appointment Weatherup is talking about. She joined Macy's board in 2014, and is a 46-year-old Asian American without any prior public board experience. She is mentored by Weatherup, and identifies personally with the roughly 70% of Macy's customers that are women. As all retailers react to the shift of shoppers who our now shopping online or researching online before heading into stores, Weatherup said it is important to have young, tech-smart board members like Young-Scrivner to advise the board. "I use my iPad and my iPhone, but I am hardly a digital board member," said Weatherup, who is 69.

"I don't feel like I am there because I am a woman," said Young-Scrivner. "I add a point of view that is different than some of the other board members and that strengthens Macy's as a company."

The result of Macy's push to bring on fresh talent is a board of directors that is high-functioning and robust with talent, said several board members. Lundgren, who has been chairman of the board since 2004, has watched four women get elected by the board and re-elected by shareholders.

Having more diverse voices on his board has "without a doubt become a tremendous advantage" as he tries to navigate a rapidly changing retail model, he said. And for now, the company's financial performance seems to be responding well to its diverse leadership: the retailer announced raised annual profit outlooks just as several of its main competitors are struggling to lure shoppers to its stores.

Macy's latest appointment of Leslie Hale represents another example of the retailer looking beyond the traditional experiences of board directors to bring in a diverse perspective. Hale, a 42-year-old African American, is the youngest member of Macy's board and had no prior board experience. Yet Lundgren is interested in Hale because of her financial acumen: At RLJ Lodging, she serves as chief financial officer.

"I was drawn to Macy's because I could add value both from my professional experience as a public company CFO in the hospitality industry and from my personal experience as a Macy's shopper with a young family," said Hale on the recent appointment. "I felt an immediate fit with the board members I met, all of whom had different backgrounds and experiences."

While Young-Scrivner acknowledged that Lundgren has led by example when searching for diverse board candidates, she added that quality recruiting firms are also essential. While companies like Macy's have made diversity a concrete criteria in their last few board searches, not all companies outline to recruiters that difference is a priority.

"By sitting in the board meetings, it becomes very clear that the Macy's board is comprised of extraordinary leaders with really diverse backgrounds," said Deirdre Connelly. "It's important to highlight that so that other companies can take the same chances on people that perhaps are not CEOs today but will be CEOs tomorrow."

SKILLS DESIRED OF BOARD MEMBERS

The PricewaterhouseCoopers LLP (PwC) 2015 Annual Corporate Directors Survey points to the pressure board members face balancing long-term strategic planning and investment with the need to meet short-term investor expectations. Among the key findings:

- **Activism, as seen on college campuses and in recent social protests, has found its way into the boardroom.** About one-third of directors now say they have interacted with activists during the last year and held extensive board discussions about activism compared to 29 percent in 2014. Activist investors desire to replace board members or management, seek fresh ideas, pressure companies to achieve diversity goals, fix problems, cut costs, or spin-off a division. As discussed earlier, activists seek change in the leadership or culture.

- **There are significant differences in male and female director views on board diversity's impact.** Female directors are twice as likely to "very much" believe diversity leads to enhanced board effectiveness.

- **Directors are less satisfied with their peers' performance.** Nearly 40 percent of directors now say someone on their board should be replaced which is a jump from 31 percent only three years ago. Directors continue to cite diminished performance due to aging, unpreparedness for meetings, and lack of expertise as the top reasons for their dissatisfaction with peer performance. Less tenured directors are more critical of their peers' performance than directors with ten or more years on the board.

The biggest hurdle to replacing an underperforming colleague lies with board leadership's discomfort in addressing the issues. Additionally, finding directors with the availability and requisite skills is not easy for most boards.

High functioning boards consist of a broad mix of individuals with the right blend of skills. Some of these skills are:

- **Governance** – knowledge of strategic planning
- **Leadership** – in areas valuable to the organization
- **Finance** – fiscal literacy
- **Performance Analysis** – seeks continuous improvement of individuals and board performance
- **Legal** – understanding of the law and its application to employee issues, management, operations, and other business functions
- **Human Resources** – effectively developing and aligning people with strategy
- **Shared Vision** – shares a passion for the vision and mission
- **Emerging Markets/Global Expertise** – the ability to think globally, and has knowledge of markets in other countries
- **Technology and Digital Media** – the ability to understand emerging technologies and employ new strategies that leverage digital tools

Of the skills listed, one of the most difficult to find in board candidates is global expertise. While this skill is typically desired in corporate board candidates for global companies, it can be just as valuable in nonprofit organizations and educational institutions that are active in different countries. The primary difficulty in finding this skill is due primarily to the lack of candidates who had opportunities to obtain global experience.

Another important skill for *all* board members, whether for profit or nonprofit, national or international, is diversity of thought. Although not generally listed on board job descriptions, understanding how to effectively address different ideas and opinions and ensure that they are considered in board meetings is a valuable skill. Board members who perpetuate the status quo by going along to get along, create destructive group think and do not contribute effectively to the organization's innovation, development, and growth. Identifying and selecting candidates who can bring fresh perspectives and viewpoints is an important function of all boards. A board that realizes its members lack the skills required to achieve and retain diversity should assess how it could reconstruct its membership.

Most boards still rely on traditional candidate criteria, which means that they source a majority of their candidates from other boards and they rely heavily on resumes. Serving on a non-profit board is a great way for D&I leaders to get experience as a director. This experience can supplement one's skills and abilities in the workplace as well. Further, certain nonprofits offer the opportunity to gain exposure to individuals who can invite you to serve on a corporate board. Some people erroneously expect corporate boards to offer positions to D&I leaders by virtue of their skills, however it is safe to say that prior board experience is a requirement.

Accordingly, D&I leaders must update their resumes and make themselves available to search firms who assist boards with finding directors. You can also attend events that connect community members with potential board opportunities. Assisting with board diversity at one's own organization or serving on a board is an important component of leadership for D&I professionals.

Figure 4 provides an example of how to assess and change the qualities required to be successful as a board member. The columns can be customized according to the board's needs. For instance, the demographics column may include race, age, gender, religion, sexual orientation, or neighborhood. Or, the age column could include the generational group (i.e., Baby Boomer, Generaton Xer, Millennial, etc.) instead of the age.

Figure 4: Board Composition Matrix - Qualities We Seek

NAME OF MEMBER OR PROSPECT	AFFILIATION		SKILLS & EXPERIENCE		DEMOGRAPHICS		FUNDRAISING	
	Constituent	Professional	Degree	Technical Skill	Race	Age	Donor	Event Planner
Kathy								
John								
Mary								
Ben								

This emphasis on diversity of leadership demonstrates that boards are proactively considering individual skills and evaluating experiences against organizational strategy. As a result of these "skills and experience" boards, directors and managers can constructively work together to achieve goals that will help the company maximize shareholder value.

A patience vs. balance approach gives the organization (regardless of size or sector) the correct corporate governance model, bypassing short-term gain in favor of embedded fiduciary and risk oversight. Outcomes are tied to individuals who foster an aggressive, value-driven, and performance-oriented culture, as well as individuals who are knowledgeable and responsive to market forces.

CHANGING THE MIX OF BOARD MEMBERS

Replacing directors is an evolving art laced with essences of traditional organizational development skills, robust team building, and effective leadership roles grounded in solid management science. The resulting best practice is the evolution of relationship-based boards into skills and experience boards. This evolution supports everything from board-succession planning to approving executive compensation.

Such an evolution requires a variety of new approaches to board composition, such as "recruiting skill sets versus recruiting names", says Peter R. Gleason, Managing Director and CFO of the National Association of Corporate Directors (NACD). Other requirements include reducing experiential overlaps and closing professional gaps. Gleason says, "You have to constantly look at what you need and what you have" both in terms of immediate assessments and the changes and challenges forecast over the next two or three years.

Figure 5 illustrates why boards decide to renew or replace members.

Figure 5: Board Renewal & Replacements

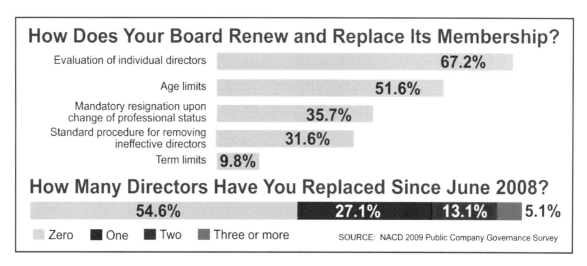

SOURCE: NACD 2009 Public Company Governance Survey

Since most boards have some latitude regarding their size, they do not need to wait for a pending term limit to expire or the looming retirement of a current member to recruit the strategic expertise necessary for critical, long-term success. These boards are not bound by a multi-month, or multi-year, member recruitment cycle either.

It is not recommended to recruit underrepresented or female board members simply for the sake of representation. The focus for board recruitment must be on skill and need. Thus, before asking "*How* do we become more diverse?", boards must ask: "Why do we need to become more diverse?" Organizations can ask other questions such as:

- Why would individuals want to serve on this board?
- What value should individual directors bring to the boardroom and beyond?
- Will diverse individuals feel comfortable serving on the board? Why or why not?
- Who is the board member of tomorrow?

The board should also ask questions pertaining to the performance of current members and regarding the group's accomplishments. According to the Blue Ribbon Commission (BRC) on Board Evaluations:

- It is imperative for boards to have standards of performance metrics. Without these, the board cannot assess its own successes and failures.

- Directors should be held accountable for the responsibilities for which they are paid. Evaluations make them aware of this accountability.

- There is not a one-size-fits-all approach to governance. Good governance is an organic process, and evaluations should relate to the unique situation of a particular company.

- The development of an evaluation process often occurs in stages, starting with a CEO evaluation to a full board evaluation to individual director self-assessments and, finally, to peer evaluations.
- To evaluate itself, a board should compose a description of its specific duties, goals, and objectives, and then set about measuring its performance against those responsibilities.

- As the evaluation process advances, it must serve one clear objective: to provide guidance that will create superior long-term shareholder value.

With this new mainstream method of determining recruitment criteria, board composition can be maintained by tools such as peer reviews and 360-degree feedback that transition a relationship board to a skill-set board committed to doing what is best for the corporation and its shareholders, regardless of countervailing pressures.

In summary, skill-set boards are the wave of the future and board evaluations are the map to accomplish the shift from relationship boards.

COMMUNITY ENGAGEMENT

There are many different models of corporate governance around the world. These differ according to the degree of capitalism in which they are embedded. The Anglo-American "model" tends to emphasize the interests of shareholders. The coordinated or multi-stakeholder model associated with Continental Europe and Japan recognizes the interests of workers, managers, suppliers, customers, and the community.

Community is a broad term. It can include individuals who are residents in a particular area, or it may refer to customers, supporters of a cause, or users (e.g., on social networking sites). In many U.S. communities, there is a perceived disconnect and alienation from local Boards of Directors.

There are several reasons for this:

1. Some board members are not visible at important functions or events.
2. Some boards are primarily focused on finances (e.g., raising funds or increasing shareholder value).
3. Some boards are uncomfortable with the community's demographics, especially in lower-income or ethnic neighborhoods.
4. Some directors are too over-committed to care about the community impact.

Helping board members understand what meaningful community engagement entails is very important. Directors must recognize that community engagement also supports the vision of attracting diverse candidates—requiring knowledge of how the two concepts are linked. To obtain this knowledge, board members must examine the difference between working for, and working with, the community.

Working FOR the community occurs when a company or organization is:

- Making in-house decisions about products, services and programs
- Determining what is best for employees, volunteers, customers, students, and/or constituents
- Including some professionals or volunteers from the community in decisions/activities
- Surveying customers or recipients of services

Working WITH the community occurs when a company or organization is:

- Acting as the facilitator of diverse community members
- Developing the product, services, or programs from their individual and collective knowledge and wisdom of the community
- Implementing ideas and programs that were created through participation from the community
- Making the products, services, or programs as effective as possible for the community
- Respecting of all community members, regardless of differences

Essentially, board members can put diversity into practice by working with the community to develop initiatives. Thus, board members must be careful not to just look at adding diversity to the board. They must also strive to be actively engaged in the diverse communities where they live and work. Moreover, they must establish the relationships, the knowledge, and the ability to effectively identify and select qualified candidates, as well as seek input from community leaders on Diversity and Inclusion policies and issues.

THE LINK BETWEEN DIVERSE BOARDS AND PERFORMANCE

Ultimately, board members are responsible for ensuring a pipeline of diverse candidates. Realizing that differences can add value to the organization will go a long way in helping to reduce other board issues in general. Nevertheless, it is absolutely crucial to understand the real reasons behind a lack of inclusion on the board. Normally, this critical issue is symptomatic of a far more serious problem. Board members need to understand what the larger issue is, why it is important, and how it relates to their overall performance.

How Diverse Boards Perform

According to a major report released in March 2011 by the international law firm Eversheds, smaller boards, more female directors, and a higher proportion of independent directors are the key boardroom components for company success.

The Eversheds Board Report is a forward-thinking study that analyzed the performance of nearly 250 of the top companies in Asia Pacific, Europe, and the US between October 2007 and December 2009 to discover whether board composition had any direct relationship to the company's ability to weather the financial crisis.

While there were some regional differences, the best performing companies were found in Hong Kong where there was an average of a 15.6% rise in share price compared to an average decrease of 29% in Europe. Better performing companies had fewer directors in total on their boards. The report shows that the optimum size for a successful board was 11 directors. Although the average in Hong Kong emerged as being slightly higher at 14, this was still lower than the European average of 19. Many of those surveyed believed that smaller boards resulted in a greater focus on the issues, better management from the chair, quicker decision-making, and better overall dynamics between the members.

Amy Hillman, a management professor at the University of Western Ontario's Ivey School of Business, recently turned up similar evidence that companies with diverse boards reap greater market returns in a study she co-wrote based on data from Kinder, Lydenberg, Domini & Co. Hillman found that companies with greater diversity make better business partners and merge more smoothly with other companies. A jarring clash of cultures can undermine these increasingly popular business deals. Diverse companies ease the transition because they more readily accept different cultures.

Hillman's study also finds that companies with diverse boards are less risky for stock market investors. Companies that are diverse in the highest ranks make better decisions about diversity and workforce management in general. According to Hillman, they are successfully channeling diverse people to the top of the organization.

Why Diverse Boards Appeal to Socially Responsible Investors

Socially Responsible Investing, also known as sustainable, socially conscious or ethical investing, describes an investment strategy which seeks to maximize both financial return and social good. In general, socially responsible investors favor corporate practices that promote environmental stewardship, consumer protection, human rights, and diversity.

Socially Responsible Investing (SRI) is a booming market in both the US and Europe. In particular, it has become an important principle guiding the investment strategies of various funds and accounts. Assets in socially screened portfolios climbed to $3.07 trillion at the start of 2010, a 34% increase since 2005, according to the US SIF's 2010 Report on Socially Responsible Investing Trends in the United States. From 2007 to 2010 alone, SRI assets increased more than 13%, while professionally managed assets overall increased less than 1%. By 2017, SRI assets exceeded $22 trillion worldwide.

SRI is a global phenomenon that can manifest itself in different ways such as positive investing. This new generation of SRI involves making investments in activities and companies believed to have a positive social impact. Positive investing suggested a broad revamping of the industry's methodology for driving change through investments. This approach allows investors to positively express their values on corporate behavior issues such as social justice and the environment through stock selections, without sacrificing portfolio diversification or long-term performance. Positive screening pushes the idea of sustainability, not just in the narrow environmental or humanitarian sense, but also in the sense of a company's long-term potential to compete and succeed.

Shareholder activism efforts attempt to positively influence corporate behavior. These efforts include initiating conversations with corporate management on issues of concern and submitting voting proxy resolutions. These activities are undertaken with the belief that social investors, working cooperatively, can steer management on a course that will improve financial performance over time and enhance the well-being of stockholders, customers, employees, vendors, and communities.

SRI has a long history of promoting corporate diversity through positive screens and shareholder advocacy. In the past, SRI filed resolutions for more race and gender diversity on boards, as well as insisted that corporations commit to non-discrimination policies based on sexual orientation and gender identity. However, no SRI portfolio exclusively focused on diversity until the launch of the Diversity Index Portfolio by Creative Investment Research, a Minneapolis-based minority owned social investment advisory firm. The portfolio consists of 40 to 60 large-cap US companies with strong performance in D&I.

Bolstering the contention that diversity is good for business, the Diversity Index Portfolio is based on the strong performance of the DiversityInc. Top 50 Companies for Diversity. Over a 10-year period, this index outperformed the S&P 500 by 24.8 percent and the NASDAQ by 28.2 percent. Senior executives, and their boards, are very interested in these types of numbers and opportunities, as it relates to the business case for Diversity and Inclusion.

The Executive Compensation Link
With a focus on good governance, boards have come under scrutiny in recent years for missteps that could jeopardize shareholder confidence and value. In the case of Apple, after the story broke in 2010 that former CEO Steve Jobs had undergone a liver transplant, the board faced severe criticism over its lack of a succession plan.

Similarly, boards have served as a rubber stamp for excessive executive compensation plans. However, in recent years, boards have become more active in reviewing executive compensation plans, ensuring that senior leadership pay is linked to results in areas such as diversity, innovation, and talent management.

The 2010 Dodd-Frank Wall Street Reform and Consumer Protection Act contained new tools to help limit CEO pay. Shareholders now have a say-on-pay vote on executive compensation, and companies must disclose the ratio of CEO-to-worker pay at each company.

In the short history of say-on-pay, these votes have attracted considerable publicity. In 2011, shareholders of Stanley Black & Decker, a tools and hardware company based in New Britain, Connecticut, issued a "no" vote on its CEO's pay. Accordingly, the company's board lowered the CEO's pay by 63%, raised minimum officer stock-holding requirements, and altered its severance pay agreements to be less CEO-friendly. In 2012, Vikram Pandit was forced out as CEO of Citigroup 6 months after shareholders rejected an increase in his compensation.

The say-on-pay has a profound effect on U.S.-based corporations, as shareholders have been demanding more accountability from senior leaders. Although the shareholder votes on compensation are not binding, they do encourage boards of directors to review their companies' executive compensation. No CEO wants to suffer the embarrassment of shareholders voting against his/her pay. As a result, companies are under pressure to eliminate practices that are red flags for investors. Tax gross-ups, golden parachutes, corporate jet travel, preferential pensions, and perquisites unrelated to performance are now under the microscope. Compensation is becoming more long-term and linked to measurable performance.

In the end, the savvy diversity executive can utilize board data to their advantage by bolstering organizational performance with strategic and measurable diversity efforts, as well as securing the long-term viability of the Office of Diversity. D&I Officers must also follow the lead of diverse boards in ensuring measurable outcomes and culture change at all levels of the organization.

References:

BoardSource, (2017). *Leading with Intent: 2017 National Index of Nonprofit Board Practices*. Available at: https://boardsource.org/research-critical-issues/nonprofit-sector-research/

Harvard Law School Forum on Corporate Governance and Financial Regulation (2017). *Gender Parity on Boards Around the World*. Available at: https://corpgov.law.harvard.edu/2017/01/05/gender-parity-on-boards-around-the-world/

Johnson, S.K., Hekman, D.R., and Chan E.T. (2016). *If There's Only One Woman in Your Candidate Pool, There's Statistically No Chance She'll Be Hired*. Harvard Business Review. Available at: https://hbr.org/2016/04/if-theres-only-one-woman-in-your-candidate-pool-theres-statistically-no-chance-shell-be-hired

Russell Reynolds & Associates. *Diversity is Better: Why Diversity in the Boardroom Matters*. Source: http://www.russellreynolds.com/insights/thought-leadership/different-is-better-why-diversity-matters-in-the-boardroom

Fairchild, Caroline. Fortune, February 2015. *How Macy's Quietly Created One of America's Most Diverse Boards*. Source: http://fortune.com/2015/02/18/macys-board-of-directors/

Rogers, William (unknown). *Will Rogers Quotes*. Retrieved From: http://www.willrogers.com/quotes

Jean-François Manzoni, Paul Strebel And Jean-Louis Barsoux Wallstrret Journal. (January 25, 2010). *Why Diversity Can Backfire on Company Boards*. Retrieved From: https://www.wsj.com/articles/SB10001424052748703558004574581851089027682

NACD (2013). *C-Suite Expectations- Understanding C-Suite Roles Beyond the Core*. Retrieved From; https://www.nacdonline.org/files/FileDownloads/PDF/C-Suite%20Expectations_1364247261983_2.pdf

Aguilar, Luis A. (Sep 10, 2009). *Diversity on Corporate Boards: When Diversity Makes a Difference*. Retrieved From: https://www.sec.gov/news/speech/2009/spch091009laa.htm

Board Diversification Strategy: Realizing Competitive Advantage and Shareowner Value (2009), available at http://www.calpers-governance.org/docs-sof/marketinitiatives/initiatives/board-diversity-white-paper.pdf.

Hillman, Amy J. (October 8, 2014). Corporate Governance. *Board Diversity: Beginning to Unpeel the Onion*. Retrieved From: https://onlinelibrary.wiley.com/doi/abs/10.1111/corg.12090

Diversity Inc. *Top 50 Companies for Diversity* https://www.diversityinc.com/news/2016-top-50-companies-diversity

Sample Test Questions:

BOARDROOM DIVERSITY

1. **A major development that shaped contemporary thinking about organizational governance was:**
   A. The 2010 Dodd-Frank Act
   B. The Sarbanes-Oxley Act (SOX)
   C. The Civil Rights Act of 1964

2. **A board composition matrix is a tool that is used to:**
   A. Assess and change the qualities required to be successful as a board member
   B. Report the demographic make-up of your board members to the EEOC
   C. Identify who serves on the Board and how long they have been in the position

3. **The Anglo-American model of corporate governance tends to emphasize:**
   A. Community re-investment
   B. Employee profit sharing
   C. Shareholder interests

4. **When board members try to minimize conflict and reach a consensus decision without critical evaluation of alternative ideas or viewpoints, they are engaging in:**
   A. Teambuilding
   B. Confirmation Bias
   C. Groupthink

5. **Boards fail in the area of diversity because of:**
   A. Socially responsible investing
   B. Initial Encounters
   C. Minimum executive support

6. **Who is responsible for ensuring diverse, new directors succeed on the board?**
   A. The Board Chairperson
   B. The Vice President of Membership
   C. The Securities & Exchange Commission

Sample Test Questions:

BOARDROOM DIVERSITY (cont'd)

7. **The nominating committee is responsible for:**
   A. Preparing the financial statements
   B. Recruiting, nominating and holding elections
   C. Nominating contractors for the organization

8. **All of the following are skills that diverse board members should possess EXCEPT:**
   A. Leadership
   B. Global expertise
   C. Self-censorship

9. **In transitioning from a relationship board to a skill-set board, directors can use tools such as:**
   A. 360-degree feedback and peer reviews
   B. Involuntary and voluntary terminations
   C. Contingency and succession planning

10. **Diverse boards benefit organizations by all of the following EXCEPT:**
    A. Presenting more risk for stock market investors
    B. Facilitating mergers and acquisitions more smoothly
    C. Making workforce management decisions better

11. **Community engagement is NOT required for effective board functioning.**
    A. True
    B. False

12. **While Hong Kong corporations have boards that are relatively larger, the province hosts the best performing companies.**
    A. True
    B. False

SUPPLIER DIVERSITY

> *Small business owners have the potential to be the lifeblood of the economy. By supporting minority and women-owned businesses, including diversity consultants, organizations can impact local communities, where small businesses are likely to create jobs, as well as demonstrate a genuine commitment to Diversity and Inclusion beyond lip service.*

OVERALL OBJECTIVES AND COMPETENCIES

This competency aims to help Diversity leaders build a diverse vendor base and enhance the organization's cost-saving opportunities with an inclusive supply chain strategy.

BACKGROUND AND CONTEXT

During the oil boom of the 1910s, the area of northeast Oklahoma around Tulsa flourished, including the Greenwood neighborhood, which came to be known as "the Negro Wall Street" (now commonly referred to as the *Black* Wall Street). The area was home to several prominent African American businessmen, many of them multimillionaires. Not only did African Americans want to contribute to the success of their own shops, but racial segregation laws prevented them from shopping anywhere other than Greenwood. Accordingly, Greenwood boasted a variety of thriving businesses that were very successful up until the Tulsa Race Riot.

Greenwood was a very religiously active community. At the time of the riot, there were more than a dozen African American churches and many Christian youth organizations and religious societies. The buildings on Greenwood Avenue housed the offices of almost all of Tulsa's Black lawyers, realtors, doctors, and other professionals. In Tulsa at the time of the riot, there were fifteen well-known African American physicians, one of whom was considered the "most able Negro surgeon in America" by one of the Mayo brothers. Greenwood published two newspapers, the *Tulsa Star* and the *Oklahoma Sun,* which covered not only Tulsa, but also state and national news and elections.

In northeastern Oklahoma, as elsewhere in America, the prosperity of minorities emerged amidst racial and political tension. But that all ended after one of the nation's worst acts of racial violence, the Tulsa Race Riot. On June 1, 1921, thirty-five square blocks of homes and businesses were torched by mobs of angry Caucasians. This act of racial hatred effectively put a dent in a legacy of successful African American business ownership until the 1960's. Following the riots, the area was rebuilt and thrived until the 1960s when desegregation allowed African Americans to shop in areas that were previously restricted.

The Emergence of Supplier Diversity

Supplier diversity has its roots in Affirmative Action. In 1963, President John F. Kennedy championed civil rights by working with Congress on HR 5271, which ultimately became the Civil Rights Act of 1974. In a "brilliant move by the arch foe of civil rights", Congressman Judge Howard W. Smith introduced an amendment to insert the word sex into the Act. This broadened Kennedy's 1961 Executive Order (E.O.) 10925 Affirmative Action which instructed federal contractors to take "affirmative action to ensure that applicants are treated equally without regard to race, color, religion or national origin."

President Johnson amended E.O. 11246, which established the Office of Federal Contract Compliance in 1967 to include affirmative action for women. This required federal contractors to make good-faith efforts to expand employment opportunities for both women and minorities. President Nixon used E.O. 11458 to create a federal Office of Minority Business Enterprise (OMBE). During 1979, the agency was renamed the Minority Business Development Agency (MBDA), a part of the U.S. Department of Commerce.

In 1971, President Nixon issued E.O. 11625, directing federal agencies to develop comprehensive plans and specific program goals for a national Minority Business Enterprise (MBE) contracting program. Then in 1983, President Ronald Reagan issued E.O. 12432, which directed each federal agency with substantial procurement or grant making authority to develop a Minority Business Enterprise (MBE) development plan. The actions of Presidents Kennedy, Johnson, Nixon and Reagan led to the formal process of identifying and vetting the credentials of businesses that claim to be owned and operated by qualified members of diverse ethnicities, veterans, women, or disabled groups.

Supplier diversity is a business strategy that ensures a diverse supplier base participates in the procurement process. It emphasizes the inclusion of a diverse supply chain in the procurement plans for government, not-for-profit and private industries. Statistics show that companies who embrace diversity in the workforce and supply chain are more profitable than companies who don't.

Today, supplier diversity is a business program that encourages the use of: minority-owned, women owned, veteran-owned, LGBTQ-owned, service disabled veteran-owned, historically underutilized businesses, and SBA defined small business vendors as suppliers.

Why is Supplier Diversity important?

Supplier diversity is important for many reasons. A common misconception is that diversity is a quota system or social program designed to benefit selected groups while adding little to no value to the bottom-line. This belief fails to grasp the fact that a competitive advantage exists for organizations that integrate supplier diversity into their supply chains, vendor pools, and operations. The following are six reasons why organizations need to consider implementing a supplier diversity program:

1. Supplier diversity promotes multiple channels in which goods and services are procured. The U.S. Census Bureau has repeatedly confirmed that consumers are becoming more diverse. Take Ford Motor Company for example. Ford has been an industry leader in supplier diversity spending for years. Ford also benefits from the diverse thinking and new ideas that come out of these relationships. Ford's diverse suppliers have provided substantial contributions to its profitable growth in the form of engineering new products and building fuel-efficient vehicles. Ford's partnership model will also be key to advancing its driverless technology and artificial intelligence.

2. Organizations can take advantage of new opportunities for business expansion by keeping in step with shifting demographics. As the makeup of the US population shifts dramatically toward increased diversity, companies must address a consumer base that is anything but homogenous. Dr. Fred McKinney, President and CEO of the Greater New England Minority Supplier Development Council (GNEMSDC) believes that changing demographics in consumer markets are the most important reasons to implement supplier diversity programs. "The issue of diversity is something that any senior executive ignores at their peril. Supplier diversity is connected to market diversity because people do care what these companies do and what effects they have in their communities," said McKinney. "Companies that are not just selling to, but also buying from, communities of color – who have been largely left out of the corporate industrial landscape until more recently – will benefit if they are doing this well."

3. Supplier diversity can be leveraged into greater market share and profitability. Let's look at Ford again. Ford recognizes how vital small, minority-owned businesses are to the U.S. economy, asserting that they are crucial to our nation's lifeblood, as well as to the identity of the Ford Motor Company. Ford internally promotes the direct and positive economic impact minority business procurement has on communities where Ford does business. For them, investing in these minority-owned enterprises helps build brand loyalty from businesses and communities who directly benefit from the jobs and wealth created by the investment in supplier diversity.

4. Organizations can attract increasingly socially conscious consumers. Companies with socially responsible business practices appeal to a broad market of consumers interested in supporting companies who make a difference. Furthermore, the extent to which a company invests in its supplier diversity program reflects the company's commitment to be a socially responsible and progressive business. According to a recent study, "87% of global consumers believe that business needs to place at least equal weight on society's interests as on the business' interests" (Source: Edelman goodpurpose® 2012). By investing in suppliers with diversity programs, companies can attract increasingly socially conscious consumers.

5. The U.S. government is the largest buyer of products and services. According to the U.S. Small Business Administration (SBA), "Purchases by military and civilian installations amount to nearly $600 billion a year and include everything from complex space vehicles to janitorial services." When it comes to supporting diversity, the government has a certain percentage of federal contracting dollars to spend with minority-owned enterprises. Every two years, the SBA works with each government agency to set their prime and subcontracting goals and their grades are based on the agreed upon goals. Each federal agency has a different small business contracting goal, negotiated biannually in consultation with SBA. The agency ensures that the sum total of all of the goals exceeds the 23 percent target established by law.

Since it may be inefficient for the federal government to buy from small suppliers in certain cases, it creates an indirect impact by encouraging its major suppliers to partner with minority businesses. Large, non-minority companies can attract government contracts by building subcontracting or supplier relationships (Tier Two) with minority-owned businesses. This demonstrates their commitment to supporting supplier diversity through their purchasing, and helps the government meet and exceed minority spend goals. If your company is working with the government, or would like to, supplier diversity needs to be on your agenda. Supplier diversity is a competitive advantage that the government evaluates when considering contracting opportunities and compliance.

6. A commitment to supplier diversity balances a company's corporate social responsibility, which is linked to employee retention. Just as the demographics of the consumer markets are changing, so is the makeup of the labor markets. As more minorities and women come into positions of corporate power, they ask their companies and employees about how well they are supporting minority businesses and communities. A 2010 study from the Center for Creative Leadership found "the higher an employee rates their organization's corporate citizenship, the more committed they are to the organization." (Source: Employee Perceptions of Corporate Social Responsibility).

Supplier diversity is beneficial to all stakeholders, not just to the companies with programs. First and foremost, supplier diversity programming adds economic value because it encourages the growth of diverse businesses. Diverse companies typically encounter barriers that challenge their start-up and sustainability, so effective supplier diversity strategies can alleviate these pain points. As small businesses grow, so will the nation's economy. Since most diverse businesses are smaller enterprises, they aid in the economic recovery and sustainability of their communities. In addition, supplier diversity is important because it provides products and services to emerging consumer markets. While traditional products and services remain available to consumers, demographic shifts create opportunities for diverse suppliers to meet the needs of emerging and/or shifting populations in the U.S. and across the globe.

According to Felecia Roseburgh in her blog, *What is Supplier Diversity and Why is it Important?* Supplier diversity is also important because it assists the country in job creation. U.S. statistics show that nearly 50% of the U.S. workforce is employed by small businesses. In December 2014, the SBA reported 57 consecutive months of new jobs added back to the U.S. workforce after the worst recession in recent U.S. history. Former SBA Administrator, Maria Contreras-Sweet reported "...this new trajectory is attributable to the success of America's entrepreneurs and the resurgence of our nation's small businesses. About 7 million of the 10.9 million jobs added back were created not by large corporations, but by startups and small enterprises."

Minority Business Enterprises (MBE)
The 2018 Minority Business Development Agency fact sheet reports that "by 2044, the Nation's prosperity will rely even more on minorities, the fastest growing segment of the population. Entrepreneurship is a sure pathway to wealth creation and a thriving national economy. Today, U.S. minority business enterprises represent 29% of all firms but only 11% have paid employees. If MBEs were to obtain entrepreneurial parity, the U.S. economy would realize 13 million more jobs."

Minority-owned firms are employment engines, demonstrating the highest level of recent new job growth and company formation compared to non-minority-owned firms. In the start-up phases, minority owned enterprises are likely to hire family members and friends who can work part-time or afford to live on a lower salary. As they grow, these companies are more likely to hire people from all races. In fact, the largest minority owned enterprises are exemplary models of Diversity and Inclusion.

The number of U.S. businesses grew 2 percent between 2007 and 2012 as the country weathered the financial crisis and entered the first three years of economic recovery. Yet, while overall business growth over this period was muted, growth in the number of minority-owned firms boomed. According to data from the Census Bureau's Survey of Business Owners, the number of minority-owned firms jumped 38 percent to 8 million. Hispanic-owned businesses ranked second in employment and sales receipts among minority groups, with Asians taking the lead in both categories in 2012.

FIGURE 1

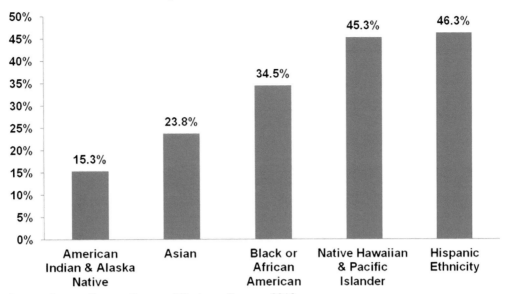

Minority Business Growth, 2007-2012

Source: Census Bureau, Survey of Business Owners, 2012

A minority-owned business is a for-profit enterprise, regardless of size, physically located in the United States or its trust territories. To qualify, the company must be at least 51% owned, operated and controlled by minority group members. For purposes of the National Minority Supplier Development Council (NMSDC) program, a minority group member is an individual who is a U.S. citizen with at least ¼ or 25% minimum of the following:

- *Asian-Indian - a U.S. citizen whose origins are from India, Pakistan and Bangladesh and the* surrounding countries.

- *Asian-Pacific - A U.S. citizen whose origins are from Japan, China, Indonesia, Malaysia, Taiwan, Korea, Vietnam, Laos, Cambodia, the Philippines, Thailand, Samoa, Guam, the U.S. Trust Territories of the Pacific or the Northern Marianas.* Includes Japan, China, the Philippines, Indonesia, Malaysia, Taiwan, Korea, Vietnam, Laos, Cambodia, Thailand, Samoa, Guam, Burma, Singapore, Brunei, Republic of the Marshall Island, Federated States of Micronesia, Hong Kong, Fiji, Tonga, Kiribati, Tuvalu, Nauru, the U.S. Trust Territories of the Pacific, the Northern Marianas [Republic of Palau].

- *Black - A U.S. citizen having origins in any of the Black racial groups of Africa or the Caribbean.*

- *Hispanic - A U.S. citizen of true-born Hispanic heritage, from any of the Spanish-speaking areas: Mexico, Central America, South America and the Caribbean Basin only. Brazilians shall be listed under Hispanic designation for review and certification purposes.*

- ***Native American*** - *A person who is an American Indian, Eskimo, Aleut or Native Hawaiian, and regarded as such by the community of which the person claims to be a part. Native Americans must be documented members of a North American tribe, band or otherwise organized group of native people who are indigenous to the continental United States and proof can be provided through a Native American Blood Degree Certificate (i.e., tribal registry letter, tribal roll register number, etc.).*

According to the 2015 U.S. Census Bureau report, minorities represented 38% of the total U.S. population and are expected to become the majority by 2060 (approx. 56%). When that happens, "no group will have a majority share of the total and the United States will become a 'plurality' [nation] of racial and ethnic groups," the U.S. Census states.

Additional Minority Business Statistics

- Minorities will account for 1 out of every 2 Americans by 2050
- Minority communities have buying power of over $2.5 trillion
- 1 in 7 small businesses is owned by a veteran
- Women-owned firms are out-pacing non-WBEs by double
- The rate of job creation by minority-owned firms increased by 27% from 2002 to 2007, compared with 0.03% for non-minority owned firms.
- Every $1.00 spent with a minority-owned firms, has a $1.74 of economic impact in their communities.
- There are more minorities in this country today than there were people in the United States in 1910. In fact, the minority population in the U.S. is larger than the total population of all but 11 countries.
- The minority population had an estimated buying power of about $2.5 trillion in 2009, larger than the purchasing power of all but five countries worldwide in 2009, including the United Kingdom ($2.1 trillion), Russia ($2.1 trillion), and France ($2.1 trillion).
- Minorities own 15.1% of all U.S. businesses, or more than 3 million firms, and 99% of these firms are small businesses.
- Minority-owned businesses account for $591 billion in revenues.
- More than one-third of minority-owned firms are owned by Hispanics:
- Hispanic..40.2%
  Asian...28.1%
  Black 28.0%
  American Indian...6.7%
- Minority-owned firms outpaced the growth of non-minority firms in gross receipts (55%), employment (27%), and number of firms (46%).

Women-Business Enterprises (WBE)

Women-Owned Business Enterprises are commonly referred to as WBE's (NOTE: The WBE is a business, not an individual). American Express Open's *2016 State of Women-Owned Businesses Report* asserts that while the total number of firms increased by 9%, the number of women-owned firms increased by 45% – meaning that between 2007 and 2016, the number of women-owned firms grew at a rate fully five times the national average. Business owners who are women of color have more than doubled since 2007, to nearly 5 million. They comprise fully 44% of all women-owned firms, but one group, in particular, has exploded. According to the Minority Business Development Agency (MBDA), "between 2007 and 2012, the number of female Hispanic-owned businesses grew an incredible 87 percent, from 800,000 to 1.5 million firms. This is the largest increase in female business ownership of any race or ethnic group."

As of January 2016, MBDA reports that the highest concentrations of women-owned businesses were in the areas of health and social assistance, educational services and administrative support. Also, California and Texas have the largest number of women-owned business enterprises, followed by New York and Florida.

To become certified as a woman owned business, an enterprise must show that:

- All prospective members have clear and documented evidence that at least 51% or more of the company is women-owned, managed, and controlled.
- The business has been open for at least six months.
- The business owner is a U.S. citizen or legal resident alien.

Evidence must indicate that:

- The contribution of capital and/or expertise by the woman business owner is real, substantial, and in proportion to the interest owned.
- The woman business owner must direct or cause the direction of management, policy, fiscal, and operational matters.
- The woman business owner shall have the ability to perform in the area of specialty or expertise without reliance on either the finances or resources of a firm that is not owned by a woman.

Veteran-Owned Businesses
Veteran-Owned Businesses (VOB) and Service Disabled Veteran-Owned Businesses (SDVOB) are some of the most prominent groups on the American entrepreneurial landscape today. In the 15+ years since the terrorist attacks of September 11, 2001, between 2.5 and three million U.S. soldiers have served in active duty. For many of them, the transition back to civilian life has been a difficult one. Veterans who find they don't enjoy, or can't fit into, ordinary working life have been turning to entrepreneurship at greater rates than the rest of the population.

According to Brian Patrick Eha's 2013 article, *By the Numbers: U.S. Veteran-Owned Businesses* in Entrepreneur Magazine, "more than 2.4 million U.S. businesses are owned by veterans, about nine percent of all American firms. They employ 5.8 million employees and dole out $210 billion in annual payroll. About 78% of veteran-owned businesses register sales of $100,000 or more, while roughly 38% of those enterprises have sales of half a million or more." Also interesting is the average age of veterans who run businesses. Whereas less than 37 percent of all business owners across the U.S. are 55 years of age or older, slightly more than 75 percent of veteran business owners are at least 55 years old, which may reflect a return to civilian life after a long military career. As for the geographic regions with the most veteran-owned enterprises, California, Texas, and Florida lead the pack.

LGBTQ-Owned Business Enterprises
LGBTQ-owned businesses (Lesbian, Gay, Bisexual, Transgender and Queer) are now included in traditional definitions and classifications of supplier diversity programs. Groups such as the National Association of Women Business Owners (NAWBO) and the National Minority Supplier Development Council (NMSDC) were founded in the early 1970s to promote the inclusion of under-utilized entrepreneurial groups. But there was nothing to provide opportunities that are more equitable to those LGBTQ+ small business owners who were also likely to face social and practical barriers to success.

The National Gay and Lesbian Chamber of Commerce began certifying LGBTQ-owned small businesses in 2002, a process that requires substantiation of majority LGBTQ+ ownership in an enterprise and verification of a business' good standing in the community.

Supplier diversity initiatives present a win-win opportunity for both the LGBTQ-owned small business and the organizations that contract them. By utilizing LGBTQ-owned businesses, companies such as IBM and Marriott International, as well as law firms like Jenner & Block, demonstrate their commitment to LGBTQ+ inclusion, as well as reap the benefits of working with businesses in the diverse communities in which they operate.

The Human Rights Campaign (HRC) Foundation's annual Corporate Equality Index surveys organizations regarding their supplier diversity efforts on an informational basis. The Corporate Equality Index has shown a steady increase in the number of organizations with supplier diversity programs that include LGBTQ-owned businesses.

CERTIFICATION & SMALL BUSINESS ENTERPRISES

Certification is an external, third party review process designed to ensure that a small business is actually owned, controlled, and operated by diverse applicants. Most certifications are granted for minority or women owned businesses, small disadvantaged businesses, and underutilized businesses. Certification agencies implement the processes for government and private sector entities and ensure that only firms that meet the eligibility criteria of the individual programs are properly certified.

Diversity certification is an important milestone in the life of a supplier because it authenticates that the business is owned, managed, and controlled by a qualifying diverse group. Organizations such as the Women's Business Enterprise National Council (WBENC), National Women Business Owners Corporation (NWBOC), and the National Minority Supplier Diversity Council (NMSDC) focus on assuring that businesses are appropriately categorized by offering third-party certification services on behalf of private industry. State and local governments also offer certification services. Certification by a governmental agency positions a supplier to conduct business in the public sector.

MBE Certification can be done at the local or state level, or nationally through The National Minority Supplier Development Council. Although local and state MBE certification is free, NMSDC and its statewide affiliates do charge a non-refundable application fee. NMSDC certification must be renewed each year along with payment of an annual fee. NMSDC was chartered in 1972 to provide increased procurement and business opportunities for minority firms of all sizes. The NMSDC Network includes a national office in New York and 37 regional councils across the country. There are 3,500 corporate members throughout the network, including most of America's largest publicly owned, privately owned and foreign-owned companies, universities, hospitals, and other buying institutions. The regional councils certify, and match more than 16,000 minority owned businesses (Asian, African American, Hispanic, and Native American) with member corporations that want to purchase goods and services.

WBE Certification is free at local and state government agencies. Formed in 1995, the National Women Business Owners Corporation (NWBOC) was the first private national certifier of women business enterprises. In 1997, the Women's Business Enterprise National Council (WBENC) was formed and became the largest third-party certifier of businesses owned, controlled, and operated by women in the United States. WBENC, a national 501c3 non-profit, collaborates with 14 regional partner organizations to designate its national standard of certification to women-owned businesses throughout the U.S. WBENC is also the nation's leading advocate of women-owned businesses as suppliers to American corporations. Both NWBOC and WBENC charge a non-refundable application fee plus annual renewal charges for a national WBE certification.

Supplier diversity programs can encourage good relationships with certain audiences. Case in point: The Women's Business Enterprise National Council reports that up to 85 percent of women said they would buy from a company that made a special effort to support women-owned businesses.

Definition of a Small Business
The Small Business Administration (SBA) defines a small business concern as one that is independently owned and operated, is organized for profit, and is not dominant in its field. Depending on the industry, size standard eligibility is based on the average number of employees for the preceding twelve months or on sales volume averaged over a three-year period. Examples of SBA general size standards include the following:

- **Manufacturing:** Maximum number of employees may range from 500 to 1500, depending on the type of product manufactured;
- **Wholesaling:** Maximum number of employees may range from 100 to 500 depending on the particular product being provided;
- **Services:** Annual receipts may not exceed $2.5 to $21.5 million, depending on the particular service being provided;
- **Retailing:** Annual receipts may not exceed $5.0 to $21.0 million, depending on the particular product being provided;
- **General and Heavy Construction:** General construction annual receipts may not exceed $13.5 to $17 million, depending on the type of construction;
- **Special Trade Construction:** Annual receipts may not exceed $7 million; and
- **Agriculture:** Annual receipts may not exceed $0.5 to $9.0 million, depending on the agricultural product.

If there is a merger or acquisition involving a small, women-owned, or minority-owned enterprise, the Small Business Administration may classify this as a change in ownership, possibly jeopardizing the entity's classification status.

There are several different types of certifications that a business may possess, and it is possible for companies to have more than one if they meet SBA criteria. These include certifications as an MBE,

WBE, DBE, and DVBE, to name a few. According to the U.S. Black Chambers Inc., the Trump Administration's proposal to increase funding for Women- and Veteran-owned businesses while eliminating the Minority Business Development Agency (MBDA) is an affront to the millions of minority entrepreneurs nationwide. The Chambers noted that Congress passed funding to keep the MBDA open in 2018, and corporations and local governments continue to support MBE's. SBA has removed the term "minority" from its main website menus. Nevertheless, minority enterprises may obtain SBA loans and other services under the broader small business category.

Small Disadvantaged Businesses (SDB) or Disadvantaged Business Enterprises (DBE)
Federal law mandates a number of requirements with respect to disadvantaged business enterprises as such entities are defined under federal law in projects where federal funds are utilized. In terms of public works and construction projects, federal funds are generally used to some extent for major transportation projects in particular.

These requirements, which are under the jurisdiction of the United States Department of Transportation, include setting DBE utilization goals, designing and implementing a DBE program, as well as monitoring and reporting.

To qualify as a DBE, the business must be owned and controlled by one or more socially and economically disadvantaged persons. Businesses must show:

- Minimum 51% ownership, control, and expertise by the individual(s) and
- Control of the daily management and operations by the individual(s)

The businesses size, as measured by average annual gross receipts over the most recent three years, must be under the specified dollar amounts for a particular industry. Depending on the company's North American Industry Classification System (NAICS) code, these limits can range from $2.5 million to $17.4 million averaged per year. Manufacturers, wholesalers, and retailers must meet an employee size standard ranging from 500 to 1,500 employees, depending on the NAICS classification, and their average three-year gross sales must be less than $17.4 million.

Recently, changes to the DBE regulations require all owner applicants to complete a Statement of Disadvantage and a Personal Financial Statement. All eligible owners must affirm that they are members of a disadvantaged group (for example, an eligible ethnic minority or a female). In addition, the personal net worth of each eligible owner applicant must be less than $750,000, excluding the values of the applicant's ownership interest in the business seeking certification and the owner's primary residence. Generally, certification is done at the local or regional level. There is no fee to apply for DBE certification.

8(a) Designation
A business enterprise meets the basic requirements for admission to the 8(a) Business Development program if it is a small business which is unconditionally owned and controlled by one or more socially and economically disadvantaged individuals. The owner(s) must be of good character, a citizen of the United States, and demonstrate potential for success. This certification is geared more for socially and economically disadvantaged individuals as defined in the Small Business Act.

The 8(a) program offers a broad scope of assistance to socially and economically disadvantaged firms. The Small Disadvantaged Business (SDB) certification strictly pertains to benefits in federal procurement. Firms achieving 8(a) designations automatically qualify for SDB certification.

Program participation is divided into two stages: the developmental stage and the transitional stage. The developmental stage is four years or less and the transitional stage is five years or more. Participants are reviewed annually for compliance with eligibility requirements.

The General Requirements for 8(a) Certification are:

- Must be at least 51% owned and controlled by a socially and economically disadvantaged individual(s)
- African Americans, Hispanic Americans, Asian Pacific Americans, Subcontinent Asian Americans, and Native Americans are presumed to qualify
- Other individuals can be admitted into the program if they show through a preponderance of the evidence that they are disadvantaged because of race, ethnicity, gender, disability, or residence in an environment isolated from the mainstream of American society (i.e., rural)
- Individuals must have a net worth of less than $250,000, excluding business equity and the owner(s) primary residence
- Must meet applicable size standards for small businesses in their industry
- Owners must show 2 full years of business operations

HUBZone Business Enterprises (HUB)

To participate in HUB (Historically Underutilized Business) contracting programs, an enterprise must be determined to be a "qualified HUBzone small business concern". A firm can be qualified if:

- It is small,
- It is located in a "historically underutilized business zone" (HUB Zone),
- It is owned and controlled by one or more US Citizens, and
- At least 35% of its employees reside in a HUBZone.

Disabled Veteran Businesses (DVBE)

The law defines a disabled veteran as a United States military, naval or air service veteran with a service related disability of at least 10 percent.

For a firm to be certified as a DVBE, it must submit a completed Small Business and/or Disabled Veteran Business Enterprise Certification Application and meet the following legal requirements:

- It is a sole proprietorship or partnership that is at least 51 percent owned by one or more disabled veterans or, in the case of a publicly owned business, at least 51 percent of its stock is owned by one or more disabled veterans; a subsidiary which is wholly owned by a corporation in which at least 51 percent of the parent company's voting stock is owned by one or more disabled veterans; or a joint venture in which at least 51 percent of the joint venture's management, control and earnings are held by one or more disabled veterans.

- One or more disabled veterans control the management and daily control of the business operations.

- The disabled veteran(s) exercising management and control need not be the same disabled veteran(s) who owns the firm.

- It is a sole proprietorship, partnership or corporation with its home office located in the United States and is not a branch or subsidiary of a foreign corporation, firm, or business.

Generally, certification is done at the local or regional level. There is no fee to apply for this certification.

BEST PRACTICES FOR SUPPLIER DIVERSITY PROGRAMS

Some organizations still have misconceptions about diverse business owners, pertaining to quality, size and capacity. However, if one peruses the Black Enterprise (BE) 100s, a listing of the largest black-owned businesses in America, individuals will learn that there are many African American owned enterprises that generate close to or even more than $1 billion in annual revenue. One thing is for sure, they didn't generate that much revenue by offering low quality or sub-par products.

The reality is, according to the SBA, small businesses consistently produce more innovations and create more jobs than Fortune 500 companies throughout the full business cycle.

Many companies have supplier diversity programs, while some organizations and educational institutions are just getting started in their diverse procurement efforts. No matter what stage an organization is in, there are many great reasons to support diverse suppliers including:

- Enhance the organization's image
- Cut costs
- Connect with new customers
- Enable the procurement process to be transparent, clean and honest
- Force non-diverse suppliers to be more competitive
- Bring in more and better ideas, and greater selections
- Improve compliance
- Stimulate the local economy
- Increase flexibility

However, some supplier diversity efforts fail because organizations of all sizes and stages have ill-defined goals for supplier diversity programs. In addition, there is no link to organizational objectives. Furthermore, the effectiveness of supplier diversity programs vary widely, depending on whether the company wants to use their program as a strategic means to lower their bottom line costs and improve profitability, or only as a public relations vehicle.

An organization's diversity spend is the percentage of procurement dollars that are spent with diverse firms. Currently, there is no benchmark for how companies define their diversity spend. A recent report from Procurementleadersnetwork.com indicates that less than 1/3 of procurement executives surveyed have high confidence in their spend data, and that 40% do not include supplier diversity spend data in their metrics. Nevertheless, tracking how much your organization spends with diverse suppliers should be a part of your evaluation plan for how Diversity and Inclusion impacts your organization.

Figure 2 provides an example of calculating the diversity spend:

FIGURE 2: CALCULATING THE DIVERSITY SPEND

$$\frac{\text{Total Diversity Spending}}{\text{Total Procurement Spending}}$$

An example would be:

$$\frac{\$15,000 \text{ in total diversity spending}}{\$167,000 \text{ in total procurement spending}}$$

Equals = 9% Diversity Spend

Your total diversity spending can include Tier 1 and Tier 2 contracts. Tier 1 (prime) suppliers invoice the buying organization directly. Tier 2 contractors invoice the Tier 1 suppliers. Tier 2 is essential since many procurement dollars are spent with MBE and WBE subcontractors.

All of these spend figures can be collected monthly, quarterly, or annually. The Society for Diversity recommends an annual total spend of at least 20%, which is average for Fortune 1000 companies, nonprofit organizations, and educational institutions. Keep in mind, if the organization's total spend is currently 6%, D&I leaders can set goals to work up to 20% over a 5-7 year period.

Buyers and Tier 1 suppliers must be educated about how to develop and manage supplier diversity and diverse supply chain programs. The best efforts include ongoing education in areas such as marketing, technology, and business alliances.

A proactive supplier diversity program will also involve attending trade fairs, providing procurement information on your web site, advertising, etc. Outreach is essential to learning the capabilities of individual MBE/WBE suppliers. Additionally, the most effective programs will understand the size, scope, and challenges that characterize diverse business owners.

Following are characteristics for Supplier Diversity best practices:

- The President or CEO provides clear commitment and support.
- The organization sets specific annual purchasing goals for diverse businesses.
- Senior management has compensation and performance plans tied to the attainment of division/department purchasing goals.
- Supplier diversity is included in the strategic plan for Diversity and Inclusion.
- The head of the supplier diversity program is at the senior management level or above and has control over corporate purchasing. Nevertheless, this individual is not inaccessible.
- The formal and informal RFP process prioritizes the inclusion of diverse businesses.

- Second-tier subcontracting requirements are written into the RFP process and prime supplier's contract. The organization verifies the minority/majority contracting partnership.

- A comprehensive database of diverse businesses is actively maintained and integrated into the purchasing process.

- The organization uses a purchasing system that tracks supplier diversity performance and can target specific contracts for additional focus, outreach, or consideration.

- The supplier diversity program is visible on the company's internet website, including program details, contacts, and a list of products and services purchased.

- The organization has strategic partnerships with ethnic/female/LGBTQ chambers, publishers, and other business organizations that can assist in diverse supplier outreach.

- The purpose of attending supplier diversity fairs is to identify new business partners and to ensure that these enterprises get contracts—not just to have a public relations presence.

It is a good idea to benchmark your organization's supplier diversity process, both internally and externally. Benchmarking is the process of measuring an organization's internal processes, and then identifying, understanding, and adapting outstanding practices from other organizations considered to be best in class. Most business processes are common throughout industries. For example, NASA has the same basic Human Resource requirements for hiring and developing employees as American Express. British Telecom has the same Customer Satisfaction Survey process as Brooklyn Union Gas. These processes, albeit from different industries, are all common and can be benchmarked very effectively.

A good source to obtain supplier diversity benchmark information is from industry groups. Since the Diversity and Inclusion industry as a whole is rather new, there may not be a plethora of current data, but you may be able to garner meaningful figures from other professionals in your network. This is why it is important to network, as well as to maintain at least one professional membership with an association that specializes in supplier diversity, minority business development, or other entrepreneurial groups.

One of the biggest mistakes organizations make when first benchmarking is that they limit their benchmarking activity to their own industry. Benchmarking within your industry is essential; however, you already have a good idea of how your industry performs so it's imperative that you reach outside and above your own industry into other sectors that perform a similar process but may have to perform this process extremely well in order to succeed in their field.

Five Tips to Developing a Supplier Diversity Strategy

1. Pick the Right Leaders (Team) and Develop Supply Chain Talent
Developing talent to lead a supplier diversity program means looking for people who have a strong supply chain, engineering, and/or finance background. While these people can be found in other organizations who have had a successful program, it is important not to overlook internal resources

with those talents. They'd know how to weave supplier diversity into the company culture and become an indispensable member of the team.

2. Keep Up with Supply Chain Technologies and Trends

When thinking about how technology will support your supplier diversity initiatives, you must go beyond supplier diversity software. It is important to understand how all technology interfaces with supplier diversity so that you can seek to integrate supplier diversity with company-critical technologies and platforms as needed. Also, remember that technology will not solve problems, processes and people do.

3. Eliminate Crippling Cross-Functional Disconnects

The biggest challenge is to prevent supplier diversity efforts from being isolated within the organization. In order to avoid this, it is critical that metrics are developed to align supplier diversity with the company's supply chain, marketing, operations, and other key business functions. Steering committees help play a key role in addressing cross functional issues; however, senior leadership support cannot be absent.

4. Collaborate with Suppliers and Customers

Robust supplier diversity efforts provide a competitive advantage for traditional businesses who are pursuing large, new customers. World-class supplier diversity initiatives magnify their efforts through active collaborations with their leading suppliers and customers. Small business owners and other traditional vendors are not only at the core of an effective supplier diversity program, they also serve as advocates and as a fountain of new ideas. On the other hand, knowing the needs of your customers not only helps to better align diverse suppliers with key projects, but it further serves as a compelling rationale for capacity-building programs.

5. Implement a Disciplined Process of Project and Change Management

When it comes to process and results, supplier diversity is not the same as supply chain management. A supply chain consists of everybody involved in getting your product into the hands of a customer. It includes raw material gatherers, manufacturers, transportation companies, wholesale warehouses, in-house staff, stock rooms, and the teenagers at the register. It also includes the tasks and functions that contribute to moving that product, such as quality control, marketing, procurement, and sourcing. In other words, procurement is the process of getting the goods you need, while supply chain is the infrastructure needed to get you those goods.

At its core, supply chain management is the act of overseeing and managing a supply chain to ensure it is operating as efficiently as possible. That said, processes to mitigate risk and manage change must not only be supported by senior leadership but must also encompass a global scope.

The keys to launching or improving a supplier diversity program are like any other effort worth doing, it's going to take time, commitment and diligence but the result may measurably impact your organization and its bottom line. In addition, you have the opportunity to impact the communities where you operate by creating jobs through diverse suppliers and stimulating local economic development. Finally, job creation through diverse supplier contracts is another item to track and report for program successes—allowing your organization to win accolades for a best-in-class program, as well as generate more publicity for your organization.

A 21st century economy demands innovation. Doing business with underutilized businesses embodies the diversity that yields true creativity as new ideas arise naturally when people with different perspectives sit around the same table. Accordingly, supplier diversity presents a win-win for everyone. It makes good business sense for any organization that seeks to be strategic, proactive, and impactful about inclusion now and in the future.

References

Diversitybiz (August 10, 2010). *Short History of Supplier Diversity*. Retrieved From: http://blog.getdiversitycertified.com/index.php/2010/08/16/short-history-of-supplier-diversity/

Edelman Study (2012). Retrieved From: https://bschool.nus.edu.sg/Portals/0/images/2012-Edelman-goodpurpose%C2%AE-Study.pdf

Eha, Brian Patrick (November 11, 2013). *By the Numbers: U.S. Veteran-Owned Businesses.* Retrieved From: https://www.entrepreneur.com/article/229886

U.S. Black Chambers Inc. (2017). Trump's Budget Eliminates Key Resource for Black Entrepreneurs. Available at: http://www.usblackchamber.org/news-events/390-trumps-budget-eliminates-key-resource-for-black-entrepreneurs

New Census Bureau Report Analyzes U.S. Population Projections (2015). Retrieved From: https://census.gov/newsroom/press-releases/2015/cb15-tps16.html

Roseburgh, Felecia (2009). *WHAT IS SUPPLIER DIVERSITY AND WHY IS IT IMPORTANT?* Retrieved From: https://blog.cvmsolutions.com/what-is-supplier-diversity

American Express (2017) Retrieved From: http://about.americanexpress.com/news/docs/2017-State-of-Women-Owned-Businesses-Report.pdf

U.S. Small Business Administration. Office of Government Contracting & Business Development (May 2013). *Module 3 Winning Contracts Pre 8(a) Business Development Program Training Series*. Retrieved From: https://www.sba.gov/sites/default/files/8abd_module3_text.pdf

Stawiski, Ph.D, Sarah, Deal, Ph.D., Jennifer J., and Gentry, Ph.D, William (June 2010). *Employee Perceptions of Corporate Social Responsibility The Implications for Your Organization*. Retrieved From: https://www.ccl.org/wp-content/uploads/2015/02/EmployeePerceptionsCSR.pdf

Sample Test Questions:

SUPPLIER DIVERSITY

1. **Supplier diversity has roots in:**
   A. Globalization
   B. The Fair Trade Act
   C. Affirmative Action

2. **Racial hatred led to the Tulsa Race Riots of 1921, which destroyed a part of town now known as the:**
   A. Black Wall Street
   B. Segregated area
   C. HUB Zone

3. **These U.S. Presidents played a role in developing supplier diversity as we know it today:**
   A. Presidents Carter, Bush Sr., Clinton, and Obama
   B. Presidents Kennedy, Johnson, Nixon, and Reagan
   C. Presidents Kennedy, Johnson, Carter and Clinton

4. **Ideally, an organization's supplier diversity program should be:**
   A. Separate from its inclusion initiative
   B. An equitable community program
   C. A proactive business process

5. **LGBTQ-owned enterprises are certified by:**
   A. The Small Business Administration (SBA)
   B. National Minority Supplier Development Council
   C. National Gay and Lesbian Chamber of Commerce

6. **Hispanic-owned enterprises can be certified by all of the following EXCEPT:**
   A. State government agencies
   B. National Minority Supplier Development Council
   C. The U.S. Hispanic Chamber of Commerce

7. **According to the Small Business Administration (SBA), a small business can be defined using the following metrics EXCEPT:**
   A. Industry
   B. Creditworthiness
   C. Sales volume

Sample Test Questions:

SUPPLIER DIVERSITY (cont'd)

8. **Who compiles a listing of the 100 largest African American owned businesses in America?**
   A. Diversity Inc. Magazine
   B. Black Enterprise Magazine
   C. Small Business Administration

9. **Supplier diversity programs fail because:**
   A. Managers do not understand supplier diversity
   B. There is limited research about best practices
   C. There is no link to organizational objectives

10. **An organization's diversity spend is the percentage of procurement dollars that are spent with diverse firms.**
    A. True
    B. False

11. **Certification is an external, third-party review process designed to ensure that a small business is actually owned, controlled, and operated by the applicants.**
    A. True
    B. False

12. **Demographic shifts create opportunities for diverse suppliers to meet the needs of emerging and/or shifting populations in the U.S. and across the globe.**
    A. True
    B. False

13. **Benchmarking is NOT a best practice in evaluating an organization's supplier diversity efforts.**
    A. True
    B. False

14. **The primary difference between procurement and supply chain resides in the:**
    A. Leadership support
    B. Community partners
    C. Infrastructure

INNOVATION THROUGH DIVERSITY & INCLUSION

Presently and in the future, advanced technology will be utilized in highly skilled and highly compensated positions. Therefore, Diversity and Inclusion leaders must shift their focus from merely recruiting diverse students and workers, towards intentionally and systemically including underrepresented groups in Science, Technology, Engineering and Math (STEM) endeavors.

OVERALL OBJECTIVES AND COMPETENCIES

This competency is designed to empower D&I leaders to investigate new and creative approaches to doing business better by promoting diversity of thought and inclusion of divergent perspectives, as well as justify the organization's ability to truly harness innovation, agility and disruption.

BACKGROUND AND CONTEXT

Some people have an innate need to express their creativity. Teenagers express innovation in the way they think, dress, wear their hair, mark their body with tattoos and piercings, and in how they act around others. However, innovation tends to drop off between the time they graduate from school and the time they enter the workforce.

Innovation is necessary for progress in business. Yet, the issue pertaining to the loss of creativity and innovation begs the question: why does the workplace encourage conformity and uniformity when the world around us is changing?

Tom Grasty, entrepreneur and business strategist, explains, "In its purest sense, *invention* can be defined as the creation of a product or [the] introduction of a process for the first time. *Innovation*, on the other hand, occurs if someone improves on or makes a significant contribution to an existing product, process, or service."

Innovation is slightly different from creativity. Shawn Hunter, author of *Out Think: How Innovative Leaders Drive Exceptional Outcomes*, (Wiley, 2013) defines creativity "as the capability or act of conceiving something original or unusual, while innovation is the implementation or creation of something new that has real life value to others. Business leaders frequently interchange creativity and innovation, without understanding what separates the two."

Hunter warns, "Creativity isn't necessarily innovation. If you have a brainstorm meeting and dream up dozens of new ideas then you have displayed creativity, but there is no innovation until something gets implemented." In other words, the innovation process is replicable and scalable; a creative individual is not.

Hunter cites the birth of Starbucks' now-popular Frappuccino drink as an example of how leaders, by giving their employees room for deviation, allowed creativity to blossom into innovation. In the early 1990s, the staff at a Santa Monica, California Starbucks, invented a new drink and asked an executive to propose the product to headquarters, where it was ultimately rejected. Later, the same store invented another drink (the Frappuccino), and the executive asked the staff to quietly make and sell the drink to local customers. It quickly became a hit, and the management group implemented the successful idea companywide once its value was proved.

At the heart of Diversity and Inclusion is **innovation**. Diversity involves valuing individuals who are unique, while innovation allows those individuals to create, express, and manage unique practices in a manner that accommodates those who need to express their creativity on a regular basis. Thus, increasing value for the organizations within which they work. Imagine what would happen if your organization had a diverse "think group" that did nothing but come up with unique ideas. Some ideas would be implemented and others ideas would be rejected. However, through the process of considering and including multiple perspectives, the organization would gain experience in innovation. The process of innovation could lead to increased productivity, time saving techniques, and other quality improvements that enhance the bottom-line.

Here, diversity moves beyond value in representation, towards value in thought variation. As leaders, we ought to encourage innovation, creativity, and revolutionary changes in thinking, processes, products, and organizations. Not only could it help the bottom-line, but it may also encourage employees to be happier, more open-minded, and more inclusive.

Complex and real-time change are the norm for organizations in the 21st century. Therefore, Diversity and Inclusion leaders need to develop the capacity to envision future opportunities as well as challenges.

Much of how business is conducted at corporations, nonprofits, health care facilities, government agencies, and educational institutions is still trapped in 19th century models.

- Employees are discouraged from straying too far away from "the way that things are done around here". Instead, they are rewarded for uniformity and "fitting in".
- From procurement to marketing, models for distribution and supply chain optimization are frozen in time and often disconnected from electronic solutions and digital efficiencies.
- Ideas about competitors are limited to traditional sources and practices.
- Lack of information about projected consumers/students/patients/constituents stymies the development of flexible, innovative and personalized products and services.
- Biased thinking frustrates the application of new business models, cross-functional leadership, different workstyles, and fair practices.

Hard questions must be asked to determine how the core competencies, strategic positioning, and corporate identity must change in order to meet the future needs of doing business.

In 2013, Forbes published an article entitled, "*Why are so few women and minorities at the top? Here's the real reason*". The article's author reminds us that, "Only 1% of the nation's Fortune 500 CEOs are Black and only 4% are women. After decades of diversity initiatives and inclusion programs, what is the problem?

That was the question Christie Smith of Deloitte Consulting and NYU Law professor Kenji Yoshino asked in their white paper, *Uncovering Talent: A New Model of Inclusion*." Hence, in thinking through these notions of invention and innovation, we have yet to solve the problem of inclusion.

Louis Byrd, Owner of Mellie Blue Branding, wrote a blog entitled, "*White Women…The New Face of Diversity*". The blog states, "Intel and Slack recently released their transparency employment reports and both companies are clear leaders with their diversity initiatives, yet their efforts in terms of bridging the ethnicity gap in tech employment pales in caparison to their growth with gender diversity. It is great that companies like Intel and Slack are seeing the growth percentage of women employees at around 40%, but when you only have white women reaping the benefits, is that truly progress? For example, Slack hired 74 people, 62 of them were White women, and only 3 were Black women, is that not a problem?" If so-called diversity efforts like this continue, the workplace will face a deficit of people of color and men.

Most people would assume that White women will help every other group in the workplace, but this is not happening because of a phenomenon that experts call "covering". In 1963, sociologist Erving Goffman coined the term **covering** to describe how even individuals with known stigmatized identities made a "great effort to keep the stigma from looming large". Goffman gave the example of how President Franklin Delano Roosevelt ensured he was always seated behind a table before his Cabinet entered the room. President Roosevelt was not hiding his disability—everyone knew he was in a wheelchair. However, he was covering; making sure his disability was in the background of the interaction.

Examples of covering in the workplace might include but are not limited to:

- A young man who removes his earring or covers a tattoo before going to his office job;
- A working mother who doesn't keep pictures of her children on her desk and makes up other reasons for leaving early to pick up her kids;
- A Latina employee who finds a place where she won't be overheard when she speaks Spanish on a personal phone call;
- A Black person who hesitates to associate with other African-American colleagues,
- An openly gay person who does not bring his/her partner to office parties.

Research has shown that covering can mitigate the negative repercussions that individuals may experience if they advocate for their own, or other, diverse groups in the workplace. In a report published in the Harvard Business Review, Kenji Yoshino and Christie Smith conclude: "Managers striving to develop a truly diverse set of leaders should recognize the fallout of even unspoken demands to conform and work to eliminate them. Just as important, they should look for opportunities to model a more authentic, inclusive culture by 'uncovering' themselves."

Research shows that most organizations hire for "fit", which means that employers seek workers who will mirror the current culture. Seeking "fit" works contrary to innovation objectives because people are hired for uniformity purposes. It is aptly said, then, that achieving breakthrough innovations requires the elimination of barriers such as conformist pressures to cover or "fit in".

A CULTURE OF AGILITY

Business agility allows organizations to adjust rapidly to changing market conditions, capitalize on emergent business opportunities, and adopt new distribution channels or supply chains. Agility simultaneously reduces costs or increases revenue streams in the process.

Business agility draws on the theories pioneered in agile project management. Project managers and their teams assess their priorities and progress frequently throughout the project lifecycle and make adjustments as needed, rather than at the end of a project. This systemic approach to change management provides senior level executives with a framework for how to respond to change, taking the needs of the entire organization into consideration.

A number of emerging technologies are useful in promoting business agility:

- **Cloud computing** allows for scalable and adjustable per-user costs;
- **Mobile devices** easily enable employees to work away from traditional office environments;
- **Collaboration software** encourages internal communication, brainstorming and problem solving among staff; and
- **Social media** permits real-time interactions with customers/students, creating a constant feedback loop to drive business agility efforts.

Business agility can be sustained by maintaining and adapting goods and services to meet customer demands, adjust to industry changes, and derive a competitive advantage from its human resources. One can say that agility is the outcome of **organizational intelligence**, the capability of an organization to comprehend and conclude knowledge relevant to its business purpose. An example of organizational intelligence is the balanced scorecard.

While employers in the past have been viewed as compilations of tasks, products, staff, profit centers and processes, today they are seen as intelligent systems that are designed to manage knowledge. Thus, terms such as "knowledge worker" and "knowledge economy" are applicable and valued in the workplace; the presence of these attributes must be treasured in the organization's culture.

The organizational culture determines how work will be performed in order to thrive. This culture can be described as the organization's atmosphere or values. Organizational culture is important because it can be used as a successful leadership tool to shape and improve the company. Once the culture is established, the chief executive can impart his/her vision. Moreover, if the leader deeply understands the organizational culture, he/she can also use it to predict a future outcome in certain situations (e.g., the engagement and inclusion of diverse groups in the workplace).

An organization with a culture of inclusion is diversity centered and opportunity oriented. They will succeed by being the best with excellence and achievement. It looks for creativity and expertise to manifest in a variety of ways from different people within the organization. The organization values efficiency, agility, and competence. A culture that fosters agility strives to make change a routine part of organizational life to reduce or eliminate the organizational trauma that paralyzes many companies attempting to adapt to new markets and environments. Because change is perpetual, the agile enterprise is able to nimbly adjust to, and take advantage of, emerging opportunities.

This means that an agile culture is one that can adapt its products, services, operations, and strategies to meet the changing needs of diverse consumers, students, patients, etc. Agile organizations are alert to the demographic data and its future impact on the culture; they are proactive and prepared. Additionally, the people in agile organizations are open to doing things differently.

An agile enterprise is not limited to the realm of for-profits. Agility may be evident in a government agency, healthcare organization, educational institution, nonprofit, or any other entity. By definition, agile enterprises include many constantly co-evolving and moving parts that require structure. Concurrently, there are several key distinctions between the agile enterprise and the traditional bureaucratic organization:

- Agile enterprises use fluid role definitions that allow for dynamic decision-making structures. Unlike the rigid hierarchies characterizing traditional bureaucracies, agile enterprises are more likely to fluidly evolve into structures that support the current direction and any emergent competitive advantage that it produces.

- Agile enterprises do not adhere to the concept of a sustained competitive advantage that typifies the bureaucratic organization. Operating in hypercompetitive, continuously changing markets, agile enterprises pursue a series of temporary competitive advantages— capitalizing for a time on the strength of an idea, product, or service then readily discarding it when no longer tenable.

- Agile enterprises are populated with individuals pursuing serial competence—they work hard to obtain a certain level of proficiency in one area but are driven to move on to the next "new" area to develop expertise. There are no "subject-matter experts" specializing for years in one topical area, as typically found in a traditional bureaucracy.

From a D&I perspective, an agile enterprise is ideal for Diversity and Inclusion work. Many companies start each year in a strategic quest for new sources of growth. Yet, the secret to innovative and organic organizational development is right under their nose. Here are a few tactics that the best employers have kept secret for decades:

Diversify talent and organizational partnerships
In *2015, HR's Year to Partner with the CEO*, Nancy Ahlrichs, CDE, reminds us that, "Employees and their intellectual capital are viewed as assets today—the Brookings Institution calculates that these intangible assets are responsible for 80 percent of the value of the company".

Today, tapping the right employees, suppliers, and other business partners are integral to an organization's success and long-term health.

Diversification, among many things, can dramatically change the financial landscape of your organization. It is a recommended tactic for investors because it provides a cushion from the risks associated with an "all-eggs-in-one-basket" strategy. In the same manner, it provides a cushion for organizations that rely too heavily on one product, one customer group, one industry, one advertising method, one funding source, one student group, or any other single entity.

As diversity implies "different", diversification implies "more than one". It creates an unlimited stream of opportunity for those willing to take the risk. You can still focus on your core groups, but diversification allows you to strategically blend your customer demographics, as well as your prospective employees, suppliers, and other business partners.

Utilize Employee Resource Groups (ERG's)

For the past 40 years, ERG's have helped a diverse range of groups obtain a voice within large corporations. ERGs got their start when Joseph Wilson, the former CEO of the Xerox Corporation took action after the violent race riots in Rochester, New York in 1964. He and many of Xerox's Black employees formed the first caucus group to address the issue of discrimination and to help create a fair corporate environment for minorities. Xerox launched the National Black Employees Caucus in 1970, then a decade later followed with the formation of the Black Women's Leadership Caucus (BWLC). Early in their history, these affinity groups were a risky and political tactic of advocating for equal pay and equal opportunity.

Today, organizations have expanded the work and the influence of ERG's. Fortune reports, Enterprises such as tech could learn a lot about gender diversity from American Express (AmEx). The financial services giant started its first women's inclusion group 22 years ago, and boasts of its 39% of women in Vice President level positions and above. Women made up 66% of their corporate executive hires in 2014. AmEx's employee affinity networks, which encompass 30% of employees globally, have grown to 16 groups with close to 100 chapters. In 2014, when AmEx looked to target multitasking moms (who control 70% of household spending), senior execs within the women's network were brought in as consultants on the project. A study co-sponsored by AmEx in 2010 discovered that women are less likely than their male peers to find advocates who champion them for promotions and raises". As a result, AmEx instituted a sponsorship program for women that led to a significant increase in promotions and strategic lateral moves.

ERG's engage workers in innovative and cross-divisional problem solving, and can offer strategic solutions to common workplace issues. The key to effectively utilizing ERGs is to make sure that they have a specific business purpose and that there is proper monitoring and support to ensure productivity. The future of ERG's will include functional groups (e.g., Business Partners for Recruiting Underrepresented Employees) versus representational units (e.g., Hispanic Business Resource Group).

Redefine Diversity Work

In 2015, Target announced that it was closing its stores in Canada. CNN Money asserts, "Target isn't the only retailer to fail in Canada, a country which seemingly has many similarities to America".

Instances like Target are where the opportunity lies for D&I work. Instead of looking at diversity as a vehicle to increase the percentages of different groups or facilitate training, view diversity as an avenue to enhance your organization's global effectiveness. Very few organizations have a person or a team dedicated to understanding the cultural nuances of doing business in other countries, and using that knowledge to help the entity succeed where others have failed.

Undoubtedly, risk management pertaining to lawsuits and negative publicity is required, but diversity work must be extended to global ethics and compliance, multicultural marketing and demographic research, as well as global talent practices via cultural operations. By redefining the scope of work, the Office of Diversity and Inclusion becomes less of a lightning rod and more of a business necessity.

Remember, great results in the field of diversity are not defined by color or gender. They are really delineated by positive, quantifiable outcomes that support organizational goals. Part of the current misalignment lies with the CEO's expectations for Diversity and Inclusion work. CEO's must educate themselves about the role of Diversity Officers, **and** D&I leaders must continually communicate how they add value.

Bloomberg Businessweek recently published an article entitled, *U.S. has Global Economic Edge in Its Minorities* by Victoria Stilwell. In it, Stilwell says that the value in diversity "represents the economic potential that could be unleashed as the U.S. makes the transition into a nation where the minority population becomes the majority in the next 30 years. At a time when countries such as China, Japan and Germany struggle to deal with aging populations, increased heterogeneity in the U.S. bolsters the outlook for its labor market and growth".

A strategic diversity plan, effective execution, and regular monitoring are key ingredients to success. With the right people leading your diversity and inclusion team, your organization will emerge as a dominant, agile leader today, and in the days to come.

THE NEED FOR DISRUPTIVE INNOVATION

Disruptive innovation is a term that was first coined in 1995. Often misunderstood, disruptive innovation is a powerful way of thinking about innovation-driven growth. However, there is an art to applying a disruptive strategy—one that requires proper timing, the right tools, and the correct approach.

Even if innovation is revolutionary, it may not necessarily be disruptive. For example, the automobile was not a disruptive innovation to the horse-drawn vehicles, because early automobiles were expensive luxury items. The market for transportation essentially remained intact until the debut of the lower-priced Ford Model T in 1908. The mass-produced automobile was a disruptive innovation because it changed the transportation market, whereas the first thirty years of automobiles did not.

Disruption describes a process whereby an organization is able to challenge its competitors by successfully targeting overlooked segments of the market and delivering more suitable functionality—frequently at a price that is attainable by the masses. Incumbents, chasing higher profitability in traditional segments, tend not to respond vigorously. Entrants then move upstream, ultimately delivering better performance and more advantages to the mainstream market. Once mainstream consumers start adopting the entrants' offerings in volume, disruption has occurred. Below are three examples of disruption:

- Rap music, also known as hip-hop, is a prime illustration because it has become a culture that has been targeted in business marketing campaigns because it generates significant revenues from coveted demographic groups. Rap music began in the 1970's and was viewed as a fad. It was disdained among the mainstream and within the older Black community. What initially began with Black youth rhyming, emceeing, DJing/scratching, break dancing, graffiti writing, sampling, and beatboxing, became an entire culture in itself.

Within 40 years, the hip-hop culture achieved mainstream—influencing everyone from young White males in America's suburbs, to youth in countries like Japan, Germany, France, Russia, and Brazil. In fact, one of the world's most valuable mainstream companies, Apple, purchased Beats Electronics from rapper Dr. Dre for $3 billion in a cash and stock deal, which was at the time, the largest acquisition in Apple's history.

- Steve Jobs, co-founder of Apple, is best known as an innovator-- but Jobs did not actually *invent* anything. The iPod was not the first portable music device. In fact, dozens of companies sold the MP3 player before the iPod was released. Additionally, Apple was not the first company to make thousands of songs immediately available to millions of users. Napster, Grokster and Kazaa were among the many companies that spawned online music sharing. What made Apple innovative was that it combined all of these elements — design, ergonomics and ease of use — into a single device, and then tied it directly into a platform that effortlessly kept that device updated with music. The iPod transformed Apple with an entire suite of innovative products, including the iPhone, iPad, iWatch, and more.

- A similar innovation occurred on August 12, 1981 when IBM released the IBM Personal Computer. Jobs would not have been as successful if it were not for IBM. The IBM PC did not contain any new inventions per se (see the iPod example above) but it was a powerful, portable device that was accessible by the masses. Ironically, the IBM team was actually under explicit instructions **not** to invent anything new because they were under pressure to complete the project in less than 18 months. The goal of the first PC, code-named "Project Chess", was to take off-the-shelf components and bring them together in a way that was user friendly, inexpensive, and compatible.

Disruption theory differentiates two types of disruption—sustaining innovations and disruptive innovations. Sustaining innovations make good products better in the eyes of an incumbent's existing customers—the fifth blade in a razor, the clearer TV picture, better mobile phone reception. These improvements can be incremental advances or major breakthroughs, but they all enable a company to sell more products to their most profitable customers.

Disruptive innovations, on the other hand, are initially considered inferior by most of an incumbent's customers. Typically, customers are not willing to switch to the new offering merely because it is less expensive. Instead, they wait until its quality rises enough to satisfy them. Once that happens, they adopt the new product and happily accept its lower price. This is how disruption drives prices down in a market (i.e., the Ford Model T, Uber, etc.).

When Diversity and Inclusion leaders understand the process of disruption, they can add more value to the organization's bottom line. Further, when a new technology or development arises, disruption theory can guide strategic choices as well as enable disrupters to improve their products/services.

Fostering Creativity in a Team
One of the most widely used methods of increasing team effectiveness and creativity is the introduction of inclusion. In practice, this means forming teams with different individuals so that the team becomes more heterogeneous or diverse. However, it also denotes configuring opportunity, interaction, and communication for these individuals so that they fully function within the entity as a whole, and they do not operate in an ineffective piecemeal manner.

To visualize this concept, think about a Lego kit. Before it is put together, there is a mixture of diverse bricks—some big, some small, and in a variety of different colors. The Lego project does not have full functionality until the kit has been completed. While it can be assembled and connected, or re-connected, in a variety of ways, all Lego bricks are designed to interlock. Additionally, Lego pieces constitute an agile universal system that can be easily updated or expanded at any time.

For a small local organization, inclusion may involve people from different disciplinary areas, age groups, sexual orientations, and/or socioeconomic backgrounds. For a multinational corporation, this might further include a mix of different nationalities, religions, or languages. Ultimately, what matters in terms of including different groups and what creativity requires by its very definition, is the diversity of thought and ideas.

We should be interested in qualities and differences beyond those visible to the naked eye. It is common wisdom that the more heterogeneous the team, the more creative the solutions it will come up with, right? Well, no; at least not necessarily. Let us take brainstorming or "thought showering" as some like to call it, as an example. The assumption is that brainstorming is a good way to generate creative ideas. Wrong! Alternatively, most believe that a clear, decisive team leader, who knows what to do, always pulls a good team together. Not so good either.

The point is that the issue of diversity does not lend itself to such simplistic suppositions. For example, a heterogeneous team may have the potential to develop creative ideas, but if the process is not managed well, the team can become immobilized by the multiplicity of ideas or the conflict that arises from such ideation. The whole issue of diversity is naturally complex with potential debates ranging from human rights issues to questions of immigration and compliance policies. But without going into the philosophical, moral, or legal implications of diversity, the general assumption is that Diversity and Inclusion should be favored, quite simply, because it improves team creativity and performance.

Creativity is an important aspect of your team(s). It is the ability to imagine or invent something new by combining, changing, or reapplying existing ideas. Creativity focuses on exploring ideas, generating possibilities, and looking for many right answers. It can be simple, practical ideas, or an attitude. Essentially, creativity is whatever you want it to be! Follow these general principles to bring out the creative genius in your employees:

- Recognize that everyone has the ability to be creative
- Understand that creativity is the ability to look at the same thing as everyone else but to see something different

Inclusion indicates that diverse perspectives are welcome! In raising the standard for D&I efforts and advocating for excellence, our research, business case, and development of resource groups should center on creative concepts, practices, and problem solving.

DARE TO RE-IMAGINE DIVERSITY & INCLUSION

The dictionary defines leadership as: The capacity to guide or conduct, to influence or induce. Leadership is not an inborn trait or inherited tendency, it is an attitude. It is developed through a process of education and reinforced through environmental experiences. Successful leaders tend to exhibit certain characteristics:

- A positive attitude that exhibits optimism and enthusiasm
- Effective communication
- Constant planning
- An ability to connect the past, present, and future
- Projection of an image of power
- The ability to motivate those around him or her

It has been said that, "into every life, a little rain will fall." The question is not whether we are going to have defeat, problems, or failures, but how do we respond to them?

The winning attitude is one that never gives up but keeps on trying, even in the face of defeat. A good example of someone who persevered in spite of defeat is Abraham Lincoln, one of our greatest Presidents. Listed among his failures are a business bankruptcy in 1831; defeat running for the legislature in 1832; failure at business again in 1833; the death of his sweetheart in 1835; a nervous breakdown in 1836; defeat in the Congressional elections of 1843, 1846, and 1848; defeat when he ran for Senate in 1855, and when he ran for Vice President in 1856 and again for the Senate in 1858. Triumphantly, he was eventually elected President of the United States in 1860, and he served two terms.

In the workplace, everyone has the capacity to demonstrate leadership in the area of inclusion, change management, and persistence. Our approach to inclusiveness and the framework within which we define diversity are principally shaped by our childhood influences and re-enforced over time by our interactions, or lack thereof, with those who are different. These experiences have created a conundrum as diversity leaders push for inclusiveness and equal opportunity, while others pull for status quo and/or a return to a storied homogeneous existence.

In spite of this, D&I leaders can be rather optimistic about the outlook for Diversity and Inclusion because more organizations are focusing on the future of work and all of the unique talents that are required to sustain a knowledge economy. This level of analysis could lead some to envision a new reality for Diversity and Inclusion. For instance, employers may:

- **Create** a fresh vision for diversity that goes beyond representation
- **Institute** additional layers, or add more tiers, to current two-party systems (e.g., Black or White, male or female, Christian or Muslim, etc.) so that our current global reality is better reflected in our dialogue, policies and programs
- **Adapt** a flexible approach to understanding the role of over-lapping or inter-connected groups within our inclusion efforts (e.g., a customer that is an employee, or the lack of diversity in local government impacting global businesses that value diversity)
- **Use** meaningful data to provide deeper insights into the future of our organizations (e.g., preparing for demographic shifts or trends in business and education)

- **Foster** more possibilities when divergent viewpoints are allowed, and managers are well-equipped to handle conflicting viewpoints
- **Integrate** Diversity and Inclusion goals within organizational operations
- **Re-evaluate** policies that mean well, but inadvertently foster divisions between groups (e.g., parental leave policies for women but not men)
- **Bring** attention to systemic disparities that serve as barriers to increased opportunities for all (e.g., unequal inner-city schools that feed the prison pipeline and disqualifies talented convicts from securing gainful employment or starting legitimate business enterprises)

Re-imagining Diversity and Inclusion is a group effort. Challenge yourself to include more people (inside and outside of your organization) and incorporate more perspectives in your prospective D&I interventions. Leadership in this space requires going against the grain, and strategically bringing concerns and/or new ideas to the table that will help the organization to solve the age-old problem of inclusion in order to achieve true innovation.

References:

Christensen, Clayton M., Raynor, Michael, E., and McDonald, Rory. *What is Disruptive Innovation?* Harvard Business Review, from the December 2015 issue.

Clark, Dorie (September 3, 2013). *Why So Few Women And Minorities At The Top? Here's The Real Reason*. Forbes. Retrieved From: https://www.forbes.com/sites/dorieclark/2013/09/03/why-so-few-women-and-minorities-at-the-top-heres-the-real-reason/#6ff2103fc9a8

Grasty, Tom. *The Difference Between Invention and Innovation*, 2012. Idea Lab. Retrieved from: http://mediashift.org/idealab/2012/03/the-difference-between-invention-and-innovation086/

Fallon, Nicole (2014). *Creativity Is Not Innovation (But You Need Both)*. Business News Daily. Retrieved from: http://www.businessnewsdaily.com/6848-creativity-vs-innovation.html

Yoshino, Kenji & Smith, Christie (March 2014). *Fear of Being Different Stifles Talent*. Harvard Business Review. Retrieved From: https://hbr.org/2014/03/fear-of-being-different-stifles-talent

Yoshino, Kenji & Smith, Christie (December 6, 2013). *Uncovering talent A new model of inclusion*. https://www2.deloitte.com/content/dam/Deloitte/us/Documents/about-deloitte/us-inclusion-uncovering-talent-paper.pdf

INNOVATION THROUGH DIVERSITY & INCLUSION

1. **Agility is the outcome of organizational intelligence, which is the capability of an organization to:**
   A. Understand and serve employees better than their competitors.
   B. Drive better business results by anticipating future customer needs.
   C. Comprehend and conclude knowledge that is relevant to its business purpose.

2. **"Covering" attempts to downplay stigmatized differences in an effort to:**
   A. Appear smarter and more productive than all other employees
   B. "Pass" as a member of the dominant group in the workplace
   C. Mitigate negative repercussions due to an individual's diversity

3. **Innovation and creativity are essentially the same.**
   A. True
   B. False

4. **Innovation is inspired in the right organizational culture, which can be described as:**
   A. The way that Diversity and Inclusion is managed
   B. The organization's atmosphere or values
   C. How managers respond to people and change

5. **_____ can be defined as the creation of a product or the introduction of a process for the first time.**
   A. Invention
   B. Innovation
   C. Creativity

6. **D&I leaders must move diversity beyond value in thought variation, towards value in representation.**
   A. True
   B. False

7. **Business agility allows organizations to do all of the following EXCEPT:**
   A. Adjust rapidly to changing market conditions
   B. Reduce business costs or increase revenue streams
   C. Manage projects better with uni-directional objectives

INNOVATION THROUGH DIVERSITY & INCLUSION (cont'd)

8. **Which of the following is TRUE about today's organizations?**
   A. They are seen as intelligent systems that are designed to manage knowledge.
   B. They are compilations of tasks, products, employees, profit centers and processes.
   C. They always adjust quickly to demographic changes and market demands.

9. **Agile enterprise models are most successful for:**
   A. For-profits
   B. Non-profits
   C. All organizations

10. **An organization with a culture of inclusion is diversity centered and:**
    A. Focused on problem solving
    B. Opportunity oriented
    C. Culturally competent

11. **Uber provides an illustration of disruptive innovation in that the company:**
    A. Saves money when drivers use electric cars
    B. Changed the ridesharing and taxi industry
    C. Raised a massive amount of money from investors

12. **The key to effectively driving innovation through Employee Resource Groups is to:**
    A. Guarantee that every group is represented
    B. Eliminate diversity councils with conflicting missions
    C. Ensure ERGs have a specific business purpose

IMPEDIMENTS TO INCLUSION & CULTURAL COMPETENCE

Many leaders believe we know what prevents buy-in to inclusion and cultural competence: fear, racism, and the good 'old boys' network. But could it be, that D&I leaders do not understand the complexity of the organizational culture? Could we lack a strategic vision for inclusion? Or have we failed to build enough of the right types of relationships?

"The greatest obstacle to diversity is not ignorance...it is the illusion of knowledge."
Deidra Dennie, D.P.A., CDE

OVERALL OBJECTIVES AND COMPETENCIES

The purpose of this competency is to correct practices that may prevent or protract organizational equity, as well as create specific strategies to eliminate institutional impediments to inclusion and cultural competence.

BACKGROUND AND CONTEXT

Inclusion by definition is a focus on creating workspaces where difference is embraced and valued. Inclusion should be a part of the organization's strategies, systems, processes and practices, or how the organization arranges people and jobs effectively to accomplish its work. Cultural competence is a skill that supports inclusive workplaces by the display of behaviors and actions that are supportive of the organization's goals. It leads to a reduction of racial and ethnic disparities. This context of inclusion and cultural competence provides the framework by which we begin to understand how organizations function around the concepts of equity, diversity, and inclusion.

Some organizations still operate from a 20th Century lens in the way work is accomplished using traditional and hierarchical organizational charts. These pyramid structural designs of organizations narrow or broaden employee access to decision makers by interspersing several layers of management in order to reach key decision makers. The 21st Century work environment recognizes talent is not compartmentalized in a chain, but is cross functional and self-directed, requiring collaboration across divisions and departments. A matrix organization brings together staff, equipment, and subject matter experts to capitalize on growth and streamline bureaucracy. This flattening of organizations allows businesses to respond quickly to rapid market segmentation.

Organizational structure and systems are indicative of where impediments start. The centric core of the CDO and diversity professional is connected to all avenues that directs the worker to rely on several vantage points to view the work: social, the business case for diversity, compliance and imbalanced efforts.

The social vantage point is indicative of creating a diverse and inclusive environment. Social responsibility is integrated into a business model that is focused on improving lives. Examples include businesses such as Burt's Bees, Tom Shoes, and Aveda. Nevertheless, even if an organization has a social responsibility component, such as a nonprofit, government agency or healthcare facility, it doesn't necessarily translate into workplace inclusion.

Patricia Pope, Diversity and Inclusion pioneer and CEO of Pope and Associates, first coined the phrase "the illusion of inclusion" in 1990. Since then, it has been the subject of Paul Mooney's 1994 comedy act and written about in books (for example, *The Illusion of Inclusion: The Untold Political Story of San Antonio* by Rudolfo Rosales). Nevertheless, this important phenomenon references the ability of women, Latinos, Asians, Native Americans, Blacks, LGBTQ+, disabled workers, etc., to be counted as added diversity in the workplace and on college campuses, while simultaneously lacking the privileges of the majority group. Using the lens of the critical race theory, authors Julian Vasquez Heilig, Keffrelyn Brown, and Anthony Brown assert that leaders must uncover the subtle ways in which diversity standards can appear to adequately address inclusion while at the same time marginalizing it.

Impediments to cultural competency and diversity in the social view attempt to make the organization's behavior more responsible for working conditions and wages. Employees can harbor a negative attitude and/or engage in unprofessional behaviors because they believe that underrepresented minorities, younger workers and nonconforming gender coworkers are protected by affirmative action, EEO laws, and company policies. In the social view, Diversity professionals are challenged during times of high unemployment, wage compression, economic downturns, and volatile socio-political environments to hold organizations accountable.

The following are ways to counteract the impediment of social views:

- **Formalize training requirements and policy.**
  The diversity council, employee resource groups, or staff in the Office of Diversity have a responsibility to inform the organization about the importance of being inclusive and culturally competent. Diversity training for all incoming employees and students should be mandatory to illustrate and inculcate the expectations of working in the organization. Policies that support inclusive, respectful behavior and stipulate the outcomes of negative behaviors are one way to hold people accountable. Another is to tie behaviors to employee performance, through ratings that articulate what behaviors (e.g., leading ERG's, facilitating training, serving as a mentor to new and diverse employees) constitute inclusive mindedness.

- **Build bridges.**
  Keep in mind, people have a right to appropriately oppose inclusion efforts so long as the opposition is respectful and civil. All leaders must be skilled in building relationships, fostering trust, demonstrating competence, and helping others to achieve their business goals and foster welcoming workplaces. Mandating anti-bias training for search and hiring committees supports the organizations goals for a respectful workplace. Mandating that all employees attend Black History Month or Women's History Month programs do not foster good will towards diversity.

- **Go beyond race and gender.**
  Too many organizations and institutions focus on race or gender alone. There are a myriad of ways to expand the construct, as well as demonstrate inclusion of other groups. Present a variety of opportunities to facilitate inclusive thinking about who your employees are and what talents they bring to work. Ask employees how the organization can do a better job of fostering inclusion. How can race, ethnicity, gender, sexual orientation, age, capability, and religion, translate into a competitive advantage for your organization?

Cultural competence describes the ability of systems to provide services and opportunities regardless of the values, beliefs, behavior, and tailoring of resources to meet social, cultural and/or linguistic needs. Unraveling centuries of institutionalized racism or systematic racism requires understanding how systems operate, function, and limit certain groups from taking part in social institutions. Organizations are complex systems, through these systems we make sense of the world and identify meaning to the contextual interactions we have socially and professionally. According to Daniel Kim in his publication *Introduction to Systems Thinking*, systems thinking recognizes that any group of interacting, interrelated or interdependent parts form a complex and unified whole that has a specific purpose. Kim simplifies this theory by stating, "understanding how systems work impacts effectiveness and proactivity". This is the social contract.

ORGANIZATIONS AND THE DIVERSITY OFFICER ROLE

The second vantage point that impedes inclusion and cultural competence is a compliance view. This viewpoint focuses on laws, compliance, training, hiring and risk mitigation to address behaviors in the workplace. Legal mandates, rooted in the U.S. Civil Rights Era, had little effect on attitudes, behaviors, or on subtle discrimination. During the 1960s and 1970s, the U.S. Federal government mandated the inclusion of diverse individuals in the workplace and at educational institutions through Affirmative Action and Civil Rights legislation. Initially, government contracts and school funding were at stake; but companies like Xerox Corporation addressed it head-on.

E. Washington et. al pointed out in their review, *Practical Resources for Recruiting Minorities for Chief Executive officers at Public Transportation Agencies,* that in a 1968 letter to managers announcing an aggressive Affirmative Action plan, Xerox acknowledged two things: (1) There was a business case for stimulating economic development in minority communities, and (2) corporate inclusiveness was a powerful way to draw talent from marginalized African-American professionals. "It will also mean the creation of an enormous and affluent market for new products and services, and of an equally enormous pool of manpower to help meet the critical shortages predicted for the future," the letter stated. Although most companies have not been able to establish a correlation between diversity and a booming business, Xerox was able to beat the odds. At Xerox, the return on investment was the subject of a Harvard Business Review case study. Between 1964 and 1974, the percentage of minorities in leadership positions grew from 1 percent to 6.9 percent, Harvard found. Over the same period, revenue grew more than tenfold, from $318 million to $3.6 billion.

Meanwhile, other employers hired diverse individuals simply because they fit into a certain category and there was no concern whether the person could do the job, or whether the organizational culture facilitated an environment for this person to succeed or move past certain positions based on merit. The few women who made it to management levels, were plagued with the suspicion that she slept her way to the top. Likewise, African Americans who were hired into management positions were considered "tokens". Both groups were left to operate in cultural isolation as there was no one who looked like them to build community and offer support. There is little doubt that Affirmative Action was necessary to level the playing field; however, it became a Damocles sword because it implied that less qualified individuals or ethnic groups would take jobs away from highly qualified, hard-working Caucasian males, and it assumed that quotas were more important than quality. The hard truth of Affirmative Action is that while it provided a few advantages to people of color, individuals with disabilities, and older workers, it benefited White females by the largest margins because Affirmative Action increased women's opportunities for education and employment. White males have experienced little if any appreciable decline in opportunity.

While organizational human resource efforts improved, the behavior of individual employees within organizations often did not. Employers found that simply hiring a more diverse workforce does not bring some of the expected benefits. Substantial evidence suggested that management needed to take a more sustained and committed approach in order to realize the benefits of diversity.

This remedial approach gave way during the 1980s, with the recognition that diversity should not be legislated or mandated but valued as a business attribute. Hence, organizations developed diversity training programs that focused on employee attitudes, awareness, and sensitivity. Diversity training then paved the way for cultural events and other celebrations of diversity that made workers feel good and caused senior leadership to think that they were doing the right thing. These efforts were usually led by a costly, external diversity consultant. However, some employers utilized internal diversity professionals.

From the mid-1980s to the late 1990s, the role of Diversity Officer, Director, or Manager lacked positive connotations in the business world and offered no career path. It was often an obscure role far down in the HR organization or otherwise occupied some anomalous and essentially powerless position on the organizational chart. The Diversity/Affirmative Action/Equal Employment Opportunity (EEO) role was often held by people who had no previous experience, individuals whose careers were in decline or someone who happened to be a visible minority with a passion for diversity. Accordingly, diversity strategies were not tied to business results and diversity professionals were not expected to be strategic business partners or demonstrate business acumen. Efforts also emphasized political correctness versus cultural competence.

Cultural competence can be defined as a system of behaviors, practices, values, and attitudes which allow cross-cultural groups to assess their own beliefs and conduct in order to effectively perform at work. Cultural competence is a process– not an endpoint– and it is achieved by communication, interaction, policies, and goals. This process of "competence" is important because it empowers individuals to become culturally skilled in order to function on their own, and within an organization, where multi-cultural situations will be present. Hence, political correctness is not required in an organization where cultural competence is expected because individuals who are culturally competent will know what is appropriate or unacceptable with different groups. They will make the proper adjustment on their own to greatly reduce offensive behaviors, languages, communications, and misperceptions.

Cultural proficiency is better. Similar to the Development Model of Intercultural Sensitivity (also known as the DMIS Scale), the stages of cultural proficiency are:

- **Cultural Destructiveness:** A person who is culturally destructive sees differences as a problem and identifies one culture as superior
- **Cultural Incapacity:** this individual lacks awareness and skill, and perpetuates paternalistic attitudes and stereotypes toward non-dominant groups
- **Cultural Blindness:** These individuals may assert that they don't "see" color and perceive that all cultures are alike
- **Cultural Pre-Competence:** A person who is culturally pre-competent may recognize differences, but is complacent in making change
- **Basic Competency:** An individual with basic competency accepts, appreciates and values differences. They may even seek out the opinions of diverse groups
- **Advanced Competency:** A person in the advanced stage seeks to actively educate those who are less informed and may seek to interact with different groups

Like organizational Diversity and Inclusion efforts, employees and supervisors should advance from one stage to the next. The work of Diversity and Inclusion must evolve as well. Figure 1 illustrates the transformation in the Office of Diversity.

FIGURE 1: THE EVOLUTION OF WORKFORCE DIVERSITY					
Model	**Ideology**	**Focus**	**Driver**	**Benefits**	**Foundation**
Affirmative Action	Remedial	Equal opportunity	Laws	Targeted groups	Assimilation model
Valuing Diversity	Idealistic	Appreciation of differences	Ethics	All employees	Diversity model
Managing Diversity	Practical	Building skills and changing policies	Corporate Strategy	The organization and all employees	Synergy model
High Performance	Inclusive	Growth, continual change, and tangible impact	Globalization and Demographics	The organization, all employees, shareholders, vendors, and other partners	Integrated business model

Over the years, it has become increasingly apparent that a strong strategy is critical for any organization that seeks to improve and maintain a competitive advantage. Focusing on a diverse and inclusive environment is not just a marketing tool, or "the right thing to do"; it offers an opportunity to capitalize on global and technologically savvy talent, changing customer/student demographics, socially responsible investors/grant makers, as well as international partners and suppliers.

The third aspect that impedes inclusion and cultural competence is "The Business Case for Diversity". The reality is that diversity, cultural competence, and inclusion are the hallmarks of future business, community and educational opportunities. Organizations that lack an appropriate strategy in these three distinct areas will run the risk of becoming irrelevant and extinct.

This issue however, presents a conundrum for many organizations who are in the initial stages of their Diversity and Inclusion journey. Once the question of whether to hire a Chief Diversity Officer has been settled, anxiety ensues over who should serve in the position. In 2017, Google hired a Caucasian female as its new CDO to address a race and gender gap that employed seven out of ten Caucasian males. Google has spent over $150 million dollars in diversity initiatives but still produces underwhelming numbers in hiring African Americans, Latinos, and women. It can be challenging for D&I leaders to facilitate change if they approach it from the context with which they are most familiar. For example, a heterosexual Christian working in D&I may frequently "forget" to include sexual orientation, gender identity and gender expression. By understanding the term "facilitator", diversity leaders can increase their effectiveness with inclusion work. A **facilitator** is neutral and takes their own personal feelings, judgements and beliefs out of the equation. He/she seeks intentional outcomes by planning and guiding groups through communication, competence, and change.

Stereotypes threaten to become a daily challenge for people of color, as well as for Whites, who are working as CDO's and diversity professionals. Regardless of who the diversity leader is, organizations must provide the resources and authority commensurate with the duties and expected outcomes of the office. Encouraging Caucasian men to serve as diversity executives and have bottom line accountability for diversity performance, will not only provide males in the majority with greater exposure, but it can also help advance careers and lend credibility to the work of diversity executives.

The following are recommendations that recognize the critical aspects of compliance and support the "The Business Case" to grow the organization toward inclusive and competent business practices:

- **Clearly define the purpose of the Chief Diversity Officer and the D&I Office**
  The outcome of diversity and inclusion work should be tied to the bottom line of the organization or institution in some way. Think of recruitment, retention, college completion, and hiring, and how the work of the diversity office can support or facilitate success in these areas. Connecting to the revenue stream of an organization is essential to the life of the diversity office. If you are not producing revenue or finding ways to save revenue, then you are a drain on the resources and easily cut from a budget line.

  The CDO is equal in role to the responsibilities of other Chief executives, Vice-Presidents, or other senior titles in the organization. If there is not an expectation of the Chief Financial Officer to write checks and train employees on how to use the financial software, there should not be an expectation of the CDO to conduct training and create programming for the organization or institution. If the Provost of the institution and the Vice President of Student Affairs are on the President's cabinets, the Chief Diversity Officer ought to be on the cabinet as well.

Diversity and Inclusion must be a business strategy, linked to organizational goals and connected to doing business better in a competitive global economy. Talented CDO's have served well as Presidents or division heads because the leadership and business skills needed to be successful for most senior executive positions are the same requirements needed to be a successful CDO. As stated earlier, institutions of higher education have been the leaders in promoting CDO's to top leadership positions in academia.

- **The Office of Diversity is mission- and vision-centric**
  Here's an opportunity to go beyond counting how many African Americans, Latinos, or women work for your organization toward a more meaningful role. Equity requires that the data educates and informs business practices, customer service, and the work environment. It is no longer acceptable to display black, brown, or female faces as proof of inclusion. Are these individuals in leadership roles to grow more diverse leaders for the organization? Can you show measurable outcomes for training and programs in diversity, anti-bias, etc.? Do your customers comment that they were treated respectfully and civilly when using your service or interacting with your employees? Have you analyzed the data that pinpoints where inequity lies in your systems?

- **First Amendment Rights**
  Many of us incorrectly assume that a leader should regulate, or police, inappropriate comments and behavior. This is not the role, or sole responsibility, of the Diversity Officer. Political Correctness (PC) prevents us from engaging in straight talk. Everyone has the right to their opinion, but they do not have a right to disrupt the work of the organization, treat customers/students badly, or negatively impact the brand. Unprofessional remarks and hateful expression should be addressed appropriately through human resource policies and procedures. It is the role of the CDO to ensure that the policies are fair, allow for due process, and are followed equitably across the organization.

IMBALANCED EFFORTS

Cultural competence is achieved by identifying and understanding the needs and help-seeking behaviors of different individuals. For example, a young lady moved to a suburb and kept her kids home on the first three days of school because she did not have the money to buy back-packs and school supplies. By middle class standards, you would simply send a note to the teacher and let her know that you didn't get paid this week but you will get the supplies next week. Or perhaps you would get school materials from a free backpack and school supply distribution. But this young woman chose not to ask for help. Older people or individuals with disabilities may do this as well, because they do not want to be a burden on anyone. Therefore, in the workplace, supervisors may notice that a person of color or an individual who is disabled or older is taking a longer time to complete an ordinarily simple assignment. Instead of assuming that the individual is not skilled to complete the task, perhaps the supervisor can ask the employee if he/she needs help, or inquire about any challenges that the employee may be facing.

One of the first steps to going beyond milk with chocolate at the bottom is to strive for transformational change. But first, you cannot assume that you know what is driving exclusion and cultural incompetence. As a Diversity and Inclusion leader, you must have data to back up your theories. This data will help you to balance your Diversity and Inclusion work.

A good doctor (or practitioner) will run tests– perhaps lots of them. In the same way, you may have to review organizational data such as promotions, hiring, and participation in mentoring programs. You may also have to gather empirical data by intentionally observing team dynamics, manager-subordinate interactions, and other meetings. In addition, you may conduct one-on-one interviews with individuals of all backgrounds and on all levels– perhaps including students, patients or customers in your fact-finding mission. You may also have to refer to historical employee surveys or conduct a climate analysis of your own. At the end of the day, you want to come to the right conclusions about what is wrong, and why it is counterproductive to organizational goals, before you launch a massive change effort. Otherwise, you are merely putting a Band-Aid on a gunshot wound.

Oftentimes, when we reflect on imbalance in the workplace, we think about the representational gaps between older and younger, Caucasians and people of color, female and male, gay and straight, and other disparate employee divisions. Nevertheless, an imbalanced effort signifies an impediment that goes beyond leveling the playing field.

Here's why: genuine culture change takes a lot of time. It may be years before policies drive behavior changes that result in fairness, or before senior executives mirror the larger employee and customer base, or before employees function effectively as a team. Nevertheless, visionary leadership is required to re-imagine culture change and the future of inclusion. What terms will no longer be acceptable in the course of work? For example, the Trump Administration in 2017, instructed policy analysts in the Centers for Disease Control (CDC) to avoid using certain terms in their budget policy documents; diversity and transgender were two of the seven banned words. In what ways does your strategy support outcomes that align with your long-term vision?

A strategic imbalance is evident when efforts, which focus on inputs such as the number of mentoring programs, event sponsorships, or resumes collected, are counted to demonstrate senior management's commitment to change. A false positive jeopardizes our credibility as business leaders because it's considered "check the box diversity". This mentality performs a simplistic task (e.g., similar to making chocolate milk by pouring milk and chocolate syrup into a glass but not stirring it up), and does not ensure follow-up, integration with business operations, or effectiveness, to name a few. The industry may be different (i.e., corporation, nonprofit, educational institution or government agency) but the vision and the organization's mission must be centric to the strategy.

According to a recent study that appeared in the Harvard Business Review, up to 70 percent of employees do not understand their company's Diversity and Inclusion strategy. Failure to understand the company's Diversity and Inclusion position can lead to poor decision making at all levels of an organization. For that reason, the first step toward crafting a diversity strategic plan is to take a careful look at where you are as a company, your place in the industry, and your realistic Diversity and Inclusion goals for the intermediate and long term that are tied to the organizational mission.

Diversity plans are actionable and measurable; they lay out the most important primary Diversity and Inclusion goals for a company. By outlining the key objectives for an organization, Diversity and Inclusion leaders enable the company's employees to develop strategies to achieve the stated goals. Ensuring employees are all on the same page and can be more productive in Diversity and Inclusion efforts.

CONCLUSION

In order to go beyond activities, Diversity Officers must think about performance as strategically as other executives in the core operating businesses: define metrics to track progress toward the vision. Diversity leaders must prioritize among competing tactics and drive increased investments toward initiatives that produce results. Use feedback to make refinements along the way. After you demonstrate mastery of one set of goals, create new objectives.

References:

Arline, Katherine. Business News Daily, Dec. 2014. What Is a Vision Statement? Retrieved December 21, 2017, from http://www.businessnewsdaily.com/3882-vision-statement.html

Bolognese, Albert F. 2002. Employee Resistance to Organizational Change. Retrieved from: http://www.newfoundations.com/OrgTheory/Bolognese721.html

Coetsee, L. (Summer, 1999). From resistance to commitment. Public Administration Quarterly, 204-222.

Folger, R. & Skarlicki, D. (1999). Unfairness and resistance to change: hardship as mistreatment, Journal of Organizational Change Management, 35-50.

Heilig, Julian Vasquez; Brown, Keffrelyn; and Brown, Anthony. Harvard Educational Review, 2012. *The Illusion of Inclusion: A Critical Race Theory Textual Analysis of Race and Standards*

Hewlett, Sylvia Ann; Luce, Carolyn Buck; and West, Cornel. Harvard Business Review, Nov. 2005. *Leadership in Your Midst: Tapping the Hidden Strengths of Minority Executives*

Kim, Daniel. 1999. Pegagus Communications Inc. Introduction to Systems Thinking. www.pegasuscommunication.com

National Association of Diversity Officers in Higher Education. *Standards for Professional Practice for Chief Diversity Officers*. 2014. www.nadohe.org/standards-of-professional-practice-for-chief-diversity-officers

Washington, E. Johnson, J., McCloskley, B., et al (2011). *Practical Resources for Recruiting Minorities for Chief Executive Officers at Public Transportation Agencies*. Pg. 6

Sample Test Questions:

IMPEDIMENTS TO INCLUSION & CULTURAL COMPETENCE

1. **Political Correctness prevents individuals from engaging in _____.**
   A. Rumor mills
   B. Arguments
   C. Straight talk

2. **Because few organizations have standards for Diversity and Inclusion work, there is little accountability for:**
   A. Boards of Directors or CEO's to understand diversity and inclusion
   B. Moving diversity and inclusion efforts beyond superficial notions
   C. Managers to apply culturally competent behaviors

3. **The entire leadership team should play a role in building bridges with Diversity and Inclusion critics.**
   A. True
   B. False

4. **Allowing Caucasian men to serve as Diversity Executives could ensure that Diversity and Inclusion is seen as a credible business imperative.**
   A. True
   B. False

5. **People have the right to protest, disagree, and be politically incorrect.**
   A. True
   B. False

6. **There are three vantage points by which Diversity and Inclusion is viewed:**
   A. Social, professional and the business case
   B. Social, compliance, the business case and imbalanced efforts
   C. Compliance, the business case, and it's the right thing to do

7. **Impediments to inclusion and cultural competence can be found in an organization's structure and systems.**
   A. True
   B. False

Sample Test Questions:

IMPEDIMENTS TO INCLUSION & CULTURAL COMPETENCE (cont'd)

8. **Zaltman & Duncan (1977) define this term as "any conduct that serves to maintain the status quo in the face of pressure to alter the status quo":**
   A. Change management
   B. Compliance
   C. Resistance

9. **The "Illusion of Inclusion" can be solved if D&I leaders focus on:**
   A. Leading with the business case for diversity
   B. Greater visibility by coordinating more activities
   C. Uncovering the diversity standards that marginalize inclusion

10. **A modern-day Diversity Officer's role is to:**
    A. Ensure political correctness by policing and enforcing policies
    B. Provide leadership in support of the organization's mission
    C. Recruit and train workers to value one another

11. **One of the ways that cultural competence can be achieved is to identify and understand:**
    A. Why workers criticize diversity and inclusion efforts
    B. How to prevent employees from doing or saying the wrong things
    C. The needs and help-seeking behaviors of different individuals

12. **The "Illusion of Inclusion" occurs when diverse groups are counted but:**
    A. HR does not file the EEO-1 report on time
    B. Conflict prevents them from being included
    C. They lack the privileges of the majority group

13. **Failure to understand the company's diversity and inclusion position can lead to:**
    A. More employees using social media to ridicule cultural competency efforts
    B. An organic decrease in discrimination and harassment lawsuits
    C. Poor decision making at all levels of an organization

UNCONSCIOUS BIAS

The concept of unconscious bias or "hidden bias" has recently come into the forefront of our work as diversity advocates. In fact, the realities of inclusion has evolved and challenged diversity leaders to confront age-old assumptions about who is, and who is not, biased.

Our traditional paradigm has generally assumed that patterns of discriminatory behavior in organizations are conscious; that people who know better do the right thing. As a result, we have developed a good person/bad person paradigm of Diversity and Inclusion: a belief that good people are not biased, but inclusive; bad people are the ones who are racist and predisposed to prejudice and exclusion.

OVERALL OBJECTIVES AND COMPETENCIES

The intent of this competency is to identify implicit associations that lead to discrimination, inequality and exclusion, as well as present effective techniques to help managers and employees overcome stereotypes and biases

BACKGROUND AND CONTEXT

Bias has been described as the inclination to hold a partial perspective. It's often accompanied by a refusal to consider the possible merits of alternative points of view. Biases are learned implicitly within cultural contexts. People may develop biases toward or against individuals, ethnic groups, nations, religions, a social class, political parties, theoretical paradigms and ideologies within academic domains, and/or a species. A person who is biased is often one-sided, lacking a neutral viewpoint towards others. It is possible that a person is unaware of his or her bias, which makes addressing it rather difficult.

Any kind of bias within an organization will cause it to miss opportunities because people will make decisions that are not objective, maintain practices that are not expedient, or foster a distrustful culture that will not lead to a competitive advantage. Nevertheless, bias can be hard to identify because it is pervasively entrenched in policies, practices, and performance expectations.

Distrust, caused by bias, creates an uncomfortable culture, where individuals misjudge other people's motives and intentions. Distrust works both ways (contrary to popular assumptions) as both the dominant and minority groups may perpetrate bias.

Social research indicates that there are over 20 ways in which bias can manifest itself. In the field of Diversity and Inclusion, the most common forms are:

- **Cultural Bias** is the phenomenon of interpreting and judging phenomena by standards inherent to one's own culture. Examples of cultural bias pertain to color, location of body parts (e.g., right hand dominant), mate selection, concepts of justice, standardized testing, acceptability of evidence, and taboos. Individuals who display cultural bias may be unaware that there are different ways of doing things or that people may have different experiences.

- **In-group Bias** refers to a pattern of favoring members of one's in-group over out-group members. This can be expressed in the evaluation of others, in the allocation of resources, and in many other ways. The opposite of in-group bias is out-group bias, where, by inference, out-group people are viewed more negatively and given worse treatment.

  In-group linguistic bias is where out-group people are described in abstract terms (which de-personifies them) when they conform to the out-group stereotype. Out-group people will be referred to in more specific, concrete terms when they act in unexpected ways.

- **Unconscious Bias** refers to a bias that we are unaware of, and which occurs outside of our control. It is a bias that happens automatically and is triggered by our brain making quick judgments and assessments of people and situations. This type of bias is influenced by our background, cultural environment, and personal experiences. Researchers say that the individual may not be racist, but a person with unconscious bias can inadvertently perpetuate racism, discrimination and other disparities.

Our focus in this competency is unconscious bias. The University of Washington's Tony Greenwald and the University of California Santa Cruz's Thomas Pettigrew make the succinct case that discrimination in the United States is not primarily a product of overt hatred for others, but rather simple preferences for people like ourselves. In a review of five decades of psychological research, they found that while most scholars defined prejudice as an expression of hostility, the more pervasive form of bigotry in the United States comes from people who favor, admire, and trust people of their own race, gender, age, religion, or parenting status.

For the most part, biases are not born from negative or positive personal experiences; rather, they are learned from watching media portrayals of certain groups of people, or taught by individuals of influence such as parents, grandparents, religious leaders, and teachers. In this sense, unconscious bias is a byproduct of others' views and experiences in cases where there is an absence of actual negative interactions with different groups. These unconscious and prejudicial influences result in bigotry, which is stronger than prejudice; a more severe mindset that is often accompanied by discriminatory behavior. According to Debbie Irving, racial justice educator and writer, bigotry is "arrogant and mean-spirited, but requires neither systems nor power to engage in".

Further, in *You're More Biased Than You Think*, Jane Porter writes that we're faced with around 11 million pieces of information at any given moment, according to Timothy Wilson, professor of psychology at the University of Virginia and author of the book *Strangers to Ourselves: Discovering the Adaptive Unconscious*, "The brain can only process about 40 of those bits of information and so it creates shortcuts and uses past knowledge to make assumptions." These shortcuts sometimes result in unconscious bias. Nevertheless, while this level of bias occurs below the surface, it does not have to remain there.

BIAS AT WORK

Most people do not exhibit bias on purpose. In *Workplace Diversity: What is Unconscious Bias & How to Manage It?,* Sahar Andrade explains that unconscious bias "is a blind spot that requires a shift in how we think about other people that we perceive different. It is a belief or attitude in our heads. Bias is the very fundamental way we look at and encounter the world to make sense of the world around us. It is driven by the hard wiring pattern of making decisions about others based on what feels safe, familiar, likable, valuable, and competent to us without us realizing it".

Bias is the ability to distinguish safe from dangerous which is a basic quality of our human brain to categorize and group information, so our brains can make sense of them. Our bias kicks in whenever we have a perception of a threat to our own survival or a threat to the safety of ourselves, loved ones, property, identity, or sense of being. It is an instinctive reaction as primal biology urges a response that brings relief to tension.

Howard J. Ross, founder of Cook Ross, was one of the first D&I pioneers to acknowledge that the brain groups people and situations into categories so that we can make decisions about our world. In *Everyday Bias*, Ross explores the impact of prejudice and encourages organizations to confront cognitive biases, as well as pre-established filters, which are perceptions, assumptions, interpretations, or preferences that we develop throughout our life's experiences. These filters enable our brains to develop patterns, or biases, which help us to effortlessly juggle or balance information about culturally complex groups of people. Nevertheless, sometimes filters result in blind spots, or unconscious bias.

So where do we get our initial filters or bias? Parents and caregivers are our first introduction to this behavior. They expose us to their beliefs, values, and cultures; then, family members, schools, religious institutions, the media/Internet, and our own life's experiences validate or reinforce our initial proclivities. If any of the above influences has a blind spot, it becomes our unconscious bias and we transfer it to the next generation that we meet.

Our unconscious bias is a "blueprint ping" throughout life. It is important to mention that it is normal that we ALL have some degree of bias no matter how open minded we think we are. Nevertheless, acting on bias is NEVER positive even if it is based on positive stereotypes (e.g., assuming that all Asians have high incomes and drive BMW's).

Bias prevents us from seeing people as individuals and is a significant challenge in the workplace. Simply stated, unconscious biases can be defined as our implicit people preferences. There are countless examples of how bias can manifest in the workplace, as illustrated below.

Joshua Bell, a world-renowned classical musician, took to a Metro station in L'Enfant Plaza, Washington, DC, in rush hour to play some of the finest classical pieces written on one of the world's most expensive violins. Disguised as a street performer, he was acknowledged by only a tiny handful of people, with the majority walking straight past the performance of a lifetime. Bell made a total of $32.17 in the performance which lasted 43 minutes and was heard by over a thousand people. Three days before, he had filled the house at Boston's Symphony Hall, where seats sold for $100 each.

Was this outcome the result of the public's unconscious bias against street performers? On the other hand, perhaps the passersby simply did not like his music. Either way, how many times has a similar situation occurred in job interview situations, and how many talented people have been rejected from jobs due to the preconceptions and unconscious biases of their interviewers?

Combatting unconscious bias is difficult because it does not feel wrong, and on the surface, it does not appear to hurt anyone. Yet, it is necessary to fight against bias in order to create a work environment that supports and encourages diverse perspectives and people. Not only is it the right thing to do, but research has shown that a diverse workforce yields higher performance and better results over the long term. That means we need to make the unconscious, conscious. The first step is education; we need to help people identify and understand their biases so that they can start to combat them.

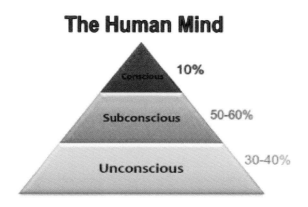

Here are four ways to reduce the influence of bias:

- **Gather Facts.** Are there patterns of behavior that work contrary to Diversity and Inclusion goals (for example, veterans who never make it past stage 2 in the interviewing process)? Which policies have a disparate outcome, and are those policies really necessary? How do you evaluate whether things are changing? It is hard to know whether you're improving if you're not measuring.

- **Create a Structure for Making Better Decisions.** Choice Architecture is the process of altering the environment in which decisions are made. Engaging in Choice Architecture can greatly reduce the subjective nature of management and encourage objectivity—not only with hiring, but in promotions, work assignments, discipline, conflict resolution, and terminations. To get started, design clear criteria to evaluate the merits of certain policies and practices. Eliminate those policies and practices that are subjective while nudging employees towards alternative and inclusive scenarios. Choice Architecture does not eliminate options, it merely redefines them in alignment with D&I values. In the words of Roy E. Disney, "When your values are clear to you, making decisions becomes easier".

Many companies have a biased view of Millennials—seeing them as unreliable slackers. At one point, FedEx faced a workplace imbalance where turnover was particularly high among Millennials. The problem concerned starting work on time. Baby Boomers, who were primarily in management positions, regarded time as finite: "If you are supposed to start at 9, you should be here by 8:45 period". Millennials, on the other hand, believed "if I am supposed to start at 9, I will get there around 9:00, 9:03, 9:05...". This generational conflict resulted in many terminations. The company had to make a choice at that point. Should the older people handle all of the packages, possibly leading to an increase in workers comp injuries? Can we afford to exclude Millennials from the management ranks? On the other hand, can we be a little more flexible with the time? Accordingly, FedEx chose the latter option: let us show some flexibility in order to be inclusive.

- **Be Mindful of Subtle Cues.** At formal meetings, look around the room, who is included and who is excluded? Are certain groups excluded from informal gatherings? For example, the employees with visible disabilities are not invited for drinks after work.

- **Foster Awareness.** Hold yourself and your colleagues accountable. For example, Google has created a "bias busting checklist". At performance reviews, it is used to encourage managers to examine their own biases and assess biased practices.

IMPLICIT & EXPLICIT BIAS

In *Prejudice, Discrimination, and Racism: Historical Trends and Contemporary Approaches,* authors John Dovidio and Samuel Gaertner assert that in the modern world, prejudice has been "driven underground". Herein lies the foundation for the two different types of bias: Implicit and Explicit.

Implicit Bias
Harvard University researchers developed the Implicit Associations Test (IAT) to measure attitudes and beliefs that people may be unwilling or unable to report. The IAT is a free tool that collects data, as well as helps people gain a realistic understanding of their own implicit biases.

Implicit bias is an understood, implied, and otherwise unspoken prejudice. While implicit bias can and does operate at the level of individual actors, it often occurs at the systems level through practices and policies applied to classifications of people. Data indicates that implicit racial bias is systemic in hiring and promotions, policing and justice, housing, media coverage, and local, state, and federal policies toward urban America. Included in this understanding is disproportionate public-school funding. Implicit bias occurs when politicians and media call Black protestors "thugs", when minorities are followed by security guards through stores as presumptive thieves, and when African Americans are paid less for the same job and performance as others.

Implicit bias is not limited to African Americans in America. It also occurs when individuals interact with veterans. Despite numerous education efforts, various myths about veterans still exist (e.g., they are less educated, they have alcohol and drug problems; they all have Post Traumatic Stress Disorder (PTSD); or they're ticking time bombs). These stereotypes prevent hiring managers from considering the unique contributions that individuals, with backgrounds as veterans, bring to an organization.

Implicit bias also affects different generations. Since the early 1970's, Generation X has been distinguished as the neglected generation. They are known for the proliferation of latch key kids, an abundance of free time that lead to explosive drug use, teen pregnancies, and rap music. Generation X's direction has been unclear to many. Even in modern day discussions and research efforts about the various generations in the workplace, GenXers are usually excluded to focus on their over-achieving Boomer and Millennial peers. Nevertheless, Boomers and Millennials are not exempt from implicit biases. Just imagine how many biases your supervisors possess pertaining to each generation.

Implicit bias refers to the attitudes or stereotypes that affect our understanding, actions, and decisions in an unconscious manner. These biases, which encompass both favorable and unfavorable assessments, are activated involuntarily and without an individual's awareness or intentional control. Residing deep in the subconscious, these biases are different from known biases that individuals may choose to conceal for the purposes of social conformity and/or political correctness. Rather, implicit biases are not accessible through introspection.

The implicit associations we harbor in our subconscious causes us to have feelings and attitudes about other people based on:

- **Primary Dimensions:** things we can see such as race, age, gender, ethnicity, physical ability, and sexual orientation (actual or presumed)

- **Secondary Dimensions:** things that can change such as marital status, parental status, income, religion, recreational habits, educational background, geographic location, and appearance

- **Organizational Dimensions:** things related to work such as division, department, union affiliation, shift, work location, seniority, job title, functional classification, and management, or tenure status

These associations develop over the course of a lifetime beginning at a very early age through exposure to direct and indirect messages. In addition to early life experiences, the media and news programming are often responsible for implicit associations.

Key Characteristics of Implicit Biases:

- Implicit biases are pervasive. Everyone possesses them, even people with declared commitments to impartiality such as judges.

- Implicit and explicit biases are related but distinct mental constructs. They are not mutually exclusive and may even reinforce each other.

- The implicit associations we hold do not necessarily align with our declared beliefs or even reflect stances we would explicitly endorse.

- We generally tend to hold implicit biases that favor our own in-group, though research has shown that we can still hold implicit biases against our in-group.

- Implicit biases are flexible. Our brains are incredibly complex, and the implicit associations that we have formed can be gradually unlearned.

- Implicit bias can influence a number of professional judgments and actions in the "real world" that may have legal ramifications.

EXAMPLE

Police officers face high-pressure, high-risk decisions in the line of fire. One pivotal research report reveals that these rapid decisions are not immune to the effects of implicit biases. Specifically, college participants in this study played a computer game in which they needed to shoot dangerous armed characters (by pressing a "shoot" button) and decide whether to shoot unarmed characters (by pressing a "don't shoot" button), as quickly as possible. Some of the characters held a gun, like a revolver or pistol, and some of the characters held harmless objects, like a wallet or cell phone. In addition, half of the characters were White, and half were Black.

Study participants more quickly chose to shoot armed Black characters than armed White characters and more quickly chose not to shoot unarmed White characters than unarmed Black characters. They also omitted more "false alarm" errors, electing to shoot unarmed Black characters more than unarmed White characters and electing not to shoot armed White characters more than armed Black characters (This research was inspired by the 1999 New York City shooting of Guinean immigrant Amadou Diallo. Police officers fired 41 rounds and killed Diallo as he pulled out a wallet). Other studies produced similar results with police officers and community members and showed that training and practice can help to reduce this bias.

EXAMPLE

A pupil with cerebral palsy, who is a wheelchair user, is told she will be unable to attend a school trip to a local theatre. The theatre is putting on a production of a play she is currently studying in English, but the building is not wheelchair accessible. The pupil and her parents are aware that the play is also being performed at a theatre in a neighbouring city which is accessible but the school does not investigate this option.

EXAMPLE

Kylar was a well-established professional at a financial institution. For several years in a row, he received stellar performance appraisals. However, there were some things about Kylar that were private; he clearly separated his work from his personal life because he never participated in the after-hours events, did not attend the holiday gatherings, nor did he share vacation stories. During a brief leave, Kylar transitioned from female to male. When he returned to the office, his co-workers were shocked. His standing weekly meeting with the department supervisor was awkward and uncomfortable, with unusually long periods of silence. Within days, Kylar began to face harassment from his supervisor and co-workers, including offensive remarks, ostracism, unreasonable demands, and restrictions on his gender identity. He was then forced out of the company and spent time being unemployed before finding another position.

EXAMPLE

Shortly after the shooting in San Bernardino, a group of 11 workers at Cargill Meat Solutions in Colorado wanted to pray at the same time in a room in the plant that is set aside for prayer and reflection. Their supervisor asked that the group break up into smaller numbers so that production is not affected. The workers complied with the supervisor's request and went in smaller groups to pray. But after their shift ended, 10 of the 11 workers resigned, turning in their badges and hard hats. News of the dispute spread to other plant employees, and about 150 Somali workers missed work for 3 days in protest. Based on Cargill's attendance policy, the company fired those who failed to come to work for three consecutive days without giving any form of notice. The plant also changed its policy which allowed short prayer breaks at various times during the day. Its 500 remaining Muslim workers were told to "go home" if they wanted to pray.

In *Detecting Hidden Bias* by Pamela Babcock, SHRM suggests that managers and/or employees take the Harvard Implicit Association Test (IAT) to identify implicit biases on an individual level. This type of assessment would be ideal before launching an unconscious bias training session. Next, D&I leaders should assess the organization with a diversity dashboard. This metric-based evaluation should consider data from hiring and promotion rates, career path movement, performance appraisals, and compensation among different employee groups to spot inequities.

Once people are made aware of implicit biases, they can begin to consider ways in which to address them. The endeavor to address these biases should not be imposed on workers, but must be a collaborative, entity-wide effort. Scientists have uncovered several promising implicit bias intervention strategies that may help individuals who strive to be unrestricted; the PAUSE Strategy is illustrated in Figure 1. The PAUSE strategy is exactly what it implies—taking a few minutes to think (e.g., about consequences) before we speak or take action.

FIGURE 1: BIAS INTERVENTION STRATEGIES

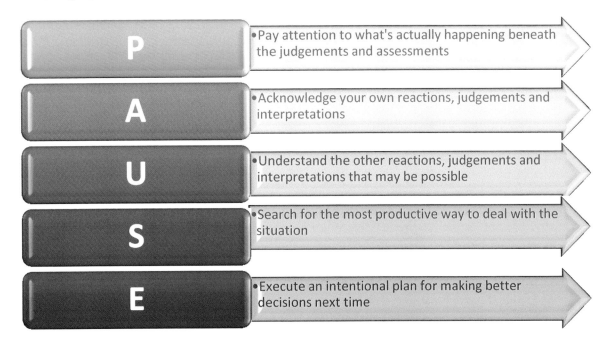

P • Pay attention to what's actually happening beneath the judgements and assessments

A • Acknowledge your own reactions, judgements and interpretations

U • Understand the other reactions, judgements and interpretations that may be possible

S • Search for the most productive way to deal with the situation

E • Execute an intentional plan for making better decisions next time

If applied long-term, people may be able to reduce or eliminate implicit bias by modifying their underlying implicit attitudes. Reductions in implicit bias have occurred as a result of longer-term exposure to minorities in socially valued roles, in the context of cultural education initiatives and even as a result of simply imagining (rather than actually encountering) counter-stereotypes.

Explicit Bias
Explicit bias is overt intolerance based on social, religious, or political views that engender antipathy towards others. Abortion and gay rights historically have been areas rife with explicit bias in which people hold fixed views of right and wrong. Recent cases, ranging from businesses refusing to provide services for gay couples, to state restrictions on restroom usage, to churches refusing to marry same sex partners, are all forms of explicit bias resulting in discrimination.

Explicit bias refers to the attitudes and beliefs that we have about a person or a group on a conscious level. Often, these biases and their expressions arise as the direct result of a perceived threat. When people feel threatened, they are more likely to draw group boundaries to distinguish themselves from others.

Research has shown that White Americans are more likely to express anti-Muslim prejudice when they perceive national security to be at risk and express more negative attitudes towards Asian Americans when they perceive an economic threat. When people perceive their biases are valid, they are more likely to justify unfair treatment or even violence. This unfair treatment can have long-term negative impacts on the victims' physical and mental health.

Expressions of explicit bias (e.g., discrimination, hate speech, etc.) occur as the result of deliberate thought. Thus, they can be consciously regulated. People are more motivated to control their biases if there are social norms in place that dictate that prejudice is not socially acceptable. Hence, bystander intervention training can be an effective tool in changing unacceptable behavior at work.

While biases can be reinforced by other people or interactions, research shows that emphasizing a common group identity (such as "everyone is at the company because they all put in the hard work and are now part of a common purpose, which is _____") can help mitigate the effects of external influences. Consistently re-affirming a shared purpose can help reduce intergroup tensions that may arise between majority and minority factions in the workplace. Also, when conducted under the right conditions, studies show intergroup contact between different employees can increase trust and reduce the anxiety that underlies bias.

Workplace Bias

Awareness of unconscious bias in the workplace is not enough; nevertheless, most training is focused on awareness. We need prescriptions, not descriptions, to change both personal and systemic behaviors; warning signs and directions can help. Here are a few warning signs that the organization, and its leadership, should consider:

1) *We have a woman at the top syndrome.* A recent study, reported by Glass Hammer from the Robert H. Smith School of Business found that there was a 'hidden negative quota' for women in top leadership. If a woman holds one of the top five executive positions at a company, the chances of a second woman being appointed in those ranks falls by 51%. Getting a second woman promoted is far more difficult, let alone attaining a critical mass or majority.

Solution: One woman at the top is only the beginning and not the reflection of a true sharing of power. Every position at the top (including line positions) should include at least two, if not more, non-dominant group members for consideration.

2) *I understand because my loved one or neighbor... defense.* Senior leaders often reference their wives, daughters, or mothers as their role models and this is what makes them truly understand women's issues and barriers to equality. A corollary to this is "Some of my best friends are..." We all use our personal experiences to help inform the world we live in, as well as show what is heartfelt and well-meaning. A male leader may think that because he wants the best for his daughter or wife he must *ipso facto* have an organization that would be good for women.

Granted, according to Catalyst, the research organization, men with daughters are more sensitive to gender issues. Unfortunately, that is not the same thing as operating the organization with all the data available and becoming competent about the differing experiences of dominant groups and non-dominant groups in the workplace. Beware too, of what Cheryl Kaiser of the University of Washington calls the "illusion of inclusion". Here is when organizations believe they MUST be fair because they have an Office of Diversity or programs directed at enhancing diversity, even in the face of statistics or other corollaries that show the opposite.

Solution: Use the data and statistics that are readily known or can be known. An example is to evaluate performance reviews and track how often men are negatively reviewed for personal communication styles versus how often women are reviewed for personal communication styles. Shelley Correll of Stanford University has found that women are three times more likely to get feedback on communication style than men are and women are 66% more likely to be coached to change their communication style.

Another study in Forbes found that 76% of women's reviews included personal comments such as "too aggressive", while only 2% of men received similar comments. Any organization that collects data on its employees can ferret out this signal of unconscious bias, not just for women, but for any non-dominant group.

3) *I never noticed that... rationalization.* Studies have shown that:

- Women are interrupted more than men are interrupted.
- Women's suggestions are less likely to be taken up and given credit; men's comments are more likely to be substantiated, given positive deference and referred to more often.
- African American men and women may code-switch their speaking styles far more than Caucasian men and women.
- Men's overconfidence may be harmful to the decisions being made.
- My "go to" person looks a lot like me.

For some, it is a normal day at the office when they are not aware that others are unintentionally excluded.

Solution: General awareness of unconscious bias is enlightening, but specific awareness is crucial for behavior change. Managers in meetings can stop interruptions or undue deference if they first know how to notice the dynamics. In one company, research assignments were thought to be given out in a gender-neutral fashion, until an actual diagram of assignments was done. Men were researching large companies in capital-intensive industries; women got the small to medium companies in the service industries. Management had not noticed until it was documented and then they were able to intervene positively. At a minimum, the decisions on who gets what assignments should be made consciously.

A data-centered approach to our proclivities regarding unconscious bias, and how our fast-thinking brains work, is part of the journey. But solutions and behavior change will be the destination for diverse, inclusive, and successful organizations.

DIVERSITY & INCLUSION HOT-SPOTS

Unconscious beliefs and attitudes have been found to be associated with language and certain behaviors such as eye contact, blinking rates and smiles. While there are many biases that may manifest in a professional environment (such as bias for right-hand dominant individuals, or for extroverts), we will explore a few common trouble spots.

Race Relations and Bias
Unconscious biases and race relations go hand-in-hand in America. They both have an impact on American organizations, schools, and neighborhoods. Housing patterns provide a great illustration of how race relations and unconscious bias are systemic issues that cannot be addressed with a simple unidimensional approach. Where someone lives affects school funding, employment opportunities, and community policing.

For example, the heavy-handed law-enforcement in urban areas is disproportionately different from what a suburban citizen experiences. In the suburbs, children learn that the police are your friends who are employed to serve and protect. Police officers may be your neighbors or involved in community sports and activities. In urban areas, children learn that the police are supposed to enforce law and order, by any means necessary.

In February 2015, former FBI Director James B. Comey delivered a speech urging United States law enforcement officials to acknowledge implicit biases toward minorities, leading to distrust between police officers and communities. Comey's belief is that police officers view Black and White men differently and that many times throughout history, "law enforcement enforced the status quo, a status quo that was often brutally unfair to disfavored groups". The speech came in the fallout of the death of unarmed Black teenager Michael Brown, who was killed by White police officer Darren Wilson in August 2014 in Ferguson, Mo., as well as the death of New York resident Eric Garner brought on by New York Police Department officers a month earlier.

While treating people inequitably because of their race is unfair, it is driven by an economic system that supports unconscious bias and segregation. In 2015, the U.S. Justice Department revealed a pattern and practice of discrimination in Ferguson, Missouri, where every branch of Ferguson government (i.e., the police, municipal court, and city hall) participated in the unlawful targeting of African-American residents for tickets and fines to the tune of $2 million in revenue from 21,000 citizens in 2012 alone. Yet Ferguson, MO., is not alone. All around America, this economic system is evident in urban supermarkets that charge a higher price for a smaller selection of goods, or in financial institutions that charge higher rates and impose more strict credit standards on individuals of color who wish to purchase homes or even cash a check.

According to Richard Rothstein, research associate at the Economic Policy Institute (EPI), segregation is no accident. Federal housing policies starting in the 1930s are largely to blame for ongoing racial segregation and its economic effects. In the last 60 years, African American families were intentionally excluded from affordable housing options across the nation's growing suburban neighborhoods. As a result, the predominantly minority laden zip codes in America's most segregated metro areas tend to be located near the city centers, while the predominantly Caucasian laden zip codes are more often found outside the city, in the suburbs. Today, as more people of color move to the suburbs, younger and older Whites are moving into urban homes or apartments with high price tags and visible security.

Research has shown that much of what is experienced in urban areas is not limited to race but is also associated with social class. Therefore, a low-income Caucasian, or any other ethnic person is likely to have negative experiences with deficient schools, lack of employment, and inadequate housing.

Social class is not insurmountable, but race in America often presents more obstacles to overcome. Studies such as, *Are Emily and Greg More Employable than Lakisha and Jamal? A Field Experiment on Labor Market Discrimination*, indicate that there is racial discrimination in the labor market based on names, race, and social class. A now classic experiment showed that Caucasian interviewers sat farther away from African American applicants than from Caucasian applicants, made more speech errors, and ended the interviews 25% sooner. Such discrimination has been shown to diminish the performance of anyone treated that way, whether a minority or Caucasian person.

Scientific research has demonstrated that biases thought to be absent or extinguished remain as mental residue in most of us. Studies show that people can be consciously committed to egalitarianism, and deliberately work to behave without prejudice. Yet, these same indivduals still possess hidden negative prejudices and/or stereotypes. A growing number of studies show a link between hidden biases and actual behavior. In other words, hidden biases can reveal themselves in action, especially when a person's efforts to control behavior consciously flags under stress, distraction, relaxation, or competition.

Sex and Gender-Identity Bias

We are all vulnerable to the influence of deeply held views and ideas that create unconscious bias. For over 1,000 years we have identified males with the words leader, provider, and driven. We like and respect men when they demonstrate these qualities. Women have been identified with emotional, supportive, and caring qualities. We find women likable when they exhibit these qualities. Many times, when a woman is seen as a leader and driven, she is perceived as unaccepting or judgmental because it goes against what a woman is supposed to represent. She is not only criticized as being cold, power hungry, and out for self; but business and industry tends to prefer a man for the same leadership role without the negative connotations.

Research has shown that senior leaders across Western Europe perceive gender stereotyping as a barrier to women's advancement. In another study, hidden personal biases are often reflected in organizations' talent management systems leading to unconsciously biased decision-making. This means those at the top of a company, who are predominantly men, will influence how the organization manages its talent pipeline so that those being promoted will often mirror the traits and biases of top leaders which is a vicious cycle in which men continue to dominate executive positions.

The think-manager-think-male perspective becomes the standard that employees expect. It is the what-you-have-is-what-you-get status quo. Interestingly, female decision-makers also enforce this status quo.

Gender bias is deeply rooted in the competencies that organizations value in a leader. In a separate study, Catalyst asked senior managers to rate leadership attributes they associated with a man or a woman and found that taking charge was perceived as a male trait, while taking care was perceived as a female trait. Traits perceived as feminine are seen as less vital to leadership which is a situation which can result in women being evaluated less positively than men for leadership positions. In fact, there are more differences between men and their colleagues and among women and their female peers, than among men and women as a whole.

Organizations must be vigilant in identifying and eliminating these stereotypes, if they want to counter gender bias and take advantage of their full talent pool. Catalyst believes this is slowly happening. The chief executive of a global company recently admitted that he expected to become a near-extinct species (a middle-aged, White man running a multinational organization) in the future. He applauded the fact that smarter organizations are already attempting to stamp out bias to ensure they better represent their customers. It is refreshing to see that gender stereotyping is becoming unacceptable in all parts of society. A recent campaign successfully ended a major UK supermarket's policy of selling children's princess and nurses' outfits labeled girls, while the outfits for the boy labels were marked on the pilot, superhero, soldier, and doctor's outfits. We are also beginning to see public restrooms with unisex and family signs. This eliminates confusion when a person who identifies with another gender uses the corresponding restroom.

The responsibility is on everyone to stamp out lazy stereotyping. Instead, it is better to listen to, and interact with, individuals without relying on unfounded generalizations. We also need organizations to redefine their stereotypical definition of an effective leader to ensure women are able to achieve their full potential.

Unconscious gender bias is not a woman's or a transgender issue. It is everyone's issue. The answer to ending gender bias and opening the gates for women to create balance in leadership, elected officials, and in traditionally male-dominated industries, is to become aware that it exists. It is about waking up, becoming conscious to bias as a function of the brains' default categorizations and then learning how to override it. After all, we cannot change what we do not see.

THE KEYS TO CHANGE: STRIVING FOR INTENTIONAL OUTCOMES

Subjectivity and the tendency to act based on unconscious biases is a business risk that companies cannot afford to ignore. It is not just Barneys or a pricey boutique in Zurich where unconscious bias can affect the bottom line. According to Huff Post writers, Kim Bhasin and Julee Wilson in their recent article entitled *Barneys' Racist Culture Deeply Ingrained in Store*, "...the situation at Barneys isn't unique, nor is it limited to upscale department stores. In the past decade, Neiman Marcus, Macy's, Dillard's, and Kohl's have each been sued for alleged racial profiling".

In many of these cases, sales associates acted on their unconscious biases and made assumptions about the worthiness of a potential customer and their ability to pay for merchandise based on the color of their skin. In the case of the Boutique in Zurich, it cost the store $38,000 when Oprah Winfrey walked out the door. It also cost them reputational capital, as the incident went viral and a public apology ensued. Undoubtedly, incidences of unconscious bias are not limited to just retailers and can cost a lot more than $38,000.

In addition to the costs associated with lost customers or students, think about the impact of a state or country losing residents or businesses. Also consider what happens when an employer under-utilizes talent. For instance, a supervisor assumes that a disabled worker is not capable of performing on a high level; or a younger employee is not included in certain client meetings because leadership assumes that the person is inexperienced. Or the hard-working Asian that is not considered for a promotion because the outgoing executive assumed that the individual would not be a good fit for a senior marketing role. All of these scenarios, and more, represent the need to re-think our commitment to inclusion.

Committing to Change

Tackling unconscious bias is one piece of making your organization a diverse workplace, and it is absolutely essential if you are going to live up to your promise to build a culture that makes life better for as many people as possible. Here is how your organization can commit to changing the environment:

1. *Ensure transparency.* Examine decision-making, social networking, policies, and procedures to determine where bias might exist. Make comparisons against similarly situated organizations and share your findings with stakeholders. Frequent communication about sensitive issues implies openness.

2. *Seek multi-dimensional feedback.* Do not just ask one African American person, or one homosexual or LGBTQ+ person, or one woman, whether bias exists. Obtain multiple perspectives to gain deeper insights about whether your business environment is fair, inclusive, and impartial.

3. *Build Trust.* Consistently making small changes over time is more effective than sweeping interventions that have no long-term strategy for sustainability. Also, leading by example is a powerful tool for building trust.

4. *Create opportunities to build relationships across differences.* Discourage the formation of cliques via the in-group/out-group phenomenon. Encourage more people to become active bystanders by challenging stereotypical information and behaviors. Form dynamic workgroups comprised of different people (managers and employees, field office and headquarters staff, various departments, etc.). Additionally, establish a formal process for handling team conflict.

5. *Provide organization-wide incentives for change.* You must establish "what's in it for me?" in order for people to really want to change. Perhaps you can tie outcomes to bonuses, raises, or promotions. Or maybe you can link better performance with diverse groups to coveted assignments.

6. *Encourage self-awareness.* We all have biases and owning up to and talking about our biases is a part of the solution. Encourage employees to explore biases during training exercises or coaching sessions.

7. *Do not blame, or shame, others when bias is acknowledged.* Personal growth cannot occur when people are fearful of making mistakes. Create a safe place for people to acknowledge their own mistakes without being judged or disciplined.

If people are aware of their hidden biases, they can monitor and attempt to ameliorate instinctive attitudes before they are expressed through action. This process can include paying attention to verbal and non-verbal communication (such as body language), as well as showing empathy toward the stigmatization felt by non-dominant groups.

If the D&I leader intends to facilitate training, instead of simply providing awareness, provide real-life examples of how unconscious bias exists in customer/student interactions, team work, assignments, communication and more. The training should also focus on delivering real-life solutions and tips for how to combat the bias. Finally, participants should be engaged in training discussions—providing them with an opportunity to share their experiences and ask questions.

It is good to reject explicit bias upon initial encounters; that is the easy part. To ask where implicit biases come from, what they mean, and what we can do about them is harder. Common sense and research suggests that a change in behavior can actually modify beliefs and attitudes. It would seem logical that a conscious decision to be egalitarian might lead one to widen one's circle of friends and knowledge of other groups. Such efforts may, over time, reduce the strength of unconscious bias when making a commitment to combat both explicit and implicit associations.

While it may not be possible to avoid automatic stereotypes and prejudice, it is certainly possible to consciously reduce it. Recognizing that the problem is in many other well-intentioned folks, as well as in ourselves, should motivate us to understand and act.

References:

Andrade, Sahar (June 18, 2014). *Workplace Diversity: What is Unconscious Bias & How to manage it?* Retrieved From: https://www.linkedin.com/pulse/20140618145805-35065017-workplace-diversity-what-is-unconscious-bias-how-to-manage-it/

Banaji, M., & Heiphetz, L. (2010). Attitudes. In S. Fiske, D. Gilbert, & G. Lindzey (Eds.)

Bhasin, Kim, and Wilson, Julee (November 7, 2013). Barneys' Racist Culture Deeply Ingrained in Store. Huffington Post. Retrieved From: https://www.huffingtonpost.com/2013/11/07/barneys-racist_n_4225710.html

Blair, I. (2002). The malleability of automatic stereotypes and prejudice. Personality and Social Psychology Review, 6, 242-261.

Bock, Laszlo, SVP of People Operations, and Welle, Ph.D., Brian, Director of People Analytics. Exposing Hidden Bias at Google. http://www.nytimes.com/2014/09/25/technology/exposing-hidden-biases-at-google-to-improve-diversity.html?_r=0

Correll, J., Park, B., Judd, C., Wittenbrink, B., Sadler, M., & Keesee, T. (2007). Across the thin blue line: Police officers and racial bias in the decision to shoot. Journal of Personality and Social Psychology, 92, 6, 1006-1023. doi:10.1037/0022-3514.92.6.1006

Dasgupta, N., & Rivera, L. (2008). When social context matters: The influence of long-term contact and short-term exposure to admire outgroup members on implicit attitudes and behavioral intentions. Social Cognition, 26,112-123

Dovidio, J., Gaertner, S., Kawakami, K., & Hodson, G. (2002). Why can't we just get along? Interpersonal biases and interracial distrust. Cultural Diversity and Ethnic Minority Psychology, 8, 88-102.

Greenwald, A., Smith, C., Sriram, N., Bar-Anan, Y., Nosek, B. (2009). Implicit race attitudes predicted vote in the 2008 U.S. presidential election. Analyses of Social Issues and Public Policy, 9, 241-253.

Lindzey, Gardner and Fiske, Susan T. Handbook of social psychology, 5th edition (pp. 348-388). New York: Wiley.

Kent, Alexander Kent and Frohlich, Thomas C. (Aug. 19, 2015) America's Most Segregated Cities, 24/7 Wall Street, http://247wallst.com/special-report/2015/08/19/americas-most-segregated-cities/

Irving, Debbie (unknown). *Are prejudice, bigotry, and racism the same thing?* Retrieved From: http://www.debbyirving.com/qa/are-prejudice-bigotryand-racism-the-same-thing/

Liswood, Laura (2015), The Warning Sign of Unconscious Thinking (Bias) and How to (Begin to) Overcome It, www.huffingtonpost.com

Penner, L., Dovidio, J., West, T., Gaertner, S., Albrecht, T., Dailey, R., & Markova, T. (2010). Aversive racism and medical interactions with Black patients: A field study. Journal of Experimental Social Psychology, 46, 436-440.

Porter, Jane. "You're More Biased Than You Think." FastCompany.com, 6 Oct. 2014. Web. 4 Oct. 2016

Sahar, Andrade, MB.BCh, Diversity, Inclusion, and Leadership Consultant- Social Media Strategist, Sahar Consulting, LLC. Retrieved from: http://www.trainingzone.co.uk/community/blogs/spicy-learning-blog/is-unconscious-bias-the-next-big-diversity-challenge

Wilson, Thomas (2004). *Strangers to Ourselves: Discovering the Adaptive Unconscious*. Belknap Press.

idc *Institute for Diversity Certification®*

Sample Test Questions:

UNCONSCIOUS BIAS

1. **Bias in the workplace can be hard to identify because it is entrenched in:**
   A. Performance appraisals, expectations, and the media
   B. Policies, practices, and performance evaluations
   C. Day-to-day interactions with diverse people

2. **The most common forms of bias are:**
   A. Racism, sexism, and classism
   B. Media, statistical and confirmation
   C. Cultural, in-group, and unconscious

3. **Unconscious bias is a byproduct of others' views and experiences in cases where:**
   A. There is an absence of actual negative interactions with different groups
   B. People make assumptions about the motivations behind negative behaviors
   C. Senior leadership does not manage equity, diversity and inclusion well

4. **Being mindful of subtle cues is <u>NOT</u> a way to reduce the influence of bias.**
   A. True
   B. False

5. **What is the role of "pre-established filters"?**
   A. To serve as fixed streams of prejudicial and biased information
   B. To confront perceptions that are contrary to our ideas and beliefs
   C. To develop patterns which help people to effortlessly juggle information

6. **One intervention strategy for implicit bias is:**
   A. F.L.E.X
   B. P.A.U.S.E
   C. P.L.A.N

7. **This term refers to the attitudes and beliefs that we have about a person or group on a conscious level:**
   A. Explicit Bias
   B. Implicit Bias
   C. Cultural Bias

Sample Test Questions:

UNCONSIOUS BIAS (cont'd)

8. **When people perceive their biases are valid, they are more likely to justify unfair treatment or:**
   A. Awareness
   B. Lawsuits
   C. Violence

9. **Reductions in implicit bias have occurred as a result of:**
   A. Strategic equity, diversity and inclusion interventions
   B. Diversity training programs that focus on unconscious bias
   C. Long-term exposure to minorities in socially valued roles

10. **Expressions of explicit bias such as discrimination can be consciously regulated because:**
    A. It originates from deliberate thoughts
    B. Management will discipline offenders
    C. Political correctness is prevalent at work

11. **To counteract "hidden negative quotas" in top leadership positions, employers should:**
    A. Maintain status quo if diversity is already visible in the lower ranks
    B. Ensure at least two non-dominant group members are considered
    C. Train senior leaders about the value of equity, diversity, and inclusion

12. **Unconscious bias can result in all of the following EXCEPT:**
    A. Lost customers or students
    B. A decrease in discrimination claims
    C. Lost or underutilized talent

EXECUTIVE COMMITMENT & SPONSORSHIP

While everyone is accountable for inclusion in the organization, the responsibility for strategy formation and modeling equity comes from senior leadership—which is a top down approach.

Further, creating a culture that values diversity and advances inclusion starts at the top. But leaders have many strategic priorities that compete for their time and attention. As such, diversity and inclusion must be clearly aligned with the organization's overall strategy and presented in a way that is relevant and meaningful.

OVERALL OBJECTIVES AND COMPETENCIES

The purpose of this competency is to secure the right type of support from, and engage, senior level leaders in equity, Diversity and Inclusion efforts.

BACKGROUND AND CONTEXT

Our Nation derives strength from the diversity of its population and from its commitment to equal opportunity for all. We are at our best when we draw on the talents of all parts of our society, and our greatest accomplishments are achieved when diverse perspectives are brought to bear to overcome our greatest challenges.
—President Barack Obama,
Executive Order 13583

Diversity provides an opportunity for each of us to be okay with, and open to, those things that set us apart, such as race, gender, sexual orientation, gender identity, nationality, religion, physical and mental ability, generational differences, language, etc. It also provides a chance for individuals to understand and accept people for who they are.

Nevertheless, the Diversity and Inclusion community has been essentially working in the dark. We do not know which leaders' support is most important or exactly what types of support are most effective. As a result, diversity strategists in some organizations have assumed from the outset that their Diversity and Inclusion performance will be limited because they do not have the visible support of the CEO. Some companies watched premier diversity programs wither in the face of regime change, reorganization, or business downturn; because the engine driving the initiative— the CEO's personal commitment disappeared.

Addressing equity, diversity, and inclusion requires a deeper commitment than most companies have made. Many companies require a few legally focused diversity-training engagements, but this is often ineffective and can be more harmful than good. Recent research suggests that mandatory diversity training that emphasizes legal risk fails to demonstrate senior leadership commitment to diversity and often backfires. It generates a perception that the company is just checking a box to protect itself.

A more effective approach is to make diversity training optional but make it clear that the senior leadership will be participating. For example, if the CEO or other senior leaders attend all the diversity training sessions and actively participate, it sends a very clear message of support for the initiative. However, some companies complain that diversity training is not important enough to warrant senior leadership time; this message is equally compelling.

The C-Suite, Culture, & Cultural Competency

For purposes of this study guide, the C-Suite will be defined as "a widely-used term that collectively refers to an organization's most important senior executives". The C-Suite gets its name because top senior executives' titles tend to start with the letter C, for chief, as in Chief Executive Officer, Chief Operating Officer, Chief Finance Officer, Chief Technology Officer, Chief Human Resources Officer, and Chief Diversity Officer. These individuals are also called "C-level executives". This group may include different variations of the leadership title, such as Chairperson, President, Executive Director, Superintendent, Principal, Managing Director, Governor, or Prime Minister.

The C-suite is considered the most influential group of individuals at an organization. Being a member of this group comes with high-stakes decision making, a more demanding workload, and higher compensation. Essential to the functioning of this group, is creating a culture of inclusion contained in an environment where individual differences and worldviews are respected.

To understand cultural competence, it is important to grasp the full meaning of the word culture. Culture is defined as the shared traditions, beliefs, customs, history, folklore, and institutions of a group of people. Culture includes the characteristics of a particular group of people, defined by everything from language, religion, cuisine, social habits, music, and arts. It is shared by people of the same ethnicity, language, nationality, or religion. It is a system of rules that serve as the basis of what we are and how we express ourselves as part of a group and as individuals.

The following descriptions indicate the most common uses of the word culture around the world. Most senior executives travel frequently and may be familiar with these descriptors.

Western culture
The term Western culture has come to define the shared traditions, beliefs, customs, history, folklore, and institutions of Western European countries, as well as the United States and other nations that have been heavily influenced by Western European immigration. Western culture has its roots in the Classical Period of the Greco-Roman era and the rise of Christianity in the 14th century. Other drivers of Western culture include Latin, Celtic, Germanic and Hellenic ethnic and linguistic groups. Today, the influences of Western culture can be seen in most countries around the world.

Eastern culture
Eastern culture generally refers to the societal norms of countries in Far East Asia (including China, Japan, Vietnam, North Korea, and South Korea) and the Indian subcontinent. Like the West, Eastern culture was heavily influenced by religion during its early development. In general, in Eastern

culture there is less of a distinction between secular society and religious philosophy than there is in the West.

Latin culture
Many of the Spanish-speaking nations are considered part of the Latin culture; the geographic region of the culture is widespread. Latin America is typically defined as those parts of Central America, South America, and Mexico where Spanish or Portuguese are the dominant languages. While Spain and Portugal are on the European continent, they are considered the key influencers of the Latin culture, which denotes people using languages derived from Latin, also known as the Romance languages.

Middle Eastern culture
Countries in the Middle East have some but not all things in common, including a strong belief in Islam. Religion is a very strong pillar of this society and it is embedded in the governance. The Arabic language is also common throughout the region; however, the wide variety of dialects can sometimes make communication difficult.

African culture
The continent of Africa is essentially two cultures—North Africa and Sub-Saharan Africa. The continent is comprised of many tribes, languages, and social groups. One of the key features of this culture is the large number of ethnic groups, some countries can have 20 or more, and the diversity of their beliefs. Northwest Africa has strong ties to Europe and Southwestern Asia. The area also has a heavy Islamic influence and is a major player in the Arab world. The harsh environment has been a large factor in the development of Sub-Saharan African culture, as there are various cuisines, art, and musical styles that have sprung up among the far-flung populations.

Broader Applications
Although culture can refer to different demographics such as race, color, ethnicity, or nationality, culture is **not** limited to an ethnic group.

The term multicultural competence surfaced in a mental health publication by psychologist Paul Pedersen (1988) at least a decade before the term cultural competence became popular. Thus, most of the definitions of cultural competence shared among diversity professionals come from the healthcare industry. This perspective is useful in the broader context of diversity work. Consider the following healthcare definitions for cultural competence:

- A set of congruent behaviors, attitudes and policies that come together as a system, agency or among professionals, and enable that system, agency or those professionals to work effectively in cross-cultural situations.

- Cultural competence requires that organizations have a defined set of values and principles, and demonstrate behaviors, attitudes, policies, and structures that enable them to work effectively cross-culturally.

- Cultural competence is defined simply as the level of knowledge-based skills required to provide effective clinical care to patients from an ethnic or racial group.

- Cultural competence is a developmental process that evolves over an extended period. Both individuals and organizations are at various levels of awareness, knowledge, and skills along the cultural competence continuum.

It is not surprising that the healthcare profession was the first to promote cultural competence. A poor diagnosis due to lack of cultural understanding, for example, can have fatal consequences, especially in medical service delivery. Accordingly, culturally competent health care programs were developed to prevent medical errors and increase access to care for vulnerable populations such as immigrants, refugees, and migrant workers.

We all develop in some type of culture. Our environment determines what we learn, how we learn it, and the rules for living with others. These rules are transmitted from one generation to the next and are often adapted to the time and locale of the communication. Children absorb the rules of the culture as they develop, whether through word-of-mouth or just osmosis.

Organizations have a culture of policies, procedures, programs, and processes, and incorporate certain values, beliefs, assumptions, and customs in its interactions with employees, Board Members, suppliers, agents, shareholders, volunteers, and customers/students/constituents. Within an organizational context, culture is known as *"the way things are done around here"*.

Organizational cultures largely echo mainstream culture in its sense of time orientation, perception, and use of resources. In many cases, an organizational culture may not lend itself to cultural competence, and that is where skill building is necessary. A culturally competent organization brings together knowledge about different groups of people and transforms it into standards, policies, and practices to make everything work well together.

Cultural competence is vitally important in education as well. With the larger population of minorities and racial integration during the 1960s and 1970s, the public-school system in the United States had to grapple with issues of cultural sensitivity as most teachers in public schools came from White, middle class backgrounds. Most of these teachers were educated, English speaking, and primarily from Western European cultures. They often had trouble communicating with speakers of limited English proficiency, let alone people of vastly different value systems and normative behaviors from that of Anglo-European culture. The purpose of training educators in the area of cultural competence was to provide new teachers with the experience and skills necessary to work effectively with children of all backgrounds and social classes.

Within the ranks of police officers, military personnel, and other public service providers, cultural competence is also a necessity. Not only can interactions with diverse cultures lead to life or death situations, but it can also result in a public and community relations fiasco.
Developing cultural competence requires examining biases and prejudices, developing cross-cultural skills, searching for role models, and spending as much time as possible with other people who share a passion for cultural competence. Studies show that new entrants to the workforce, and local communities, increasingly will be people of color, immigrants, and White women because of differential birth rates and immigration patterns. Therefore, cultural competence in every workplace is non-negotiable.

There are many benefits to building an organization's cultural competence,

- *Increasing respect and mutual understanding among those involved.*
- *Increasing creativity in problem-solving through new perspectives, ideas, and strategies.*
- *Decreasing unwanted surprises that might slow progress.*
- *Increasing participation and involvement of other cultural groups.*
- *Increasing trust and cooperation.*

- *Helping to overcome fear of mistakes, competition, or conflict. For instance, by understanding and accepting many cultures, everyone is more likely to feel more comfortable in general and less likely to be fearful of making a mistake when interacting with under-represented groups.*
- *Promoting inclusion and equality.*

EVIDENCE OF THE CEO'S COMMITMENT

From an organizational development perspective, cultural competence may be associated with a diverse culture, or an environment that is open to different ways of getting things done. Hence, diversity **must** be prevalent and valued before one may be considered a culturally competent organization.

Studies suggest multiple obstacles to diversity in C-Suite positions include:

- *Lack of line management experience or career opportunities.*
- *Lack of role models and mentors.*
- *Gender differences in socialization or exclusion from informal networks.*
- *Gender-based stereotypes and tokenism.*
- *The "old-boys network" persisting at the top and in boardrooms.*
- *The pace of work and the necessity to always be "on" or connected*
- *The complexity that comes with a matrixed organization and multiple teams.*
- *Constant travel or demands to relocate.*

Some definitions of cultural competence emphasize the knowledge and skills needed to interact with people of different cultures, while others focus on attitudes. A few definitions attribute cultural competence or a lack thereof to policies and organizations. Executives who are working on this problem should continue to examine the aforementioned factors, treating them as hypotheses to be tested and refined. But we need more thoughtful inquiry into real-world phenomena— without preconceived notions of gender roles and stereotypes—and we need to be open to the idea that there are fundamental differences at play in the workplace, including brain function, evolutionary inheritances, and socialization factors.

The problems that diverse executives and other leaders grapple with concerning the glass ceiling and the retention of diverse talent has less to do with overt discrimination in the corporate suite, dated ideas about limitations, or the mommy track. These problems, and the solutions that we require, have more to do with outdated succession planning and career development systems. And deep down, the solutions concern the pace of work, corporate culture, and the ability to find meaning in the workplace.

Many organizations are focusing on helping women to experience fairness and advancement in the workplace. Typically, women decide to enter the running for the C-suite in their early 40s. At that phase of life, women with children already have a lot on their plates. These women usually are expected to handle the home front. Their children are becoming teens, while their parents and in-laws are aging. No matter how good these executives think they are at multitasking, the mental and emotional pressure is real, and it is constant.

For reasons important to the survival of the species, women in childbearing years undergo changes that intensify their focus on the viability of offspring. It is a passing phenomenon, but ill-timed for those with career ambitions. To expect some women to add the demands of a C-suite role to their plates at this stage in life may not be realistic. Yet, in most organizations, the succession plans pick a cohort as they enter their late 30s and early 40s. Therefore, many high-potential women may opt out because the timing is just wrong.

Organizations have it within their power to create new patterns that work for all employees. If a company is serious about bringing individuals that are more diverse into top management, open the window of promotability wider. Also, when you dangle the brass ring of advancement and someone qualified fails to grab it, do not permanently write that person off. When senior leaders understand these options, they can make better choices.

In order for workplace Diversity and Inclusion efforts to truly be successful within an organization, there must be involvement and commitment from the top. Here are five ways CEOs are demonstrating their commitment to workplace Diversity and Inclusion, as determined by Diversity Best Practices' 2014 benchmarking assessment. The CEO:

1. Embeds D&I into the business growth strategy
More than half of companies (64 percent) that participated in Diversity Best Practices' most recent diversity assessment and benchmarking survey have CEOs who embed Diversity and Inclusion into the business growth strategy.

2. Meets regularly with the D&I executive to review diversity goals and progress
Nearly three quarters (72 percent) of Diversity Best Practices' assessment and benchmarking companies meet regularly with diversity executives to review goals and performance.

3. Requires the D&I executive to report back to him/her with metrics
Almost three-quarters (72 percent) of companies participating in Diversity Best Practices' assessment and benchmarking survey have a CEO who requires diversity executives to report back to her/him on diversity metrics.

4. Provides an annual update on Diversity and Inclusion to the Board of Directors
Nearly eight in 10 companies (72 percent) that participated in Diversity Best Practices' most recent benchmarking and assessment survey have a CEO who provides annual updates on diversity and inclusion to their board of directors.

5. Makes a personal Diversity and Inclusion statement available on corporate website
CEOs at 80 percent of companies participating in Diversity Best Practices' assessment and benchmarking survey made their personal diversity and inclusion statement available on the corporate website and in other corporate materials. Public statements given by an executive level supporter (i.e., the CEO or President) demonstrate a top-down commitment to the organization's diversity and inclusion efforts. Strategically placing the statements on websites and other printed materials, such as brochures and annual reports, are ideal for the success of an initiative.

Examples of Current & Former
Diversity Commitment Statements

Executive Commitment to Diversity and Inclusion at Blue Cross Blue Shield of Kansas City:

At Blue Cross and Blue Shield of Kansas City (Blue KC), we know that success starts with a diverse and inclusive workforce. That's why the Blue KC executive leadership team is committed to ensuring that diversity and inclusion are a part of our everyday business by continually recognizing, respecting and valuing the differences and similarities in our workforce, workplace and marketplace.

Our ability to work effectively as individuals and collectively as teams is a direct reflection of our ongoing dedication, and our award-winning service is based on the unique perspectives of our employees. That is why we as the executive leadership team are truly committed to fostering an inclusive culture through equity, opportunity, and respect.

The Blue KC business philosophy is to leverage diversity and inclusion to meet the complex and ever-changing needs of our employees, partners and the customers we serve. We recognize that diversity and inclusive culture breed opportunities. Therefore, we hold ourselves, management and all individuals at Blue KC accountable for promoting an environment that celebrates the richness of diversity for the benefit of those who entrust us with their health and wellness. We ask that our employees, customers, other local businesses and the KC community join us in our commitment to diversity and inclusion.

-Executive Team, Blue KC

Executive Commitment to Diversity at Microsoft

The collaborative energy that is created when talented people from different backgrounds come together to focus on innovation has helped fuel Microsoft's success for more than 30 years. As we bring our innovations into more and more markets around the world, and as we strive to bridge the digital divide so that people at all levels of society can benefit from the opportunities of the global knowledge economy, we recognize that it's more important than ever to honor diversity, both inside Microsoft and in the communities where we live and work.

- Bill Gates, Microsoft Founder

By providing access to technology, Microsoft strives to help all people realize their potential. This means that diversity and inclusion are not just words on paper for us; they are core values and business imperatives. We promote diversity at every level within our organization and strive for inclusiveness in everything we do. We believe that employing the world's top talent from all groups within our communities—from many backgrounds and with varied experiences—helps us to better serve our customers and gives us a competitive advantage in the global marketplace.

- Steven A. Ballmer, former Microsoft Chief Executive Officer

Diversity and inclusion are part of Microsoft's long-term business strategy. Because our leadership team is deeply committed to this effort, we've developed a comprehensive plan to promote and integrate diversity at every level within our organization and in everything we do as a company. We broadly promote Diversity and Inclusion worldwide by encouraging multicultural perspectives and conversations among key Microsoft publics—current employees, prospective employees, customers and partners. Building the best software means recognizing the diverse needs of our customers and partners—and that is reflected in our employee base around the world.

We also strive to:

- *Understand and value the differences in all parts of the globe;*
- *Respect the values of every culture and country;*
- *Give back to the diverse communities in which we work, live and do business.*

- Bob Muglia, former President, Server and Tools Business

Commitment to Diversity, UC San Diego

Diversity is a defining feature of the State of California, and is a source of innovative ideas, creative accomplishments, and a variety of values and worldviews that arise from differences of culture and life experiences. The University of California strives to reflect this diversity in its students, faculty, and staff. Achieving such diversity is a high institutional priority and is integral to UC San Diego's achievement of academic excellence.

Diversity has an educational, social, economic, political, and ethical value for our university. It enriches the ability of UC San Diego to accomplish its academic mission by broadening and deepening the educational experience through interactions of students and faculty from multiple backgrounds and perspectives. Diversification offers social participation and mutual understanding to all Californians regardless of their heritage, orientation, or situation. It provides equality of access and opportunity so that every segment of society can contribute to and benefit from our economic future. It enlightens and empowers constituencies of all types to engage in our democracy in an increasingly multicultural state, where voters and political leaders are likely to be more supportive of an inclusive, representative, and heterogeneous university. Finally, embracing faculty, students, and staff from all social sectors constitutes a moral obligation in a nation with a long history of unequal treatment of disadvantaged groups. For all these reasons and more, UC San Diego must continue and strengthen its commitment to diversity.

Through the campus Principles of Community, we strive to create a climate of respect, fairness, cooperation, and professionalism and to promote innovation and leadership by utilizing the talents and abilities of all. In creating an environment of equity for all, an effort is made to remove any barriers, which hinder equal opportunity in employment, particularly for those groups who historically have often experienced discrimination in the area of employment. Academic Affairs values diversity, equity, and inclusion as essential ingredients of academic excellence in higher education, and we have established the office of the Vice Chancellor for Equity, Diversity and Inclusion (VC-EDI) to actively advance these values as an institutional priority. The VC-EDI was charged to lead the development of a diversity strategic plan for UC San Diego. This work will be integrated into the overall campus-wide strategic plan and will provide an important foundational element in furthering our academic mission. The VC-EDI also works to develop broad-based partnerships throughout the campus, across the UC system and with external constituents including our local and K-12 communities, donors, industry partners and other supporters.

– Executive Chancellor

Building and sustaining a diverse workforce is not the responsibility of one person in an organization, but rather a shared responsibility. Management must lead by example and make a definite commitment to diversity. Kenneth Blanchard, author of the best-selling book *One Minute Manager*, once said, "There's a difference between interest and commitment. When you're interested in doing something, you do it only when it's convenient. When you're committed to something, you accept no excuses, only results."

Managers need a solid understanding of the various cultures represented on their team to eliminate any stereotypes or preconceptions. Open communication helps team members better understand the unique aspects of various cultures, and prompts discussion as to how these attributes can be incorporated into the work environment.

Boards of directors and senior management teams need to set the tone and ensure that their own behavior aligns with organizational values and missions. An organization's ability to attract, retain, and support diverse employees also reflects the way an organization can approach diversity more broadly – with volunteers, board members and the larger community.

Imagine if the Office of Equity, Diversity, and Inclusion focused on organizational culture versus Political Correctness (PC). What IF we empowered supervisors to handle P.C. and we executed the D&I strategy? What IF we played a role in helping our workforces understand the various cultures that interact with the organization? How would the power structure, and our impact, shift?

A CEO CASE STUDY

(Source: "Great Leaders Who Make the Mix Work" | by Boris Groysberg and Katherine Connolly | The Harvard Business Review, Sept. 2013)

The Role of Personal Experience
A CEO's commitment often arises from his or her own understanding of what it means to be an outsider. Take Andrea Jung of the personal care products firm Avon.

(Note that Jung, like a number of other CEOs they talked with, has stepped down since our interview with her.) Describing her career, she said: "I was often the only woman or Asian sitting around a table of senior executives. I experienced plenty of meetings outside my organization with large groups of executives where people assumed that I couldn't be the boss, even though I was."

MasterCard's CEO, Ajay Banga—a Sikh from India who was hassled in the United States after 9/11—shared something similar: "My passion for diversity comes from the fact that I myself am diverse. There have been a hundred times when I have felt different from other people in the room or in the business. I have a turban and a full beard, and I run a global company—that's not common."

Carlos Ghosn of Nissan Motor Company told how bias had affected his own family. "My mother was one of eight children," he said. "She used to be a very brilliant student, and when the time came to go to college, she wanted to become a doctor. Unfortunately, her mother had to explain to her that there was not enough money in the family, and that the money for college was going to the boys and the girls would instead have to marry. When I was a kid and my mother was telling me this story—without any bitterness, by the way, just matter-of-fact—I was outraged because it was my mother. After hearing that story, I said I would never do anything to hurt someone based on segregation."

To Ghosn, gender bias is a personal affront. "When I see that women do not have the same opportunities as men, it touches me in a personal way," he said. "I think it's refusal related to my sisters or to my daughters."

Even White male CEOs had stories to share. Kentucky native Jim Rogers of the electric-utility holding company Duke Energy felt like an outsider at the start of his career. "When I went to Washington to be a lawyer, I felt like I had to work harder, be better, and prove myself because I had a southern accent and came from a rural state," he said. The self-awareness, insight, and empathy that Rogers and other chief executives acquired from personal experience have clearly shaped their attitudes toward diversity and inclusion and informed their priorities as leaders.

Persistent Institutional Barriers

The CEOs were generally disappointed with the lack of progress on diversity in the C-suite. While several women have risen through the ranks to become leaders of multibillion-dollar corporations, the statistics are grim overall. Only 4% of companies on the 2013 Fortune 500 list are led by female CEOs. As Banga acknowledged, "That's more than what it used to be 20 years ago, but it's nowhere near where it should be." The disparity also persists in other senior leadership positions and on boards. Ken Frazier of Merck offered a harsher assessment: "I think that the progress of women in the last two decades has been so limited, so slow, so inadequate, that it would defy even the most skeptical people from 20 years ago."

We asked the CEOs what they perceived to be the greatest obstacles to women's advancement in their own companies and industries. Although there's no one truth about what holds women back, the leaders we spoke with offered candid views based on years of observation.

If there's a single barrier that affects all women, it's exclusion from networks and conversations that open doors to further development and promotion, according to seven of the CEOs. Woods Staton of Arcos Dorados, the largest operator of McDonald's restaurants in Latin America, defined the offending mechanism as "social cliquishness," a pattern of interaction in which men seek out the company of other men and ignore women. "The men come out of a meeting, hang out with each other, and then go out at night for drinks," Staton explained. "It's subtle discrimination, and it's difficult to work around." Barry Salzberg of the professional services firm Deloitte described this pattern as a tangible, negative consequence of "the old boys' network."

Frazier went so far as to say, "I'm an African-American, and I've worked in the business world all my life, and I believe very strongly that whatever barriers race presents in the workforce, they pale in comparison to the barriers that women face when creating the close mentoring relationships that are necessary to be promoted." We find that this kind of discrimination is often unintended, unconscious, and embedded in a company's culture.

The CEOs also reported that the contributions of women are often underappreciated. As an example, Jim Turley of Ernst & Young described an incident when he himself was called out: "I like to facilitate our board discussions by getting right into the more contentious points, and we were having a discussion around a particular topic. Three women on the board made individual comments that were similar in direction, which I didn't respond to. Not long after they spoke, a fourth person, who happened to be a man, made a comment in line with what the women had been saying, and I picked up on his comment. I said, 'I think Jeff's got it right,' not even aware of what I had just done. To their great credit, the women didn't embarrass me publicly. They pulled me to the side, and they said, 'Jim, we know you didn't mean for this to be the way it was received, but this is what happened.' They played it back to me, and they said that that's what happens to women throughout their careers. It was a learning moment for me."

Clearly, even leaders passionate about building inclusive cultures can inadvertently allow unconscious biases to shape their behavior.

Five of the CEOs asserted that unexamined assumptions also constrained women's chances to progress. As Frazier explained, "If a job requires a woman to travel a lot, sometimes people decide preemptively that she's got a young child at home—this won't be something she's interested in." Double standards can also trip up women in line for promotions, as when characteristics prized in male leaders are viewed as negative qualities in women. "When men come into the environment and they're tough, they're perceived as strong business leaders," said Block. "When women come in and they're tough, it's not always as valued."

Geographic immobility due to family constraints was another problem, mentioned by three of the CEOs. "People often require geographic mobility to get the appropriate amount of exposure to the various aspects of the business that they need to understand," Randall Stephenson of AT&T noted.

"As managers mature, we observe that some female managers get to a place where they want to begin families, or their spouse also works, which makes them less inclined to move and physically relocate their families." Jung concurred: "In my experience, where part of career development and part of talent management was getting a 'global passport' stamped, one of the barriers for women could have been mobility. I saw that beyond the opportunity for the individual, we also had to try to create all of the opportunities necessary to make sure the whole family could in fact move."

Another three CEOs cited insufficient support for women who were rejoining the workforce after taking time off to raise children. Any organization that hopes to encourage women to succeed needs to address that, noted Rogers. "If a woman is pregnant and leaves, you must have the flexibility to allow her to do that but not lose her place or her momentum," he said.

Unsurprisingly, five CEOs brought up barriers related to childbearing and child rearing, and six mentioned a lack of flexible work hours. They observed that the push-and-pull between work and family, though increasingly an issue for men too, remains predominantly a barrier for women. George Chavel of Sodexo North America drove home that point, asking, "Why should women have to be superhuman, have these reputations of 'They can do it all,' and make these major sacrifices, and men don't have those kinds of expectations placed on them?"

Do Women Lead Differently?
Eight of the CEOs perceived a distinction between male and female leadership styles. Though social scientists may not agree with their take on things, the CEOs said that women were less political, less likely to define themselves by their careers, more collaborative, better listeners, more relationship-oriented, and more empathetic and reasonable. We also heard that women were more likely to focus on completing the job at hand and to neglect to position themselves for recognition or promotion, while men were more apt to seek attention.

This tendency not to assert themselves could hold women back. George Halvorson of the California-based managed-care consortium Kaiser Permanente explained the problem this way: "There are cultural barriers, in that leaders who are looking for the next generation of leaders, for the people to promote, are less likely to see and understand the capable women that they have in their shop, probably because the male style tends to focus more on being in the spotlight, and the female style tends to focus more on bringing people together to get things done. The very thing that makes the best female leaders very successful also makes them less visible, and that's an incredibly important distinction. A good leader knows to look for things that have gone really well and then drills down to find the person who really did it, as opposed to just looking for whoever has a lot of accolades and did the dance."

But some differences in leadership style can work to women's advantage, said several CEOs. "When you've got a complex project involving multiple layers, you need a leader who is collaborative, and more often than not I have found that leader to be a woman," said Halvorson.

What Is an Inclusive Culture?
Resoundingly, the CEOs agreed on what an inclusive culture meant for their organizations. They defined it as one in which employees can contribute to the success of the company as their authentic selves, while the organization respects and leverages their talents and gives them a sense of connectedness. "In inclusive culture employees know that, irrespective of gender, race, creed, sexual orientation, and physical ability, you can fulfill your personal objectives by aligning them with the company's, have a rich career, and be valued as an individual. You are valued for how you contribute to the business," said David Thodey of Telstra, the Australian telecommunications firm.

Brad Wilson of Blue Cross and Blue Shield of North Carolina described an inclusive workplace as "one where all who come with the professional skills sufficient to perform the requirements of the job feel welcome, supported, and rewarded, and are inspired to succeed based on their ability." That's similar to the point that John Rowe of Exelon, a U.S. energy producer and distributor, made when he noted that a culture of mutual respect helps his company address the complexities of its business. "A big organization needs only a few generals and a lot of sergeants," he said. "The sergeants deserve respect too."

Some CEOs observed that the proof is not only in how individual employees feel about opportunities for growth but also in how teams operate, and decisions are made. "In an inclusive culture, we create and support heterogeneous teams," said Chavel. "They may take longer to make decisions than homogeneous teams, but it's worth the investment because their decisions will be better informed." To these CEOs, inclusiveness is not merely a matter of the composition of the organization or of teams (though such metrics can be helpful); it also has to do with how people relate to one another. "Board diversity is necessary, but if you just walk away after you have it, you may not get the outcomes you want," said Steve Voigt of King Arthur Flour, a company where women account for three of eight board members and three of six senior executives. "You really have to manage it, grow it, and educate around it."

Practices That Make the Difference
Turley drew an important distinction: "Diversity itself is about the mix of people you have, and creating an inclusive culture is about making that mix work." HBR asked the CEOs which of their organizations' practices had been most effective at harnessing diversity.

Here's what they said:

1. Measure Diversity and Inclusion.
The CEOs agreed that metrics are key because, as we know, what gets measured gets done. Bank of America, for example, puts questions about diversity and inclusiveness into its biannual employee engagement survey and compares the results for any team that gets at least seven responses against those of a normative group of companies.

"We've also built a diversity-and-inclusion index that tells us if people here feel they are treated fairly and to help us ensure that people of diverse backgrounds can succeed at Bank of America," said Moynihan. "With this data, each team can have a dialogue to determine what we're doing well and what we can improve to make Bank of America a better place to work."

2. Hold managers accountable.
Merck, Nissan, General Mills, Telstra, and ABB North America are among the many organizations that make diversity and inclusion goals part of their managers' performance objectives. "Each of my direct reports has things that they're going to do personally to help promote diversity, not things that they can assign to their team," explained Moynihan. "I say, 'What are *you* going to do to get involved?' For example, they can mentor somebody individually or sponsor diversity events." AT&T takes a different approach. "We benchmark

diversity objectives at the senior levels of management, and we have regular meetings around my table about how we're advancing," said Stephenson. "A portion of our officers' compensation is based on achieving those objectives." Many CEOs also reported that managers who embraced diversity were more likely to be considered for promotion at their companies.

In some organizations a favorable attitude toward diversity even determines whether an employee is viewed as a good fit for the organization. "We really have challenges when the leadership group is not diverse, and they don't get it. And so you have to educate them—and if they still don't get it, I let them go," said Tim Solso of the engine manufacturer Cummins.

He elaborated: "We hit a serious downturn in the second half of 2000 through the first half of 2003. I mean, we were on the brink as a company, but I didn't back off on diversity. One of the senior officers basically said to another officer, 'Why doesn't Solso get off this diversity stuff? We need to save the company.' I fired him. It was well known why he was fired. After that, people either got it or didn't talk that way."

3. Support flexible work arrangements.
Many of the CEOs reported that their organizations offered benefits that helped employees balance their professional and personal commitments—such as flexible hours, on-site child care, and onboarding support after a leave of absence. Ken Powell of the U.S. food processor General Mills explained his company's efforts this way: "I've had officers at General Mills say to me, 'I realize that I'm one of several people who could be the brand manager for Cheerios, but I'm the only person who can be the mother to my children.' While some of those women make the decision to leave the company—sometimes permanently—we've learned that we can retain many of them by providing greater flexibility during those hectic childbearing years."

At Sodexo North America, Chavel and his leadership team have made work/life balance a personal matter. "Although the job is 24/7, I try to send the message that I'm open and receptive to any kind of flexible arrangement," Chavel said. "For example, I will end a meeting early to get to one of my sons' athletic events or travel somewhere for a family commitment."

4. Recruit and promote from diverse pools of candidates.
Workforce diversity begins with the search for talent. At General Mills, Powell's leadership team tracks metrics during and after the hiring process. "From the beginning, we're looking at the composition of the pool of candidates that we interview on campus, because that's an important early indicator," Powell told us. "Then we look at the composition of the group of people we hire in any given year. We track the retention rate for different groups, such as women or African-Americans. Even interns. At what rate are they leaving? At what rate are they getting promoted? What percentage advances to each level in the company? Our metrics help us diagnose and understand what's going on—enabling us to develop action plans to address any issues we see. It's important, and that's why I review those metrics myself on a quarterly basis."

Ghosn has taken a different approach at Nissan in Japan, where women are strikingly underrepresented in management ranks. "We've implemented quotas in hiring, particularly in the populations where there are fewer women—like engineering—and we make sure that in the succession plans of the company we always have a specific number of female candidates," he explained. "This forces management to identify women in their own ranks or to hire more women. So, when it comes time for promotions, we have a diverse group of candidates from which we can choose. I believe quotas are a great way of advancing diversity, particularly when you have a long way to go and you don't want to wait forever. After a company attains a certain level of diversity, I think quotas lose their effectiveness. But when you're moving from 1% female managers to 5%, if you don't enforce a quota, it's going to take forever to reach that number."

Owing in part to this strategy, the representation of women in Nissan's management has increased three times as fast as the average rate in Japan over the past decade.

5. Provide leadership education.
Another key practice is providing leadership development opportunities for women at the lower levels of the organization, which tend to be more diverse. Bloomberg described Discovery Health's CEO Program like this: "It's a brilliant two-year program which involves candidates in intensive internal and external training, significant exposure to senior executives, and travel to the U.S. to do a course at Duke. It includes external candidates and young candidates from previously disadvantaged backgrounds already in the company. It's a big financial investment for us, but we've been able to add quite a lot of muscle to our recruitment capacity and also invest significantly in the more rapid advancement of existing internal candidates."

And Johnson & Johnson's Bill Weldon noted that diversity training cannot be hived off from the rest of the operation. It has to be woven into the culture. "About 10 years ago one of the women's leadership initiative programs was being held across the street, and I asked the people running it if I could go to the program," he recalled. "They said no. I asked why not, and they said I couldn't go because I was a man. My response was that that may be the problem—you have to broaden it beyond women. We evolve and learn and grow to make sure we're capturing not just the people involved but the views of the whole community."

Needless to say, companies should also offer their high-potential employees opportunities for external education and development. But according to Harvard Business School, only 23% of participants in executive education programs on the Boston campus in 2012 were women. Companies also need to invest in women-only leadership development programs and in educating both men and women about subtle gender biases and how they manifest themselves in firms.

6. Sponsor employee resource groups and mentoring programs.
Several of the CEOs' companies offered less structured professional development opportunities to various subgroups of employees. One approach is employee resource groups, or networks of employees who share an affiliation (such as women, ethnic minorities, or young professionals). Angela Braly of the U.S. managed-care firm WellPoint underlined the importance of leveraging such groups in substantive ways. "I visit each group twice a year and give them real assignments," she said. "I am very clear about my expectation that they will have a real impact on the business."

Companies must also invest in these groups, according to Banga. "Here at MasterCard we have many business resource groups, or BRGs," he said. "We have women's leadership networks, a YoPro group for young professionals, a group for employees of African descent, a pride community, a Latino community, and an 'East' community for Asian employees. Each BRG has a business sponsor, who's normally a direct report of mine. We do a ton of things with them, from employee-networking events to multicultural summits to a women's forum for which we get outside speakers as well as panels comprised of me and members of my board."

7. Offer quality role models.
It's no surprise that diversity at the top promotes diversity throughout an organization. A varied array of leaders signals an organizational commitment to diversity and also provides emerging leaders with role models they can identify with. Several of the CEOs, including those from Kaiser Permanente, Sodexo North America, King Arthur Flour, Duke Energy, and Cummins, said that putting women in leadership roles was key to attracting, retaining, and developing other female talent.

Rogers described how Duke did this: "This historically has been a man's industry. So, early on, we worked to move a woman into a plant manager position. That set an example. You have to be intentional and make sure you populate your organization with leaders who represent diversity. That creates an environment that allows those with diverse backgrounds to say, 'If they can, I can.' That is a very important feeling that needs to be embedded in the people in the company."

As for individualized employee development, many CEOs cited the importance of mentorship and sponsorship opportunities. Ohlsson explained IKEA's unique approach to mentorship this way: "We have a grandfathering/grandmothering principle at IKEA—that is to say that a hiring boss has to have another manager say yes to a candidate before that person can be hired. Two people then share the responsibility for the development of that individual." Such double sponsorship increases the likelihood that talented employees of any background will feel supported and stay with the company.

But Halvorson warned against tokenism—the practice of putting people into jobs because of their classification, not their ability. "If you put someone in place who fits a certain category but doesn't have the skill set needed to do the job, then you basically set the whole agenda back significantly," he said. "My sense is to hire stars, and the constellation is far more effective if it's a diverse constellation."

8. Make the Chief Diversity Officer position count.
As this relatively new role proliferates across industries, CEOs must decide how to maximize its effectiveness. At the time of his interview, Enrique Santacana of ABB North America had just received approval from the firm's North America Executive Committee to create a chief diversity and inclusion officer position, reporting directly to him. "We want to make sure that people understand that it has full support from the top, and it's not just a communications message that goes out there with no follow-up," he explained. "It institutionalizes the process and the intent, and it establishes a formal means by which we will develop programs as well as metrics, so that we can track our progress."

> *Lead by Example*
> Once the vision of an inclusive culture has been articulated and best practices have been put in place, what is the CEO's daily contribution to seeing that the vision becomes a reality? Nearly half the CEOs said their most important role was to set the tone for the organization's culture by demonstrating a commitment to inclusion.
>
> Perhaps the most meaningful way to do that is by dedicating time to work personally on diversity and inclusion initiatives. A quarter of the CEOs we interviewed mentioned direct involvement with diversity programs, such as meeting regularly with employee resource groups and diversity councils. Banga, Moynihan, and Thodey even chair diversity and inclusion councils themselves. By pointing the way, CEOs will help their organizations attract and develop the best, most diverse talent, giving them the edge they need to succeed.

Companies with the most successful records on diversity and inclusion tend to share the following characteristics:

- *The organization's statement of values explicitly includes diversity and inclusion (as opposed to "respect for individuals" or other more general statements).*
- *The CEO is held responsible by the non-executive Board of Directors (the Board) for the company's diversity initiative and his/her compensation is linked to diversity performance.*
- *The Board itself is ethnically and nationally diverse.*
- *The Board reviews the diversity of high potential pools and succession slates.*
- *The CEO talks frequently to his/her direct reports (the Executive Committee) about diversity, demands regular reports from them on the progress of diversity initiatives, and holds them accountable for both their personal behavior and for meeting objectives such as developing and mentoring diverse people.*
- *Managers are trained to recognize "micro-inequities" and "micro-aggressions".*
- *Many companies have created special marketing strategies and performance goals for diverse market segments (e.g., women, racial/ethnic minorities, specific regions or countries).*

Too often, leaders are motivated to seek diversity measures simply to avoid discrimination lawsuits that can occur if employees believe an organization has not complied with EEOC regulations. To protect against such legal fallout, a leader may require cultural awareness programs in which employees are trained to avoid problems such as insensitivity, stereotypes, prejudice, and labeling. Developing awareness is a fundamental step in managing diversity. Sociologists who studied company managers concluded that the best practices in an organization create a sense of responsibility through a comprehensive strategy that includes affirmative action plans, diverse staff, and diversity task forces.

Leaders should create and maintain environments where diverse groups of people are integrated into the overall cultural context of an organization. Challenges such as intolerance, discrimination, segregation, and bias are not always avoidable. However, diversity prospers when every person in an organization feels affirmed. Organizational leaders can capitalize on diversity by ensuring that inclusion initiatives are a central part of planning and not just peripheral activities. While leaders may be key players in structuring a diverse workforce, the people they lead can enhance their effectiveness, which is why leaders must ensure that their employees have a genuine interest and commitment to establishing an inclusive environment. Mutual accountability helps leaders make positive strides in diversifying their organizations.

COACHING, MENTORING & SPONSORSHIP

Talent retention is one of the most important goals for CEOs and other senior level executives. More companies are striving to retain their high performers who drive their organization's performance, productivity, and profitability. One of the most fundamental ways you can retain and develop diverse and/or talented employees is through a timely performance planning and evaluation process.

Performance evaluations serve as the foundation for goal setting, performance measurement, and talent development. Goals are set successfully when the employee and manager have a shared understanding of the objectives, behaviors and competencies necessary to execute the goals—as well as the performance measures that assess whether the goals were achieved.

Coaching vs. Mentoring
The performance evaluation process also provides an excellent opportunity for coaching—a key role of managers. The "manager as coach" arrangement pays huge dividends because it helps employees set the direction for their careers. It gives both employees and managers time to communicate their expectations and concerns. It fosters employee motivation and commitment, as well as provides your organization with an opportunity to revise performance-development goals.

Often, managers and employees believe that coaching and feedback takes place only when performance is lagging. Certainly, when performance does not meet expectations, employees need specific constructive feedback to improve their performance. However, coaching should support all types of employee performance. When an employee's work meets or exceeds expectations, managers should recognize high performance and give feedback that helps them to understand why their accomplishment is outstanding.

Accordingly, managers play an instrumental role in driving the performance evaluation process. The only way employees will understand that they are meeting certain standards is through specific and timely feedback from their managers. Employees want to know that what they are contributing and what they are being held accountable for has value. If rewards are not tied to performance, employees will not continue to perform effectively over the long term and will seek opportunities outside your organization.

Managers must play a role in driving employee engagement and performance. A great way to do this is through mentoring. Mentoring is different from coaching.

Differences between Mentoring and Coaching		
	Mentor	**Coach**
Focus	Individual	Performance
Role	Facilitator with no agenda	Specific agenda
Relationship	Self-selecting	Comes with the job
Source of influence	Perceived value	Position
Personal returns	Affirmation/learning	Teamwork/performance
Arena	Life	Task related

Mentors are typically selected through a couple of processes—a formal mentoring program or via an informal relationship. A mentor focuses on the protégé, his or her career, and their plan for individual growth and maturity. Alternatively, the coach is job-focused and performance oriented.

A mentor can give advice with the protégé free to select what they choose to do with the information. The context does not have specific performance objectives. A coach is trying to direct a person to some end result; the person may choose how to get there, but the coach is strategically assessing and monitoring the progress and giving advice for effectiveness and efficiency.

Essentially, mentoring is biased to the advantage of the mentee. Coaching is impartial, focused on improvement in behavior. In summary, the mentor has a deep personal interest or personal involvement—such as a friend who cares about the mentee and their long-term development. The coach develops specific skills for the task, challenges and performance expectations at work.

Role
Mentoring is a power-free, mutually beneficial relationship. Mentors are facilitators and teachers allowing the protégé to discover their own direction.
A coach has a set agenda to reinforce or change skills and behaviors. The coach has an objective/goal for each discussion. From an employee perspective, the top four words chosen to best describe a mentor's dominant style were—friend/confidant, direct, logical, questioner.

Relationship
Even in formal mentoring programs, the protégé and mentor have choices—to continue, how long, how often, and the focus. Self-selection is the rule in informal mentoring relationships with the protégé initiating and actively maintaining the relationship. If I'm your mentor, you probably picked me. Coaching comes with the job—it is a defined competency for managers and leaders.

Source of influence
Interpersonal skills will determine the level of effectiveness and influence for both the coach and mentor. The coach also has an implied or actual level of authority by nature of their position—ultimately, they can insist on compliance. A mentor's influence is proportionate to the perceived value they can bring to the relationship. It is a power-free relationship based on mutual respect and value for both mentor and protégé. Your job description might contain "coach", or you might even have that job title—it is just a label or expectation. "Mentor" is a reputation that has to be personally earned; you are not a mentor until the protégé says you are.

Return
The coach's returns are in the form of more team harmony and better job performance. Conversely, the mentoring relationship is reciprocal; the mentor learns from the feedback and insights of the protégé.

To ensure that you have an effective mentoring program, take the following steps:

1. *Clarify objectives.* An effective mentoring program supplements coaching from managers, and it should be positioned as a way to make the organization, not just the individual employees, more successful. From there, you can add a more specific goal, such as helping new employees get up to speed quickly.

2. *Define mentoring selection criteria.* Mentors need to be more than willing. They need to have a coaching attitude and ability. Mentors will need these characteristics and other traits, such as particular business knowledge or specific skills.

3. *Equip other mentors.* Provide tools and training to help mentors fulfill their role. This process goes beyond basic coaching skills to include an emphasis on:

   - Individualized partnerships. "Do unto others as you would have others do unto you" may serve people well most of the time, but it can actually get in the way of successful mentoring. Effective mentors understand their individual mentees' needs and work with everyone differently. What works great for one person can derail another. It is best to use the Platinum Rule of Diversity: Treat others the way they want to be treated.

   - Career coaching. Although employees may look to their mentors for career "navigation" advice, research indicates that few protégé's are clear on what is important to them. Mentors need to help people get behind the core values that create job satisfaction for them. What do they like to do and why? What would enrich their work each day? Only then can mentors help employees create a plan for professional development, career progression, or job enrichment.

Reinforce mentoring

To reap the benefits that mentors provide, executives need to make mentoring a way of life. Senior leaders must be role models and discuss with employees the impact that mentoring has on business and personal success.

The more a leader mentors, the more successful their mentoring becomes. A virtuous cycle may be created: They believe in mentoring, they have seen how it works, and they are motivated to build their own competence.

In addition, do not forget to factor in accountability, metrics, and recognition systems. Without these, mentoring can fall by the wayside instead of remaining a core strategy for building an engaged workforce and thriving business.

For many years, organizations thought of mentoring only as a tool to help women and people of color. Mentoring lacked widespread support within most organizations because it was wrongly viewed as a remedial program. Mentoring can be of great value to women and people of color. These employees have often been disenfranchised within organizations and have not been "chosen" by informal mentors.

Nevertheless, if mentoring is to be successful as a tool for empowering employees, it needs to be truly diverse—representing everyone within the organization and not just women and people of color. By including the broadest spectrum of people, mentoring offers everyone the opportunity to grow professionally and personally without regard to gender or race. A successful mentoring program needs to balance the need for inclusion with the need for fair representation.

Engaging an Executive Sponsor

An executive sponsor is a C-level administrator who has a vested interest in seeing a project to completion. An executive sponsor can be useful in succession planning efforts, Employee Resource Groups (ERG), and other key D&I initiatives.

For example, in an ERG, the executive sponsor fills an important and multi-faceted role. He or she alternates between coach and tiebreaker, advocate and adversary. Additionally, he or she can clearly proselytize the value of equity, diversity, and inclusion to the business. A 2005 research study reported that project success rates were proportional to the organization's sponsorship capabilities. Unfortunately, the combination of fuzzy role definitions and the misinterpretation of priorities mean that more often than not, executive sponsors do not measure up.

You have doubtlessly seen an ivory tower manager somewhere in your company. This is the supervisor who never leaves his or her office, and sometimes shuts the door to avoid interruptions.

In this case, the acronym MBWA does not mean, "management by walking around," but "management by *waiting* around". If no one walks through the doorway or schedules a meeting, it is all good.

This type of figurehead may agree to be an executive sponsor. Regrettably, this person will do little to support Diversity and Inclusion efforts by sponsoring exactly what is requested—no more, no less. If the ERG initiative is successful, this individual will be proud to represent it at the next executive management meeting off site. If the initiative fails, he/she will point an index finger in the direction of the D&I leader. Then he/she will close the door and hide behind the undeserved title that invited the sponsorship request in the first place—until the next sponsorship opportunity rolls around.

Generally, there is no rulebook for executive sponsors; therefore, each sponsor must personify the role as he or she sees it. The executive sponsor is most likely adding the role to an already full plate. Thus, he or she must be comfortable with the additional time demands. Additionally, Diversity and Inclusion practitioners should understand how the potential sponsor operates in crisis mode in the event that a problem arises.

With most Diversity and Inclusion initiatives, there is an executive at a high enough level to envision the desired outcome and make it happen. He or she has the energy to propel things forward, the organizational authority to get people to listen, the passion to evangelize the benefits, and the time management skills to participate at the level needed. In this role, he or she performs a service to the project and to the company by setting an example of good project sponsorship and solid leadership.

Of course, the best way to choose an executive sponsor is not to choose one at all, but for the sponsor to self-select. The second-best sponsors are those who vet the role that is requested of them. They ask what needs to be done, decide whether they could contribute, and inherently know that they will be effective before saying yes.

Ideally, each ERG would have an Executive Sponsor. This helps ensure senior management accountability for Diversity and Inclusion objectives, and it is a good way for executives to maintain visible support of equity efforts. The role of Executive Sponsor can be for a term (e.g., for one year) and/or the position can rotate—giving senior executives an opportunity to learn about multiple facets of diversity as well as absorb employee concerns and objectives. From the employee perspective, it provides an opportunity to build relationships with senior level executives and stay focused on organizational objectives.

Today, securing Executive and Leadership support for ERG's is no longer the challenge. The biggest challenge is overcoming the passive resistance exhibited by business-unit leaders and middle managers during program execution. Leaders often tend to withhold support of initiatives perceived to be a distraction or are perceived to be less important than other drivers of productivity and goal achievement. However, by establishing a clear and measurable approach, it often becomes illogical for leaders to withhold their support as they come to realize the real potential to enhance key business drivers that Employee Resource Groups can provide. Again, this is where Executive Sponsors can play a key role in garnering support by, and making a connection to, mid-level managers and business unit leaders.

Besides resource groups, executives can serve as sponsors for:

- Succession planning
- Research initiatives such as culture climate surveys, White papers, reports, etc.
- Supplier diversity efforts
- Diversity and inclusion training
- Work-Life Programs such as pay-equity efforts, new parental leave policies, etc.

The key to engaging an executive sponsor is not to assume that they know what to do. We may have to explain what is expected of them, as well as discuss the scope of the role. Executive sponsors can be the key to providing the right amount of exposure for your D&I work, while at the same time, building the cultural competence of your C-Suite.

References:

Elder, Jeff. *Expanding Diversity Requires Executive Commitment, Speakers Say.* Wall Street Journal, Dec. 2014. Retrieved from: http://blogs.wsj.com/digits/2014/12/10/expanding-diversity-requires-executive-commitment-speakers-say/

Diversity Best Practices. *Top Five Ways CEOs Show Commitment to Diversity.* Retrieved from: http://www.diversitybestpractices.com/events/top-five-ways-ceos-show-commitment-diversity?pnid=7880

Groyberg, Boris and Connolly, Katherine. *Great Leaders Who Make the Mix Work.* Harvard Business Review, Sept. 2013. Retrieved from: https://hbr.org/2013/09/great-leaders-who-make-the-mix-w

Sample Test Questions:

EXECUTIVE COMMITMENT & SPONSORSHIP

1. **Individuals in the C-Suite are an organization's:**
   A. Most important executives
   B. Culture & ethics workgroup
   C. Cohort of "fast-track" leaders

2. **Diverse executives grapple with glass ceilings and retention issues because of:**
   A. Dated ideas about limitations
   B. Outdated succession planning systems
   C. Overt discrimination in the C-Suite

3. **The difference between diversity and cultural competence is that diversity is a broad mix of different people and cultural competence is:**
   A. The process of including under-represented groups in employment opportunities
   B. The ability to effectively interact with people from different cultures
   C. A quota system designed to stimulate equity and fairness in the workplace

4. **The term "C-Suite" includes all of the following EXCEPT:**
   A. Front-line managers
   B. Superintendents
   C. Prime Ministers

5. **Use of the word "culture" should be limited to ethnic groups.**
   A. True
   B. False

6. **According to Diversity Best Practices' 2014 benchmarking assessment, all of the following are ways that a CEO can show support for D&I EXCEPT:**
   A. Meeting regularly with the Diversity Officer to review goals and progress
   B. Making a personal statement about equity, diversity and inclusion
   C. Assigning complete responsibility for D&I to a Chief Diversity Officer

7. **In "Great Leaders Who Make the Mix Work", if a company requires a global passport for career development, this could cause a mobility barrier for executives who are:**
   A. Disabled
   B. Aging
   C. Females

Sample Test Questions:

EXECUTIVE COMMITMENT & SPONSORSHIP (cont'd)

8. **While intolerance, discrimination, segregation, and bias are not always avoidable, diversity can prosper when:**
   A. Inclusion is a peripheral component of the company
   B. The Board of Directors prioritize Equity & Inclusion goals
   C. Every person in the organization feels affirmed

9. **These individuals drive an organization's performance, productivity, and profitability:**
   A. High performers
   B. Front line supervisors
   C. Board of Directors

10. **The difference between a mentor and a coach is that a mentor:**
    A. Was formally asked to serve in that role
    B. Has a set agenda to change behaviors
    C. Comes with a position in management

11. **Instead of being a core strategy for engagement, mentoring can fall by the wayside if:**
    A. Managers focus only on coaching
    B. Accountability and metrics are missing
    C. It is not included in the succession plan

12. **An executive sponsor is a C-level administrator who may have a vested interest in:**
    A. Talented employees who are females or people of color
    B. Ensuring a project is executed and measured properly
    C. Strategic equity, diversity and inclusion planning

13. **This serves as the foundation for goal setting, performance measurement, and talent development:**
    A. Strategic Planning
    B. Succession Planning
    C. Performance Evaluations

STRATEGIC PURPOSE & PARTNERSHIPS

The ability to strategically partner across disciplines requires personal awareness, collaboration, and motivational skills. However, most Diversity and Inclusion leaders marginalize their inability to galvanize support and believe that they can push a D&I agenda without internal and/or external corroboration. This is a faulty and dangerous assumption, and it should be avoided at all costs.

OVERALL OBJECTIVES AND COMPETENCIES

This competency is designed to help diversity leaders assemble strategic and mission-centered teams, as well as build relationships with division leaders, mid-level managers, resource groups, and community partners.

BACKGROUND AND CONTEXT

According to Annie McKee, educator, author, and founder of the Teleos Leadership Institute, "We know from research (and common sense) that people who understand and manage their own and others' emotions make better leaders. They are able to deal with stress, overcome obstacles, and inspire others to work toward collective goals. They manage conflict with less fallout and build stronger teams; and they are generally happier at work. However, far too many managers lack basic self-awareness and social skills. They do not recognize the impact of their own feelings and moods. They are less adaptable than they need to be in today's fast-paced world. And they don't demonstrate basic empathy for others: they don't understand people's needs, which means they are unable to meet those needs or inspire people to act."

Your ability to inspire others to act lies at the heart of partnering across disciplines. This means that strong communication skills, the ability to resolve real or perceived conflicts, build bridges, and assemble a powerful group of individuals are essential. In other words, you must form a cross-functional team.

A cross-functional team is a group of people with different functional expertise working toward a common goal. The team may include people from finance, marketing, operations, and human resources departments. Typically, it includes employees from all levels of an organization, and may consists of members from outside the organization (in particular, from diverse suppliers, key customers, and/or consultants).

Cross-functional teams often operate as self-directed teams assigned to a specific task, which calls for the input and expertise of numerous departments. Assigning a task to a team comprised of multi-disciplinary individuals increases the level of creativity and out of the box thinking. Each member offers an alternative perspective to the problem and a potential solution to the task at hand. In business, innovation is a leading competitive advantage, and cross-functional teams promote innovation through the creative collaboration process. Members of a cross-functional team must be well-versed in multi-tasking as they are simultaneously responsible for their cross-functional team duties as well as their normal day-to-day work tasks.

Cross-functional teams can be likened to a board of directors or advisory council. In the D&I space, a cross functional team can exist in the form of a Diversity Task Force, Diversity Council/Committee, or Resource Group. This is where a group of qualified individuals of various backgrounds and disciplines are assembled to collaborate in an efficient manner in order to better the organization or solve a problem. Decision making within the team may depend on consensus, but often is led by a team leader (who, for purposes of this guide, may be the Diversity & Inclusion Officer, Diversity Council Chairperson, Resource Group President or Vice President, etc.).

Leadership can be a significant challenge with cross-functional teams because leaders must transform different variations of input into one cohesive final output. Nevertheless, employing cross-functional teams will influence Diversity and Inclusion decision-making, engagement, and outcomes. In particular, D&I leaders can expect to observe the following:

- **Fewer Unidirectional Objectives**
  Instead of all of the decisions and objectives originating from the Office of Diversity, intra-team dynamics will allow these processes to become multi-directional rather than hierarchical.

- **Greater Scope of Information**
  An inherent benefit of a cross-functional team is the breadth of knowledge brought to the group by each member. Each team member is a representative of a department and therefore can leverage their familiarity with accessing and providing knowledge of that department for the team. This increases the efficiency of a cross-functional team by reducing time spent gathering information.

- **Broader Appeal to Employees**
  Modern D&I efforts lack middlemen, or laymen, to combine, sort, and prioritize the data. The cross-functional team, however, is a game-changer.

  Technical, financial, marketing, and all other types of information will come in a form that all members of a cross-functional team can understand. This involves reducing the amount of specialized jargon, sorting information based on importance, hiding complex statistical procedures from the employees, interpreting results, and providing clear explanations of difficult issues.

Hence, instead of relying solely on an endorsement from the President or CEO, D&I leaders must prioritize striving for cross-functional support and teamwork. This will allow the Office of Diversity to conserve resources, create more effective interventions, and demonstrate better results. The process of forming a diverse work team, however, may inevitably produce conflict.

HOW TO HANDLE CONFLICT BETTER

There are multiple types of conflict that may arise throughout the course of Diversity and Inclusion work. Conflict may exist with another division head, between different employee groups, with your supervisor or direct report. Interestingly, conflict is rarely about what is being outwardly argued. Rather, it steams out of a stew of slights, misunderstandings, irritating incidents, and never-discussed tensions that have simmered for weeks, if you are lucky, but often for months or years.

For example, in 2015 there was an interesting article entitled, *How Equal is American Opportunity? Survey Shows Attitudes Vary By Race* by Brakkton Booker on the NPR news site. Unlike many other websites with a comments section, this article elicited a respectful dialogue. One of the readers commented that there is a huge disparity in workplace opportunity because diversity leaders have done a poor job in communicating the benefits for all. Another reader replied, "You're just a racist". To which the original poster said, "Am I a racist because I am giving an honest critique?"

That question resonates in the D&I field because many diversity practitioners believe they are being attacked on a daily basis from people within their organizations. At the end of the day, someone must ask, "Is some of the criticism justified?"

Figure 1 outlines how some division leaders view Diversity & Inclusion Officers.

FIGURE 1: HOW MANAGERS CLASSIFY DIVERSITY & INCLUSION LEADERS

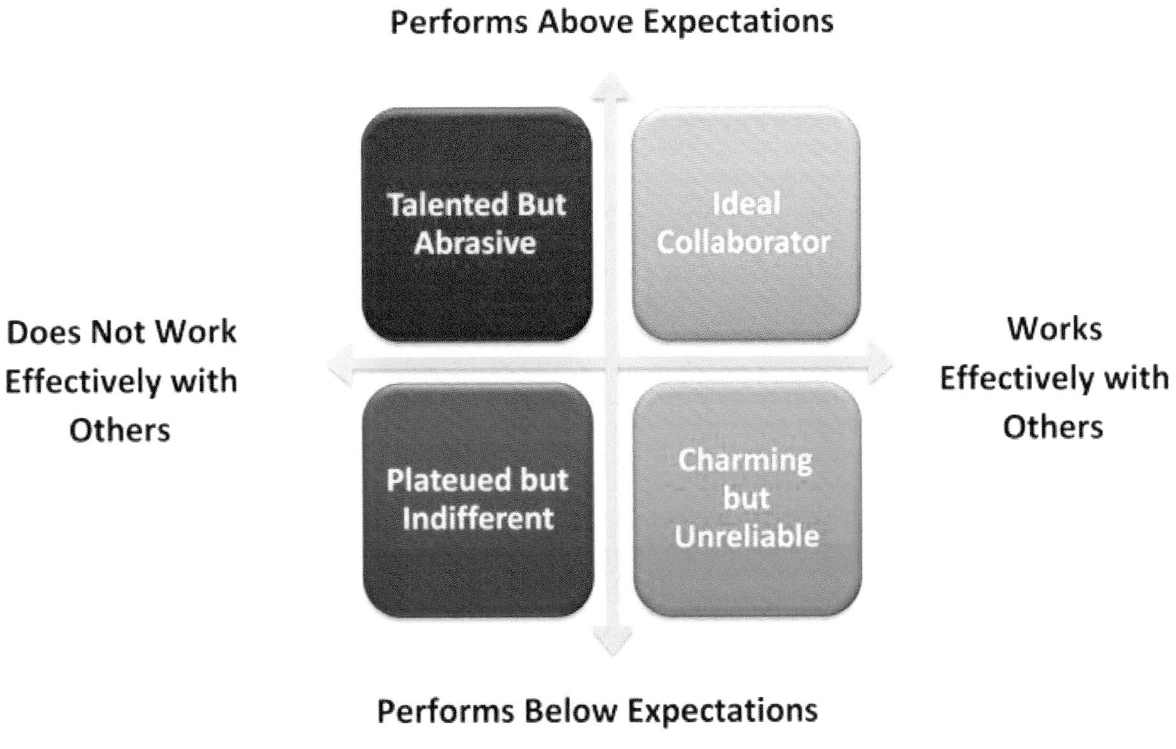

Performs Above Expectations

| Talented But Abrasive | Ideal Collaborator |

Does Not Work Effectively with Others — Works Effectively with Others

| Plateued but Indifferent | Charming but Unreliable |

Performs Below Expectations

Conflict management is a vital component of effective D&I performance. While playing the roles of disturbance handler and negotiator in the workplace or on college campuses, many diversity officers often find themselves in the midst of conflict. Some Diversity and Inclusion leaders are typically labeled as troublemakers because they ask too many questions, object to disparate impact, or serve as a conscious reminder of workplace diversity. Such individuals are likely to be dismissed as having personality deficiencies rather than being viewed as an "ideal collaborator".

Nevertheless, the D&I leader must continue to advocate for the disenfranchised and underrepresented. How else will change occur? As a caution, D&I leaders must strategically determine when to engage in battle, and which fights to surrender. Waging war over every issue is counterproductive, while avoiding battles altogether indicates weakness. However, compromising on, or winning the right issues will establish your fortitude and leadership.

As far as managers are concerned, they have great difficulty handling conflict, especially when diverse workers or students are involved. This is why training is required. When confronted with a problem, managers need to guard against the tendency to assume that bad behaviors implicate a bad person. Instead, managers should learn productive ways in which conflicts can be objectively resolved.

CASE STUDY #1:
Resolving Conflict

Jane, a white woman, goes to Paul, the team supervisor, and says, "Can I talk to you for a minute? I'm really frustrated." Paul stops what he is doing because he realizes that his star employee is completely flustered. "Sure, what's going on?"

Jane begins to tell Paul that she hates this new Diversity and Inclusion effort. "As a result, less qualified people are hired." Jane adds, "LaTonya is a perfect example." She shows Paul a print out where every customer name is entered incorrectly. The last name is in the first name field, and the first name is in the last name field. Paul responds, "Sheesh, how long has this been going on?" Jane says, "Since she was hired two weeks ago." Paul asks, "Have you talked to her?" Jane shakes her head no. "I figured I would leave that up to you." Jane gets up to go back to her desk.

Instead, Paul stops her. "Wait—stay right here," he says. He buzzes LaTonya and asks her to come to his office. When LaTonya gets there, he asks Jane to tell LaTonya what is wrong, and how it impacts her work. LaTonya explains that she was trained to enter the data in this fashion. Julie, from HR, trained LaTonya using the 2.0 system versus the current 4.0 software. Paul immediately dials Julie and advises her of the error. Paul tells LaTonya to pay attention to the field descriptions when entering data; then he instructs Jane to take issues directly to LaTonya first, before bringing it to him. Afterwards, Jane apologized to LaTonya and they worked together to correct the data that had been entered inaccurately.

Fortunately, Paul participated in the Diversity Training session on Conflict Management. Instead of ignoring the problem or taking sides, he was able to quell negativity about the new diversity effort, as well as refute the claim that LaTonya was not qualified.

Contrary to the usual prescriptions for helping a person with a problem, most executives believe that sticky situations must be handled with kid gloves or in a detached, counseling-like way. Yet, this is no time to offer a "positive sandwich"—praise followed by criticism, followed by praise again—because most subordinates are smart enough to perceive its contents as "baloney". The goal is to clarify the unwanted conduct and redirect the employee to desired behaviors. Consequences must be spelled out and enforced. From the start, managers must be prepared to take a tough stand. Blaming and fault finding will not work. Both parties must accept the fact that each is responsible at some level for allowing the situation to continue.

If a D&I leader is in a position where inappropriate language or conduct must be addressed, understand that the situation calls for straight talk. Both managers and employees must have clear-cut performance expectations that are established and connect to organizational incentives. Help these individuals face central questions, such as: Why do they behave as they do? In what way does their performance help the organization to achieve its goals? Are they aware that their behavior impacts how other employees/clients/students/patients/donors perceive the organization? Are there legitimate personal reasons or priorities that have caused them to behave as they do? Are they having trouble admitting that they are not well suited for their jobs? A big first step to resolving problem behavior is to engage in some honest dialogue.

Bear in mind that no one expects you to be a miracle worker. Establishing a pattern of coaching and feedback, perhaps supplemented with training and scheduled follow-up, will definitely make an impact. Leaders can also empower supervisors and other employees to take action. Nevertheless, there are no quick fixes or guarantees that your interventions will avert termination. One week of training is not the answer, nor is a simple heart-to-heart talk. You must accept the fact that behavior change, or culture transformation, will take time.

Better Communication Skills Resolve More Conflicts

When confronting personal attacks in a professional setting, hold what we call a crucial conversation. Start by assuming the other person is not fully aware of the impact of his or her actions. Hence, isolate the person from the behavior.

First, time your approach well. Do not wait six months after the incident, the person may have forgotten what he or she did. Also do not address the issue in front of a public forum. Next, describe the problem, starting with the facts: "Here's what just happened" as opposed to what you want to see happen. Another example: "You raised your voice and called John incompetent. I was hoping we could keep our conversations civil—free from labels or a harsh tone." Then stop and check for the other person's point of view. "Is that what just happened, or am I misinterpreting your comments?"

When a Diversity and Inclusion leader is in search of information, consensus, or building a working relationship, attentive listening is a must. With that, speaking in a way that will garner a response is required; however, it is not necessary to dominate the conversation. Use silence confidently as a tool to encourage hesitant speakers. Repeat key words silently to ensure that you remember the critical points of the conversation.

Active listening is a communication technique that requires the listener to understand, interpret, and evaluate what (s)he hears. The ability to listen actively can improve personal relationships through reducing conflicts, strengthening cooperation, and fostering understanding. This is a vital skill for individuals in the field of Diversity and Inclusion.

Active listening is best demonstrated by asking open-ended questions. This can further engage and stimulate audiences if you keep your responses brief. Figure 2 shows the degree to which an individual listens to the responses by repeating, paraphrasing, and reflecting.

FIGURE 2

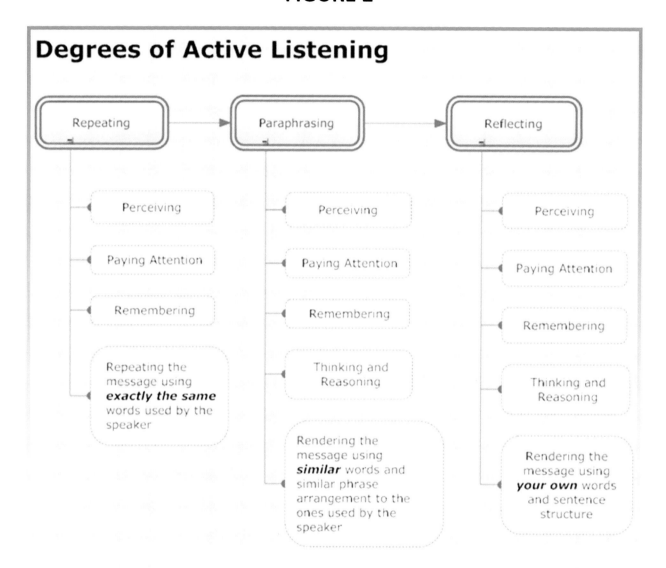

When interacting, people often are not listening attentively. They may be distracted, thinking about other things, or contemplating what they are going to say next (the latter case is particularly true in conflict situations or disagreements). Active listening is a structured way of paying attention, and responding to others by focusing attention on the speaker.

Barriers that can impede the flow of conversation may affect all elements of communication, including listening. Such barriers include distractions (such as cell phones), trigger words, vocabulary, and limited attention span.

Listening barriers may be psychological or physical (e.g., noise and visual distractions). Cultural differences, including speakers' accents, vocabulary, and misunderstandings due to cultural assumptions, often obstruct the listening process as well.

Noise is evident in Figure 3:

FIGURE 3: MODEL OF COMMUNICATION

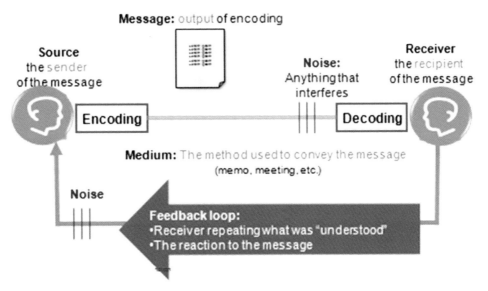

Source: Project Management Global Solutions, 2010

Frequently, the listener's personal interpretations, attitudes, biases, and prejudices lead to ineffective communication. At any rate, Diversity and Inclusion practitioners must become skilled at listening if we are really interested in getting to the heart of the problem. Sometimes, managing a difficult conversation can be a matter as simple as listening without walls of resistance.

What is more important than getting people to see things your way? Being able to demonstrate respect in communications, as well as displaying a willingness to listen, is more important than anything you can verbalize. Remember, people watch what you do before they listen to what you say.

Confronting Difficult Issues
Oftentimes, people say that we need to facilitate conversations about Diversity and Inclusion in order to engender better understanding, foster teamwork, and resolve conflict. Conversely, how do you initiate a conversation about an issue that has the potential to spiral out of control? For instance, if someone asserts that your work is racist, what do you do? If an employee claims that your senior leadership team is not doing enough about discrimination, how do you respond? Or how do you tell a senior executive that his or her behavior is inappropriate?

First, you cannot ignore it, because it won't go away on its own. Not only can the problem escalate into a lawsuit, it usually affects other employees. Second, allowing diversity problems to linger is counterintuitive to your efforts to change the organizational culture.

There are several ways to handle a potentially contentious conversation. We must understand that some White individuals may claim that they are a victim of racism or reverse discrimination. There may also be African American's, Latino's, Asian's, or Native American's who feel that they have been victims of racism or discrimination and no one has taken them seriously.

In any situation that a person alleges an "ism"—racism, sexism, ageism, whatever—it is up to you to ask, "What makes you say that?" Finding out what happened and demonstrating empathy may actually solve the problem. Make sure that you keep it professional and do not let it devolve into a negative "Me-too" exchange or an argument.

If merely venting their frustration does not help, continue to ask the employee questions such as "What could have been done differently?" or "How do we prevent this in the future?" Suggest that you take their concerns to management. Also, before doling out advice, first ask if they would like to hear your views about the situation. This approach where you should aspire to be an active and constructive listener is illustrated in Figure 4.

FIGURE 4: ACTIVE LISTENING FOR D&I LEADERS
Source: Amplify Disturbance, 2010

FOLLOWERS			
Passive & Silent	Unquestioning faithful	Uncomplaining Optimists	Silent Majority
Active & Negative	Combative Contestants	Disillusioned Cynics	Potential Converts
Active & Constructive	Potential Deserters	Potential Cynics	Creatively Engaged
	Don't Listen	Say They're Listening	Actively Listening

LEADERS

For a group conversation about a workplace conflict, you want to avoid "stacking the deck" where everyone is complaining about some unfair and unfortunate situation. Instead, begin the meeting with a non-threatening topic. You could inquire about how individuals grew up, and how today's families are different. Alternatively, you could ask long-time employees to describe how the organization was different when they first started or probe how your industry has changed over the years. Discussing change in a neutral context will set the stage for your hard-core discussion. Once you begin the conversation, do not simply ask "What is wrong?", make sure you seek solutions.

Asking, "How do we fix it?" is a great way to get employees thinking and engaged in the healing process.

According to Charles M. Blow, writer for the New York Times, whenever you initiate a conversation about race, gender, LGBT, age, different abilities, or other unique characteristics, it cannot be an insular, circular, or one-dimensional dialogue. It should be a multi-directional discussion that includes historical information, presents data, and shares personal experiences. Additionally, the group should explore the stereotypes and privileges of the majority group. Much more than a training session, this type of dialogue presents an opportunity for employees to learn from each other, build relationships across differences, and explore new paradigms. Do not forget to follow-up on the conversation. Change will not occur with one discussion, but over a series of gatherings. Be sure to plan an agenda for each meeting.

Excerpt from "If You Want to Win, You Have to Learn How to Fight"
by Steve Tobak

Open conflict is a critical aspect of an effective decision-making process, which in turn drives optimum outcomes and performance. In other words, the best performing teams handle conflict often, openly, and constructively.

Now let's talk about those three words, "often," "openly" and "constructively."

When I say "often," that doesn't mean all the time, anytime. Once a decision is made, that becomes the plan and everyone should get behind it until an outcome, unless something important changes, like the competitive landscape. I'm talking about appropriate meetings where issues are debated and decisions made.

Likewise, "openly" doesn't mean knock-down drag-outs in the hallway or in front of customers and investors. In general, a management team should show its stakeholders a reasonably united front. But during decision-making meetings, everyone should air their views openly and without holding back.

And "constructively" means attacking the problem, not the person. It means providing concrete reasons why you think an idea is flawed and offering an alternative view, not shooting it down with hyperbole or shouting someone down with insults and aggression.

A group conversation is the perfect setting to obtain feedback about Equity, Diversity and Inclusion work. There are several reasons why you may receive negative, and perhaps unwanted, feedback:

- There is no apparent link to organizational objectives or business imperatives.
- People are not clear what Diversity and Inclusion means or what your role is within the organization, and how it includes them.
- Diversity efforts center around one or two dimensions, such as race or gender.
- Equity efforts do not adequately address fairness, or the culture of favoritism.
- The Diversity Officer does not demonstrate or model inclusion.

- The Diversity Officer is not open to change or receptive to feedback.
- Employees fail to understand "What's in It for Me?" concepts.

Before labeling someone as a hater, racist, homophobic, or sexist, stop to consider whether you could do a better job communicating or building relationships across differences. Although some organizations have been doing Diversity and Inclusion for years, every employer has NOT had clear and effective leadership in this arena.

There are two ways that you can demonstrate better leadership: (1) by developing an elevator pitch (e.g., as a diversity officer/chair/leader, I am responsible for connecting the organization's people, practices, and profits to the long-term competitive benefits of diversity and inclusion") and (2) by going beyond your current circle of support to include and communicate regularly with critics.

Instead of shying away from critics, seek them out. This is the only way that you can grow and develop, as well as ensure that your Diversity and Inclusion efforts are on track. While not every critique may be justified, the least you can do is show a willingness to listen. Additionally, criticism presents an opportunity for you to enlist Diversity and Inclusion champions. Employees, who see that your effort values them and their opinions, are more likely to be receptive and supportive when you can turn the criticism into a compliment.

The following are steps to resolve conflict:

1. Calm Down - If your heart is racing or your temple is pulsating, nature is telling you to walk away. In this emotionally charged state, you are not likely to have a rational or collaborative conversation. Become attuned to what signs your body sends you when you are really upset, and learn to say, *"I really do want to talk about this, but I need some time to calm down. Let's talk later."*

2. Talk Later - Just because the anger goes away, it does not mean the conflict does. Remember the first step is committing to having the conversation, no matter how difficult. Use your cooler head to discuss the problem—not to let yourself off the hook.

3. Share Negative Emotions in Person – Emails, text messages, and written notes cannot convey the nuances that facial expressions, voice intonation, and body language can. If you absolutely must, discuss the problem over the phone, but face-to-face is always better.

4. Abandon Blame - Although people should be held accountable for their behavior, blaming is counterproductive to conflict resolution. Take responsibility for your feelings to avoid blaming others. For example, you might be tempted to tell your co-worker that she drives you crazy because she is always late, but that will invite nothing but defensiveness. Instead, try saying, *"I get really anxious when you come in late. Mornings are hectic, and when I have to answer your phone in addition to my own work, I'm afraid I'm going to miss important deadlines."*

5. Turn Your Anger Into Requests - You might be tempted to stay silent, but that will only compound the conflict, especially if this is not the first disagreement between you and your co-worker. Let's say your supervisor criticizes you in front of students or confronts you in front of colleagues. Take her aside when the two of you can be alone, remind her of the incident that bothered you, and ask, *"If you'd like me to do something differently, or you have a problem with my work, could you call it to my attention in private?"* By not making an issue of it at the time she angers you (in front of students and colleagues), you model the kind of behavior you are hoping for from her, and you deescalate the conflict.

6. Learn to Listen Like a Neutral Party -This is extremely difficult because it takes great self-discipline. But it can be done, with practice. This kind of listening requires the listener to hear what the other party is saying from the other party's point of view by asking questions designed to gain understanding, not to challenge. Mastering this skill will make you an asset at work, and it sure will help at home too.

7. Engage in Behaviors Designed to Elicit Cooperation

- Use "I" statements
  Example: *"I am often afraid to ask you a question for fear that you will think I don't know what I am doing."* This is much better than, *"You make me feel like an idiot every time I ask you a question."*

- Make appropriate, but not laser-like, eye contact.

- Show that you have been listening by asking questions or confirming what you have heard.
  Example: *"It sounds like your greatest concern is. . ."*

- Acknowledge responsibility for your part in the dispute.
  Example: "I've had time to think about this, and I realize that I could have approached this differently. Could we discuss how to resolve this problem?"

- Acknowledge the other person's point of view.
  Example: *"I can see how it looked that way to you. . ."*

- Do not make the next word in that sentence "but". Try, "*I can see how it looked that way to you, and I'd like to share with you how I see it".*

- Allow the other person to vent. This is also hard, but the pay-off can be big. To do this, listen to the other person's story until he/she is done, and then ...

- Ask questions. Resist the urge to argue your point or comment on how ridiculous your opponent's point is. You might want to say, *"That decision makes no sense!"* Instead, ask a question like, *"Can you tell me more about how the group made that decision?"* This approach encourages dialogue instead of debate, and again, reduces the intensity of the conflict.

- Avoid assumptions. Another way of putting this is, stop inventing intentions. You might assume you understand the intentions behind the other person's behavior, but unless you ask, you cannot know for sure why anyone does anything. Instead of telling your opponent, *"You are trying to make me look bad to our boss"* try, *"Can you explain why you spoke to our boss before discussing the problem with me?"*

These tips are useless if you are unwilling to actually have the tough conversation. Avoiding a difficult conversation is completely natural. It is also totally counterproductive to managing diversity conflict.

ASSEMBLING A STRONG TEAM

People resist diversity efforts for a number of reasons. For example, groups who are not made to feel included in the process, such as White men, may feel blamed for inequities in their organizations and react with defensiveness. Individuals who feel excluded may also believe that their own concerns and issues are not being addressed by organizational efforts. Alternatively, people who are specifically included in diversity efforts (such as women or people of color) may express resistance because they do not want to be singled out or perceived as having succeeded purely as a result of change efforts. Finally, individuals are cynical and reluctant to get involved with new diversity efforts when past change initiatives have not been successful.

Resistance may take many different forms, depending on the stage of the diversity initiative. In some organizations, the most marked struggle can come at the introduction of a new initiative when individuals do not understand what changes will be made and why. Alternatively, people may be curious about what is happening and thus remain neutral in the early stages. Their resistance may become more pronounced in the purposeful phase, when changes that are more concrete directly affect their day-to-day experiences.

Without clear communication, individuals create their own perceptions of the true nature of the initiative's goals and rationale as well as the methods by which these goals will be achieved. In the workplace, employee perceptions of diversity efforts may include:

- A belief that unearned benefits or advantages will be given to a specific group, such as younger individuals, White women, or people of color
- A perception that one has to be part of a specific group in order to be promoted
- Equating the goal of the diversity effort with tokenism
- A view that Diversity and Inclusion efforts will separate employees because it emphasizes groups over individuals
- A perception that the development of some employees necessarily impedes the advancement of others
- A sense of being singled out or punished
- A sense of being dominated by political correctness

Resistance may be passive or active. Some examples of resistant employee behaviors include:

- Propagating rumors about why certain promotions, or development opportunities, are given, perhaps openly insinuating preferential treatment
- Charging that ill-considered promotions are made for the sake of making quotas
- Ignoring or giving very low priority to program implementation and policy compliance related to a diversity initiative (e.g., ensuring a diverse slate of candidates when recruiting, or attending a mandatory professional development session on managing diversity effectively)
- Making dismissive jokes regarding inclusion efforts (i.e., making up disrespectful nicknames for employee resource groups and networks)
- Taking legal recourse because an individual believes his/her retention and advancement has been adversely impacted by diversity programs or policies
- Believing or communicating that the team-building process is time consuming, arduous, or doomed to fail

Building a Bridge of Inclusion

Serving in a senior executive capacity may be glamorous, but in some cases, the risk negates the rewards. Consider these recent high-profile CEO terminations (source: Entrepreneur Magazine):

- Ehab Al Shihabi was replaced as CEO of Al Jazeera America after it was sued for $15 million, over alleged sexism and anti-Semitism at the company. Al Shihabi was reportedly blamed by one departing executive for presiding over a "culture of fear." Consequently, the American division of Al Jazeera news ceased operations in April 2016.

- After a 6-month suspension from American Apparel, Dov Charney was officially fired after allegations that he had misused corporate funds. In general, Charney's time as CEO was plagued by controversy. In 2009, the company came under fire for hiring illegal immigrants to work in its Los Angeles factory. Charney himself had been accused of sexually harassing several female employees, and of diving at and then choking a male employee before rubbing dirt in his face.

The question of the day is: How do you improve the quality of one's leadership before it is too late? Instead of providing a list of recommendations, it may be more helpful to consider the answers to these questions:

- Are you having trouble meeting goals? If so, what can you do differently?
- If you do not have trouble achieving goals, how many different people helped you with your latest accomplishments? How can you keep these individuals engaged?
- How diverse is your inner circle? Could it use more diversity (e.g., intellectual, racial/ethnic, gender, age, geography, status, etc.)?
- How do you treat other people? How do others perceive your interaction with, or treatment of, different people?
- How can you improve communication?
- What advantage will you experience from setting aside pride and resolving conflict with another person or group?
- How can you inspire others to achieve the greatness within?

By definition, quality means the standard of something as measured against other things of a similar kind; the degree of excellence of something. Whether from a professional or organizational perspective, the quality of leadership determines:

- The culture
- The breadth of aspiration and innovation
- The ability to achieve desired outcomes

D&I executives often operate from the perspective of "How can I achieve my goals?" However, becoming a leader involves more than setting and achieving goals. Accomplished leaders become better when they can (1) enhance their own performance; (2) motivate others to live up to their fullest potential; and (3) galvanize action around a shared vision. In the words of Brian Tracy, author and motivational speaker:

> *"Become the kind of leader that people would follow voluntarily;*
> *even if you had no title or position."*

Part of fostering inclusion involves asking for help. Think about your organizational culture. Is it shameful to admit mistakes or to ask for help?

Perhaps help is just bouncing an idea off someone's head, or sharing frustration about the lack of support, or asking for guidance. At any rate, "winging it" is no longer acceptable in this field. Admitting we need help from others is a strategy to invite other leaders to join you in changing the organizational culture. Diversity and Inclusion leaders are not invincible or omnipotent. We need help in order to get more done. The first step in getting the help we need is to ask for it.

The Power of Teamwork
Diversity and Inclusion is about empowering people and promoting the human spirit. It makes an organization effective by capitalizing on all of the strengths of each employee. It is not EEO or Affirmative Action; these are laws and policies. Rather, diversity is about understanding, valuing, and making the most of the individual differences found in each and every person.

Simply enforcing government regulations will not make your organization the best that it can be. To obtain the best competitive advantage, great teams need to be created by utilizing the full potential of every individual. Teams are much more than a group. A group is a collection of individuals where each person is working towards his or her own personal goal or agenda, whereas a team is a collection of individuals working towards a common goal or vision. This creates a synergistic effect within the team.

An individual, acting alone, can accomplish much; but a group of people acting together in a unified force can accomplish great wonders. This is because team members understand each other and support each other. Their main goal is to see the team accomplish its mission. Personal agendas do not get in the way of team goals. In fact, personal agendas become a huge waste on an organization's resources because they do not support its mission or goals.

Using the synergy effect of teams can help you harness a competitive edge over other organizations that are merely employing individuals acting alone. If team members do not accept others for who they are, they will be unable to use the abilities of each team member to compensate for their own individual weaknesses. Hence, team effort develops knowledge and bridges skill gaps that often lead to failure.

Embracing diversity is the first step in building strong teams. Almost every team building theory states that to build a great team, there must be a diverse group of people on the team. Essentially, avoid choosing people who are alike. Choosing people like yourself to be team members will multiply the flaws of the team. Compare this to the other end of the continuum, having an assorted group of individuals diminishes the flaws of each person.

Nevertheless, our biases and prejudices are deeply rooted within us. From the moment we are born, we learn about our environment, the world, and ourselves. Families, friends, peers, books, teachers, idols, and others influence what is right and what is wrong. These early experiences, rooted deeply within us, shape our perceptions about how we view things and how we respond to them.

Embracing diversity is more than tolerating people on your team who are different. It is actively welcoming and involving them by:

- Developing an atmosphere in which it is safe for all individuals to ask for help. People should not be viewed as weak if they ask for help. This is what builds great teams - joining weaknesses together with strengths to get a goal or objective accomplished.

- Actively seeking information from people from a variety of backgrounds and cultures in order to develop a broader picture. Also, engaging everyone in the problem solving and decision making process.

- Including people who are different from you in informal gatherings such as lunch, coffee breaks, and spur of the moment meetings.

- Creating a team spirit in which every member feels valued and involved.

If an organization does not take on this challenge, it will soon become extinct or left far behind. There are too many competitors who are striving to become the best, and they want to be the best in more than one area. They know that customers, students, patients, and/or funders will not tolerate lackadaisical service.

Great organizations who remain competitive in one or more areas do not sit around patting themselves on the back; they know there are dozens of others who want to take their place. They do, however, celebrate accomplishments and achievements. This celebration is important because it shows employees what success looks like and what is important to the overall team. When tough goals are partially met, it is important to celebrate and acknowledge the success. Difficult goals provide learning experiences that cannot be simulated in training classes. These experiences allow the individual to operate outside of their comfort zone, extend critical thinking, and improve team cohesion. In addition, they provide opportunities for leaders to instill new skills into employees. Setting a difficult goal and not reaching it is far more important than setting and meeting a mediocre goal.

Although some organizations never become the best, they must compete to do things better than their competitors. This not only allows employees to grow, but also lets their clients know that they are willing to go out of their way to serve them in their area of expertise.

Team building activities have always been popular, but organizations must take care not to divide workers! For example, one company's Christmas party was highly offensive instead of festive.

Because of accident liability, the company chose not to serve liquor, but instead, let employees buy it at a cash bar. Many employees only made slightly above minimum wage and found the charge per drink high and consequently complained about the party. Meanwhile, the employees from the higher socioeconomic levels did not find the drink charge a problem. The two groups also approached the party differently. The more affluent group enjoyed dressing up for the occasion while the rest were annoyed about having to purchase a dress or suit. To further complicate matters, a small faction objected to Christmas altogether and stayed away from the party. As a result, a company function that was designed to build teams actually ended up dividing the employees into three camps.

It stands to reason that events and other activities may not be the most effective way to build a team. If you want to develop effective working relationships with diverse people, you must start with the similarities, not differences. Diversity in the workplace adds a special richness, and special challenges. As a Diversity and Inclusion leader, effective and multi-cultural work relationships are critical to your success.

In recent years, D&I leaders have emphasized honoring and appreciating the diverse needs, skills, talents, and contributions of different people. While this is critical, do not let the pendulum swing too far in this direction. We are in danger of forgetting to honor and appreciate our similarities. By acknowledging the similarities and likenesses, we create a starting point for understanding and appreciating diversity in the workplace.

In Watson Wyatt's WorkUSA research, they asked 7500 workers at all job levels across various industries to respond to 130 statements about their workplaces. Watson Wyatt broke down the responses to look for diversity patterns across demographics including whites versus people of color, men versus women, and individuals over and under 30 years old. They found more similarities than differences, especially in the categories respondents rated as most important to them. Among the key findings, people agreed about what inspires their commitment to a particular employer, such as:

- Their company's mission or business
- Using their skills on the job
- A competitive compensation package
- The company taking action on employee suggestions

People also agreed on what organizations need to improve: employee input and promoting the best performers while helping the worst performers get better. Additionally, employees want to know how their job affects internal and external clients. They want to understand how their job contributes to the accomplishment of organizational goals. They want a safe work environment with highly rated services.

In response to this research, look at your peers or direct reports with new eyes. Think about the factors that you share in common with them. You will find:

- You are all human beings with complex emotions, needs, interests, outlooks, viewpoints and dreams. Share something about yourself to create an environment in which your coworker wants to share information with you. Listen and do not pry. Polite and continuing interest in your coworkers will contribute to workplace harmony.

- You have family and other interests outside of work. Listen to what your coworkers tell you about their personal lives. Remember to demonstrate respect and attentiveness.

- You have similar work needs and interests. Acknowledge this and note the commonalities.

Work is more exciting when you feel as if you are accomplishing mutual goals. Act as if you are part of a winning team. Emphasize, with peers, your common interest in your team's success and the success of the organization. You will get to know people as individuals if you participate in activities planned by other departments/divisions. Better yet, join the team that plans them!

Start by recognizing the ways in which you are similar to your coworkers. This will build a base of understanding and acceptance that will withstand the stormy times when your differences come to the forefront.

Team diversity is paradoxical: well managed heterogeneous teams can create better, more innovative services, and they can outperform homogenous teams. Yet the opposite can also be true: homogenous teams can outperform heterogeneous teams, which tend to have more conflicts and higher personnel turnover. Hence, the key here is that heterogeneous teams must be managed well.

For the same reasons, brainstorming can prove both effective and ineffective. After all, it is teams that carry out the brainstorming and other problems can present themselves such as social loafing, lack of preparation, lack of personal accountability, etc. Nevertheless, how helpful can brainstorming be if each member of the team contributes, feels valued, and brings a different skill to the table? This may sound complicated, but in many ways, it means going back to the basics. It means giving greater consideration to teamwork and to our colleagues around us.

Teams are often their own worst enemy, believing the illusion that they can function perfectly well on their own. However, when partnering across disciplines, D&I leadership is required to create cross-functioning teams that understand the advantage of "outside" help. The D&I leader keeps the team motivated, productive, and engaged by demonstrating the right balance. No one likes an overly decisive team leader, yet an indecisive leader is not actually a leader at all. Regardless, whether you like teamwork, brainstorming, or neither, the fact remains that ideas, concepts, and decisions develop better in a collective environment.

GET THE HELP YOU NEED

If you normally force change on people, problems will arise. Once again, an effective change management strategy entails thoughtful planning and sensitive implementation. Above all, you must consult with, and involve, the people affected by the changes. The following is a great example of partnering in change:

CASE STUDY #2:
Prince Sports' New Policies

Several years ago, when Prince Sports separated from Benetton, the U.S. based employer adopted traditional American business practices—including the Employee Handbook. However, instead of simply issuing new policies and asking managers to enforce the policies, Prince Sports prepared a draft employee handbook. The draft was circulated to nearly 20 supervisors and division heads. Each manager was provided with a deadline for providing feedback. If managers made suggestions or noted exceptions, these were incorporated into the final version. Once the final Employee Handbook was released, divisional leaders communicated the new policies to workers.

References

McKee, Annie. *How to Hire for Emotional Intelligence.* Harvard Business Review, February 5, 2016. Retrieved from: https://hbr.org/2016/02/how-to-hire-for-emotional-intelligence?utm_source=feedburner&utm_medium=feed&utm_campaign=Feed%3A+harvardbusiness+%28HBR.org%29

Booker, Brakkton (September 21, 2015). *How Equal is American Opportunity? Survey Shows Attitudes Vary By Race.* NPR. Retrieved From: https://www.npr.org/sections/thetwo-way/2015/09/21/442068004/how-equal-is-american-opportunity-survey-shows-attitudes-vary-by-race

Sample Test Questions:

STRATEGIC PURPOSE & PARTNERSHIPS

1. **All of the following behaviors are designed to elicit cooperation EXCEPT:**
   A. Using "I" statements
   B. Shouting and interrupting
   C. Making eye contact

2. **_____ is a group of people, with different functional expertise, who are working toward a common goal:**
   A. An Employee Resource Group
   B. A cross-functional team
   C. The Office of Diversity

3. **For group conversations about workplace conflicts, avoid stacking the deck where everyone is complaining.**
   A. True
   B. False

4. **All of the following are ways that you could show better D&I leadership EXCEPT:**
   A. Developing an elevator pitch
   B. Going beyond your circle of support
   C. Creating and solving more conflict

5. **Conflict management is a not vital component of effective D&I performance.**
   A. True
   B. False

6. **Whenever you initiate a conversation about race, gender, LGBTQ+, etc., it can't be:**
   A. Multi-directional
   B. Circular or insular
   C. Fair or inclusive

7. **In order for cross-functional teams to accomplish specific tasks with the input and expertise of others, they must:**
   A. Ask diverse workers to lead
   B. Conduct anonymous surveys
   C. Operate as self-directed teams

Sample Test Questions:

STRATEGIC PURPOSE & PARTNERSHIPS (cont'd)

8. **Intra-team dynamics allow decision-making processes to be multi-directional rather than:**
   A. Hierarchical
   B. Inconsequential
   C. Remedial

9. **Active listening is best demonstrated by:**
   A. Paying attention to the speaker
   B. Asking open-ended questions
   C. Thinking about what to say next

10. **Allowing diversity problems to linger is counterintuitive to your efforts to:**
    A. Recruit and retain diverse workers
    B. Market to multicultural audiences
    C. Change the organizational culture

11. **A positive approach for executives to resolve problems or conflicts is to:**
    A. Clarify unwanted conduct
    B. Offer a "positive sandwich"
    C. Provide detached counseling

12. **Pertaining to conflict, D&I leaders must strategically determine:**
    A. How to demonstrate empathy for majority groups
    B. How to confront people without being confrontational
    C. When to engage in conflict and when to surrender

13. **Instead of relying solely on an endorsement from the CEO, D&I leaders must:**
    A. Establish a rapport with the Board of Directors and customers
    B. Prioritize striving for cross-functional support and teamwork
    C. Develop an elevator pitch that purposefully satisfies all critics

CONNECTING DEMOGRAPHIC SHIFTS TO ORGANIZATIONAL STRATEGY

> *Demographics are a vital component of Diversity and Inclusion work. Population data and projections help organizations make informed decisions and gain deeper insights into the needs of different groups. Smart organizations regularly review this information during product development and strategic planning sessions.*
>
> *Additionally, the most recent social population data and its corresponding projections must be applied to discussions and decisions pertaining to service delivery, talent management, marketing, communications, competitive positioning and more.*

OVERALL OBJECTIVES AND COMPETENCIES

The purpose of this competency is to empower diversity leaders to research, forecast and interpret how global demographic changes and user trends will impact the organization, as well as equip D&I leaders to advise flexible, long-term strategies to respond to market fluxes.

BACKGROUND AND CONTEXT

According to the Statistics Division of the United Nations Department of Economic and Social Affairs, "*Vital statistics* constitute the collection of statistics on vital events and relevant characteristics throughout a person's lifetime. Vital statistics provide crucial and critical information on the population in a country. For statistical purposes, *vital events* are events concerning the birth and death of individuals, as well as marriage, adoption, and other significant occasions in one's life."

Acquiring knowledge of the size and characteristics of a country's population on a timely basis is a prerequisite to socioeconomic planning and informed decision-making. Vital statistics and their subsequent analysis and interpretation are essential for setting targets and evaluating social and economic plans. These statistics include the monitoring of health and population intervention programs, and the measurement of important demographic indicators pertaining to levels of living or quality of life, including the expectation of life at birth and the infant mortality rate.

Population increases with the addition of live births, decreases with the subtraction of deaths, and is impacted by migration. Information about the number of live births and deaths occurring in a population is crucial for estimating the natural increase (or decrease) and the annual change in size and structure for that population. Knowledge of the size and growth of a population is a prerequisite for planning and resource allocation.

Births, deaths, marriage rates, and data on family size and composition are important sources of the information needed in planning related to public housing. The trends in the birth and marriage rates are indicators of future housing needs and can predict the size of the school population. Data on those trends are essential in planning for the provision of school facilities, as well as for training teachers. Marriage rates and trends in marriage influence the construction industry, business (clothing and furniture manufacturing), and many other attributes that affect a community.

Vital statistics are useful in planning related to future markets for consumer goods such as medicine, food, clothing, and furniture. If the birth rate remains high, it can be expected that the demand for maternity clothing will remain high; that medicine, food, clothing, equipment, and furniture will continue to be in demand; and that housing and house furnishings will be at a premium price. Birth projections and statistics are useful to commercial firms and enterprises when planning for inventory in clothing, toys, and play equipment for growing children.

Vital statistics from different sources need to be of the highest quality to serve as the basis for better decision-making. Quality is indicated in terms of completeness, correctness, availability, and timeliness. For example, in 2008, Scientific American published an article entitled, *There Are More Boys Than Girls in China and India*. The article's subheading was *Preference for Sons Could Spell Trouble for China and India*. The author, Jeremy Hsu, asserted that "the ratio of boys to girls is so lopsided that economists project there may be as many as 30 to 40 million more men than women of marriageable age in both countries by 2020." The gender imbalance began when the Chinese government started enforcing its one child per family policy in the early 1980's. Hsu adds, "The Chinese have traditionally preferred sons because of their potential to financially support their parents, carry on the family name, and lead ancestor worship, population experts say, and this holds particularly true for rural areas where sons provide much-needed labor."

In India, there are no laws mandating one child per family. However, the male bias continues to exist as females are viewed as 'financial burdens' largely because of "the dowries that are required before marriage". Hsu stated that more males without marriage prospects will pose a "hidden danger that will affect social stability". Over the years, both nations have seen an increase in the 'brain drain', where talented males left the region to find partners in other nations. The effect of years of male bias is also evident in a surge in sexual assaults on young female children, as well as in sexual violence against women in India. When one factors in higher levels of human trafficking and prostitution, Hsu's assertions more than a decade ago suggest that the data could have led to more proactive policies. China changed its one-child policy, effective on the first day of 2016. Nonetheless, between the two countries, there were 50 million excess males are under age 20 by 2018 according to a Washington Post report entitled, *Too Many Men*.

Every organization has the potential to utilize demographic data to its advantage through the employ of Diversity leaders. However, the work must be meaningful and strategic. Diversity leaders must also have regular access to data that will inform policies, strategies and sustainability efforts, as well the ability to provide insight into what demographic changes could mean to the organization.

For purposes of Diversity and Inclusion work, demographic data may include:

- Changes in population patterns and statistics;
- Shifts in behaviors, preferences, priorities, and expectations;
- Demographic group, or industry, trends.

THE LINK TO BIG DATA

Evolving customer needs and fluctuating stock prices aren't the only challenges that companies must navigate these days. The workforce is changing too, and the future success of organizations rests on their ability to change with it. Generational differences, shared household responsibilities and longer, healthier lives create new opportunities for managers to harness the expertise and talent that so many have to offer. To effectively retain great employees and sustain innovation in the 21st century, employers must first recognize where these shifts are occurring and understand what to do about them.

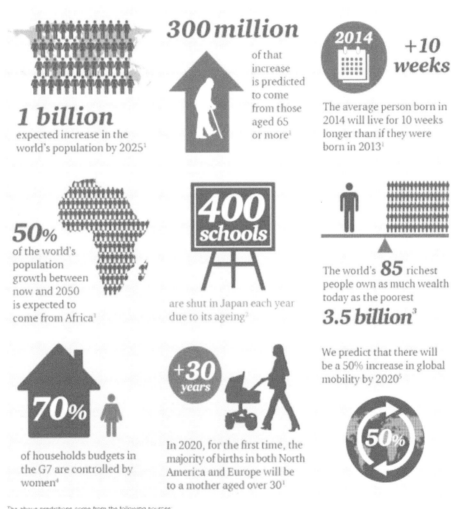

Demographic and social change
Did you know?

1 billion expected increase in the world's population by 2025[1]

300 million of that increase is predicted to come from those aged 65 or more[1]

2014 +10 weeks The average person born in 2014 will live for 10 weeks longer than if they were born in 2013[1]

50% of the world's population growth between now and 2050 is expected to come from Africa[1]

400 schools are shut in Japan each year due to its ageing[2]

The world's **85** richest people own as much wealth today as the poorest **3.5 billion**[3]

70% of households budgets in the G7 are controlled by women[4]

+30 years In 2020, for the first time, the majority of births in both North America and Europe will be to a mother aged over 30[1]

We predict that there will be a 50% increase in global mobility by 2020[5]

The above predictions come from the following sources:
1 UN Population Division, World Population Prospects (2012) • 2 FT (2014) • 3 Oxfam (2014) • 4 The World's Women, UN (2010) • 5 PwC Talent Mobility 2020 and beyond (2012)

Smart phones, satellite imagery, social media, and the internet allow us to access data everywhere at any time. These technologies generate data "Big Data" faster and more detailed than ever before. Technology also offers new measurement opportunities and challenges for statistical systems around the world. For instance, different internet sites allow users to rate their experiences with everything from hotel stays, to restaurants, to employers. The opportunity lies in harnessing that data to determine what customers/employees prefer. The challenge resides in weeding out responses about companies who paid for positive reviews.

Big Data is the next frontier of Diversity and Inclusion work. As with everything in D&I, Big Data presents huge opportunities to:

- Drive incremental revenue
- Predict customer behavior across all channels
- Understand and monetize customer expectations
- Improve operational effectiveness
- Predict machine failures and network attacks
- Manage financial risk by reducing fraud and increasing security
- Increase the value of Diversity and Inclusion

People, processes, and machines generate Big Data. It is the future of analytics. Forbes and HP conducted research in April 2014 and found two things: (1) Top economic performers believe finding new consumer insights is the most valuable focus; and (2) The most successful businesses place a 25% greater emphasis on using Big Data to find social and consumer insights compared to lower performing peers.

For example, parents realized that tablets, cell phones, iPods, iPads, and iPhones were great babysitters by the early 2000's. In many ways, some of these parents thought they were preparing their kids for a Science, Technology, Engineering and Math (STEM) career by providing earlier exposure to electronics. Changes in parental behavior, such as these, should have led Toys R Us to adjust its business strategy a decade earlier. It's possible that the company thought the changes were a fad, or perhaps organizational leaders assumed the market would shift back to their favor. At any rate, by the time Toys R Us went out of business, kids did not miss the retailer (although their parents may have). Thus, not only did their customer base change, Toys R Us' competitors also changed. Previously known as a category killer because there was no other competition in the same category, Toys R Us lost millions in business to Walmart, Target and Amazon before closing in 2018.

Like diversity, Big Data is an asset, but we must know how to leverage it properly so that we do not drown in it. There are different types of data: Relational Data (e.g., Tables, Transactions); Text Data; Semi-Structured Data (e.g., Excel Spreadsheet); Graph Data; and Streaming Data (e.g., Single Use). Each type of data is subject to streams, which are continuous, huge, fast, and changing.

In connection-oriented communication, a **data stream** is a sequence of digitally encoded coherent signals (packets of data or data packets) used to transmit or receive information. While data streams allow for real time processing, the arriving speed of streams and the huge amount of data are beyond our capability to store through normal means. Therefore, it must be clustered. Clustering can be used to predict patterns in buying behavior, trends, expectations, and more.

Clustering is the task of grouping a set of objects in such a way that objects in the same group are more similar to each other than to those in other groups. It is a way to simplify and easily store the data obtained via streams.

FIGURE 1: AN EXAMPLE OF CLUSTERING

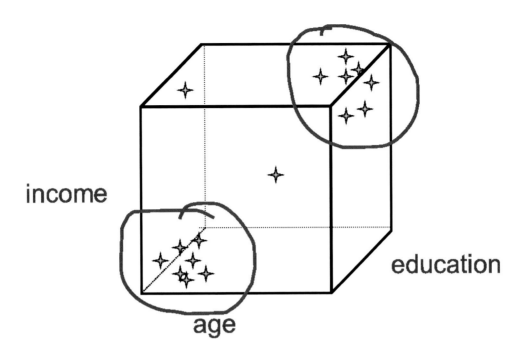

Clustering models identify relationships in a dataset that you might not logically derive through casual observation. For example, you can logically discern that people who commute to their jobs by bicycle do not typically live a long distance from where they work. The algorithm, however, can find other characteristics about bicycle commuters that are not as obvious. In Figure 1, education, age, and income can be clustered to gather more information about these bicycle commuters and help target these particular groups more effectively.

For example, clustering may lead some organizations to discover that bicycle riders are environmentally conscious or eat healthier. In fact, some supermarkets now have a bigger produce section. Not only are they following in the lead of Whole Foods and Trader Joes, but they are catering to a growing multicultural consumer population that is willing to pay more for fresh food items. According to Nielsen, "The biggest and most obvious hurdle to reaching multicultural consumers is that the "multicultural" umbrella covers a vast range of people, cultures and backgrounds. But a closer look at shopping behaviors across multicultural shoppers reveals one important commonality—they are particularly influential in fresh groceries (i.e., more likely to expect fresh meat, produce, deli, bakery and seafood). Multicultural shoppers spend $40 billion on fresh products annually and devote 21% of their annual food spend to fresh. These consumers also spend 4% more on fresh products than white non-Hispanics, which amounts to $60 million in sales annually."

Clustering is a technique that helps organizations to identify key demographic characteristics in clusters so that targeting different consumers, students, clients, patients, etc., occurs in a systematic pattern. Clustering, however, requires that the organization properly understands and interprets key demographic information.

HOW DEMOGRAPHIC PROJECTIONS SUPPORT MARKET SEGMENTATION

Diversity and Inclusion leaders must become fluent in demographic changes and projections. This requires the ability to connect the dots from who an organization served 40 years ago, to who is served today, to who *will be* served in the next 40 years. For example, instead of simply stating that there are not enough television shows featuring diverse individuals, a stronger business case for diversity in television programming would center around Nielsen ratings and Twitter use—which USA Today also reports on a regular basis. One could also make the case based on the quantity and quality of advertisers.

Figure 2 exemplifies how the U.S. population has changed as a whole.

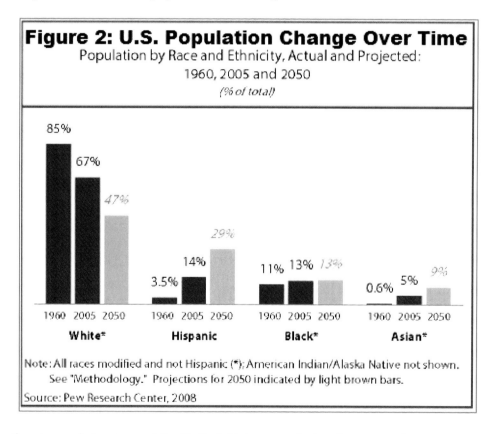

Projecting the size and structure of the United States population, in terms of age, sex, race, and origin has implications central to both public and private interests. School enrollment and participation in programs such as Social Security and Medicare are affected by how quickly and the extent to which the population grows. Population changes are also central to urban and regional planners, who help create communities, improve infrastructure to accommodate population growth, and revitalize physical facilities in towns, cities, counties, and metropolitan areas.

Over the next 40 years, the United States is expected to experience rapid growth in its older population <u>and</u> a large increase in racial and ethnic diversity. Like most European nations, net international migration has played an important role in shaping changes in the size, growth rate, age structure, racial, and ethnic composition of the United States population.

The Asian and Hispanic populations have engendered the greatest effects on international migration. The size and age structure of the Asian population is strongly linked to projected levels of net international migration. For the Hispanic population, the level of net international migration has enhanced (but is not the only determinant of) trends in population growth and aging for this group. Even in the absence of net international migration, the size of the Hispanic population is expected to increase substantially in the coming decades. This is largely due to the current age distribution of the Hispanic population and the higher fertility rates for them, which is properly termed a natural increase in the population.

The level of net international migration is found to affect the timing of the majority-minority crossover, whereby higher levels of net international migration cause the crossover to occur sooner. This data serves as the core for changes to American immigration policies. Nevertheless, similar to China's childbirth policy, changes to U.S. immigration laws will have little effect on population projections at this point.

Demographic trends reveal developments and changes in human population. More specifically, demographic trends relate to changes in a population's age, gender, geographical location, marital status, educational attainment, employment status, household income, race, religion, and health.

Demographic changes will influence businesses in both positive and negative ways, as well as across various sectors. The list below provides some examples.

- Diverse groups continue to face barriers to educational opportunity. Current changes to immigration laws, and a negative global perception of the U.S., will result in fewer individuals desiring to come to America even if they are legally permitted to work. Therefore, the failure to educate or remove barriers to a high quality education for the next generation of children in the United States (where diversity is already the majority) will have a negative effect on economic growth.

- Businesses need to offer flexible work schedules and fair pay to both men and women due to long work hours, substantial travel responsibilities, and increased demand for a balanced or integrated work/family lifestyle.

- The aging population will require the healthcare industry to provide for more people for a longer period of time. The growing, aging population will impact the global health-care market in years to come—where low-cost drugs, non-invasive medical procedures, and alternative treatment options must be balanced with diverse expectations for high quality care.

- The varying characteristics, styles, and preferences among larger and more affluent diverse populations around the world will have a direct effect on all types of consumer product/service offerings.

Demographic trends may also be helpful in workforce projections. Figure 3, for example, shows projected labor force participation by age.

FIGURE 3:
Labor Force Participation By Age

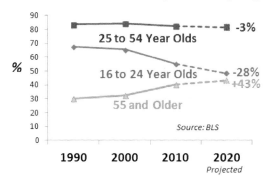

Source: BLS

Diversity and Inclusion leaders can glean valuable insight from demographic trends. For example, a satellite office in a certain geographic location might experience a decline in customers. Without understanding the demographic trends for the area, an organization could make decisions about the customer segment based on conjecture. Upon a deeper analysis of demographic trends for the area, however, it might be revealed that there was a change in the population's average age, employment status, income, or wealth—all of which could help the organization make better business decisions.

The more information about a population that decision-makers can appropriately group together, or cluster, the more valuable the data will be to them. This can yield additional insight such as trends in a population's socioeconomic status, life stage, and lifestyle. Socioeconomic status is determined by measuring income, education, occupation, and wealth of an individual or a family. Life stage is based on an individual's age, family status, and relationships. Lifestyle is determined by education, location, activities, interests, opinions, socioeconomic status, and life stage. All of these characteristics are helpful to organizations as they are valuable predictors of consumer spending trends and other behaviors.

Organizations can also utilize the latest demographic trends to identify existing and emerging markets for their products and services. By evaluating this data, decision-makers can identify changing marketplace needs and appropriately adjust to them. Periodically reviewing demographic trends can also help organizations recognize future opportunities earlier. For example, a college may discover that Baby Boomers are going back to school to prepare for a new line of work after retirement. The sooner an institution recognizes this, the stronger it can position itself competitively.

When combined with behavioral and attitudinal data, demographics can be used to improve marketing effectiveness by helping organizations target new market segments with the right messages at the right time. When done well, your organization can increase awareness, improve customer/student acquisition efforts, and bolster client retention rates.

How Does Market Segmentation Work?
Few organizations are able to adequately serve an entire market because different customer groups have diverse preferences, needs, and expectations. For example, some customers want to be style leaders. They will always buy certain styles first and usually pay a higher price for them. Other customers are bargain shoppers. They try to find contemporary styles at the lowest price. Accordingly, a company with premium products would not appeal to bargain shoppers.

For this reason, market segmentation is a strategy that offers an opportunity to position your organization and its products/services to targeted groups that perceive the full value of products/services differently. An athletic footwear company might have market segments for basketball players and long-distance runners. As distinct groups, basketball players and long-distance runners will respond to very different advertisements.

The concept of marketing segmentation is necessary to identify and target certain demographic groups. It is a model that is applicable to for-profit enterprises, nonprofits, educational institutions, and government agencies—whether targeting customers/students/constituents or employees.

The most common forms of market segmentation are based on:

- **Geographic Segmentation-** An organization can segment according to geographic criteria—nations, states, regions, counties, cities, neighborhoods, or postal codes. The geo-cluster approach combines demographic data with geographic data to create a more accurate or specific profile.

- **Demographic Segmentation-** Segmentation according to demography is based on variables such as age, gender, ethnicity, occupation, education level, or household income. In a business-to-business (B2B) environment, the market may be segmented by number of employees, revenue, or industry.

- **Behavioral Segmentation-** Behavioral segmentation divides consumers into groups according to their knowledge of a product's features; attitude towards changing from a current supplier; or current readiness stage, usage rate, or loyalty status with a product. This subset provides extra connectivity with the other segments. Many marketers believe that behavior variables are the best starting point for building market segments.

- **Psychographic Segmentation-** Psychographic segmentation, which is sometimes called lifestyle, is measured by studying the activities, interests, and opinions (AIOs) of different groups. It considers how people spend their leisure time and which external factors most influence them. Mass media has a predominant influence in psychographic segmentation.

Organizations that use market segmentation and targeting properly stand to gain greater business benefits. The first step in this process is to determine the basic characteristics of your largest customer/student/constituent groups. Next, you must determine which communication channels (direct mail, social media, television, radio, etc.) are most effective, as well as what types of messages best appeal to and generate a reaction from these groups. This may require testing, which can be a lengthy process. Finally, it is a good idea to link diversity recruiting to your market segmentation efforts as multiple perspectives about different groups can help you to better research and serve these audiences.

STRATEGY 101

Regardless of the industry, diversity leaders should primarily focus on the strategy. Often, when we reflect on great strategists, we think of Sun Tzu, Chinese military general, or Jack Welch, former CEO of General Electric. For most executives, business strategy is a complex concept that is difficult to master. Introspective and retrospective thinking might reveal that good strategy is simple and obvious. Business strategy does not pop-out of a fill-in-the-blanks template, matrix, triangle, or other strategic management tool.

Using these devices may lead to bad strategies indicated by:

- **Failing to address the problem (also known as "passive management")**
  Police departments in New York, San Diego, Chicago, Baltimore, and Ferguson, Missouri, have all been in the news recently for police misconduct. Instead of addressing errant behavior and the culture that fosters the negative conduct, leadership in these cities choose to ignore the problems or temporarily placate the complainants with monetary settlements.

  In *The Perils of Bad Strategy*, McKinsey & Company asserts, "A strategy is a way through a difficulty, an approach to overcoming an obstacle, a response to a challenge. If the challenge is not defined, it is difficult or impossible to assess the quality of the strategy. And, if you cannot assess that, you cannot reject a bad strategy or improve a good one. To summarize, if you fail to identify and analyze the obstacles, you do not have a strategy. Instead, you have a stretch goal or a list of things you wish would happen."

  When organizational leaders are too passive, they expect the problem to solve itself. Passive leaders wait and wait—secretly hoping that the problem will go away on its own. Unfortunately, it never happens because no one takes charge, and no one is accountable.

- **Mistaking goals for strategy**
  A goal, or objective, is defined as the desired result that a person or organization anticipates and plans to accomplish. Some management theorists propose S.M.A.R.T. goals, which are defined as goals that are specific, measurable, achievable, results-focused, and time-bound. Goals can be either short-term or long-term, depending on the strategy. Many organizations for example, have a goal of increasing women in leadership positions. However, how does one go about breaking the proverbial glass ceiling?

  Strategies are the methods that one uses to achieve the goals. There are three types of organizational strategies: **corporate strategy**, which deals with achieving long-term, entity-wide objectives; **business unit strategy**, which deals with how different divisions/departments function or thrive in certain markets; and **operational strategy**, which deals with the utilization of systems (e.g., work processes, management, etc.) and resources (e.g., time, treasury and talent) that can help achieve an organization's goals.

  Hence, a goal serves as the specific aim, while the strategy serves as the pattern, system, or means by which the goal is reached or achieved.

- **Unrealistic strategic objectives**
  When an organization plans a merger/acquisition, everyone hopes for a great outcome. Reality has consistently demonstrated that failed cultural integrations are often at the heart of merger difficulties. In fact, in a 2004 Mercer survey of executives involved in Merger and Acquisition (M&A) deals, 75% cited "harmonizing culture and communicating with employees" as the most important factors for successful post-merger integration.

A textbook example of this is the merger of Daimler Benz and Chrysler. Initially, the merger was seen as the perfect transatlantic union between automakers; the product portfolios were diverse and both companies had complementary geographies. However, the structural and financial merits of the deal were rendered irrelevant when the two companies could not find a way to operate productively under competing cultural identities.

To quote Miami University economics professor John Brock, problems arose when an "upright, hierarchal approach to things at Daimler Benz and … a risk taking, entrepreneurial, loose organization [at Chrysler]" were forced together. Indeed, many analysts cited friction between the American and German management teams from the outset because the corporate leaders failed to conduct cultural due diligence prior to the merger.

- **Too much fluff**
  A final hallmark of mediocrity and bad strategy is the application of superficial concepts (a flurry of fluff) designed to mask the absence of thought. Fluff is a restatement of the obvious, combined with a generous sprinkling of buzzwords that masquerade as expertise.

  Virtually every college has a web site in which they state how much they value diversity. They use buzzwords such as diversity, inclusion, and equity; then they take actions that seemingly contradict what they say they value. For example, the University of Missouri had a "Show Me Respect" campaign, which was designed to promote civility. According to the school website, "Civility means consistently treating people with consideration and respect, valuing the culture and humanity of others. Show Me Respect is our effort to create a culture of civility at the University of Missouri. Just as each student, staff member, and faculty member makes a unique contribution to the university community, so we ask that each of us contribute to the culture of civility." This is the same school where the President <u>and</u> Chancellor resigned amid a campus climate of incivility while they had a Show Me Respect campaign running for months prior to the terminations.

  Simply calling an initiative strategic does not necessarily mean that it is strategic. Most strategy documents do not include important details such as what should be done from day-to-day and how the strategy's progress can be tracked. When we are unable to break the concept into specific, doable actions, we fail to execute the idea.

A true business strategy is different from the vision, mission, goals, priorities, and Diversity and Inclusion plan. Good strategy works by focusing energy and resources on one, or a very few, pivotal objectives whose accomplishment will lead to a cascade of favorable outcomes. The key word here is *works*, meaning that there must be a bridge between the critical challenge at the heart of the strategy and the action(s).

According to the Harvard Business Review, there are *Five Questions to Build a Strategy*:

1. What are the broad aspirations for our organization and the concrete goals against which we can measure our progress?
2. Within the potential field available to us, where will we choose to play and not play?
3. In our chosen place to play, how will we choose to win against the competitors there?
4. What capabilities must we build and maintain in order to win in our chosen manner?
5. Which operating and/or management systems are necessary to build and maintain the key capabilities?

Strategy can help determine what to do, as well as what you should not be doing. Nevertheless, developing a strategy can be a lengthy process. That is why it is best to create stages for a strategy so that in the event that the market changes, the organization can adjust accordingly.

How can the Office of Equity, Diversity, and Inclusion help the organization successfully transition from Point A to Point B? The best way to achieve this is to create a subset of the organization's overall strategy, which will be called the D&I strategy. A **Diversity and Inclusion Strategy** is the proactive process of steering an organization toward sustainable, long-term success through inclusion, cultural competence, market segmentation, and equitable service. These elements are critical to the proper growth and development of the organization, as well as vital components of employee recruitment, retention, and engagement.

CONCLUSION

Diversity and Inclusion efforts must properly center on organizational dynamics and demographics. It is imperative for a D&I leader to understand market and organizational demographics, as well as ascertain how they pertain to employees, communications, and prospective business opportunities. The D&I leader must also use this knowledge to drive strategy, sustainability efforts, and results. Finally, a keen emphasis on strategy prevents your organization from losing focus and concentrating on the wrong things. A German proverb sums it up this way: "What's the use of running, if you are not on the right road?"

References:

United Nations Department of Economic and Social Affairs, Statistics Division, Statistical Papers, *Principles and Recommendations for a Vital Statistics System*, Series M No. 19/Rev.3, page 3

Hsu, Jeremy (2008). *There Are More Boys Than Girls in China and India.* Scientific American. Available at: https://www.scientificamerican.com/article/there-are-more-boys-than-girls/

Denyer, S. and Gowen, A. (2018). *Too Many Men.* The Washington Post. Available at: https://www.washingtonpost.com/graphics/2018/world/too-many-men/?noredirect=on&utm_term=.5670e2664651

Nielsen Insights (2016). *Fresh Foods and Flavors: How Multicultural Consumers are Driving Fresh Grocery Trends.* Available at: http://www.nielsen.com/us/en/insights/news/2016/fresh-foods-and-flavors-how-multicultural-consumers-are-driving-fresh-grocery-trends.html

U.S. Census Bureau, *United States Population Projections: 2000 to 2050*. Available at: (http://www.census.gov/population/projections/files/analytical-document09.pdf?cssp=SERP)

Difference Between Goals and Strategies | Difference Between | Goals vs Strategies
http://www.differencebetween.net/business/difference-between-goals-and-strategies/#ixzz3uA3Zh9ga

Martin, Roger L. *Five Questions to Build a Strategy.* Harvard Business Review. May 26, 2010. Retrieved from
https://hbr.org/2010/05/the-five-questions-of-strategy.html

Rumelt, Richard. (June 2011) McKinsey Quarterly. *The perils of bad strategy.* Retrieved From: https://www.mckinsey.com/business-functions/strategy-and-corporate-finance/our-insights/the-perils-of-bad-strategy

Rowley, Claudette. (Producer) *How to Integrate Culture During a Merger or Acquisition.* Retrieved From:
https://www.onlinecompliancepanel.com/webinar/How-to-Integrate-Culture-during-a-Merger-or-Acquisition-501566

Sample Test Questions

CONNECTING DEMOGRAPHIC SHIFTS TO ORGANIZATIONAL STRATEGY

1. **The difference between vital statistics and vital events is that vital events pertain to:**
    A. Relevant characteristics throughout one's lifetime
    B. Marriage, births, deaths, and other significant occasions
    C. Population data and various intervention programs

2. **This is the next frontier of D&I work. It is generated by people, processes, and machines:**
    A. Technology
    B. Big data
    C. Innovation

3. **_____ is an example of semi-structured data.**
    A. An Excel spreadsheet
    B. Streaming data
    C. A table or transaction

4. **High quality vital statistics are indicated by completeness, correctness and:**
    A. Carefulness
    B. Effectiveness
    C. Timeliness

5. **All organizations must prepare for an American demographic shift in racial and ethnic diversity that will be driven by:**
    A. Undocumented workers and a natural increase in births
    B. Corporate equity, diversity and inclusion programs
    C. Net international migration and an aging population

6. **One of the most common forms of market segmentation is:**
    A. Behavioral Segmentation
    B. Cluster Segmentation
    C. Migration Segmentation

7. **Relating to bad strategies, failure to address the problem is also known as dismissive management.**
    A. True
    B. False

idc Institute for Diversity Certification™

Sample Test Questions

CONNECTING DEMOGRAPHIC SHIFTS TO ORGANIZATIONAL STRATEGY (cont'd)

8. **The three types of business strategy are:**
   A. Marketing, operational, and financial
   B. Long-term, short-term, and intermediate
   C. Business unit, corporate, and operational

9. **The concept of market segmentation allows organizations to:**
   A. Identify and target certain demographic groups
   B. Have a successful Diversity and Inclusion initiative
   C. Increase revenue by marketing to all segments alike

10. **Clustering is the task of grouping a set of objects in such a way that objects in the same group are more similar to each other than to those in other groups.**
    A. True
    B. False

11. **Good strategy works by focusing energy and resources on _____ pivotal objectives that will lead to favorable outcomes.**
    A. 1-3
    B. 10-12
    C. 20-25

12. **The difference between strategy and goal is that a strategy serves as:**
    A. The competitive impetus that drives victory
    B. The specific aim that one seeks to accomplish
    C. The pattern, or system, used to reach the goals

13. **Psychographic, or lifestyle, segmentation considers how people spend their leisure and is predominantly influenced by:**
    A. Families
    B. Mass media
    C. Hobbies

INTEGRATING CULTURES AMIDST MERGER & ACQUISTION ACTIVITY

> *There are 3 reasons why workplace Diversity and Inclusion efforts are not going away: (1) shifting demographics, (2) changing competition, and (3) globalization.*
>
> *The Financial Times posted a March 2018 article by three authors in New York, London and Hong Kong entitled, "Record Mega-Deals Push Global Takeovers Beyond $1.2 Trillion". The multi-national authors wrote, "Despite a heightened level of political uncertainty, a potential US-led trade war, and fraught Brexit negotiations, companies have embarked on an unprecedented number of big acquisitions this year." This means that while politicians are inducing anti-globalization hysteria, there is an extraordinary amount of global business activity that continues to bridge international cultures.*

OVERALL OBJECTIVES AND COMPETENCIES

Mastering this competency will allow Diversity and Inclusion leaders to reconcile cultural expectations and practices amidst a unification of companies, departments, or agencies. D&I leaders will also be uniquely positioned to consult with leadership about potential problems and opportunities that may arise from a merger or acquisition.

BACKGROUND AND CONTEXT

There are 195 countries in the world today. Globalization has brought about many changes in the ways that companies conduct business—affording unprecedented opportunities to hire talented workers and market products in countries that most of us barely know.

The United Nations says that globalization "is a widely-used term that can be defined in a number of different ways. When used in an economic context, it refers to the reduction and removal of barriers between national borders in order to facilitate the flow of goods, capital, services, and labor" although considerable barriers remain to the flow of labor.

Globalization is not a new phenomenon. It began towards the end of the nineteenth century, but it slowed down during the period that began with the start of the First World War until the third quarter of the twentieth century. This slowdown can be attributed to the inward-looking policies pursued by a number of countries in order to protect their respective industries. Economists have linked inward-looking policies to the Great Depression, which began with the United States and triggered a worldwide economic crisis.

U.S. President Herbert Hoover was a moderately successful businessman who never held elected office. His campaign ran on the promise that he would create jobs for Americans by slashing immigration. Hoover introduced themes of efficiency in the business community and provided government support for standardization, efficiency and international trade. Nevertheless, as President, his domestic programs were overshadowed by the Great Depression from 1929 to 1933.

Wall Street's sudden and devastating crash on October 29, 1929 was considered a symptom of the Great Depression. Even after "Black Tuesday", optimism persisted, and U.S. stocks rebounded by April 1930. Then interest rates dropped and Great Plains drought crippled American farmers. These issues were compounded by trade tariffs. At first, Hoover attempted to coerce businesses to forgo cutting workers or slashing wages, but many companies could not resist.

Hoover's tenure in the White House not only reflected economic struggle, but also racial resentment and xenophobia. Hoover encouraged Congress to pass the Smoot-Hawley Tariff Act on June 17, 1930. The Act raised U.S. tariffs on over 20,000 imported goods and resulted in retaliatory tariffs by America's trading partners. The tariffs exacerbated the destruction of life and property from World War I—leading to over-production, unemployment, and business failures. By 1931, there were German and British banking crises, and soon countries around the world reported severe economic conditions. The League of Nations labeled Chile as the country hardest hit by the Great Depression because 80% of government revenue came from exports. Nevertheless, some nations such as Portugal, China, Japan, and Russia were largely unaffected by the Depression.

Sweden was the first country to recover from the Depression, and over time, the rest of the world recovered. The pace of globalization picked up rapidly during the fourth quarter of the twentieth century. Today, employees and consumers around the world have more choices than ever before. It's finally becoming clear that globalization does not merely increase corporate profitability in western countries. Globalization's greatest impact has been on people in developing nations and it has fostered a level of international equity that was previously unachievable. Educated workers in developing countries are now able to compete in the global job market for high paying jobs. Further, production workers in developing countries are not only afforded an equal opportunity to compete, their language and culture offers them a stronger advantage over their counterparts in the industrialized world.

In centuries prior to the Great Depression, a scramble for colonization led to American and Western European nations amassing great wealth that was not shared with those who were annexed. Globalization has had the opposite effect. According to the Brookings Institute, Asian and African nations are estimated to be far wealthier than previously imagined. Brookings states, "The changing distribution of middle-class spending toward new entrants will have an effect on markets. Households just entering the middle class will seek to purchase consumer durables, as well as services including tourism, entertainment, health, education, and transport."

As many American and Western European citizens witness the shift in middle class opportunities, some have denounced the unfairness of globalization. Learning about imperialism caused many of these individuals to believe that the advantages of superiority are still possible today. Yet Brookings asserts, "Unless globalization can be reframed into a win-win for the middle class in each country, the political narrative can be distorted into one of colliding interests between the middle class in emerging economies and those in advanced economies. A new package of "inclusive growth" must be constructed based on the common theme that continued widening of income and opportunity inequality, and the barriers these create to social mobility, must be forcefully tackled while preserving the benefits afforded by globalization and technological change and innovation."

FIGURE 1: GLOBAL MIDDLE CLASS PROJECTIONS

A term that has materialized from globalization is *emerging market*. Emerging markets are countries that are restructuring their economies along market-oriented lines to offer a wealth of opportunities in trade, technology transfers, and foreign direct investment. By nominal Gross Domestic Product (GDP), the six largest emerging markets in 2018 are China, India, Brazil, Russia, South Korea and Mexico.

Although it is difficult to compile a complete list of emerging markets, other countries that are also considered to be high potential markets include Indonesia, Argentina, South Africa, Poland, Turkey, Nigeria, Israel, and United Arab Emirates, to name a few. These countries made a critical transition from a developing country to an emerging market. Each of them is important as an individual market and the combined effect of the group as a whole will change the face of global economics and politics.

In fact, Brazil, Russia, India, China, and South Africa are collectively known as the BRICS countries. This diverse association is comprised of population and regional powerhouses on four continents. Since 2009, these nations have hosted an annual summit. The aim of the BRICS Summit is to improve the global economic outlook and reform financial institutions so that global markets are not dependent on the U.S. dollar. The formation of BRICS is a direct challenge to the clout of the G-7, as the intercontinental nations created their own rival to the International Monetary Fund (IMF). The New Development Bank, or BRICS Development Bank, is a multilateral development financial institution, where lending primarily focuses on infrastructure projects. Additionally, the nations created the BRICS Contingent Reserve Arrangement in 2014, which is a framework that provides protection against global liquidity pressures—in the event that another Great Depression occurs.

In the 1970s, "less developed countries" (LDCs) was the common term for markets that were less "developed" (by objective or subjective measures) than the developed countries such as the United States, Western Europe, and Japan. The term "less developed country" was thought by some to be politically incorrect so the emerging market label was created. These markets were supposed to provide greater potential for profit but contained more risk from various factors.

Figure 2 compares the E-7 (Emerging 7) with the G-7 (Group of 7).

FIGURE 2: GLOBAL POPULATION VS. GDP

E-7	Population (million)*	Nominal GDP (bn USD) 2010*	G-7	Population (million)*	Nominal GDP (bn USD) 2010*
China	1330	5879	USA	310	14582
India	1173	1729	Japan	127	5498
Indonesia	243	707	Germany	82	3310
Brazil	201	2088	France	65	2560
Pakistan	184	175	UK	62	2246
Russia	139	1480	Italy	61	2051
Mexico	112	1040	Canada	34	1574
Total	3382	13098	Total	741	31821
	49% of world total	21% of world total		11% of world total	50% of world total

Source: U.S. Global Research
*As of December 2010

Globalization is tantamount to the mythological "Pandora's Box". Once the box is opened, it is virtually impossible to recollect all of the complexities that arise from the container. A company generating $3 billion globally cannot easily scale back to $325 million in one country alone.

Not only should D&I and human resource professionals be aware of economic concerns pertaining to international developments, but they should also be aware of issues related to business operations. In the event of a merger or acquisition, these professionals must ensure that business conditions are ethical and aligned with the image that the organization desires to portray. This means emphasizing core standards such as no sweat shops, no child labor, no forced labor, freedom of association, right to organize and bargain collectively, and the right to decent working conditions.

FOREIGN WORKERS & THE U.S.

With new and improved transportation options, people are able to move around the world for better housing, education, healthcare, and employment opportunities. As of 2017, more than 258 million people don't live in the country where they were born, according to the United Nations (UN). The United States is the world's leader by far as a destination for immigrants. Saudi Arabia and Germany come in second and third place, while Russia holds the number three spot. Although Germany is home for a little over 1% of the world's population, the nation now views immigration as an advantage due to historically low birth rates.

U.S. organizations can employ foreign workers in America or send American employees abroad for short- or long-term assignments. American employers can temporarily employ foreign workers in specialty occupations in the U.S. through the H-1B Visa Program. The H-1B is a non-immigrant visa under the Immigration and Nationality Act, through the Department of Homeland Security. It allows an employee to stay in America for 3 years or 6 years if granted an extension. Recent changes to the law provide that U.S. Immigration officers can seek detailed documentation from employers to establish that they have specific assignments in a specialty occupation for the H-1B beneficiary. The changes also make it more difficult to obtain extensions.

The regulations define a *specialty occupation* as requiring theoretical and practical application of a body of highly specialized knowledge in a field of human endeavor. This includes but is not limited to architecture, engineering, mathematics, physical sciences, social sciences, biotechnology, medicine and health, education, law, accounting, business specialties, theology, and the arts, and requiring the attainment of a bachelor's degree or its equivalent as a minimum (with the exception of fashion models, who must be "of distinguished merit and ability"). Likewise, the foreign worker must possess at least a bachelor's degree or its equivalent and state licensure, if required to practice in that field. H-1B work-authorization is strictly limited to employment by the sponsoring employer.

Currently, the law limits the number of H-1B or otherwise provided visas to 65,000 aliens each fiscal year (FY). In addition, excluded from the ceiling are all H-1B non-immigrants who work at (but not necessarily for) universities and non-profit research facilities. This means that contractors working at, but not directly employed by, the institutions may be exempt from the cap. While there are some exceptions to the annual cap, annual shortfalls in the number of available visas cause employers to advocate for immigration reform.

The U.S. Department of Labor (DOL) is responsible for ensuring that foreign workers do not displace or adversely affect wages or working conditions of U.S. workers. While an employer is not required to advertise the position before hiring an H-1B non-immigrant pursuant to the H-1B visa approval, the employer is required to complete and submit a Labor Condition Application (LCA).

By signing the LCA, the employer attests that: (1) the prevailing wage rate for the area of employment will be paid, (2) working conditions of the position will not adversely affect conditions of similarly employed American workers, (3) the place of employment is not experiencing a labor dispute involving a strike or lockout, and (4) that the foreign employee will be given benefits comparable to those offered to other workers with similar jobs. The law requires H-1B workers to be paid the higher of the prevailing wage for the same occupation and geographic location, or the same as the employer pays to similarly situated employees. Other factors, such as age and skill were not permitted to be taken into account for the prevailing wage. Congress changed the program in 2004 to require the Department of Labor to provide four skill-based prevailing wage levels for employers to use.

The taxation of income for H-1B employees depends on whether they are categorized for tax purposes as either *non-resident aliens* or *resident aliens*. A non-resident alien for tax purposes is only taxed on income from the United States, while a resident alien for tax purposes is taxed on income from both inside and outside the United States.

The classification is determined based on the "substantial presence test": If the substantial presence test indicates that the H-1B visa holder is a resident, then income taxation is like any other U.S. person and may be filed using Form 1040 and the necessary schedules; otherwise, the visa-holder must file as a non-resident alien using tax form 1040NR or 1040NR-EZ. The individual may claim benefits from tax treaties if they exist between the United States and the visa holder's country of citizenship. Persons who are in their first year within the United States may choose to be considered a resident for taxation purposes for the entire year and must pay taxes on their worldwide income for that year. This "First Year Choice" can only be made once in a person's lifetime.

A U.S. company can also send employees to work abroad. An expatriate (in abbreviated form, expat) is a person who is temporarily or permanently residing in a country and culture other than that of the person's upbringing or legal residence. In common usage, the term is often used in the context of professionals sent abroad by their companies, as opposed to locally hired staff. The differentiation found in common usage usually comes down to socio-economic factors—skilled professionals working in another country are described as expatriates, whereas a manual laborer who has moved to another country to earn more money might be labeled an "immigrant". The term *expatriate* in some countries also has a legal context used for tax purposes. An expatriate living in a country can receive favorable tax treatment. In this context a person can only be an expatriate if they move to a country, other than their own, to work with the intent of returning to their home country within a period of no more than 5 fiscal years.

Lately, a different type of expatriate emerged where commuter and short-term assignments are becoming more common and often used by organizations to supplement traditional expatriation. Additionally, personal motivation is becoming more relevant than company assignment. Families may stay behind when work opportunities amount to months instead of years. The cultural impact of this trend is more significant. Traditional corporate expatriates did not integrate and commonly only associated with the elite of the country they were living in. Modern expatriates form a global middle class with shared work experiences in multi-national corporations, working and living in the financial and social centers.

The continuing shift in expatriates has often been difficult to measure. In Dubai, the population is predominantly comprised of expatriates from countries such as India, Pakistan, Bangladesh, and the Philippines; with only 20% of the population made up of citizens. In terms of outbound expatriation, the UK has the highest number of expatriates among developed countries with more than three million British living abroad, followed by Germany and Italy. On an annual basis, emigration from the UK has stood at about 400,000 people per year for the past 10 years. In terms of expatriate influx, the most popular expatriate destinations are currently Spain, followed by Germany and the UK.

In dealing with expatriates, an international company should recognize their value and have experienced staff to develop written policies and employee benefit programs for expatriates. Salary of internationally assigned personnel customarily consists of standard salary and monetary benefits such as cost of living and/or hardship allowances, supported by non-monetary incentives, such as housing and education. Some companies will completely cover the cost of the education, even at relatively expensive international schools; while others, usually smaller companies, encourage families to find local schooling options. Family relocation is an important element of successful long-term international assignments. International corporations often have a company-wide policy and coaching system that includes spouses at an earlier stage in the decision-making process, giving spouses an official voice. Few companies provide compensation for loss of income of expatriate spouses, although they often do provide other benefits and assistance. The level of support varies, ranging from offering a job-hunting course for spouses at the new location to full-service partner support structures, run by volunteering spouses supported by the organization.

There are several advantages and disadvantages of using expatriate employees to staff international company subsidiaries. Advantages include, permitting closer control and coordination of international subsidiaries and providing a broader global perspective. Disadvantages include high transfer costs, the possibility of encountering local government restrictions, and possibly creating a problem of adaptability to foreign environments.

Research indicates that a significant amount of international business is lost due to ineffective communication such as a lack of foreign language skills. Many English-speaking business people do not bother to learn other languages because they believe that most of the people they do business with in foreign countries can speak English, and if they do not speak English, interpreters can be used. The lack of foreign language knowledge puts the English speakers at a disadvantage. In meetings, for example, the people on the other side can discuss things amongst themselves in their own language without the English speakers understanding, and using interpreters slows everything down. While socializing after the meetings, the locals probably feel more comfortable using their own language rather than English.

INTRO TO MERGERS AND ACQUISITIONS

In recent years, long-standing competitors have been combining their efforts to achieve scale and dominance. Mergers and Acquisitions (M&A) have proven far more attractive and easier to pitch to investors than an expansion, which might require increased talent, plant, equipment, and other expenses. For the world's largest companies, the M&A race is energized by the need to acquire the best talent, increase market share, respond to industry consolidation, and innovate.

What is the difference between mergers and acquisitions?
By Brian Beers, Investopedia | Feb. 7, 2018

Mergers and acquisitions are two of the most misunderstood words in the business world. Both terms are used in reference to the joining of two companies, but there are key differences involved in when to use them.

A merger occurs when two separate entities combine forces to create a new, joint organization. Meanwhile, an acquisition refers to the takeover of one entity by another. Mergers and acquisitions may be completed to expand a company's reach or gain market share in an attempt to create shareholder value.

In an acquisition, a new company does not emerge. Instead, the smaller company is often consumed and ceases to exist with its assets becoming part of the larger company, who takes over all of the operational management decisions. Acquisitions – sometimes called takeovers – generally carry a more negative connotation than mergers. Due to this reason, many acquiring companies refer to an acquisition as a merger even when it is clearly not.

Legally speaking, a merger requires two companies to consolidate into a new entity with a new ownership and management structure (ostensibly with members of each firm). The more common distinction to differentiating a deal is whether the purchase is friendly (merger) or hostile (acquisition).

In practice, friendly mergers of equals do not take place very frequently. It's uncommon that two companies would benefit from combining forces with two different CEOs agreeing to give up some authority to realize those benefits. When this does happen, the stocks of both companies are surrendered, and new stocks are issued under the name of the new business identity.

Both mergers and acquisitions have pros and cons. Mergers require no cash to complete but dilute each company's individual power. Acquisitions require large amounts of cash, but the buyer's power is absolute.

The Nonprofit Hub reports that nonprofit organizations may consider merging for several reasons including when two organizations seek to:

1. Reduce financial instability
2. Eliminate competition
3. Combine skill sets or service offerings
4. Replace key staff

The *Metropolitan Chicago Nonprofit Merger Research Study* found that nonprofit mergers hold great promise. The study, a partnership between Northwestern University's Kellogg School of Management, Mission and Strategy Consulting, and eight Chicago foundations, analyzed 25 nonprofit mergers that occurred in the Chicago area between 2004 and 2014. The "most important finding was that in 88 percent of the cases that the researchers studied, both acquired and the acquiring nonprofits reported that their organization was better off after the merger, with 'better' being defined in terms of achieving organizational goals and increasing collective impact."

Similarly, changes in international student enrollment due to U.S. immigration laws, as well as other mounting fiscal pressures have created a ripe environment for mergers between colleges and universities. At the National Association of College and University Business Officers 2017 annual meeting, panelists concurred that "Mergers are extremely difficult, and neither trustees nor college administrators know how to manage a transition that involves high stakes and high rewards." The panelists convened just days after Inside Higher Ed reported that "one in eight chief business officers said senior administrators at their institutions had serious internal discussions about merging with another college or university in the last year."

According to panelists, "Reasons for institutions to merge are many. They can save money by becoming larger organizations. Large institutions might want to acquire smaller ones if it adds to the depth or breadth of their operations. Merging into larger institutions can also give small colleges the protection of a better-known brand name or additional institutional resources with which to improve their performance."

For example, University System of Georgia completed a number of mergers between its institutions when demographic projections determined that the 15-24 year old population was expected to decline. Acquisitions are also occurring at a steady pace in the educational sector. Nonprofit Purdue University acquired for-profit Kaplan University Online in a global deal to reach new students and enhance educational offerings. Critics were outspoken about their concerns that Purdue's values would change. Yet in 2018, Purdue received accreditation approval to augment its online education presence, an area where the institution has traditionally lagged.

Government agencies are not exempt. President Trump plans a massive federal government overhaul, where his administration intends to merge several agencies. Johnathan Breul, Executive Director of the IBM Center for The Business of Government, says, "In government, mergers are typically undertaken to streamline services and reduce costs. It is harder to judge whether a public sector merger is successful, though." Unlike the corporate sector, government agency mergers are rather mysterious as the literature about public consolidations is almost nonexistent. Nevertheless, state and local governments have a fair share of experience from which to draw upon. In Singapore, two government agencies merged to help more for-profit companies grow and internationalize. Singapore officials say the 2018 merger will allow government agencies to, "Evolve and re-organize themselves as needed, to better support local businesses and prepare them for the future economy."

In the corporate sector, 2017 was the third year in a row with more than 50,000 M&A deals announced worldwide according to Thomson Reuters. From Amazon and Whole Foods, to Aetna and CVS, to Disney and Fox News, the corporate landscape is quickly changing as unlikely companies acquire and merge and acquire and merge again. For these for-profit enterprises, the purpose is clear: to protect or improve the strength or profitability of the dominant company.

The South China Morning Post reports that, "Trade tensions have failed to hold Chinese companies back from pursuing their 'go global' ambitions." Chinese acquisition deals are being led by private equity firms as opposed to corporations, and investors expect to increase its strategic outbound deals. CNBC asserts that "Most of the deal-making will likely happen in sectors aligned with the Belt and Road Initiative, which is China's massive plan to connect Asia, Europe, the Middle East and Africa with a vast logistics and transport network. The Belt and Road Initiative involves 65 countries, which together account for one-third of global GDP and 60 percent of the world's population, according to Oxford Economics."

With a projected increase in global, national, statewide and local merger and acquisition activity, the Office of D&I can play an instrumental role. For example, helping organizational cultures to mesh, and ensuring that underrepresented groups are not adversely impacted by M&A activity are key goals for Diversity and Inclusion leaders.

As globalization continues to shrink boundaries, workforce diversity will be an imperative for the long-term sustainability of organizations, both large and small. As companies race to become bigger globally, there are a myriad of complex issues to address such as safety– which includes everything from terrorism to kidnappings to internet security. Further, D&I and human resource leaders can help employers maintain a sense of consistency and quality employee engagement. As the Financial Times puts it, "Trying to fit employees worldwide into one cultural straitjacket could seem detrimental." Alternatively, D&I leaders must advocate for one global purpose and identity but allow for geographical differences. In other words, don't erase geographic or functional identities; build upon them. Also, instead of an approach that doesn't 'see culture', organizations should seek to understand the cultures in local markets.

Regardless of industry, organizations will require workforces with unique perspectives in order to remain competitive in fields where the preferences, expectations, and needs of customers/students/patients are continually evolving. Additionally, organizations must prepare for the nature of competition to change, where big companies to compete against smaller enterprises in distant markets, or for-profits compete with nonprofits. This means that mega-employers must develop a culture of agility. Employers must also have a clear plan to move forward.

A CLEAR PATH FORWARD

In a Bain and Company survey of executives who have managed through mergers, a culture clash was the number one reason for a deal's failure to achieve the promised value. In a culture clash, the companies' fundamental ways of working are so different and so easily misinterpreted that people feel frustrated and anxious, leading to demoralization and defections. Productivity lags, and no one seems to know how to fix it.

A company's culture is all the shared values, beliefs and behaviors that determine how people do things in an organization. Three key elements in combination define the culture:

1. The **behavioral norms** exhibited by everyone from senior leaders to frontline employees

2. The **critical capabilities and decisions** about where and how to compete, as defined by the company's strategy

3. The **operating model** of the company—the structure, accountabilities, governance mechanisms and ways of working that make up the blueprint for how work gets done

To integrate two cultures, the organization must first define the cultural objectives in broad terms. This is invariably a job for the Chief Executive—and the CEO has to be willing to sustain his or her commitment until the objective is realized.

Setting the cultural agenda necessarily involves hard choices. What is the culture you want to see emerge from the combination of the two organizations? An acquirer can assimilate the acquired company, or it can create a blend of cultures. In some cases it can even use the merger to import the acquirer's culture into its own organization. The focus and the organization's objectives naturally depend on where the deal's greatest value lies. If cross-selling product lines is a key to the merger's success, for example, integrating the salesforce culture will be essential.

CASE STUDY: HAIER AND SANYO
Excerpt from "How to Bring Cross-Cultural Teams Together"
By Alicia Clegg | Financial Times, March 30, 2017

Few would have bet on a good outcome when Haier, China's leading home appliances maker, formed a joint venture with Sanyo Electric to develop refrigerators in Japan — a 2007 episode in corporate history studied by researchers at Iese Business School in Spain.

Speculation was rife among the Japanese workforce that Haier, the majority partner, merely wanted to rip off Sanyo's know-how. "There was a lot of uncertainty," says Du Jingguo, Haier's Asia chief executive, of the deal. "Would we cooperate long term or did we just want to take the technology?"

Culturally, the two companies were poles apart. While Haier promoted staff on merit and paid by results, Sanyo was wedded to the Japanese tradition of promoting by age and length of service. In the end, Mr. Du arranged an informal gathering where employees could share their concerns over drinks. Haier eventually bridged the gap by making concessions that allowed younger workers to advance, while sparing the pride of older employees.

In *How to Bring Cross-Cultural Teams Together*, Alicia Clegg suggests, "Organizing exchange visits and opportunities to collaborate on shared projects may be one way to foster a sense of collective identity. At Infosys, workers from across the group are encouraged to dial into monthly forums and present their top innovations so that good ideas can be shared." Employers will also have to think through local customs and operations. Clegg cautions, "Local differences in the protections that workers enjoy on matters such as disability, health and safety, gender and LGBT rights are another hazard that companies must negotiate. Though respecting local law may be all that is required to operate legally, applying different policies internationally can expose companies to accusations of hypocrisy."

Combining the Office of Diversity
The Office of Diversity may seem like a small piece of a large pie, but there are many factors to consider if a merger is announced. First, which organization has a more advanced diversity effort? It doesn't make sense to take two steps back in the realm of equity and inclusion, even if the acquire is smaller. A better scenario is to adopt the strategy and approach that is taken by the more advanced department. This requires a careful evaluation of each department's:

- Diversity Plan, with up-to-date evidence of tactical execution
- Standard Operating Procedures and/or Structure
- Visible Senior Management Support & Employee Participation
- Formal annual evaluation of D&I efforts

The more advanced effort will have next generation practices (i.e., those interventions that are not heavily focused on Affirmative Action, Political Correctness, or Intro to Diversity), and the office will have more formal documentation in place.

An audit will also:

- Weed out duplication of effort
- Determine management styles and priorities
- Use short surveys to determine employee perceptions about accepted behaviors, the culture, equity and inclusion
- Ascertain where the biggest cultural gaps exist (e.g., regarding customer service, management, etc.)

There are many areas where D&I can provide tools and resources to address potential problems and opportunities before or after a merger or acquisition. It will be critical to allay the fears of different groups by defining the shared vision for culture, diversity, and inclusion.

After a merger or acquisition, there is no one-size-fits-all approach to managing talent worldwide. Nevertheless, there are areas to consider, such as the following:

- **Understand how cultural perspectives shape career paths in emerging markets.** In developed nations, there is a human capital trend toward flatter organizational models. However, in emerging markets like India, progression through job titles really matters, reflecting the fact that attitudes about career progression are different.

  Another important area where employee perspectives vary considerably is global mobility. Cultural attitudes can affect what role international assignments play in an organization.

The traditional north-south mobility assignment, which lasts three to five years and is typically reserved for senior executives who return to the home country, may not be attractive to emerging-market employees.

Tactics developed in emerging markets have produced a variety of mobility models that grew out of sensitivity to different employee expectations. The models include much more fluid solutions like short project-based assignments, rotational programs, intra-country mobility, virtual mobility, and global-nomad assignments.

- **Develop country-specific rewards strategies.** Different cultures, environments and regulatory regimes may drive different needs and employee priorities in your rewards practices. Health care is a great example of this. Some countries rigidly regulate health care, while in other countries there are no requirements at all. While it may seem obvious that workers in countries with universal health care do not value employer-provided medical benefits, it may require deeper analysis to understand if those same workers are attracted to employer-provided transportation or onsite day care.

  Global employers in growth economies need to keep pace with rapidly changing employee priorities. For instance, while pay continues to be one of the most important tools for worker retention in China, other factors, such as benefits that support work-life balance, are increasingly important. Something as seemingly minor as the timing of a paycheck disbursement can be a significant differentiator, based on the needs of residents in those areas to meet their cash-flow issues. Hence, paying employees through direct-deposit debit-card accounts has become more common in emerging markets such as Mexico.

- **Leadership development.** The leadership pipeline needed to drive growth may be lacking in emerging markets. Long-term leadership development, not just technical training, is critical.

  Deploying senior executives is the traditional north-south model and has been very successful for many companies in emerging markets. That model is being augmented, or in many cases replaced, by models that develop talent locally. An example is IBM, which has established software centers of excellence in India with more than 100 locations. As more companies expand into newer emerging markets, the ability to develop local leaders will likely become a key differentiator.

- **Flexibility and innovation.** It is essential that international businesses tap into the ideas and innovations coming out of emerging markets. Some organizations are seizing this opportunity by investing in emerging market design centers or by moving entire operations to emerging markets from traditional strongholds. Bayer MaterialScience, for one, relocated the global headquarters for its polycarbonates business to Shanghai to increase its access to customers and innovative ideas. Business leaders and staff in established markets also need to be receptive to new ideas and innovations from their counterparts in emerging markets.

Understanding what is happening during a merger or acquisition is critical for D&I leaders. Keep in mind, a merger or acquisition can literally result in your organization operating in dozens of markets around the world overnight. Even if an organization does not operate globally, staying abreast of trends in emerging markets, immigration issues, and merger activity within the industry will be beneficial from a best practices and benchmarking perspective.

References:

Platt, E., Espinoza, J., and Weinland, D. *Record Megadeals Push Global Takeovers Beyond $1.2 Trillion.* Financial Times. Available at: https://www.ft.com/content/a0b4c0ce-327c-11e8-ac48-10c6fdc22f03

Kharas, Homi (2017). *The Unprecedented Expansion of the Global Middle Class.* The Brookings Institute. Available at: https://www.brookings.edu/research/the-unprecedented-expansion-of-the-global-middle-class-2/

United Nations Department of Economic & Social Affairs (Dec. 2017). *Population Facts.* No. 2017/5. Available at: http://www.un.org/en/development/desa/population/migration/publications/populationfacts/docs/MigrationPopFacts20175.pdf

Beers, Brian (2018). *What is the difference between mergers and acquisitions?* Investopedia. Available at: https://www.investopedia.com/ask/answers/021815/what-difference-between-merger-and-acquisition.asp#ixzz5K3ua922M

Hawthorne, Randy When Nonprofits Should Consider a Merger. Nonprofit Hub. Available at: http://nonprofithub.org/board-of-directors/nonprofits-consider-merger/

Haider, Donald (2017). *Nonprofit Mergers that Work.* Stanford Social Innovation Review. Available at: https://ssir.org/articles/entry/nonprofit_mergers_that_work

Seltzer, Rick (2017). *The Merger Vortex.* Inside Higher Ed. Available at: https://www.insidehighered.com/news/2017/08/01/higher-ed-mergers-are-difficult-likely-grow-popularity-speakers-say

Breul, Johnathan (2010). *Making Mergers Work in Government.* Governing. Available at: http://www.governing.com/blogs/bfc/Making-Mergers-Work-in.html

3E Accounting (2018). *Singapore Government Agencies Merge for Greater Effectiveness.* Available at: https://www.3ecpa.com.sg/regulatory-and-business/singapore-government-agencies-merge-for-greater-effectivness/

Choudhury, Saheli Roy (2017). *Money will start flowing out of China again, but it'll be much more targeted.* CNBC. Available at: https://www.cnbc.com/2017/11/12/chinese-ma-china-outbound-mergers-and-acquisitions-to-rise-in-2018.html

Clegg, Alicia (2017). *How to bring cross-cultural teams together.* Financial Times. Available at: https://www.ft.com/content/01503bd8-fd00-11e6-8d8e-a5e3738f9ae4

Sample Test Questions:

INTEGRATING CULTURES AMIDST MERGER & ACQUISTION ACTIVITY

1. **An employee may obtain an H1-B visa for all of the following work EXCEPT:**
   A. Theology
   B. Biotechnology
   C. Factory production

2. **Excluded from the employment visa limit are all H-1B non-immigrants who work at:**
   A. Federal government agencies
   B. Small businesses
   C. Universities

3. **An employer must submit this form in order to hire a foreign worker with an H1-B visa.**
   A. EEO-1 Form
   B. Labor Condition Application
   C. Fair Trade Agreement

4. **A resident alien for tax purposes is taxed on income from:**
   A. Inside the U.S.
   B. Outside the U.S.
   C. Both inside and outside the U.S.

5. **Before the term "emerging market" was coined, developing nations were called:**
   A. Less developed countries
   B. Newly industrialized nations
   C. Frontier markets

6. **The key difference between a merger and an acquisition is that an acquisition is:**
   A. Not going to require cash
   B. Sometimes called a takeover
   C. A combination of two entities

Sample Test Questions:

INTEGRATING CULTURES AMIDST MERGER & ACQUISTION ACTIVITY (cont'd)

7. **Friendly mergers of equal entities take place:**
   A. Never
   B. Often
   C. Rarely

8. **An example of an advanced Diversity and Inclusion effort will be evident through:**
   A. External awards & recognition
   B. Formal documentation
   C. Higher paid D&I staff

9. **D&I leaders can utilize short surveys to determine _____ perceptions about accepted behaviors, the culture, equity, and inclusion.**
   A. Employee
   B. Customer
   C. Shareholder

THE NEXT GENERATION OF EQUITY, DIVERSITY AND INCLUSION WORK

Generation Z is a diverse and complex group that is projected to transform education, the workplace, the marketplace, technology, philanthropy, the environment, and more. As the world welcomes this large new cohort into its institutions, the most effective Diversity professionals will have already made advanced preparations to adjust their definitions, practices and strategies in order to usher in the next frontier of equity and inclusion work.

OVERALL OBJECTIVES AND COMPETENCIES

The purpose of this competency is help D&I professionals evaluate how workplace Diversity and Inclusion efforts have changed over the years and prepare the organization to adopt forward-thinking practices and strategies.

BACKGROUND AND CONTEXT

We are living in a world that few could have imagined 50 years ago. As we envision the future, the question is: *"What will the workforce and workplace look like half a century from now?"* We can begin to tackle that question by examining where we have been, where we are, and where we are going.

The American economy is the strongest in a generation—perhaps in history. Unemployment is at a 30-year low. The sea of budget red ink has been turned to black. Wages are up, productivity is rising, and inflation is in check. Even in today's dynamic economy, there are some things that consistently remain important. In particular, there are three pillars providing stability in workers' lives:

1. **Economic Security Over a Lifetime**—where workers can have food on the table, a roof over their head, health care when needed, and a secure income for retirement.

2. **Work and Family Balance**—the resources and the time to enjoy family life and meet the needs of children and aging parents.

3. **Safety and Fairness in the Workplace**—free from health hazards, discrimination, and other unfair employment practices.

Globally, countries such as Singapore, Hong Kong, Niger, Liberia, Japan and Switzerland are posting strong economic results and historically low unemployment rates as well. Nevertheless, within the next few years, the workplace and workforce will undergo a major transformation. Some of these changes include:

Diversity in the Marketplace and Workplace
Diversity involves making sure that your organization reflects the markets in which you operate. It is about maintaining an employee base as diverse as the consumers/patients/students in the broader market, as well as making sure your employee selection is reflective of those served by your organization in local communities. This means that your employees (i.e., men and women of all generations from all types of ethnic and racial backgrounds, sexual orientations, abilities, etc.) will parallel multiple demographic segments, understand the needs of the market, and enable your organization to serve these different groups better than the competition.

By 2050, the U.S. population is expected to increase by 50 percent and groups of color will make up nearly half of the population. International immigration will play a role in shaping the future ethnic and racial composition, as well as impact the minority-majority crossover. In a 2018 report, the U.S. Census Bureau outlines several possible scenarios, "Under the assumption of a high level of net international migration, the population is expected to grow to 458 million by 2050. For the Low Net International Migration series, the population is projected to reach 423 million in 2050. Even under the assumption that net international migration is maintained at a constant level, the population will grow to 399 million by 2050. In contrast, for the Zero Net International Migration series, the population will increase slightly by 2050 to 323 million."

In other words, the current changes to immigration laws will only serve to slow down a demographic trend that has been in the works for decades. Current American immigration and trade policies would have the greatest impact on: (1) American employers who would experience a severe labor shortage; (2) the price of goods and services, which would increase with higher labor costs and global tariffs; and (3) social safety net programs such as Social Security, which could experience insolvency sooner.

The Social Security issue is particularly troubling as the population of older Americans is expected to more than double, and individuals will live longer. Some people may be forced to stay in the workplace longer or re-enter the workforce (both of which could increase workers comp injuries, depending on the type of work being performed).

One-quarter of all Americans will be of Hispanic origin. Almost one in ten Americans will be of Asian or Pacific Islander descent. And more women and people with disabilities will be in the job market. In short, there will be more diversity where we live, work, and do business. Organizations who wish this reality would simply go away, will soon wish that they did more to prepare for the future. Today's diversity and organizational leaders understand that progress in the equity and inclusion space takes years, or even decades. Therefore, employers with diversity leaders now will have a stronger competitive position in a world that is destined to change in more areas than demographics.

Five Upcoming Trends in Workplace Diversity
(source: Bersin by Deloitte)

1. *More CEO's Are Piping Up:* In top companies, CEOs are prioritizing and spearheading the diversity and inclusion dialogue; meanwhile in not-so-great workplaces, CEO's aren't saying a word. Outside of the surge in corporate webpages that now include <u>a diversity statement from the CEO</u>, more executives are using their platforms to address inclusion issues. Several CEO's are using LinkedIn to publish articles about diversity and inclusion, while <u>Intel's former CEO, Brian Krzanich</u>, used his time on the platform at the 2015 International Consumer Electronics Show (CES) to announce a major Diversity in Technology initiative. Intel's project includes new hiring and retention goals, and a $300 million allotment for building a pipeline of female and under-represented engineers and computer scientists.

   Intel's 2015 goal was to fill 40 percent of open positions with diverse candidates, which included women and underrepresented minorities (Asian men are overrepresented). The company tracked 43.3% diverse hires in 2015, which exceeded their 40% goal. By releasing more data and ensuring transparency, Intel hopes to be a leader in making its U.S. workforce more diverse by 2020.

2. *Semantics Aren't So Subtle Anymore:* What's in a title? When it comes to diversity, if you're not tying inclusion efforts to innovation, then you're thinking archaically. More and more employers are explicitly tasking diversity roles with innovation, in part by titling key jobs accordingly. The Corporation for Public Broadcasting employs a <u>Senior Vice President for Diversity and Innovation</u> among its senior staff—while Genentech recently posted an advertisement for a <u>Senior Director of Innovation, Diversity & Inclusion</u>. <u>Abbott</u>, a company long recognized as an employer of choice, has installed a Director of Next Generation Recruitment, Diversity & Innovation position, the purpose of which is to help the organization maintain its positive employer brand and harness the newest technology to source top applicants and predict their success. For a function that's long been marginalized, framing Diversity in terms of its inventiveness, imagination, and competitiveness is a smart practice for re-enlisting employees in organizational change.

3. *Diversity's Definition Has Changed:* In addition to fostering a workplace inclusive of race, gender, and sexual orientation (to name a few), many organizations are seeking value in something even simpler, <u>diversity of thought</u>. In some industries that are known for being limited in diversity – think law firms or high-tech companies – seeking out talent with different thinking and problem-solving backgrounds is critical.

   <u>Deloitte research</u> underscores that diverse thinker's help guard against groupthink, a dynamic observed firsthand with a large corporate client. Partnering with the company just after they had experienced a major product failure, the CEO lamented that the failure resulted from too much internal blind agreement – something Deloitte's study calls "expert overconfidence." Forward-thinking companies who see the danger in this lack of diversity continually question their own hiring and retention practices, as well as their everyday operating norms.

   While diverse representation is naturally required, it's how organizations utilize their diverse talent that will make the difference between an effort that provides lip-service and one that obtains great results.

4. *It's Less About Being a Good Corporate Citizen:* The <u>business case for diversity</u> has never been more front and center than it is now...and why not? Basic economic theory suggests that consumers will remedy a company's lack of diversity by simply not spending money there—making slow-to-change organizations extinct. The same can be said of employees, who are constantly balancing the costs of working somewhere against the personal benefits they derive, including a match in values. Gains in <u>employee engagement, effort and retention</u> alone make for a compelling diversity proposition. Add to that <u>customers who evangelize your inclusive philosophy</u> and products—and diversity ROI is hard to ignore.

5. *Technology Will Move from Burden to Benefit:* HR analytics experts say that the average large company has more than 10 different HR applications (including diversity data), taking considerable effort to bridge and synthesize that data into meaning. Luckily, startups are building new "diversity technology" that drives more precise, actionable change. "<u>Gap Jumpers</u>" came up with software that allows for blind interviewing and testing via the computer, helping to sidestep the risk of biased hiring decisions. <u>These</u> systems help employers write more inclusive job descriptions and creates accountability during interviews, for example calling out if a hiring manager disregards criterion they initially said was very important to them in a hire. Not surprisingly, those companies seen as most mature in terms of HR also spend the most on HR—and predict technology will be their largest future HR investment.

Technology + Inclusion

The use of the Internet and social media in workplaces will become more pervasive and the functions performed using portable electronic devices will dramatically increase. The influence of technology will go beyond new equipment and faster communications, as work and skills will be redefined and reorganized.

Increased global competition will continue to affect the type of functions being performed in workplaces, creating new high-skilled jobs and lessening the demand for low-skilled labor. The impact of globalization will continue to grow as more of the economy becomes involved in producing exports or competing with imports.

Between now and 2020, businesses will have nowhere to hide from the disrupting yet energizing effects of new technology. Those with flexible processes, structures, and culture will be able to adjust quickly and will find technology-led change invigorating and loaded with opportunity. Innovative working processes are arguably more vital to business model changes than innovation in technology.

According to recent research from the Economist Intelligence Unit, almost one third (31 percent) of business leaders worry that new technologies, and not business needs, will dictate the future direction of their company and how it will be managed. More than one third (37 percent) believe that by 2020 their organization will be unable to keep up with technology and they will lose their competitive edge. They need to be prepared with the right tools and expertise to ensure that they are maximizing technology and implementing innovative business processes for the future.

There is no doubt that technology will be a key source of change for the workplace of the future, but Diversity and Inclusion leaders do not need to be held hostage by it. It is essential that information processes are led by organizational needs, instead of by technology alone. Technology is already disrupting existing jobs and creating new jobs that never existed before.

In fact, change is happening so rapidly that 65 percent of today's grade school kids in the U.S. will end up working jobs that haven't even been invented yet. Hence, Generation Z workers will have different training needs and expectations from employers.

The pace of technological change—whether through advances in information technology (IT), biotechnology, or such emerging fields as nano-technology, will almost certainly accelerate in the next 10–15 years, with synergies across disciplines generating advances in research and development, production processes, and the types of products/services offered.

In the IT field for example, advances in micro-processors will support real-time speech recognition and translation, and artificial intelligence and robotics are likely to further advance. In terms of Diversity and Inclusion work, these advances will impact the disabled population as well as international travel assignments. For example, supersonic jets promise to cut travel time from New York to London to 3 hours and Tokyo to San Francisco in 6 hours.

The use of more intelligent robotics in manufacturing will support the ability to quickly reconfigure machines to produce prototypes and new production runs, with implications for manufacturing logistics and inventories. It will also impact healthcare, with less intrusive procedures; nevertheless, different religious groups may still object to advanced treatment options. Further technological advances are expected to continue to increase demand for a highly skilled workforce, support higher productivity growth, and change the organization of business, as well as the nature of employment relationships. Warehouses are a perfect example of how technology has changed work. For example, some Midwest cities are witnessing the development of huge warehouses on previously undeveloped land. These ultra-modern buildings house robots and drones than can stack products, conduct inventory, and perform other routine tasks. The robots and drones reduce injuries and turnover, as workers perform duties that are less tedious and physically taxing. Without a high level of automation, companies like Amazon would not be able to operate at low costs, or pass the savings on to customers.

Varying Degrees of Culture

The phrase "varying degrees of culture" is a silent nod to the fact that people will identify themselves in a variety of different ways. Accordingly, living and working in our society will require that each of us become increasingly aware of the challenges pertaining to cultural change. For example, White males should not be made to feel uncomfortable around multi-ethnic groups because of their race, gender, sexual orientation, or history. White men and women may also have to adjust to sharing some of the privileges that were once restricted to their group. The key is to ensure that Caucasians are not focused on losing, but excited about the future and its potential.

When you have a diverse workforce, it alters the way that people in the organization think and work. In a diverse workplace, you are more likely to be around different types of people who can introduce new approaches at work. Individuals from different cultures and backgrounds often bring unexpected and fresh perspectives to problem solving, design, and product development.

Having a diverse workplace is not only about race and cultural backgrounds; it encompasses a wide variety of contributions. Some people are more analytical while others are artistic. People from varying religious, political, and socioeconomic backgrounds possess different perspectives on the world and other specific issues. Additionally, there are individuals who are introverts and others who are extroverts; one could also factor in low-context and high-context cultural characteristics into these personality styles. Bring all of these types of people together and you are likely to see more creativity, new and better ideas, and improved service delivery.

Acclimating the workplace culture for diversity requires inclusion on all levels of the organization, especially in work assignments, strategic planning, and decision making to name a few. While new ways of organizing will be increasingly important for employers to succeed in the future, it will also be important to take into account the profound generational changes that are predicted to occur in the workplace. Indeed, companies are already facing the challenge of transforming their structures and ways of organizing to incorporate the new age of working.

THE NEW AGE OF WORKING

More than a third of the workforce are Millennials

% of the U.S. labor force

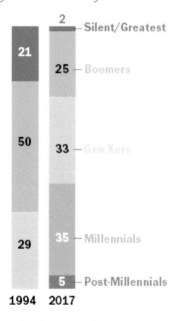

1994   2017

Note: Labor force includes those ages 16 and older who are working or looking for work. Annual averages shown. Source: Pew Research Center analysis of monthly 1994 and 2017 Current Population Survey (IPUMS).

PEW RESEARCH CENTER

Never before have organizations seen three and even four generations working together. These overlapping generations have great implications; not only for the way work is performed, but also for the way employers need to think about their future human capital and talent management strategies. In this age, heterogeneity and diversity have replaced the homogeneous workforce that pervaded previous eras.

The generations working together in today's workforce are: Baby Boomers, Generation X, and Generation Y. Baby Boomers refers to the post-war generation, born between 1946 and 1964; Generation X (GenX) refers to individuals born between 1965 and 1980; and Generation Y (Millennials) refers to persons born between 1981 and 2000. Although they comprise the smallest percentage of the workforce, Traditionalists were born between 1922 and 1945. Some Traditionalists still work (in paid and volunteer roles) to stay physically and mentally active.

The number of US workers over the age of 40 has increased significantly. By 2010, 51% of the US workforce was 40 years of age or older, while Millennials represented only 22% of the workforce. However, in 2016, Millennials became the largest generation in the labor force, according to Pew Research Center Analysis of U.S. Census Data. These figures suggest that an impressive replacement of the workforce occurred over a relatively short period of time, and this underscores the emphasis that companies will have to place on adapting to the fast-changing demographics.

Traditionalists or Silent

Traditionalists served their countries during the Second World War. But they also witnessed the First World War and participated in the Korean War. Loyalty, respect, and honor define the values of the traditionalists. Many of them have military experience and as a result, the managerial style of this generation tends to follow a top-down approach to getting things done, and they are accustomed to an assembly-line style of work. Not surprisingly, traditionalists embrace the idea of working for large institutions, as they view such institutions as the source of a stable career that one can be proud of.

Baby Boomers

Baby Boomers are still a large percentage of the workforce. However, as of 2015, Baby Boomers are between their early fifties and retirement age. The fact that a large proportion of the current workforce is near retirement is a huge challenge for organizations that need to build a bridge between generations to prepare for their continued success in the future.

Baby Boomers witnessed the Cold War, the Vietnam War, Watergate, the first time a man walking on the moon, the civil rights struggle, and the assassination of President Kennedy. Moreover, they were able to watch many of these events on television; indeed, one could say this generation was raised with the television. Power was being shared by two generations, Baby Boomers and Traditionalists. Boomers were raised to "pay your dues" or work long hours. Boomers were raised under a top-down managerial approach but needed to learn how to build consensus. This is an optimistic generation that has been able to live in a wealthy, prosperous world, and could afford to influence idealistic social change.

Generation Xers

After the Baby Boom generation, the birth rate declined dramatically. This new smaller generation, GenX, accounts for managers in their late-30s through early-50s. This generation has witnessed great technological developments and is technologically savvy, though GenXers are digital immigrants. The toppling of the Berlin wall, the AIDS epidemic, divorce, teen pregnancy, the crack cocaine crisis, and the Gulf War were among the most important events this generation witnessed in its formative years. The skeptical GenXer has seen parents' multiple divorces, corporate scandals, corruption, and well-established institutions called into question.

While Boomers' lives were impacted largely by the TV, many inventions have changed GenXers' ways of working: cable TV, fax machines, video games, Palm Pilots, pagers, mobile phones, and personal computers among others. Not surprisingly, GenX has clashed with the other generations still in the workplace. The managerial style of the three generations can be described as "chain of command" (Traditionalists), "change of command" (Baby Boomers), and "self-command" (GenX). Given these different management styles, such clashes have been predictable in a sense.

The "Millennial" Effect

Realistic is the best adjective to describe this new workforce. Consider for a moment where Millennials are coming from: for the most part, they are children of later-year Baby Boomers and earlier-year GenXers who dedicated their lives to companies and ended up having to jump from job to job over the course of their lives and careers. As a result, the millennial generation did not grow up in an era of increased job security as their parents had, but instead in a period of reduced job security and a time when ties between employee and employer are weak. Millennials' loyalty thus rests more with themselves and less with the company. For example, if they feel the company is not providing the opportunities they are looking for, Millennials are quick to move on, that is, to quit their jobs and offer their talent to competitors.

As millennials flood the workforce, companies are seeing a massive drop in employee engagement, the lowest it's been in the past eight years. Why? Perhaps because 21st century employees are different from those in previous generations — such as their attention spans, how they consume content and how fast they'll leave an employer when they're dissatisfied. Further, replacing them is a massive challenge costing companies billions of dollars annually.

Generation Z or iGeneration

The word iGeneration is derived from Apple's suite of popular products, encompassing the iPod, iPhone, iPad, and iWatch, to name a few. This generation prefers to play video games with multiple users, send text messages with emojis, FaceTime, use touch screens, watch short video clips online (e.g., YouTube), and wear headphones. To them, the Internet is not limited to home or work computers, it is something you can access in your pocket.

From social media, to reality television, to the proliferation of mobile technology, iGen has the potential to be among the smartest and most competitive employees yet. But iGen represents change in methods, attitudes and values. For instance, a larger proportion of iGen members are multi-racial. In fact, Census 2010 reported that the multi-racial population has increased almost 50% since 2000, making it the fastest growing youth group in the country.

A marked difference between Generation Y and Generation Z is that older members of the former remember life before the takeoff of mass technology, while the latter have been born immersed within it. This generation has also been born completely into an era of postmodernism, multiculturalism, and globalization. Additionally, parents of Generation I are working part-time or becoming stay-at-home parents so that children are raised by them and other family members instead of a day care facility, which forces children to be in groups.

FIGURE 1:

Source: Good&Co., The Multi-Generational Workforce: A Personality Analysis, 2015

DOMINANT PERSONALITY TRAITS ACROSS GENERATIONS

Gen Z	Gen Y	Gen X	Baby Boomer	Greatest Generation
Leads by (%)	Leads by (%)	Leads by (%)	Leads by (%)	Leads by (%)
Liking for Stress, 12	Risk-taking, 11.2	Competitiveness,10.9	Idealism, 18.39	Flexibility, 6.35
Creativity, 9.74	Emotional Stability, 10.97	Social Adaptability, 9.4	Democraticness, 7.64	Empathy, 5.04
Motivation, 6.84	Intellectual Curiosity, 7.2	Collaboration, 8	Social Confidence, 7.54	

THE NEXT GENERATION OF WORK

Instead of Diversity and Inclusion professionals identifying stereotypical descriptors about different generation groups, leaders must identify what impact these different groups will have on education and the workplace.

New Intergenerational Terms

Within the D&I space, there are terms that cross multiple generations. In some way, all of these terms impact people in the workplace.

- A *Boomerang Kid* is someone who leaves the household and then comes back. In previous generations, you left at age 18, with no questions asked. But this generation of parents actually welcomes their kids to move into the basement or their old bedroom. A 2013 Pew report found that more than three-quarters of "boomerangs" — the young adults ages 25 to 34 who move back in with their parents — were satisfied with their living situation.

- The *Sandwich Generation* is a group of people who are in the middle of caring for their aging parents while supporting their own children. The Sandwich phenomenon is due in part to what the U.S. Census Bureau calls the "Delayer Boom", or the number of American women who decided to have children later in life. In this scenario, highly educated women initially delay childbearing but are more likely to have children in their 30s. Unfortunately, by this time, their parents have aged and require some level of support while the individual is working and raising a young family.

- A *Helicopter Parent* is a mom or dad who pays extremely close attention to a child's (or children's) experiences and problems, particularly at educational institutions and in the workplace. Helicopter parents are so named because, like helicopters, they hover overhead. The term gained wide currency when American college administrators began using it in the early 2000's as the Millennial Generation began reaching college age. Their Baby-Boomer parents earned notoriety for practices such as calling their children each morning to wake them up for class and complaining to their professors about grades the children had received. Employers also reported similar behavior with parents attending job fairs and showing up with candidates for job interviews. The rise of the cell phone is often blamed for the explosion of helicopter parenting.

- A *Snow Plow Parent* seek to "plow the way" for their children. In Today's Parent, Emma Waverman asserts that Helicopter Parents are old news. In *Snowplow parenting: The latest controversial technique*, Waverman defines a snowplow parent as "a person who constantly forces obstacles out of their kids' paths. They have their eye on the future success of their child, and anyone or anything that stands in their way has to be removed." She adds that while helicopter parents are motivated by fear, snowplow parents are driven by something else. Waverman says, "Snowplow parents may also micro-manage when it comes to diet and education, but they do so with an eye on the future. They want to remove any pain or difficulties from their children's paths so that their kids can succeed. They are the parents sitting in the principal's office asking about extra courses or for special allowances for their child. According to educators, there is a sense of entitlement to snowplowers: They blame the school when things go wrong and never accept anything less than first place for their child."

Keeping Workers Motivated

Millennials and Generation Z value (1) multitasking, (2) the role of technology and being connected, (3) work-life integration, and (4) social consciousness. These four values will impact an organizations' way of organizing in the future.

To elaborate, first, these generations have been noted for its ability to juggle many things at the same time. For example, a person can use FaceTime on the phone and watch a You-Tube video that provides instructions on how to advance from one stage to the next in a video game—all while playing a video game on the Xbox. Additionally, some individuals enjoy the ability to play video games like Roblox and Fortnite in teams (with friends and/or family) while text messaging live updates or recording their ability to play. Games like Fortnite combine dancing and real teamwork to sustain global popularity.

Younger people have been raised in a context of great stimulation, which has allowed them to develop strong multitasking skills. This young workforce can perform business tasks while listening to music and interacting on Facebook from time and time. Some managers might consider attention given to non-work tasks disrespectful. However, this is a common practice that many Millennials and iGen welcome.

Second, for much of their lives, Millennials have been connected to the world through texting, internet chats, surfing on the web, or social networks. Podcasting and blogging complement the diverse communication forms that this generation embraces. All of the time they spend on the internet makes Millennials masters of multitasking. They are able to work on many things at the same time, and they expect their jobs to offer and resemble the diverse world they have grown up in with respect to access to technology.

A great example of using robust activity to capture a young person's attention exists in digital and object animation. Children who watch cartoons today expect to see many moving parts, in comparison to the relatively static cartoons of the 1970's and early 1980's. Even on the Big Screen, more movies are offered in 3-D and 4-D. Additionally, a 2014 study from The Council of Research Excellence found 16.1 percent of survey respondents claimed to have used social media (Facebook, Twitter, etc.) while watching prime time television.

In a survey conducted by Accenture, Millennials indicate that they want to choose which technologies they use rather than being forced to use those supplied by their employer, and they expect to be able to access the applications of their choice. This study suggests that 52% of all Millennials surveyed consider state-of-the-art equipment and technology in the workplace as crucial considerations when selecting an employer. While this generation is able to multitask and is technologically savvy, both Millennials and iGen are easily distracted. Not surprisingly, companies and schools alike are changing their approach towards capturing the attention of this attention deficient generation.

Third, this generation will pressure organizations to re-think work-life integration. As the term work-life integration suggests, Millennials aim to integrate their work and life, not just to balance their work and life. Their diverse activities (of which work is just one) require blending their work, workplaces, and personal lives. This trend has spread throughout all generations and is apparently evident in the number of people working from home, working while on vacation, and/or sending e-mails or doing work at non-traditional hours.

Finally, organizations should respond to the greater importance this generation places on solving social and environmental problems. Millennials expect employers to drive a social responsibility strategy that makes a difference in the community. Millennials also want their work to reflect their personal interests and ethics. They are proud to work for companies that have a positive social or environmental impact. For iGen, they have learned to work with diverse teams to solve complex problems. In some schools, the team rotates every month or every quarter so that students can gain experience working with different groups. In K-12 school, iGen is also learning how to utilize various techniques to arrive at the same answer. For example, in prior generations, students memorized multiplication tables. Today, the multiplication table is one of 8 or 9 tools that students can utilize to attain the right answer. Some of these mathematical tools employ techniques that originate from different countries.

In order to successfully integrate the different generations, it may be necessary to address varying management styles and values. Some companies are working hard to avoid generational clashes by supporting interventions that aim to build intergenerational connections. A few organizations are experimenting with diversity workshops, mentoring, and reverse mentoring as ways to connect the different generations.

IBM Corporation, for example, has developed Mentor Me, which allows employees to use the company's intranet to request a mentor. Employees can seek mentors in a variety of areas, such as general career development or technical skills enhancement, and the system identifies suitable matches from a pool of volunteers. IBM also offers a reverse mentoring program for senior executives who wish to learn from recent college graduates how technology is being used by consumers. These exchanges help ease senior employees' fear of passing on power while readying the next generation to lead.

Companies should build bridges between generations in the workplace to ensure that the different groups are able to coexist productively. Organizations must aim to optimize the talents of all age groups, reconciling intergenerational conflicts and leveraging diversity for an individual and organizational advantage. The case of IBM is one of many in which employers are trying to be open minded and innovative while working within the context of different generational needs.

With more Millennials entering the workplace, organizations may have to change the way that they are structured. The new workforce encourages companies to move away from older management paradigms in favor of freedom and flexibility. Millennials and Generation Z can easily work within the scope of a wider organizational structure that accommodates different educational and family needs, career aspirations, medical situations, and personality types. However, integration is a critical issue to make sure that this new generation positively focuses its energy into the organization.

For example, because some Generation Xers were latch key kids, many were told by parents that they needed to get certain tasks completed before mom or dad came home at 6:00. It didn't matter what time one started, or how one got it done, GenXers did their homework, cleaned up, and got dinner completed by the deadline. When GenXers entered the workforce, there were some that rejected the theme song from the 80's, "*Working 9 to 5*" by Dolly Parton. These individuals felt they were better suited with a later start, and the workplace provided an accommodation with the introduction of Flex Time. Alternatively, the Millennial generation saw the introduction of Open Concept offices, where individuals do not have "walls" to stop the flow of information. An example of how to adjust the organizational structure for the future workforce is indicated in Figure 2.

FIGURE 2: The "Age-Appropriate" Organizational Structure

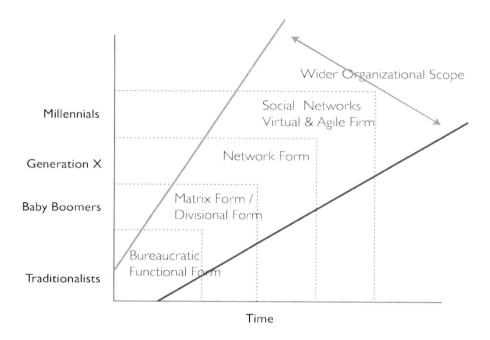

As evidenced in Figure 2, generational influences encompass multiple workplace policies and practices, and D&I leaders must think through how these influences will shape work. For example, Millennials also seek companies that align with their core values. Some of the values include:

- **Millennials recognize that professional development is the pathway to success.** According to a <u>recent survey</u> from Kleiner Perkins Caufield & Byers, training and development is the No.1 perk millennials seek when evaluating prospective employers. This generation is clamoring to advance professionally, and they don't want to wait for the slow climb up the corporate ladder; they want to take a rocket ship.

- **Nothing is more important to millennials than doing work that matters.** Millennials are on a constant search for meaning. Educate employees on why the organization exists and what it's doing to help others; this will increase the organization's chances of retaining young talent.

- **Millennials demand autonomy to do their best work.** Today, global businesses run with just a laptop and an internet connection. More than wearing a suit and filling up a seat, millennials know success comes from putting in the effort to get outstanding results, no matter where they are, what they're wearing, or what time they clocked in.

- **Millennials don't want to play by the rules. And that's good for business.** Today's Millennials understand there's always a faster, smarter, better way to do things. Some are born hackers, always on the lookout for the next smart-cut or workaround. They know that getting more done in less time is the greatest chance they have at shaping the organizations of tomorrow.

- **Too much information? To a Millennial, there's no such thing.** Millennials can't get enough communication. A generation of information junkies, the Millennials are hooked on how-to, they're programmed to seek out answers and ruthless when it comes to demanding honesty and authenticity.

Following are 10 tips on how to give millennials more of the development, meaning, autonomy, transparency, and efficiency they want at work:

1) **Create learning in short bursts.**
   Traditional learning is too slow for today's employees. Rather than long videos and boring lectures, use a micro learning-based approach to make content easily searchable, accessible and consumable on the job.

2) **Personalize diversity training.**
   Too many employees waste time on awareness training they don't need, failing to get the skills that actually help to make them more productive. Personalize learning paths for employees around the skills they actually use every day.

3) **Rethink management approaches.**
   More than bosses and managers, millennials want coaches and mentors. Adopt this mentality to foster a learning-driven culture.

4) **Teach the mission during onboarding.**
   Instill a company's mission and vision in a clear, uniform and inspiring way during the onboarding process; celebrating the organization's history and values to new hires who are still fresh and excited to be joining the ranks.

5) **Help them learn by doing.**
   The entrepreneurial way is to shoot first, aim later. Make relevant learning content available at the point of need and provide realistic practice opportunities so that acquiring new skills simply becomes part of doing the job.

6) **Offer a wide range of skills training.**
   Make training available on soft skills like negotiation and innovation, as well as on hard skills like Search Engine Optimization (SEO) or digital tools. Train Millennials like they're the CEO's of themselves.

7) **Update content continually.**
   The skills needed to do good work today are evolving constantly. Make sure learning materials are up-to-date with high-quality training, particularly on digital tools that expire fast.

8) **Put learning in the workflow.**
   Abandoning the task at hand to learn a new skill or technique is not efficient. Make learning available whenever and wherever employees are working — at the office, in the field, at home, and on mobile devices.

9) **Educate employees about the business.**
   How does the organization make money? What deals are in the works? How are the economics of the organization evolving? The more materials that employees have on how the company functions, the more invested they'll be.

10) **Make real-time announcements and updates.**

Without the most recent information, employees are incapable of making the best decisions possible on the job. Keeping employees informed will have a direct impact on their engagement and performance.

Finally, be wary against stereotyping individuals based on their generation. Figure 3 illustrates how Millennials perceive themselves in comparison to how human resource professionals (and others) perceive them.

FIGURE 3.

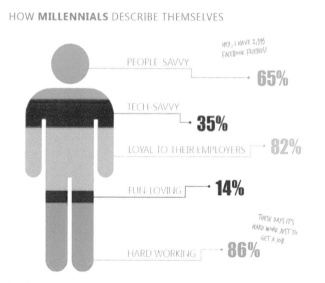

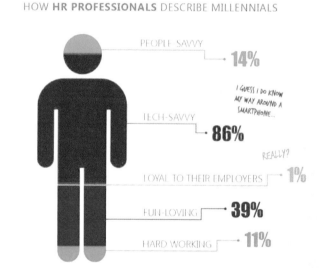

Millennials can be used as a model to prepare organizations to attract, develop, engage, and retain Generation Z in the future. Key areas to consider are:

- Multi-tasking and Multi-functional Approaches (such as concurrently teaching and learning)
- Teamwork
- How Technology is Used and What it is Used for
- Transparency (e.g., the ability to explain why certain individuals have different experiences)
- Diverse Identities and Diversity of Thought (i.e., in relation to problem solving)
- Social Responsibility

A NEW APPROACH TO INNOVATION

As innovation becomes a key differentiator for the world's best and/or largest employers, organizations will increasingly see a diverse and inclusive workforce as critical to driving the creation and delivery of new products, services, and business processes. For leaders in charge of Diversity and Inclusion, describing opportunities for innovation is paramount to building the business case.

As globalization continues to shrink boundaries, workforce diversity will be an imperative for the long-term sustainability of organizations, both large and small. These entities will require workforces with unique perspectives to remain competitive in fields where the preferences, expectations, and needs of customers/students/patients/constituents are continually evolving.

Larger organizations will have the resources to employ Artificial Intelligence (AI), which can improve the speed, quality, and cost of available goods and services. Nevertheless, in *How robots, artificial intelligence, and machine learning will affect employment and public policy* the Brookings Institute reports that, "Emerging technologies like industrial robots, artificial intelligence, and machine learning are advancing at a rapid pace, but there has been little attention to their impact on employment and public policy."

The impacts of automation technologies are already being felt throughout the economy. For example, in 2014 Google was valued at $370 billion with only 55,000 employees, a tenth the size of AT&T's workforce in the 1960s. Still, Google has a sizable workforce because there is some work that is simply performed better by humans.

Globally, innovations from the cotton gin to electricity to the computer have created dramatic changes in the way that we work and the jobs that are available—and to whom they are given to. The Brookings Institute also reported, "The worldwide number of industrial robots has increased rapidly over the past few years. The falling prices of robots, which can operate all day without interruption, make them cost-competitive with human workers. In the service sector, computer algorithms can execute stock trades in a fraction of a second, much faster than any human. As these technologies become cheaper, more capable, and more widespread, they will find even more applications in an economy."

Will AI eliminate the need for Equity, Diversity, and Inclusion interventions? Not exactly. Experts disagree on the size of the impact that automation technologies will have on the workforce. While some warn of staggering unemployment, others point out that technology may create new job categories that will employ displaced workers. A third group argues that the technology will have little effect on employment in the future.

From a systemic perspective, this only means that Diversity and Inclusion efforts must do better at increasing the quantity and quality of diverse workers in the high-tech, high-wage pipeline, starting with K-12 education. Connecting STEM education with careers could include targeting children that enjoy building Legos or playing video games. In fact, hackers initially learn how to exploit technological flaws by advancing through various video game levels. Likewise, robots and drones allow kids to learn how to program code. Indeed, schools and workplaces miss out on a whole population of diverse workers with advanced technology skills because they are not 'packaged' the right way. These groups can do a much better job of linking a child's hobbies to a profession that the individual will enjoy, as well as working with others in the D&I field to solve systemic STEM issues.

All of these efforts must work hand-in-hand with supply chain management, philanthropy, and sustainability efforts. Also, comprehensive supplier diversity efforts will ensure that smaller enterprises continue to create local jobs that will not be replaced by Artificial Intelligence.
In previous eras, the D&I field as a whole was reactive in its approach to managing the impact of multiple generations. Today, Diversity leaders have an opportunity to get in front of projected changes in the workplace and marketplace. The next generation of Equity, Diversity and Inclusion leaders must be ready to face a complex set of unknowns never faced before: competition for talent, managing rapid change and creating real-time agility. Additionally, Diversity and Inclusion executives must be prepared to design long-term strategies to solve business problems, as well as meet the dynamic needs of the future workforce.

Future trends in technology, globalization, and demographics will likely affect the distribution of jobs and wages. In the absence of a strong increase in the supply of skilled workers in response to the higher returns in education, wage dispersion (particularly as measured by the gap between more- and less-educated workers) will likely remain at current levels or even continue to widen. Unsustainable imbalances between supply and demand will put huge additional strains on governments struggling to adjust as public-sector finances become stressed beyond tolerance.

Diversity, historically considered an initiative in corporate America, will become a workforce and marketplace reality, according to FutureWork Institute, a consulting firm that evaluates workplace trends. FutureWork further maintains that the fastest-growing domestic markets for goods and services will be ethnic communities. Therefore, smart companies must carefully balance changing demographics and increased buying power, with organizational realignments and technological endeavors.

While the Next Generation of Equity, Diversity & Inclusion will be very different than it is today, the old adage says, *fortune favors the prepared.*

References:

Next Generation Talent Management *(Palgrave, 2010) and* The New Workforce Challenge *(Palgrave 2013).*

Karsten, Jack and West, Darrell M., 2015. *How robots, artificial intelligence affect employment and public policy.* The Brookings Institute, October. Retrieved from: http://www.brookings.edu/blogs/techtank/posts/2015/10/26-emerging-tech-employment-public-policy-west

Lynn A. Karoly and Constantijn W.A. Panis, "The 21st Century at Work: Forces Shaping the Future Workforce and Workplace in the United States", MG-164-DOL, 2004

Diversity Best Practices https://www.diversitybestpractices.com/events/top-five-ways-ceos-show-commitment-diversity?pnid=7878

Ortman, Jennifer M. and Guarneri, Christine E. (2018). *United States Population Projections: 2000 to 2050.* U.S. Census Bureau. Available at: https://www.census.gov/content/dam/Census/library/working-papers/2009/demo/us-pop-proj-2000-2050/analytical-document09.pdf

Wingfield, Nick (2017). *As Amazon Pushes Forward with Robots, Workers Find New Roles.* The New York Times. Available at: https://www.nytimes.com/2017/09/10/technology/amazon-robots-workers.html

Fry, Richard (2018). Millennials are the largest generation in the U.S. labor force. Pew Research Center. Available at: http://www.pewresearch.org/fact-tank/2018/04/11/millennials-largest-generation-us-labor-force/

Waverman, Emma. Today's Parent (Jan. 14, 2015). *Snowplow parenting: The latest controversial technique.* Available at: https://www.todaysparent.com/blogs/snowplow-parenting-the-latest-controversial-technique/

idc Institute for
Diversity Certification™

Sample Test Questions:

THE NEXT GENERATION OF EQUITY, DIVERSITY & INCLUSION WORK

1. **In the labor market, it is very important to Millennials to:**
   A. Do work that matters
   B. Get paid high wages
   C. Take time off to travel

2. **In the "Age Appropriate Organizational Structure", Traditionalists were best served in:**
   A. Social Networks
   B. A divisional form
   C. A bureaucratic form

3. **Artificial Intelligence (AI) will eliminate the need for Diversity and Inclusion efforts.**
   A. True
   B. False

4. **All of the following are pillars that provide stability in a workers life EXCEPT:**
   A. Pay inequities
   B. Safety and fairness
   C. Work-life balance

5. **Millennials do not face stereotypes in the workplace.**
   A. True
   B. False

6. **As employers prepare for Generation Z, they should evaluate how:**
   A. Supervisors manage
   B. Employee benefits vary
   C. Teams function

7. **All of the following provides Millennials with more meaning at work EXCEPT:**
   A. Holding back pertinent information
   B. Rethinking management approaches
   C. Teaching the mission while onboarding

Sample Test Questions:

THE NEXT GENERATION OF EQUITY, DIVERSITY & INCLUSION WORK (cont'd)

8. **With more Millennials entering the workplace, organizations may have to change how:**
   A. They approach equity
   B. They are structured
   C. Service is delivered

9. **Lack-key kids, from the Generation X era, ushered this into the workplace:**
   A. Boomerang kids
   B. The notion of Flex Time
   C. Open concept offices

10. **This group currently comprises the largest percentage of the workforce:**
    A. Millennials
    B. Generation Xers
    C. Baby Boomers

11. **How have organizations changed the definition of diversity to add more value?**
    A. From Affirmative Action/EEO to inclusion
    B. From cultural competence to inclusion
    C. From representation to diversity of thought

12. **In the future, it will become more apparent that the employee base must reflect:**
    A. The preferences and whims of the Millennial generation
    B. The racial composition of the senior leadership team
    C. The demographics of the communities being served

13. **Comprehensive supplier diversity efforts will ensure that _____ continue to create local jobs that will not be replaced by Artificial Intelligence.**
    A. Government agencies
    B. Smaller enterprises
    C. Multi-national employers

ADVANCED DATA INSIGHT & ANALYSIS

It is not enough for D&I leaders to simply collect data or share the findings from research reports. Diversity professionals must provide insight, which is an accurate and deeper level of understanding into how the data will impact the organization today and in the future.

Beyond assumptions or opinions, data allows one's insights to result in the creation of new ways of thinking about an organization's Strengths, Weaknesses, Opportunities and Threats.

OVERALL OBJECTIVES AND COMPETENCIES

The purpose of this competency is to establish a diverse and inclusive environment where leaders can collect timely and relevant data for measurement and evaluation purposes; benchmark the organization's D&I progress against similarly situated employers; and compile analytic insights to drive organizational culture change and reconstruct inequitable inter-connected systems.

BACKGROUND AND CONTEXT

According to Vriens and Verhulst, a business insight is:

A thought, fact, combination of facts, data and/or analysis of data that induces meaning and furthers understanding of a situation or issue that has the potential of benefiting the business or re-directing the thinking about that situation or issue which then in turn has the potential of benefiting the business.

Providing insight focuses attention on increasing understanding for the purposes of benefiting the organization. These insights will also allow D&I leaders to demonstrate impact in a meaningful way. There are two primary conversations paramount among Diversity and Inclusion professionals— one focuses on accountability and the other focuses on performance, particularly impact. For years, many practitioners have been disappointed with the inability to demonstrate measurable impact through Diversity and Inclusion. There are two points to make here: accountability should be addressed in the evaluation process and impact should be demonstrated with progressive illustrations, examples, and empirical evidence.

Point #1: You need a Strategic Diversity & Inclusion Plan
The successful evaluation process begins with a formal, written Diversity and Inclusion plan. If you already have a plan, then you are well on your way to demonstrating measurable outcomes.

Conversely, if you do not have a plan, it will be difficult to demonstrate that you made an intentional and strategic impact. The establishment of desired outcomes, activities, and indicators should take place during the strategic Diversity planning stages.

Think of the desired **outcomes** *as what you ultimately want your Diversity and Inclusion effort to accomplish;* **activities** *as what you will do to get there; and* **indicators** *as the gauge of whether, and to what degree, you are making progress.*

Outcomes should be consistent with what could reasonably and realistically be accomplished and not overly idealistic. Reasonable and realistic does not mean limiting your effort or the expanse of the outcomes. A properly designed Diversity plan is clearly defined, with measurable outcomes, which translates into benefits for the business and its stakeholders. The plan should also indicate who is responsible for which tasks.

Outcomes provide a foundation for *all* subsequent program implementation and evaluation activities, and each of the outcomes will need to be evaluated. While you and your internal Inclusion partners will undoubtedly seek to obtain a vision that is much bigger and beyond the scope of the Office of Diversity & Inclusion, focus your outcomes on what can realistically be accomplished within a designated timeframe (e.g., 6 months or 1 year).

Activities are the interventions that your Diversity and Inclusion effort will provide in order to facilitate or bolster the intended outcomes. Programs can be created for many different activities to achieve desired outcomes. For purposes of this course of study, activities will be classified as any type of direct service or information provided to employees, students, customers, patients, constituents, or other stakeholders, that will facilitate an outcome.

Indicators act as the gauge of whether, and to what degree, your Diversity and Inclusion effort is making progress. The progress needs to be examined in two distinct ways:

1. The quantity and quality of the **program activities you are delivering** (commonly referred to as process indicators), and

2. The quantity and quality of the **outcomes that your program is achieving** (commonly referred to as outcome indicators).

Therefore, indicators must be developed to measure both types of progress. *Process indicators* help track the progress that your Diversity and Inclusion effort is making as you work toward achieving the desired outcomes. Process indicators often provide important feedback to senior leadership long before you can expect to see evidence that outcomes are being achieved. *Outcome indicators* provide the most compelling evidence that the Diversity and Inclusion effort is making a difference in the lives of employees, students, customers, constituents, or other stakeholders.

Now that an understanding of what outcomes, activities and indicators entail, the question becomes, what is the best way to develop them for your particular organization? That brings us to our next point.

Point #2: Plan your evaluation strategy based on where you fit on the Diversity Development Continuum

The problem with most evaluations is that some people assume that their organization's evaluation results should yield the same outcomes as other organizations that are more or less mature in their Diversity and Inclusion journey. Since organizations are at different stages on the Diversity development continuum, it is necessary to determine where your organization is situated before developing a comprehensive evaluation strategy.

Figure 1 illustrates the various stages on the Diversity development continuum. Essentially, this tool determines the organization's competency in the realm of Diversity and Inclusion. Each stage of the continuum will use different measurement tools to assess the impact of Diversity on business operations or the organization's climate. As the organization progresses through the continuum and the Diversity and Inclusion efforts grow more complex, the evaluation methods should also become more elaborate to reflect bottom-line impact. Nevertheless, evaluation data should not be so intricate that it is confusing to the average person. However, it should reflect standard business measurement practices.

FIGURE 1. DIVERSITY DEVELOPMENT CONTINUUM

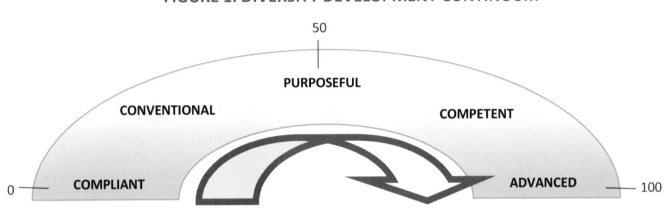

THE COMPLIANT ORGANIZATION

In the Compliant mode, an organization is doing the minimum to ensure compliance with the law. This type of activity does not register on the Diversity continuum because the organization is not attaining Diversity or Inclusion. The organization is ensuring compliance with Equal Employment Opportunity law (or applicable national/state/local legislation), which is a separate, although related, matter.

Thus, the goal for compliant organizations is to move beyond compliance toward conventionalism. In order to satisfy this goal, the organization's readiness must be assessed. To this end, a model (see Figure 2) is provided as a guide. This model can be incorporated into a more comprehensive assessment tool included in an online survey sent to your employees or used during a focus group meeting.

FIGURE 2. ASSESSING YOUR ORGANIZATION'S READINESS FOR DIVERSITY & INCLUSIVENESS

1. ***Level of Commitment to Diversity & Inclusion***
    - *What is driving your need for Diversity and Inclusion?*
    - *Do you have a formal Diversity plan? Is it integrated into your organizational Strategic Plan?*
    - *Is there a dedicated professional responsible for Diversity and Inclusion (e.g., a Chief Diversity Officer, Director of Diversity, etc.)? Does he or she have decision-making authority and a budget?*
    - *Is there visible senior management support for D&I goals? Are there executive sponsors for key Diversity initiatives?*

2. ***Training & Professional Development***
    - *Have you conducted a formal assessment to determine what type of Diversity and Inclusion training would best suit employees?*
    - *What other professional development programs would benefit from a Diversity and Inclusion component (i.e., coaching, mentoring, consultation, etc.)?*
    - *Do New Hire Orientations indicate your Diversity & Inclusion values?*
    - *Is Diversity management a required competency for new supervisors or promotions?*

3. ***Operations & Internal Support Systems***
    - *How could a Diversity Council or Employee Resource Group best support organizational objectives?*
    - *How should business units/departments integrate Diversity and Inclusion goals (e.g., customer service unit strives to increase diverse client retention by 0.05%)?*
    - *Are field offices involved in Diversity planning and Inclusion efforts?*

4. ***Performance Management & Accountability***
    - *Have employee policies been updated and distributed to workers and managers? Are existing policies enforced?*
    - *Are Diversity and Inclusion goals (e.g., recruiting, retention, training, etc.) incorporated into managers' performance evaluations and bonus requirements?*
    - *Are there managers who receive more discrimination/harassment complaints than others? What interventions are available to remediate behavior?*

5. **Marketing & Communications**
   - *What are the projected demographics for your customer, student, patient, or constituent base in the next 10 years? Are you currently marketing to these audiences?*
   - *How has the industry changed? What has your organization done to adjust to these changes?*
   - *Are your marketing and communications materials available in other languages?*
   - *Are corporate visual images consistent with your Diversity and Inclusion values (e.g., your website, social media, printed materials, etc.)?*
   - *If you operate in other countries, are social media and online marketers knowledgeable about the cultural nuances in each region?*

6. **Community Relationships & Philanthropy**
   - *What diverse community-based organizations can help you reach your target audience for employees, customers, students, board members, etc.?*
   - *Do you have a supplier Diversity program?*
   - *Do you sponsor or financially support diverse organizations and events?*

In the compliant mode, the evaluation of success is measured by moving beyond legal compliance toward deriving organizational value from serving different groups better than competitors. In "valuing" Diversity, most evaluation data will be qualitative or "soft" data. A good strategy for gathering data might be to start by defining Diversity, locating a consultant to help with Diversity training, or designing and distributing an employee survey.

THE CONVENTIONAL ORGANIZATION

In the Conventional mode, an organization truly begins its Diversity and Inclusion journey. This is where an employer may hold a mandatory Diversity training session on how to value differences. In this mode, the company is looking for ways to deal with issues that have surfaced. When discriminatory behavior is detected, sometimes only involving one or two people, a training date, time, and location is set, and a consultant is hired by HR. Employee feedback will generally be negative, reflecting resistance to change. However, the goal for conventional organizations is to keep the momentum going; don't stop with one mandatory training session for all employees.

In this mode, evaluation criteria may be based on how many people attended the session and whether the training laid the foundation to help solve "the problem". To inculcate the conventional mentality into the company, it may be advantageous to conduct a cultural climate audit before and after the training. Some organizations may even create a Diversity plan in this phase.

It is important to note that in this stage, the strategic Diversity and Inclusion plan should be simple. This means that the plan may be one-page and the goals are very easy to accomplish. *Simple.* Not only will this approach give employees and senior leadership confidence toward the change management process, it will increase buy-in for future D&I efforts. In this phase, employees resist Diversity because it is HR-led; therefore, it is important to utilize communication to keep senior executives engaged and excited about D&I's potential so that they can eventually play a key role in leading it to the next stage.

These small, incremental steps are necessary to ensure that everyone is on board, in the right seat, at the right time. Achieving Diversity is a journey, while Inclusion is a process. Initial resistance is normal, and it will be significantly less than a whirlwind campaign with a lot of conflict, minimal support, and few results.

THE PURPOSEFUL ORGANIZATION

In the Purposeful mode, an organization understands that it needs to do more than hold an annual Diversity training session. In this phase, the organization may develop a business case for Diversity, create a multifaceted Diversity plan, and/or design a recruitment strategy for diverse employees. Hence, the company recognizes that there is a genuine purpose for Diversity and Inclusion efforts. This stage is transformative because it is where senior leadership typically buys-into Diversity and Inclusion. At this juncture, a senior executive calls for D&I versus HR initiating it. A higher level of employee support for D&I is evident when a senior executive launches the effort.

In this mode, "how to value" Diversity training sessions are no longer presented unless one is facilitating a new hire orientation. During this stage of the continuum, training should focus on Diversity and Inclusion skills—communication, customer service, team building, conflict resolution, management, etc. If the organization is an educational institution or non-profit, training could focus on researching different demographic groups in an effort to attract new students, constituents, donors, or volunteers. Concurrently, training for the Information Technology (IT) department could revolve around working with employees and/or customers from different generational groups. For a corporation, ensuring that the sales and marketing team is culturally competent with different groups will go a long way in appealing to, or generating new revenue from, diverse sources. Essentially, all Diversity and Inclusion training in this stage should focus on skills that employees can take back to the job and apply immediately.

In this mode, the Diversity plan should be revised to reflect growth. With the initial goals accomplished, what is next? At this point, it may be necessary to comb through the organizational plan and map out a strategy to link Diversity and Inclusion efforts to specific organizational goals. Again, do not go overboard in setting goals, keep it simple! Everything at this point should have a purpose.

Begin preparing managers for the next stage, **Competence**. To assist in achieving competence, keep managers engaged in the process. Ideas include:

- Identifying what the organization rewards and ensuring that supervisors are rewarding behaviors that align with D&I values.
- Empowering managers with tools to address bullying, harassment, and other unprofessional behavior.
- Holding leadership retreats that are not focused on Diversity, but includes a Diversity and Inclusion component.
- Publicly acknowledging managers who are making an effort in hiring, developing, and promoting personnel who are diverse.
- Providing coaching, and follow-up, for supervisors who are challenged by the demands of Diversity and Inclusion.
- Utilizing a pre-determined schedule to regularly update managers about D&I successes.

In the Purposeful stage, your efforts can be evaluated by whether you accomplished Diversity and Inclusion goals, which should be linked to business objectives. You can also measure how the culture has changed, and what impact the changes have had on customers, students, patients, volunteers, donors, etc. Are there reportable increases? Are there more compliments from external stakeholders? Is there greater employee satisfaction?

Evaluation data at this point will be considerably "soft". The data does not get entirely "hard" or quantitative until after this phase. Nevertheless, there should be adequate documentation of your processes, progress, and outcomes. This documentation should include **at least** one annual report. The Office of Diversity and Inclusion can also prepare a monthly, quarterly, or semi-annual report.

THE COMPETENT ORGANIZATION

What makes an organization competent is the integration of D&I practices into everyday business operations, and its focus on setting Diversity and Inclusion goals that are more intricate. Thus, instead of the D&I leader being solely responsible for equity and inclusion, responsibility for goal-setting and achievement spreads throughout the enterprise. For example, pay increases and bonuses for managers may be linked to achieving departmental Diversity and Inclusion objectives. Intercultural curriculum and co-curriculum may be developed. Several employee resource groups may be formed and trained. A supplier Diversity program for Tier 1 and Tier 2 vendors may be rolled out, with training for procurement officers/corporate buyers, traditional vendors, or diverse suppliers. Alternatively, the organization may apply the research from the previous phase to a marketing campaign targeting a diverse segment.

There is a saying that goes, "that which gets measured, gets done". The same could be said in the converse: "That which gets done, gets measured". However, not all activities need be measured, unless they are deemed important and are tied to the overall success of the organization's core business. This will engender a competitive advantage. Too many organizations spend time trumpeting the success of activities that yield no measurable impact or benefit to their strategic goals or customer needs. As a result, they experience the absence of key stakeholder support, employee resistance to change, and shareholder distrust.

Practitioners must approach Diversity and Inclusion management in the same manner as other business objectives measured by tangible and specific results. This will also help reinforce the business case established in the previous phase.

In a Society for Human Resources Management (SHRM) Study on Workplace Diversity, *How Can the Results of Our Diversity Initiative Be Measured?,* it was suggested that measurement is done by a "comparative process that includes both baseline data detailing the starting conditions <u>and</u> clear objectives against which change can be measured". Therefore, as a rule, **never start a change process without collecting baseline data**.

The measurement process requires that you clearly define a starting point for change and collect two to three months of baseline data before "transforming" anything. This process anchors the change and enables your organization to measure the impact of the change over time. Determining a starting point also ensures that evaluation is a forethought, rather than an afterthought. When evaluation is an afterthought, the D&I leader performs a lot of work and then asks, "How can I measure D&I's impact"? However, there were never any intentional targets set, or data collected throughout the process to ascertain whether the impact is net positive, negative or neutral.

There are a number of sources from which baseline data can be gathered, such as:

- *Collecting existing organizational data.* Information from various internal departments (e.g., human resources) can be used in your measurement process. For example, existing staff satisfaction survey results can tell you a lot about what is on the minds of your rank-and-file employees that may not surface in face-to-face interviews. Look for patterns or recurrent themes in groups such as women or underrepresented ethnic groups.

You can also initiate inquiries into policies and processes. For example, determine the impact of turnover among diverse groups, as well as the cost to hire and replace people who have left your organization within a short amount of time. Is there an inordinate amount of absenteeism within a particular group or department? What about an increase in EEO complaints in mono-cultural or less diverse divisions or teams? Is there a disparity in the levels of dissatisfaction of employees according to ethnicity, job classification, and gender? How often does the organization "innovate", and what has been the customer response to new products/services?

- *Facilitating focus groups.* Convene small groups of 6-10 employees, customers, or students to talk about the perceptions, challenges, values, and expectations of your organization. To ensure constructive discussions, these meetings must be led by skilled facilitators who can guide meaningful group conversations while important anecdotal information is being captured.

Once baseline data has been gathered, work with your business partners to identify, monitor, and measure the key metrics. From a Human Capital perspective, employing more diverse individuals is not the goal, engaging more diverse perspectives that lead to breakthrough thinking is the goal. From a marketing perspective, more multicultural marketing is not the goal, deeper penetration into new and emerging markets is the goal. From a Procurement perspective, collecting more small business qualification surveys is not the goal, awarding more contracts to diverse suppliers is the goal. Look for tangible measures, and be specific and intentional from the onset. Make sure the metrics clearly support business goals and note past criticisms.

In addition to collecting the baseline data, you want to:

- **Establish a Clear Aim**
  Establish a clear improvement aim or target. Such a target should: (a) be realistic yet ambitious (e.g., do not expect 100 percent completion), (b) be linked to organizational objectives, and (c) avoid confusion, especially with percentages (e.g., say reduce turnover from 65 percent to 25 percent, rather than 'improve turnover by 62 percent').

- **Consistently Collect Data**
  The ability to establish consistent channels for collecting measurement data on a regular basis is a crucial part of the change process. These channels may exist in current data systems; however, you may need to collect the data manually. Often it is easier to rely on manual collection for quick and direct feedback on the success of the intervention. This means relying on small samples collected over short periods of time to measure progress.

- **Chart Your Progress**
  Over time, your organization will collect both pre-change (baseline) and post-change data, and the data should be shared with stakeholders within your organization. The most effective tool for sharing this information is charting your progress over time using simple line graphs. These powerful visual aids should follow one simple axiom: one graph, one message.

- **Ask Questions**
  The most important step in the process is to ask questions. For example, what is the information telling me about change in my organization? If the Diversity initiative was unsuccessful, why did it fail? If the intervention worked, what contributed to the effectiveness of this effort? How can we make improvements? If change is successful, the information you have collected may affirm which intervention(s) had the most success in meeting your goals.

To set good goals, use the SMART model: Specific, Measurable, Achievable, Relevant, and Time Bound. Working closely with internal business partners will allow you to set goals that meet these criteria. The next step is to establish who will do what, when it will be done, and what are the rewards and consequences. Serious attention must be paid to monitoring each step of the implementation process. As always, everything done in each step of the process should be documented.

FIGURE 3. ENSURING ORGANIZATIONAL COMPETENCY	
Method	**Activities**
Establish corporate-wide goals	• Review strategic plan • Interview senior executives • Document and confirm objectives and goals • Review bonus goals for all senior level executives
Pinpoint departmental goals	• Review departmental plans • Interview department managers • Document and confirm objectives and goals • Review bonus goals for each manager • Confirm alignment with senior management goals. If not aligned, review with Senior leadership and seek alignment
Ascertain supporting initiatives	• Review departmental level projects • Discuss program specifics with the project manager
Select appropriate interventions	• Assess current organizational projects and proposals • Identify high impact, high visibility projects that can be influenced by D&I
Identify business partners	• Interview department managers • Identify D&I champions • Assess D&I skills and capabilities • Select business partner(s) with unique perspectives
Review and understand departmental jargon	• Discuss with the department manager • Review past projects • Identify the most successful projects • Isolate the key areas of focus and reporting • Use the language of the department, not HR or D&I • Align language and terminology with specific bonus goals for managers and senior leadership
Develop key metrics	• Link interventions with corporate strategic targets • Connect goals with departmental objectives • Align projected outcomes with bonus goals • Design SMART (Specific, measurable, achievable, realistic and time bound) goals • Monitor team generated goals

By helping departments and managers achieve key goals, D&I efforts present a win-win for everyone. This builds enthusiasm, teamwork, engagement, and Inclusion. Accordingly, the outcomes will also contribute to the accomplishment of key organizational goals.

THE ADVANCED ORGANIZATION

As we progress up the Diversity development continuum, you will note that Diversity and Inclusion efforts become more involved. Hence, the evaluation of business impact becomes more complex as well.

In the final phase—Advanced—there is a specific expectation for results and a push toward integrating Diversity and Inclusion into corporate growth strategies and everyday business operations. The Advanced phase deals with tangible and intentional outcomes. Here, the Diversity and Inclusion expert can fully demonstrate that D&I can be evaluated according to commonly accepted business principles—that is, quantitative hard-core metrics. Moreover, because of programs like the Institute for Diversity Certification, D&I practitioners will speak on one accord versus everyone using different standards. Thus, success will no longer be an anomaly; it will be the expected norm.

The advanced phase involves:

- Solving a business problem that threatens sustainability (e.g., how to increase foot traffic in malls),
- Coordinating interventions across systems (e.g., connecting D&I across a university system, on the federal/state level, or other multi-state initiative)
- Enhancing product/service offerings (e.g., introducing a scalable 'customization' feature to an existing product/service),
- Venturing into new markets (e.g., developing a new app that traverses different ages, genders, races, nationalities, etc.),
- Facilitating simultaneous cultural developments (e.g., translating your website into 23 different languages while building an international call center),
- Achieving other inherently complex feats.

The advanced phase allows for revolutionary ideas and enterprise-wide transformations. At a university, the D&I office may lead an initiative to establish a sister campus in Dubai. At a corporation, the D&I office and African American Employee Resource Group may lead a delegation consisting of business, government, nonprofit and academic leaders to an African country to discuss international business opportunities. At a nonprofit, the D&I office may lead an effort to expand international services, as well as publicity and fundraising. At a state government agency, supplier diversity efforts may result in robust economic development. At any of these entities, the D&I office may establish a job rotation program that allows American personnel to gain work experience overseas, and international employees to gain experience working in the Americas.

International business strategies are the way of the future. Not only has the Internet expanded global opportunities, but the proliferation of Asian, African, and Latino middle class families has facilitated emerging markets overseas with unmet or under-served needs. Thus, a global focus allows organizations to seize more financial opportunities through Diversity and Inclusion. A state government agency may have an interest in attracting foreign businesses to the state in order to create jobs, stimulate foreign investment, or model best practices. Likewise, a hospital may want people to come from outside of the local area for specialized treatment at the facility. Finally, a multinational organization may want to ensure that it has a diverse, global supply chain. Each of these strategies presents opportunities for the Office of Diversity and Inclusion to capitalize on increased economic activity in partnership with other business units within the organization.

If you remember one thing in this phase, remember this: **do the math, or the math will do you.** In other words, operating a fully functional diversity and inclusion effort is expensive. If you don't demonstrate a positive benefit, a negative value proposition will *not* work in your favor.

Diversity words should not be used to show positive benefits. In order to speak the language of the CEO, President, Executive Director, Secretary, or other senior leaders, the savvy Diversity and Inclusion professional must speak the language of the Corporate Suite (C-Suite)—*revenue generation or cost savings*. Keep in mind, whether you work at a for-profit, educational institution, nonprofit, or government agency, **every executive has some level of concern for finance**. Accordingly, in the advanced phase, D&I professionals are more fluent and transparent in business dealings, and they are more comfortable talking about money and/or operating in other nations. Therefore, we will reference D&I outcomes in financial terms (i.e., the language of executives).

This is fairly new for the D&I industry, and it is the next generation of Diversity thought leadership. In our capacity as experts in the field, we will use words such as "asset", "calculate", "measure", "return on investment", "value", and "bottom line". Each of these terms must be used in order to establish and maintain the importance of Diversity and Inclusion to organizations.

Value implies usefulness or something of worth. It can also denote principles or character. In transferring values (i.e., passion for Diversity and Inclusion) to an organization, and creating *more* value, it is important to move beyond warm and fuzzy (soft) data toward cold, hard facts.

Andres Tapia, Senior Partner at Korn Ferry, was the 2011 keynote breakfast speaker at the annual Forum on Workplace Inclusion in Minnesota. He spoke on the topic, "*Diversity 1.0 is Tired, Spent, and Obsolete: It's Time to Invent the Next Generation of Diversity Work*". Mr. Tapia's presentation centered on retiring Diversity and Inclusion tenets that do not work. He proposed adapting a new Diversity and Inclusion platform that is strategic, successful, and sustainable. Otherwise, if D&I practitioners resist moving past Diversity 1.0, they eventually succumb to the math.

Life generally requires movement, transition, or advancement because time and change are constant. Moving or progressing requires change, the same thing that we are asking others to do, and change is not easy; however, change is necessary. Over time, what makes people feel good— valuing one another (the beginning of the Diversity development continuum)—is not perceived as valuable to the company. That is why, at this level, organizations need the Office of Diversity and Inclusion to produce a tangible bottom line impact.

It is important to remember that bottom line impact differs from organization to organization. For example, the American Red Cross counts volunteers and donations, not profits; and government organizations, like the IRS, may have a service-oriented bottom line. Still all employers, whether for-profit or not-for-profit, depend on their ability to get the best possible return on dollars invested. Thus, it is necessary to understand how your organization makes money and its long-term goals. Additionally, you will have to know how to operationalize key terms such as:

- *Bottom Line:* The final outcome of a process, showing a gain or loss; the most important fundamental aspect of a situation
- *Return on Investment:* A form of cost-benefit analysis that measures the costs of a program (i.e., the investment) versus the financial return realized by that program
- *Measurement:* A collection of quantitative data; allowing for comparison against accepted standards

In the field of Diversity and Inclusion, ***impact*** can be defined as the quantifiable change, or potential change, in one or more key areas:

- *Economic* (including sales, donations, enrollments, and other factors that affect finances)
- *Environmental* (such as the organizational climate or culture)
- *Professional* (including hiring, training, advancement, and retention)
- *Legal* (such as the number of complaints or lawsuits filed)

Essentially, there are four components involved in measuring impact.

1. ***Combining*** quantitative and qualitative data to get deeper insights.

2. ***Customizing*** the metrics to reflect what is important in the organization's culture, its business results, and industry.

3. ***Collaborating*** in both traditional and nontraditional ways to acquire information, allow for innovation, and activate integration throughout the organization.

4. ***Communicating*** both expectations and accomplishments in a predetermined format on a predetermined schedule.

Impact focuses on corporate benefits in terms of:

- *Knowledge gained and how that knowledge is applied.*
- *Behavior or attitude changes.*
- *Practice or situation changes.*
- *Results of those behavior, attitude, practice, or situation changes.*

Impact can be positive or negative. Sometimes, when it comes to Diversity and Inclusion, as is the nature of most people, it is easier to remember the negative impacts than the positive impacts. Nevertheless, almost every organization has experienced unsuccessful projects—programs that go astray, cost too much or that fail to deliver on promises. Critics of the projects suggest that failure could have been avoided if:

1. The project was based on legitimate need from the beginning
2. Adequate planning was in place at the outset
3. Data was collected throughout the project to ensure it was on track
4. Greater emphasis was placed on accountability

Calculating impact has been difficult because, in the Diversity industry as a whole, activity has been confused with impact. Unlike other departments and business units that have a definitive career path and expectation for results, the Office of Diversity and Inclusion often has two problems: (1) Some organizations hire or promote practitioners without prior experience or formal education in the field of Diversity and Inclusion (2) Some individuals have experience and/or the education, but they are used to "winging it" (e.g., no definition of Diversity, no strategic Diversity plan, no annual evaluation, etc.). In either case, there may be a lot of activity (i.e., travel, events, meetings, training sessions, etc.), but none of these endeavors have real bottom-line impact.

Figure 4 compares and contrasts activity to impact.

FIGURE 4. D&I ACTIVITY VS. IMPACT	
Activity	**Impact**
• Organizing cultural events throughout the year	• Creating a formal Diversity plan with regular interventions and evaluation criteria
• Revising Policies, such as Paid Time Off (PTO)	• Soliciting input and feedback from Supervisors about how the new policies will affect operations and management practices
• Mandatory Diversity Training for all employees	• Providing Diversity & Inclusion Training by Business Unit to demonstrate the link to day-to-day tasks & responsibilities
• Hiring a Diversity Coordinator	• Creating a Succession Plan for the Office of Diversity
• Participating in a Supplier Diversity Fair	• Following up to ensure that those small businesses are added to your list of vendors and that they get contracts
• Recruiting Diverse Candidates	• Training supervisors "how to" model inclusion and manage diverse teams

As figure 4 indicates, some organizations spend thousands of dollars recruiting diverse candidates to no avail. How could a greater impact be created? Before spending money recruiting diverse candidates, find out whether the organization is inclusive in policies, practices, and communications. A simple way to determine the level of inclusiveness at the organization is to ask current employees. Don't just ask the women or the people of color, ask everyone. If or when they make suggestions, vet the ideas. If the ideas are viable, implement them. Not only will this build an inclusive workplace, but it will also stimulate innovation, creativity, and engagement.

When Eli Lilly, a Fortune 500 pharmaceutical giant, conducted its first employee survey more than 20 years ago, senior management was surprised at the Diversity of its workforce. This led to the creation of many work-life programs. Ultimately, Eli Lilly became an award winning, best place to work for talented scientists and health care professionals. Today Eli Lilly does not consider Diversity to be an add-on to their business, nor is it vulnerable to changes in strategic direction. The organization's commitment to Diversity and Inclusion is embedded in the way the company operates. The success of Diversity and Inclusion in an organization as vast as Eli Lilly is the result of it being attached to as many key business metrics, goals, and targeted wins as possible.

Understanding and communicating the essence of true organizational impact, or the business benefits, is key. Diversity representatives often report things like attendance figures, what people like about an event, the number of meetings held, business units served, and/or a new award, as impact. While some of this information provides context, at this stage, none of it indicates impact.

Impact can be indicated by demonstrating changes in sales, productivity, the ability to recruit and retain high quality talent or attract exceptional students, and any other bottom line data point. Similarly, these items are factors that can be incorporated in your business case for Diversity. Other data that signifies impact includes savings from diverse suppliers, favorable publicity, product development, decreases in EEO Complaints/Lawsuits, and other statistics. Additionally, buying patterns, trends, and demographics are changing, thus requiring an adjustment to the organizational strategy for Diversity.

Ralph V. Gilles is a Haitian-American automobile designer. He formerly served as the President and CEO of the SRT Brand and Senior Vice President of Design at Chrysler Group LLC until he was promoted to Head of Design for Fiat/Chrysler. Mr. Gilles served as the executive sponsor of the Chrysler African American Network (CAAN) and is a leading player in The Chrysler Global Diversity Council. Mr. Gilles was responsible for re-designing the Chrysler 300 luxury sedan, which won the most new car awards in history and resulted in over one million vehicles sold around the world. This example of Diversity in Chrysler's senior leadership has led to innovations in product development, efficiencies, and increased sales and publicity—impacting employees, customers, and shareholders.

You can also indicate impact with soft data. However, care must be taken not to base your entire case for Diversity and Inclusion on soft data. In the industry, we have been doing this for years and it has led critics to assume that Diversity does not work. A better strategy is to utilize both soft and hard data to validate impact.

An example of hard data is a quantifiable measure of the turnover rate; an example of soft data is employee satisfaction. Soft data can be converted into hard data, if there is enough statistical evidence to support it. For example, a Sears metric demonstrated that employee attitudes (soft data) were linked directly to customer retention. Sears found that a 0.05% rate of employee dissatisfaction equaled a 1.3% rate of customer dissatisfaction, which translated into a 0.05% revenue loss or $200 million in lost sales. In this instance, it is clear that soft data, quantified in numerical terms, can be valued information for determining the impact on the bottom line.

STRATEGIC ANALYSIS & INSIGHT

Bernard Marr, Forbes contributor, asserts, "The goal of any business analytic tool is to analyze data and extract actionable and commercially relevant information that you can use to increase results or performance." In *The 18 Best Analytics Tools Every Business Manager Should Know*, Marr identifies several tools that will be particularly effective in analyzing D&I needs and/or outcomes:

- **Business experiments:** Experimental design and AB testing are all techniques for testing the validity of something – be that a strategic hypothesis, new product packaging or a marketing approach. It is basically about trying something in one part of the organization and then comparing it with another where the changes were not made (used as a control group). It's useful if you have two or more options to decide between.

- **Visual analytics:** Data can be analyzed in different ways and the simplest way is to create a visual or graph and look at it to spot patterns. This is an integrated approach that combines data analysis with data visualization and human interaction. It is especially useful when you are trying to make sense of a huge volume of data.

- **Correlation analysis:** This is a statistical technique that allows you to determine whether there is a relationship between two separate variables and how strong that relationship may be. It is most useful when you 'know' or suspect that there is a relationship between two variables and you would like to test your assumption.

- **Scenario analysis:** Scenario analysis, also known as horizon analysis or total return analysis, is an analytic process that allows you to analyze a variety of possible future events or scenarios by considering alternative possible outcomes. Use it when you are unsure which decision to take or which course of action to pursue.

- **Data mining:** This is an analytic process designed to explore data, usually very large business-related data sets – also known as 'big data' – looking for commercially relevant insights, patterns or relationships between variables that can improve performance. It is therefore useful when you have large data sets that you need to extract insights from.

- **Video analytics:** Video analytics is the process of extracting information, meaning and insights from video footage. It includes everything that image analytics can do plus it can also measure and track behavior. You could use it if you wanted to know more about who is visiting your store or premises and what they are doing when they get there.

- **Cohort analysis:** This is a subset of behavioral analytics, which allows you to study the behavior of a group over time. It is especially useful if you want to know more about the behavior of a group of stakeholders, such as customers or employees.

- **Meta analytics/literature analysis:** Meta analysis is the term that describes the synthesis of previous studies in an area in the hope of identifying patterns, trends or interesting relationships among the pre-existing literature and study results. Essentially, it is the study of previous studies. It is useful whenever you want to obtain relevant insights without conducting any studies yourself.

The objective is to utilize standard business practices with which organizational leaders are already familiar. Oftentimes in the field of Diversity and Inclusion, we create new techniques or utilize big words (e.g., cultural competence, diversity, inclusion, etc.) that the average everyday executive does not know. It doesn't necessarily mean that they think big words make us smarter; in their minds, all of the terms mean the same thing. This is why it's possible for some executives to assert that it is necessary to substitute the word *diversity* with the term *inclusion*. Part of the process of providing insight is to use clear and concrete, real life examples of how the terms are different.

The SWOT Analysis
An analysis allows organizations to identify opportunities for improvement in operations and/or processes. The process of analysis consists of gathering, documenting, evaluating and synthesizing data in order to develop new solutions. The SWOT Analysis is one tool that D&I leaders have used successfully in this process. A SWOT Analysis is a strategic planning method used to evaluate the **S**trengths, **W**eaknesses, **O**pportunities, and **T**hreats involved in your Diversity initiatives. The SWOT analysis can evaluate several initiatives, or one particular intervention, such as Supplier Diversity, Diversity Training, or Diversity Recruiting. For example, University of Massachusetts at Dartmouth once did a SWOT Analysis on Student Diversity in Enrollment. The analysis compared the SWOT findings with institutional goals.

Alternatively, the SWOT analysis can assess the overall effectiveness and potential success of the organization's Inclusive business practices. The findings can help your organization plan, prioritize and identify a strategic starting point for change or allow the organization to ascertain what's next. The SWOT Analysis addresses both internal and external factors. The organization's strengths and weaknesses are internal factors; the external factors are opportunities and weaknesses.

FIGURE 5: SWOT ANALYSIS

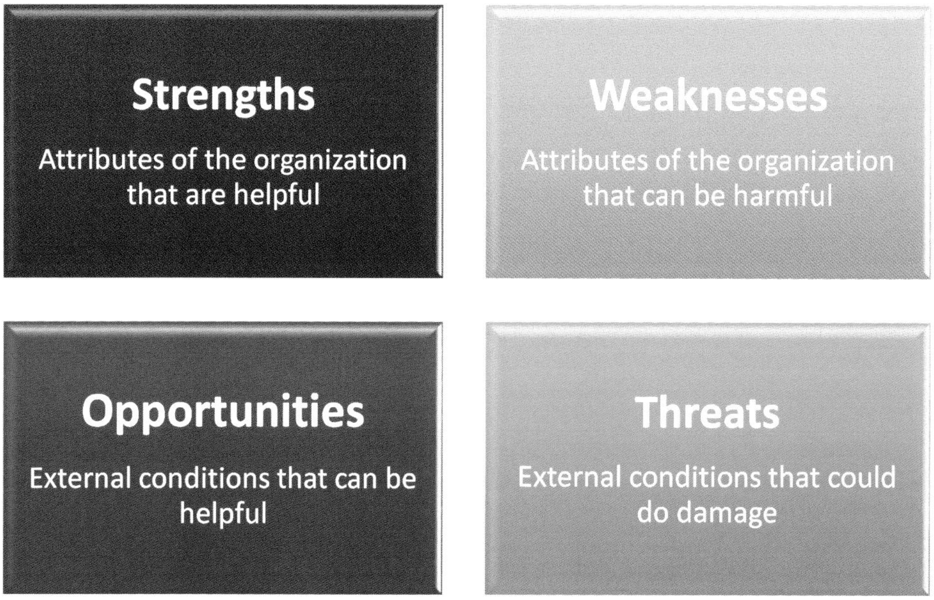

Strengths
Attributes of the organization that are helpful

Weaknesses
Attributes of the organization that can be harmful

Opportunities
External conditions that can be helpful

Threats
External conditions that could do damage

In conducting a SWOT analysis, ask these questions and generate as many ideas as possible to develop strategies:

- *How can we use and capitalize on each strength?*
- *How can we improve each weakness?*
- *How can we exploit and benefit from each opportunity?*
- *How can we mitigate each threat?*

An example of a SWOT Analysis follows:

FIGURE 6: SAMPLE SWOT ANALYSIS

Strengths	Weaknesses	Opportunities	Threats
• Reputation in marketplace	• No formal Diversity plan	• Well established position in the market	• Weak Economy
• High Employee Satisfaction	• No streamlined D&I policies across business units	• Diverse employee groups	• Competition for Talent

Benchmarking
Benchmarking is the process of comparing your own organization, operations, or processes against other organizations in your industry or in the broader marketplace.

Internal benchmarking is the process of evaluating how your work, processes and policies compare to other internal divisions and departments. While it is important to measure and monitor performance for all critical processes, organizations should beware of developing a simple internal or insular view of their operations. If an organization is preoccupied with itself, it can easily lose track of competitors and broader-world innovations, as well as changing demands of customers.

Looking beyond your own industry for best-in-class performance for particular processes or functions is an excellent way to challenge your firm to rethink long-standing assumptions and practices. For example, Southwest Airlines famously analyzed the processes, approaches, and speed of automobile racing pit crews to gain ideas for improving their airplane turn-around time at the gate. The outcome of this benchmarking study is reported to have helped Southwest reconfigure their gate maintenance, cleaning, and customer loading operations, and to have saved the firm millions of dollars per year. This is a great example of Strategic benchmarking.

We define benchmarking as a process because D&I leaders should not take a simplistic approach to continual improvements or quality control. Some of the steps include:

- Comparing your work to competitors
- Pinpointing performance gaps
- Identifying Improvement initiatives
- Enhancing Enterprise value

Similar to the Business Process Improvement method, we want to improve quality, productivity and response time for handling diversity and inclusion issues.

The *Global Diversity & Inclusion Benchmarks: Standards for Organizations Around the World (GDIB)* provides a universal framework to support the development of best practices in benchmarking. Julie O'Mara, Alan Richter, Ph.D., and 95 expert panelists associated with The Center for Global Inclusion identified several organizational uses for a benchmarking analysis. These are:

- To set and stretch standards and agree on your desired state
- To assess the current state of D&I
- To engage employees
- To determine short-term and long-term goals
- To measure progress
- To assist in hiring D&I staff & consultants
- As a "gift" to organizations in your community

Developed in 2017, the purpose of the GDIB standards is to create a better world by improving organizational performance. All Diversity leaders can utilize this free data to determine strategy and measure progress, as well as access a suite of user tools and other downloads (available at: http://centreforglobalinclusion.org). The framework is illustrated in Figure 7.

FIGURE 7: GLOBAL DIVERSITY & INCLUSION BENCHMARKS

Source: ©The Center for Global Inclusion, 2017

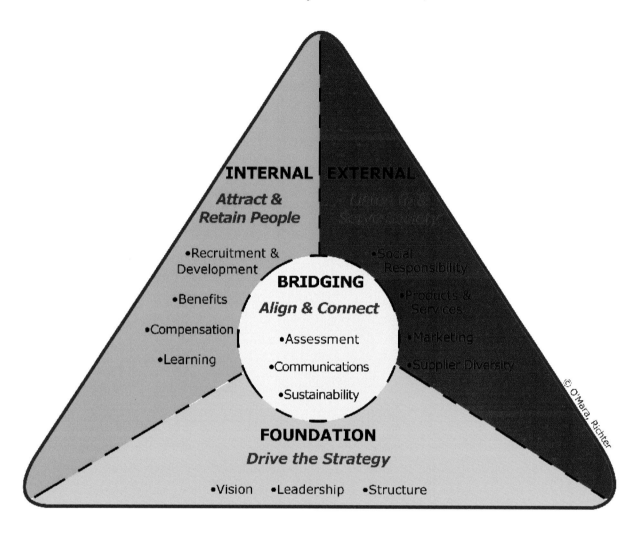

The approach to GDIB is based on five areas that ultimately connect to sustainability:

1. *Competence:* Improving skills, knowledge and ability
2. *Compliance:* Complying with laws and regulations
3. *Dignity:* Affirming the value and interconnectedness of every person
4. *Organization Development:* Improving organizational performance
5. *Social Justice:* Treating people equitably and ethically

According to the report, focusing on these areas "can help improve the quality of D&I work of all organizations in the world, regardless of how the work is named." In addition to the GDIB, there are multiple sources where D&I leaders can gather benchmarking data including: surveys; professional and trade associations (e.g., Diversity Best Practices, Human Rights Campaign, etc.); publications (e.g., DiversityInc., Black Enterprise Magazine, etc.); Diversity and Inclusion conferences; industry analysts and consultants (e.g., Deloitte, McKinsey, etc.); university white papers and reports (e.g., The Harvard Business Review); Diversity and Inclusion annual reports; and competitor websites.

IN CONCLUSION

Essentially, there are four (4) components involved in measuring D&I impact.

1. *Know what you want to measure; then figure out how to track and calculate impacts over time.*
2. *Regularly assess where you are on the Diversity Development Continuum. Combine quantitative and qualitative data to get deeper insights into how D&I impacted the organization.*
3. *Customize the metrics to reflect what is important to the organization's culture, the business results, and the industry.*
4. *Communicate expectations and accomplishments in a predetermined format on a predetermined schedule.*

Today, there is a plethora of data available in the field of Diversity and Inclusion that can help inform our work, and enable us to report overall program outcomes, not just individual events or activities. Providing insight into the data and our work is key. Providing insight takes time and should be intentional. Likewise, measuring impact is not a haphazard activity. It encompasses a strategic approach that takes time and effort to demonstrate the effect that inclusion, interconnectivity and innovation has on your organization.

References:

Vriens, Marco and Verhulst, Rogier (2008). Unleashing Hidden Insights. Available at:
https://www.ama.org/Documents/MRWinter08Vriens.pdf

SHRM Study on Workplace Diversity, 1999. *How Can the Results of Our Diversity Initiative Be Measured?* (pp.27-29)

Jayne, M. E., & Dipboye, R. L. *Leveraging diversity to improve business performance: Research findings and recommendations for organizations.* Human Resource Management, 43, 4, 409-424. 2004.

Kaplan, Robert S., and David P. Norton. *The Balanced Scorecard: Translating Strategy into Action.* Boston: Harvard Business School Press, 1996.

Hubbard, Edward E. *The diversity scorecard: Evaluating the impact of diversity on organizational performance.* Burlington, MA: Elsevier Butterworth. 2004 (first edition: 2003)

Hubbard, Edward E. *Diversity Return on Investment Fundamentals.* Global Insights Publishing. 2015

Hubbard, Edward E. *Diversity Training ROI: How to Measure the Return on Investment of Diversity Training Initiatives.* Global Insights Publishing. 2010

Hubbard, Edward E. *The Power of Diversity ROI Measurement Alignment — Part 2.* Diversity Executive Blog, December 14, 2012. Available at http://blog.diversity-executive.com/2012/12/14/the-power-of-diversity-roi-measurement-alignment-%E2%80%94-part-2/

Marr, Bernard (2016). *The 18 Best Analytics Tools Every Business Manager Should Know.* Forbes. Available at: https://www.forbes.com/sites/bernardmarr/2016/02/04/the-18-best-analytics-tools-every-business-manager-should-know/#4f504f4d5d39

O'Mara, Julie, and Richter, Alan, Ph.D. (2017). ACPA Edition, *Global Diversity & Inclusion Benchmarks.* Available at: http://centreforglobalinclusion.org/

Sample Test Questions:

ADVANCED DATA INSIGHT AND ANALYSIS

1. **This is the process of comparing an organization, its operations, or processes against others:**
   A. Providing insight
   B. Benchmarking
   C. Evaluation

2. **In compliant mode, an organization is doing the bare minimum, which is:**
   A. Holding mandatory diversity training
   B. Recruiting veterans with disabilities
   C. Ensuring compliance with the law

3. **The final outcome of a process, showing a gain or loss, is the:**
   A. Bottom line
   B. Return on Investment
   C. Cost-benefit analysis

4. **A collection of quantitative data that allows for comparison against accepted standards is called:**
   A. Impact
   B. An Asset
   C. Measurement

5. **In the field of diversity and inclusion, impact can be defined as the quantifiable change in economics, professionals, legal or:**
   A. Social
   B. Planning
   C. Environment

6. **The purpose of providing insight into D&I data is to:**
   A. Increase understanding
   B. Improve productivity
   C. Benchmark progress

Sample Test Questions:

ADVANCED DATA INSIGHT AND ANALYSIS (cont'd)

7. **Calculating impact has been difficult because, in the diversity industry as a whole, we have:**
   A. Linked diversity efforts with organizational goals
   B. Been too effective with Affirmative Action programs
   C. Confused D&I activities with impact

8. **A SWOT Analysis is a tool that can be used to assess and improve all of the following EXCEPT:**
   A. The organizational culture
   B. Employee's mindsets
   C. Diversity recruiting

9. **The following is an example of video analytics in the Diversity and Inclusion space:**
   A. Extracting information, meaning and insights from You-Tube Diversity and bias videos
   B. Creating short, new videos about the organization's Diversity and Inclusion efforts
   C. Synthesizing videos and literatures to identify patterns, trends and relationships

10. **The limitations of internal benchmarking include all of the following EXCEPT:**
    A. Neglecting broader-world innovations
    B. Losing track of competitors
    C. Understanding how departments compare

11. **Diversity is valuable to international business strategies, which is the way of the future.**
    A. True
    B. False

12. **Competence is the second level of the Diversity Development Continuum.**
    A. True
    B. False

13. **Indicators act as the gauge of whether, and to what degree, your diversity and inclusion effort is making progress.**
    A. True
    B. False

ANSWER KEY

CDE ANSWER KEY

Personal Awareness & Managing Blind Spots

1. B
2. A
3. C
4. A
5. C
6. B
7. B
8. A
9. C
10. A
11. B
12. A

Improving Your Approach to the Bottom Line

1. C
2. B
3. C
4. A
5. C
6. A
7. C
8. B
9. A
10. A
11. C
12. A
13. B
14. A
15. B

Global Best Practices

1. A
2. B
3. C
4. C
5. A
6. A
7. A
8. B
9. C
10. A
11. B
12. A
13. A
14. C

The Elements of Leading a Large-Scale D&I Effort

1. C
2. B
3. C
4. B
5. C
6. B
7. C
8. B
9. C
10. A
11. A
12. A
13. B

Race, Power & Privilege

1. B
2. C
3. B
4. A
5. B
6. C
7. B
8. C
9. A
10. A
11. B

Boardroom Diversity

1. B
2. A
3. C
4. C
5. B
6. A
7. B
8. C
9. A
10. A
11. B
12. A

CDE ANSWER KEY

Supplier Diversity

1. C
2. A
3. B
4. C
5. C
6. C
7. B
8. B
9. C
10. A
11. A
12. A
13. B
14. C

Impediments to Inclusion & Cultural Competence

1. C
2. B
3. A
4. A
5. A
6. B
7. B
8. C
9. A
10. B
11. C
12. C
13. C

Executive Commitment & Sponsorship

1. A
2. B
3. B
4. A
5. B
6. C
7. C
8. C
9. A
10. A
11. B
12. B
13. C

Innovation Through D&I

1. C
2. C
3. B
4. B
5. A
6. B
7. C
8. A
9. C
10. B
11. B
12. C

Unconscious Bias

1. B
2. C
3. A
4. B
5. C
6. B
7. A
8. C
9. C
10. A
11. B
12. B

Strategic Purpose & Partnerships

1. B
2. B
3. A
4. C
5. B
6. B
7. C
8. A
9. B
10. C
11. A
12. C
13. B

CDE ANSWER KEY

Connecting Demographic Shifts to Organizational Strategy

1. B
2. B
3. A
4. C
5. C
6. A
7. B
8. C
9. A
10. A
11. A
12. C
13. B

The Next Generation of Equity, Diversity & Inclusion Work

1. A
2. C
3. B
4. A
5. B
6. C
7. A
8. B
9. B
10. A
11. C
12. C
13. B

Advanced Data Insight and Analysis

1. B
2. C
3. A
4. C
5. C
6. A
7. C
8. B
9. A
10. C
11. A
12. B
13. A

Integrating Cultures Amidst Merger & Acquisition Activity

1. C
2. C
3. B
4. C
5. A
6. B
7. C
8. B
9. A

CDE References

"2007 State of Workplace Diversity Management Report," Society for Human Resource Management, March 2008, http://www.shrm.org/Publications/HRNews/Pages/DiversityBusinessImperative.aspx.

Ashford, Jose B. & LeCroy, Craig W. "Human Behavior in the Social Environment: A Multidimensional Perspective", 4th Edition. Belmont, CA. Cengage Learning, 2009.

Bennett, Janet M. "Cultural Marginality: Identity Issues in Intercultural Training," in R. Michael Paige, ed. Education for the Intercultural Experience. Milton J. Bennett and Janet M. Bennett, 2000.

Bennett, Milton J. "Towards a Developmental Model of Intercultural Sensitivity" in R. Michael Paige, ed. Education for the Intercultural Experience. Yarmouth, ME: Intercultural Press, 1993.

Bennett, M. J. (1993). Towards ethnorelativism: A developmental model of intercultural sensitivity (revised). In R. M. Paige (Ed.), Education for the Intercultural Experience. Yarmouth, Me: Intercultural Press.

Bertrand, Marianne & Mullainathan, Sendhil. "Are Emily and Greg More Employable Than Lakisha and Jamal? A Field Experiment in Labor Market Discrimination". *American Economic Review* 94 (4): 991–1013.) September 2004.

Blauner, Robert. *Racial Oppression in America* (New York: Harper and Row, 1972).

Buchanan, D. & Boddy, D. "The Expertise of the Change Agent: Public performance and backstage activity". Prentice Hall. 1992.

Butrica, Barbara B.; Iams, Howard M.; and Smith, Karen E. "The Changing Impact of Social Security on Retirement Income in the United States", Social Security Bulletin, Vol. 65 No. 3, 2003/2004.

Cabot, L. "Professional development for IT leaders". *Education Quarterly. 1*:54-56. 2006.

Canterucci, Jim: "Are You a Change Leader?" Available at http://www.corpchange.com/archives/article_archives/a19_are_you_a_change_leader/a19_are_you_a_change_leader.htm

Carnevale, A. *The Coming Labor And Skills Shortage.* T&D, 59(1), 37–41. (2005, January).

Day, H. R. "Race relations training in the military". In D. Landis & R. Brislin (Eds.), Handbook of Intercultural Training, Vol. II: Issues in training methodology (pp. 241-289). New York: Pergamon Press. 1983.

'Deadly Trend' of Hispanic worker deaths on top of agenda at OSHA. *Labor Relations Week, 16*(41), 1257. (2002, October, 17).

Devine, P. G., & Monteith, M. J. "The role of discrepancy-associated affect in prejudice reduction". In D. Mackie & D. Hamilton (Eds.), Affect, cognition, and stereotyping: Interactive processes in group perception (pp. 137-166), San Diego, CA.: Harcourt, Brace, & Jananovich. 1993.

Digh, P. "Creating a new balance sheet: The need for better diversity metrics". November 2001. Retrieved from www.centeronline.org/knowledge/whitepaper.cfm?ID=813&ContentProfileID=122197&Action=searching

Dittman, M. "Generational differences at work." Monitor on Psychology. 2005. Retrieved from http://www.apa.org/monitor/jun05/generational.html

Dong Olson, Valerie. "Generational Diversity: Implications For Healthcare Leaders". *Journal of Business & Economics Research –Volume 6, Number 1.* November 2008.

Durose, Matthew R.; Schmitt, Erica L.; and Langan, Patrick A. "Contacts Between Police and the Public: Findings from the 2002 National Survey. U.S. Department of Justice", (Bureau of Justice Statistics), April 2005.

Ferdman, B. M., & Gallegos, P. I. "Racial identity development and Latinos in the United States." 2001.

Gailbraith, Jay R. "Designing Organizations". Jossey-Bass Publishers: San Francisco, CA. 1995.

Ganderton, P. T. & Santos, R. *Hispanic College Attendance And Completion: Evidence From High School And Beyond Surveys.* Economics of Education Review, 14 (1), 35 – 46. (1995).

Gates, S. "Measuring more than efficiency: The new role of human capital metrics." 2004. Retrieved from www.conference-board.org

Goldsmith, Marshall. "4 Tips for Efficient Succession Planning", Harvard Business Review Blog. May 2009. Available at http://blogs.hbr.org/goldsmith/2009/05/change_succession_planning_to.html

Gratton, Brian and Gutmann, Myron P. "Hispanics in the United States, 1850-1990: Estimates of Population Size and National Origin," *Historical Methods 33*, no. 3 (2000): 137-53.

Greenberg, Josh. "Increasing Employee Retention Through Employee Engagement", Ezine Articles. 2004. Available at http://ezinearticles.com/?Increasing-Employee-Retention-Through-Employee-Engagement&id=10575

Hansen, Fay. "Diversity's Business Case Doesn't Add Up", p. 28-32, Workforce Management Magazine, April 2003.

Hastings, Rebecca R. "Diversity Training May Contribute to Diversity Fatigue", SHRM Online, April 17, 2008. Available at http://www.shrm.org/Publications/HRNews/Pages/diversityfatigue.aspx

Heistad, Kari. "Diversity Fatigue Blog Series: Seven Causes of Diversity Fatigue", Culture Coach Blog: The Global Voice. June 26, 2013. Available at http://www.culturecoach.biz/wordpress/diversity-fatigue-blog-series-seven-causes-of-diversity-fatigue/#sthash.EmfuaxXi.dpuf

Hubbard, E. E. "The diversity scorecard: Evaluating the impact of diversity on organizational performance". Burlington, MA: Elsevier Butterworth. 2004.

Hubbard, Edward E. "The Power of Diversity ROI Measurement Alignment — Part 2". Diversity Executive Blog, December 14, 2012. Available at http://blog.diversity-executive.com/2012/12/14/the-power-of-diversity-roi-measurement-alignment-%E2%80%94-part-2/

Jayne, M. E., & Dipboye, R. L. "Leveraging diversity to improve business performance: Research findings and recommendations for organizations". Human Resource Management, 43, 4, 409-424. 2004.

Kanter, Rosabeth Moss: "The Enduring Skills of Change Leaders." In Leader to Leader, Nr. 13 Summer 1999. Available at http://www.pfdf.org/leaderbooks/l2l/summer99/kanter.html

Kirkpatrick, D. "The Human Resources Program Evaluation Model, *Evaluating Training Programs*", 1994.

Kochhar, R. The occupational status and mobility of Hispanics. (December 15, 2005). Retrieved from http://pewhispanic.org/files/reports/59.pdf

Kohn, Sally Kohn. "Affirmative Action Helps White Women More Than Others" (June 17, 2013) Retrieved from TIME.com http://ideas.time.com/2013/06/17/affirmative-action-has-helped-white-women-more-than-anyone/#ixzz2p1jkx863

Kupperschmidt, B. "Addressing multigenerational conflict: Mutual respect and carefronting as strategy". *Online Journal of Issues in Nursing,11*(2):4. 2006.

"Labor Force Characteristics by Race and Ethnicity, 2009", Report 1026, US Department of Labor Bureau of Workforce Statistics, 2009.

Lamb, Robert, Boyden. "Competitive strategic management," Englewood Cliffs, NJ: Prentice-Hall, 1984.

Langfield, Amy. *When It Comes to Diversity, White Male Managers Not Doing So Hot* (April 4, 2013). Retrieved from http://www.cnbc.com/id/100616408

"Latino Shoppers: Demographic Patterns and Spending Trends among Hispanic Americans, 8th Edition", Packaged Facts, 2011.

Leibman, M., Bruer, R., & Maki, B. "Succession management: The next generation of succession planning". *Human Resource Planning, 19.* 1996.

Manzoni, Jean-Francois, Strebel, Paul, and Barsoux, Jean-Louis. "Why Diversity Can Backfire on Company Boards" The Wall Street Journal, January 25, 2010.

Miles, Stephen A. "Succession Planning: How To Do It Right", Forbes.com, July 2009. Available at http://www.forbes.com/2009/07/31/succession-planning-right-leadership-governance-ceos.html.

Munnell, Alicia H., and Annika Sundén. "Coming Up Short: The Challenge of 401(k) Plans." Washington, DC: Brookings Institution Press, 2004.

Noble, S., Schewe, C., & Kuhr, M. "Preferences in health care service and treatment: A generational perspective". *Science Direct, 57*(9):1033-1041. 2004.

Norris, Donald M., Joelle, M.C. *"Winning with Diversity – A Practical Handbook for Creating Inciusive Meetings, Events and Organizations,"* Fignole Lofton, 1995.

Ogunjimi, A. "What are the benefits of diversity councils?" Ehow. November 2010. Available at: What Are the Benefits of Diversity Councils? | eHow.com http://www.ehow.com/about_7549534_benefits-diversity-councils.html#ixzz1McSJMvLv

Oney, Angie. "How to Measure Diversity Training". e-How. 2011. Available at: How to Measure Diversity Training | eHow.co.uk http://www.ehow.co.uk/how_8320277_measure-diversity-training.html#ixzz1M9EePOFI

Ostrower, Francie. "Nonprofit Governance in the United States", The Urban Institute, 2007.

Perez, S. M. (Ed.). *Moving up the economic ladder: Latino workers and the nation's future prosperity.* National Council of La Raza. Washington, D.C.: 2000.

PricewaterhouseCoopers LLP "Boards confront an evolving landscape: PwC's Annual Corporate Directors Survey", 2013. Available at http://www.pwc.com/us/en/corporate-governance/annual-corporate-directors-survey/assets/pdf/pwc-annual-corporate-directors-survey-full-report.pdf

Puckett, C. "Administering Social Security: Challenges Yesterday and Today". Social Security Bulletin, Vol. 70, No. 3, 2010.

Raines, C. "*Connecting Generations: The Sourcebook.*" Crisp Publication. 2003.

Recklies, Dagmar. "What Makes a Good Change Agent?", October 2001. Available at http://www.themanager.org/Strategy/change_agent.htm

Saenz, Rogelio. "Latinos and the Changing Face of America". T*he Russell Sage Foundation and Population Reference Bureau,* August 2004.

Sardar, Ziauddin. "What Do Muslims Believe? The Roots and Realities of Modern Islam". New York: Walker Publishing Company. 2007.

Schoen, Robert. "What I Wish My Christian Friends Knew About Judaism". Illinois: Loyola Press. 2004.

Shelton, Chuck. "Equip and Engage White Men to Lead Diversity". Diversity Executive Magazine, September 2009.

Sherman, R. "Leading a multigenerational nursing workforce: Issues, challenges and strategies". *Online Journal of Issues in Nursing, 11*(2):3. 2006.

Smola, K. & Sutton, C. "Generational differences: revisiting generational work values for the new millennium". *Journal of Organizational Behavior. 23*(4):363-382. 2002.

Stachura, Jim & Murphy, M. "Multicultural Marketing: Why One Size Doesn't Fit All", 2005. Available at: http://www.marketingprofs.com/articles/2005/1652/multicultural-marketing-why-one-size-doesnt-fit-all#ixzz1MBa4J0WC Available at: http://www.marketingprofs.com/articles/2005/1652/multicultural-marketing-why-one-size-doesnt-fit-all#ixzz1MBZcONBO

Stanley, K. "Age to age: Insight into managing a multigenerational staff". *Journal of Medical Practice Management, 22*(5):269-75. 2007.

Schwarz, R. "Why managing generational differences is important." Retrieved from http://www.marsvenusatwork.com/generations/htm

Vaughn, B.E. "Diversity Pioneers In The History Of Diversity Education", Ezine Articles, 2008. Available at: http://EzineArticles.com/988500

Vaughn, B. E. "Heuristic model of managing emotions in race relations training". In E. Davis-Russell (Ed.), Multicultural Education, Research, Intervention, & Training (pp. 296-318). San Francisco, CA.: Jossey-Bass. 2002.

Whalen, Charles & Barbara. "The History of Affirmative Action Policies; Americans for Fair Chance", The Longest Debate, page 116, Seven Locks Press, 1985.

Wijeyesinghe, C. L. & Jackson, III, B. W. (Eds.), *New perspectives on Racial Identity Development: A theoretical and practical anthology* (pp. 32-66). New York: New York University Press.

Wildman, Stephanie M.; Armstong, Margalynne; Davis, Adrienne D.; Grillo, Trina. "Privilege Revealed: How Invisible Preference Undermines America". New York: NYU Press. 1996.

Wiseman, M. & Yčas, M. "The Canadian Safety Net for the Elderly", Social Security Bulletin, Vol. 68 No. 2, 2008. Wuthnow, Robert. "America and the Challenges of Religious Diversity". New Jersey: Princeton University Press. 2005.

Diversity/The Bottom Line Beyond HR, "Creating A Culturally Diverse Organization: 10 Keys to Success", The Kaleel Jamison Consulting Group.

"How Can the Results of Our Diversity Initiative Be Measured?" *Workplace Diversity- A Product of the SHRM Diversity Initiative*, 1999.

FREQUENTLY UTILIZED WEBSITES

- www.wikipedia.org
- www.eeoc.gov
- www.dol.gov
- www.ssa.gov
- www.census.gov
- www.ehow.com
- www.shrm.org
- www.diversityinc.com
- www.hbr.org